Kallimachos

*The Alexandrian Library and
the Origins of Bibliography*

Rudolf Blum

Kallimachos

*The Alexandrian Library and
the Origins of Bibliography*

Translated from the German
by

Hans H. Wellisch

The University of Wisconsin Press

The University of Wisconsin Press
114 North Murray Street
Madison, Wisconsin 53715

3 Henrietta Street
London WC2E 8LU, England

Library of Congress Cataloging-in-Publication Data
Blum, Rudolf, 1909–
[Kallimachos und die Literaturverzeichnung bei den Griechen. English]
Kallimachos: the Alexandrian Library and the origins of bibliography
Rudolf Blum: translated from the German by Hans H. Wellisch.
294 pp.   cm. — (Wisconsin studies in classics)
Translation of: Kallimachos und die Literaturverzeichnung bei den Griechen.
Includes bibliographical references and indexes.
ISBN 0-299-13170-X (cloth)
1. Aliksāndrīnā (Library) 2. Callimachus—Knowledge—Book arts
and sciences. 3. Libraries—Egypt—Alexandria—History—To 400.
4. Greek literature—Bibliography—Methodology. 5. Bibliography—
Egypt—Alexandria—History. 6. Cataloging—Egypt—Alexandria—
History. 7. Greece—Bibliography—Methodology. 8. Callimachus—
Influence. I. Title. II. Series.
Z722.5.B58 1991
027.032—dc20   91-28997

Contents

Translator's Preface

GREEK NAMES in this work are not rendered in their commonly used Latinized form but by transliteration, using the system employed by the Library of Congress (which is identical with the one used in the German original). Only a few names have been retained in their Latinized form, e.g. Alexandria, Aristotle, Byzantium, Plato, Socrates. My authority for this is George Sarton who in the introduction to his *A History of Science* said:

> There is really no reason for giving a Latin ending to
> a Greek name, when one is writing not in Latin but in
> English. Hence, we write Epicuros, not Epicurus (the two
> *u*'s of that Latin word represent different Greek vowels!).
> . . . There remain inconsistencies in our transliteration
> because we prefer to be inconsistent rather than pedantic
> and do not wish to disturb our readers more than we can help.
> . . . They should realize that English usage is full of
> inconsistencies, e.g., one writes habitually Aristarch*us* of
> Sam*os* and Eudox*us* of Cnid*os*.[*]

Titles of Greek works have also been rendered in transliteration, with the exception of *Iliad* and *Odyssey*, and titles of works by Plato and Aristotle which are best known in their Latin form as given in the Loeb Classical Library and in other editions. Direct quotations from Greek works available in Loeb Classical Library editions have been given in that translation; those editions also allow the interested reader to compare the Greek text to which the author occasionally refers.

The German text generally distinguishes between "Gelehrte" and "Forscher" or "Fachleute", the former referring to ancient scholars, the latter to those of our own times. I consistently used the term "scholar" for the ancients and "researcher" for modern classical philologists, who indeed in the most literal sense of the word re-search for clues on authors in the fragments of their lost works, as ably demonstrated by the author himself. The use of the term "philologists" instead of "grammarians" (a term generally employed in writings about the Alexandrians) is explained by the author on p. 7. The term "autopsy" which is used several times in relation to the compilation of the *Pinakes*, is quite common in German as a bibliographical *terminus technicus*, but it is less well known in English in this sense. The *Oxford English Dictionary* gives as its first definition "personal observation or inspection" and this is indeed what is meant: the bibliographic description of a work, based on personal inspection by the bibliographer (and not on somebody else's description).

---

[*]George Sarton, *A History of Science* (New York: Norton, 1952) vol. 1, p. xvii.

The German text distinguishes between "Abschrift", "Exemplar" and "Vorlage", all of which are generally expressed in English by the single word "copy". While it was possible to use the word "exemplar" for "Vorlage" and thus to distinguish it from "Abschrift" (a copy made from it), there are no good synonyms for "copy" in its two other senses, i.e. something that has been copied, as distinct from a book that is another specimen of the same work. The context will make clear what is meant when the terms "Abschrift" and "Exemplar" occurred in the same original sentence and had to be rendered into English.

The original bibliography has been augmented by English or French works cited by the author in German translations, and by English editions of German works; in addition, all English translations of Greek authors, passages of which are quoted in the text, have also been included.

Most of the Greek passages quoted in the original footnotes have been omitted (with the consent of the author) and references to the sources have been given instead. In a few instances, where this is necessary for the understanding of a note, the Greek text has been reproduced from the original.

Footnotes in the original which merely refer to passages in the text itself have been omitted; instead, the index is more comprehensive than the original one, so that the reader will find there references to persons or topics. All explanatory footnotes and those referring to cited sources have been retained.

The following abbreviations have been used in the notes:

sc.	=	scilicet, "namely"
s.v.	=	sub verbo, "under the word"
T.	=	Testimonium

I wish to express my appreciation for the painstaking and tireless work of Mrs. Golda M. Haines without whose expert typing and word processing this book could not have been produced.

I am also grateful to the Harvard University Press for permission to use the English translations of passages from Aristophanes (1924), Athenaeus (1927), Callimachus (1921), and Strabo (1929), bibliographical data of which will be found in the bibliography under the dates indicated in parentheses.

Finally, I wish to thank the staff of the University of Wisconsin Press, and in particular Barbara Hanrahan, Ruth A. Semmerling and Elizabeth Steinberg, who spared no effort in overcoming numerous technical problems and succeeded in presenting the book to its readers in a pleasing format.

—Hans H. Wellisch

Preface

THIS WORK deals with the beginnings of bibliography. Kallimachos of Kyrene, a Hellenistic scholar and a famous poet, created about 260 B.C. a fundamental list of Greek authors with biographical and bibliographical data, the first national author bibliography, based on the holdings of the Alexandrian library. But what he, his predecessors, and successors achieved in the field of bibliography, that staging area for the history of literature, is almost unknown outside the circle of experts. In addition, there are some important related issues which are still in need of clarification.

The investigations which I have undertaken for this purpose pertain to questions in the history of ancient scholarship and librarianship. But I endeavored to write in such a manner that not only students of Classical Antiquity will be able to follow me. Therefore, I inserted explanations of issues pertaining to Antiquity wherever I deemed them to be appropriate. Greek quotations are rendered in translation. Greek titles of books, typical Greek expressions, and shorter sayings of Greek scholars are always transliterated. Some passages in the footnotes are also given in the original Greek.

Bibliographic works of the Romans and those of Christians in Antiquity have been omitted because I am treating these, together with those of the Middle Ages and the early modern period, in another work.[*]

—R.B.

---

[*]Rudolf Blum. *Die Literaturverzeichnung im Altertum und Mittelalter. Versuch einer Geschichte der Biobibliographie von den Anfängen bis zum Beginn der Neuzeit* (Frankfurt a.M.: Buchhändler-Vereinigung, 1983).

Kallimachos

*The Alexandrian Library and
the Origins of Bibliography*

1. Introduction

THE TERM "bibliography" is generally understood to mean the compilation of lists of books. Some bibliographies contain also biographical data about the authors whose works are being listed. These are known by the technical term "biobibliographies," and often they are also called biographical dictionaries. Almost all ancient and medieval bibliographies were biobibliographies. The making of a bibliography entailed in those days also the collection of information on the lives and works of authors.

The first bibliographies compiled and published after the invention of printing were likewise biobibliographies.[1] Although most bibliographers gradually ceased to include biographical data, biobibliographies continued to appear from time to time and appear even today, most often as general national or regional biographical dictionaries, less frequently as international or subject-oriented biobibliographies. The national biographical dictionaries are still among the most important sources of information on the lives and works of persons who were active as authors, irrespective of the subject field. Since the 19th century we have also biographical dictionaries which list only living authors. Thus, for German belles-lettres, we have in addition to Kosch's *Deutsches Literatur-Lexikon* also Kürschner's *Deutscher Literaturkalender*.

The first bibliography, or more precisely, the first biobibliography to appear in print was the work of a German prelate, the *Liber de scriptoribus ecclesiasticis* of Johannes Trithemius, published in Basel in 1494.[2] It continued the long line of biobibliographies of ecclesiastical authors that had been started by St. Jerome's *Liber de viris illustribus* in the latter part of the 4th century, but it was more correctly named. The successors of the Church Father had also given the title *de viris illustribus* to their own similar works. Jerome himself admitted that it would have been better to give the title *de scriptoribus ecclesiasticis* to his work, because it listed only authors and no others than ecclesiastical ones.[3] The Church Father was not the first to use the term *viri illustres* solely for authors; this usage went back, for example, to Suetonius whom he mentioned as one of his models. The limitation to ecclesiastical authors was however an issue in the controversy between Christianity and paganism.

Trithemius published also the first printed national biographical dictionary of the modern period. His *Catalogus illustrium virorum Germaniae* (Mainz, 1495) was, to be sure, only a somewhat enlarged extract from his *Liber de scriptoribus ecclesiasticis*, published one year earlier. He did not list all famous Germans but only German writers; Trithemius did not simply give the title *Catalogus scriptorum Germanicorum* to this book, in analogy to his biobibliographic main work, but resorted here, where he dealt with the authors of his own nation, to the sonorous expression *viri illustri*.

As a compiler of a national biographical dictionary of authors Trithemius had no immediate predecessors. The Middle Ages knew only the international lists of ecclesiastical authors and their works, compiled by St. Jerome's successors. But both in Greece and in Rome there had been national biographical dictionaries of authors. The oldest and most important was the work of Kallimachos, always cited as *Pinakes* (Lists). According to the *Suda,* the great Byzantine encyclopedia of the 10th or 11th century (formerly erroneously ascribed to an author named Suidas) to which we are indebted for most of the information about the lives and works of Greek authors, the complete title was: *Pinakes tōn en pasē paideia dialampsantōn kai hōn synegrapsan* (Lists of those who distinguished themselves in all branches of learning, and their writings). Since this work and its author form the main subject of the following investigation, they will be presented here in brief outline.

Kallimachos (ca. 305-240 B.C.) was a native of Kyrene, but spent the larger part of his life in Alexandria at the court of King Ptolemaios II Philadelphos, one of the centers of Greek Culture in Hellenistic times. He was held in high esteem as a poet and scholar and was certainly a member of the Museion, a kind of academy of arts and sciences founded by Ptolemaios I. It is likely that he was also a director of the library of the Museion. This library, which had been founded by the first Ptolemaios, and had been further developed by the second one, was the largest collection of books in Antiquity, and served as a model for all subsequent libraries. A circle of learned men who were his pupils surrounded him. Foremost among these was Hermippos of Smyrna, known as the Kallimachean, who is mentioned by Jerome (following Suetonius) as his principal model in his work *De viris illustribus.* Kallimachos has been considered as the greatest of the Hellenistic poets ever since his poetic works, previously transmitted only through medieval (Byzantine) manuscripts, were substantially complemented by the discovery of papyri. His fame as a scholar rests however primarily on the *Pinakes.* This gigantic work, said to have comprised 120 books, has not been preserved, but it is possible to reconstruct it in outline from quotations by later Greek scholars. It listed Greek authors by classes according to literary forms or by scholarly disciplines. The bibliographies of individual poets, philosophers, orators, etc. were preceded (as in later biographical dictionaries) by concise biographical data.[4] This biobibliography was presumably based on a catalog, compiled under the direction of Kallimachos at the library of the Museion.

Classical philologists have long since agreed that most of the information transmitted by later Greek scholars on the lives and works of authors of the archaic, classical and early Hellenistic periods originated in the *Pinakes* of Kallimachos. It seems to me, however, that Kallimachos's own achievements as a librarian and bibliographer have so far not been fully grasped. This already points to the main goal of my investigation. The *Pinakes* were for me as a classical philologist a well-known concept ever since my student days. But only when I began to deal with them more thoroughly (after many years of work as a librarian and bibliographer, and after much research into the history of libraries and bibliography), I realized that it was both necessary and possible to determine more precisely what this man, whose name is linked to one of the most important works of Greek scholarship, had achieved as librarian and bibliographer.

All historians of classical philology have dealt with the *Pinakes* of Kallimachos, most extensively Pfeiffer in his *History of Classical Scholarship*[5] which is far superior to earlier accounts; this eminent Kallimachos scholar and editor of his works was qualified for this task like no one else. But even he did not elaborate on what to me seems to be the real achievement of Kallimachos as librarian and bibliographer. Nevertheless, his work was useful to me, even concerning those issues on which I do not see eye to eye with him, because if one wishes to comprehend the work of the author of the *Pinakes* one must start with the history of philology.

This will not astonish those readers who are familiar with the compilation of library catalogs and bibliographies (the methods are largely the same). They know of course that the bibliographic description of books in catalogs, the determination of the entry, is often preceded by long and difficult bibliographic searches which at times take on the character of genuine philological research. Most people think of course that all a librarian has to do is to copy the bibliographic data found in books, mostly on the title page (author, title, place and year of publication, etc.) in a certain form and sequence onto catalog cards, and then to file these according to the purpose of the catalog, e.g. alphabetically by authors' names. But unfortunately, the bibliographic data as found in books are often incomplete and incorrect. If a publication appears, for example, anonymously or under a pseudonym, the cataloger must find out the real name of the author with the aid of reference books, or, if these fail, by other means. A library catalog must not only reflect the data printed in the book, but, if these are incomplete or incorrect, it must also show who was the (real) author of the work in question, including the differentiation of authors with the same name and their works, also what was the title of the work as given by the author, whether the present edition is a complete or abridged one, whether it contains the original version of the work or any other version, where and when that version was actually published, etc. One wants to collocate with the help of the catalog all editions of a particular work by the same author which are available in the library, and one wants to see which editions and what kind of editions they are. This is possible only if each cataloged book has been uniquely identified. One can hardly imagine how much research is needed for the identification not only of older publications but even of newer and quite recent ones. This can be observed in every library, most clearly in a national library in which all publications appearing in a certain region are collected and cataloged for a national bibliography. Most problems of identification arose and still arise due to the carelessness of publishers, editors and also authors. But sometimes the true bibliographic facts (e.g. the author's real name, the actual place of publication) were and still are obscured or falsified for political, commercial or other reasons.

The cataloging of medieval manuscripts, especially those containing medieval texts, is however even more difficult than that of older or the earliest printed publications.

This can be explained by the practices of those centuries in which literary works were reproduced not mechanically but manually. Books did not have title pages in those days. Conscientious copyists indicated the author and title of the copied work immediately before or after the text, but others omitted these data either partially or entirely; at times, this was even done on purpose because of personal, theological or other motives. If data on the author or the title were missing from the original copy, learned scribes tried to supply them, but while trying to do this they frequently made mistakes. Therefore we have not only innumerable texts without data on authors or titles or with false data, but also many identical texts under the most varied names of authors and titles. The identification of such copies, not to speak of their localization and dating, constitutes a philological problem that is not always easy to solve. In many cases, the ascription or naming of such texts remains therefore controversial for a long time. Even if the name of an author is indicated, but only by his given name without differentiating addition, it is at times troublesome to clarify which of the many bearers of this name, which Peter or Paul, is meant. Whether or not a work is presented in its original form is only possible to ascertain after a study of the text and a comparison with other versions.

Librarians entrusted with the cataloging of medieval manuscripts created various bibliographical aids during the 19th and 20th century, such as lists of incipits of certain works for the identification of copies without author's names or title. The librarians of the 16th, 17th and 18th century who lacked such aids, had a much more difficult task. But even their successors are frequently faced with difficult philological problems, especially when the contents of collected manuscripts (*codices miscellanei*) from the 14th and 15th century must be identified.

The Alexandrian scholars of the 3rd century B.C., who had to catalog the scrolls acquired by the Ptolemies for the library of the Museion, were in a situation similar to that of modern librarians who have to catalog medieval manuscripts. They too had often to solve difficult problems of identification because, as is evident from many accounts and observations, the scrolls contained many texts which had incorrect, incomplete or even no data on authors and titles, or texts were contained in other scrolls under different names of authors or with different titles. Some works existed in different versions which in part were widely divergent, so that it became questionable which version was the authentic one. The task faced by the Alexandrians was therefore also eminently philological, but philology had in those days not yet a tradition of many centuries, but was still a young branch of scholarship.

Pfeiffer says that "Scholarship is the art of understanding, explaining, and restoring the literary tradition".[6] This art, applied to the literature of the Greeks and Romans, constitutes today as "classical philology" the main part of the scholarly study of Antiquity which established itself during the 19th century, based on several different disciplines, with the aim of exploring historically the entire culture of Graeco-Roman or Classical Antiquity.[7]

Classical philology already existed, however, albeit under a different name, in Antiquity itself. During the third century B.C. it developed into a discipline in its own right whose subjects were the works of the great Greek poets, particularly so in the framework of the Museion at Alexandria.[8] In the second half of that century it reached its first culmination with Aristophanes of Byzantium who became the director of the library of the Museion around 200 B.C., and with his successor, Aristarchos of Samothrake. The explanatory notes on literary works from Antiquity known as *scholia* which have come down to us are based, as far as they pertain to the classical literature of the Greeks, on the works of the great Alexandrian philologists and their pupils.[9] But it is possible to trace the prehistory of philology back to the sixth century B.C. We may consider those Greek scholars of the fourth century B.C. who pursued among their many studies also philological and literary-historical research—above all Aristotle and his pupils, the members of the Peripatos of Athens—as the immediate predecessors of the Alexandrian philologists.[10]

The other subdisciplines of the study of Classical Antiquity, e.g. those that deal with politics, religion, and other "antiquities" of the Ancient world, are almost all as old as philology, and they too grew largely out of the requirements of an understanding of the literature.

The Greek name for philology was *grammatikē* (sc. *technē*), that is, the art of scholarly study based on experience that deals with the *grammata* (letters, *litterae* in Latin) in the sense of *syngrammata* (writings, works of literature).[11] Modern researchers are therefore wont to call the philology of the ancients "grammar" and its representatives "grammarians". What was once seen as its proper task becomes clear when we look at the subdivision of grammar in Antiquity. The so-called *Technē* of Dionysios Thrax is the oldest extant Greek grammar, and it was used extensively over a long period of time. In the scholia from the 6th century to this work we are told, in accordance with the explanations of two Roman scholars, Varro (1st century B.C.) and Quintilian (1st century A.D.), that in old times four "parts" (*mere*) – Varro says more correctly "duties" (*officia*, Greek *erga*) – of philology were distinguished,[12] namely the following:

1) the *anagnōstikon* (sc. *meros*) the reading (*anagnōsis*, *lectio*) as well as the recitation of literary texts which were written without word division, without accents and without *spiritus*;[13]

2) the *exēgētikon*, their explanation (*exegesis*, *enarratio*);

3) the *diorthōtikon*, their correction (*diorthōsis*, *emendatio*), the correction of mistakes made when a text was copied or written down from dictation;[14] and

4) the *kritikon*, their critical evaluation (*krisis*, *iudicium*) regarding aesthetic aspects and authenticity. The latter pertained not only to entire works, but also to all parts of a work, e.g. the individual verses of a poem.[15]

Dionysius Thrax calls the *kritikon* "the most beautiful part of grammar" and one of his commentators calls it "the consummation, the crown, as it were, of the entire art".[16] In three scholia we are reminded that grammar was previously known as criticism and the grammarians as critics.[17] All commentators on the *Technē* consider criticism of aesthetic aspects as an aid for the establishment of authenticity; some verses of the *Iliad*, so they say for example, should not be considered genuine, because they are not worthy of Homer.[18] They stress, however, time and again that the philologist is not a poet, and that he ought not to judge whether, for instance, certain verses or poems are beautiful, but that he should only determine whether they are similar to other verses or poems of the same author, i.e. whether they are genuine.[19] One of the scholiasts points out how many spurious works there are, in order to emphasize the importance of critical evaluation of authenticity; as examples he mentions the *Antigonē* of Sophokles, which is said to have been written by his son Iophon, as well as the epic works of Homer (*Kypria* and *Margitēs*), Aratos (*Thytika* and *Peri orneōn*) and Hesiod (*Aspis*). A later Byzantine commentator mentions in addition a didactic poem by Nikandros (*Thēriaka*).[20] Thus, we see that the critical examination of the authenticity of literary works was deemed to be highly important by ancient philologists.

The commentators of Dionysius Thrax had, however, too narrow a conception. The Hellenistic grammarians, especially Aristophanes of Byzantium and his successor Aristarchos of Samothrake, had used aesthetic criteria not only in order to separate the genuine works of an author from the spurious ones, but also, in order to choose the best authors of each literary genre, for the compilation of lists (so-called *canones*) of first-class, exemplary poets and prose writers, the "classics".[21]

Since the *kritikon* includes the critical evaluation of the authenticity of individual verses and sentences, it is, according to our conception, also textual criticism. But the *diorthōtikon*, the correction of copying or listening errors is also textual criticism. The activity of a textual critic was even always designated by the verb *diorthun*, "to correct" (which will appear in an important section of this investigation), and the textual critic was called a *diorthōtēs*, "corrector".[22] The scholars of Antiquity pursued in their textual criticism the same goal as modern philologists, though they were not as methodical. They too wanted to reconstruct as far as possible the original wording of a literary work those text had been corrupted, enlarged, or abridged in the course of time by being copied again and again. They did this by using the extant copies, by comparing the different variants and versions, and by choosing the best among these. Therefore they endeavored to correct the errors which had crept in, to eliminate the additions made by other hands, etc. Initially they used quite simple methods, but in the course of time their methods were refined, and especially the edition of Homer's texts by Aristarchos of Samothrake (Alexandria, first half of the 2nd century B.C.) came quite close to modern textual criticism. In any case, it went far beyond mere correction of copying errors, because it contained much *krisis*. Nevertheless, this kind of textual criticism and its results, the critically edited text, were also called *diorthōsis*.[23]

The solution of the many interwined problems confronting the grammarians demanded the most varied knowledge. The scholars who were of the opinion that grammar consisted of four "parts" distinguished also between four "tools" (*organa*) of that art; the *glōssēmatikon* (sc. *organon*) the *metrikon*, the *technikon* and the *historikon*, i.e. lexical, metric, grammatical and historical knowledge; the latter comprised also mythological, antiquarian and geographical knowledge.[24] But a philologist who investigated, say, the poems of a lyric poet had also to be conversant with his life and work and that of other lyric poets, as well as with the history of lyric poetry and even that of the art of poetry in general. To our historically oriented way of thinking, literary history and its basis, the biography of individual authors and their bibliographies, are integral elements of philology. After all, the work of an author is indeed the most important thing in his life. It is therefore the history of literature that occupies the largest part in outlines and handbooks of philology.

So far as I can see, the ancient grammarians did not express any opinion on the relation between philology (in the narrower sense) and literary history,[25] but

6

they conducted also biographical and bibliographical studies as well as studies on literary history. They could not help doing so, if they wanted to fulfill their proper obligations—I shall revert to this issue in a moment—but they dealt of course very soon also with problems of literary history for their own sake. Presumably they considered knowledge of literary history as one of the "tools" of their art, as one of the parts of the *historikon organon*.[26] Both literary history and cultural history were indeed considered as branches of history. This is evident from the fact that events in literary history were recorded also in general historical reviews as early as about 300 B.C.

The grammarians were primarily interested in the history of poetry and the lives of poets whose works, as already indicated, formed the primary subject of their discipline. The literary history of oratory and historiography was dealt with in part by orators, that of philosophy and the sciences largely by philosophers and practitioners of the respective branches of science. There were many works on the lives and works of famous authors, as well as on the character and origin of individual literary genres, as well as works that presented a characterization of a genre and its stages of development, with a chronological survey of its representatives, their peculiarities, innovations and creations. To be sure, very little of all this has come down to us,[27] but the data that these works contained have been partially transmitted to us by later compilers and compilers of compilers, especially the editor of the *Suda*. A literary history in the modern sense was, however, not created in Antiquity, even though there are certain beginnings in Aristotle. Leo attributes this to the interest in biography which always remained predominant.[28]

The activities of the ancient grammarians, especially those at Alexandria, were, however, largely similar to those of modern philologists and literary historians. The only debatable issue is whether one ought to distinguish between pre-Alexandrian philological endeavors in the narrower sense and research on the biography and bibliography of authors and on literary history, and whether one may say (as Leo and Pfeiffer do) that the former were not combined with the latter until Hellenistic times.[29] The scholarly endeavors which were later designated as "parts" of philology, were in my view connected from the very beginning with biographical, bibliographical and literary-historical reconstructions.[30] The study of the texts was normally the only way in which one could obtain insights into the lives and works of authors and other writers mentioned by them. Conversely, one needed knowledge of literary history, and especially of biography and bibliography, in order to solve problems of textual explanation and critical evaluation of authenticity. The latter in particular formed the link between philology in the narrower sense and literary history. The scholars who dealt with a particular author had always to take into consideration that among the works ascribed to him, i.e. in the scrolls bearing his name, there might also be spurious ones, given the conditions of textual transmission in those times. Their first task was therefore to distinguish between an author's genuine works and those that were falsely ascribed to him. But not all scholars were content to do only this; some tried even at a very early stage to find also the real authors of spurious works. Later on, those who did not do so were reproached. (That is why I prefer the broader concept of literary criticism, ascertaining the real author, to the narrower one, critical evaluation of authenticity.) The bibliographies of authors that were subsequently compiled constituted the results of literary critical research in the form of lists. In this way literary criticism contributed substantially to literary history. Where knowledge of literary history already existed, it helped in turn to answer questions of literary criticism.

The identification of texts with incomplete or incorrect data about authors or titles, or of texts transmitted without such data was the task of the librarians, and that too belonged to the field of literary criticism. If a work was extant in various versions, the librarian who had to catalog it was even confronted with a task involving textual criticism, because he had to decide which version was the authentic one. For this reason, it is indispensable to deal also with textual criticism in the present study which is mainly devoted to literary criticism.

Literary and textual criticism ran mostly in parallel, but occasionally they also touched each other tangentially or intersected. They had the same goal: the reconstruction of the literary *oeuvre* of ancient authors, especially that of classics, in its original form. To do this, one had to find the works that they had actually created, and had to establish their authentic texts.

Literary criticism was made difficult for the ancient philologists (similar to what their modern colleagues experience when they deal with medieval literature) because among Greek authors as well as among medieval ones there are so many namesakes (Apollonios, Alexandros, etc.). Thus, for example, we find that Diogenes Laertios (3rd century A.D.) lists for 29 of the 82 philosophers with whom he deals in his work on the lives and opinions of famous philosophers (the most recent are from the end of the 2nd century A.D.) several known namesakes, most of whom had also been authors.[31] Quite a few bearers of the same name were active in the same field, were compatriots and contemporaries.[32] It also happened frequently that an author had the same name as his father, equally well-known as an author. In such cases the customary procedure for the identification of persons—complementing the personal name by an indication of the father's name (in the genitive) and the place of birth or domicile (in adjectival form)—was not sufficient. One had to find further biographical details and to add them.[33]

The large number of authors with the same name was a corollary of the large amount of Greek literature, the sheer bulk of which alone would have been enough to keep the ancient biobibliographers busy. The small nation of the Greeks was immensely productive in art and scholarship. Although it is impossible to ascertain the total number of all works written by Greek authors, there were certainly many more than those that have been preserved or are merely known to have existed. For example, we have no adequate idea of the multitude of works which Kallimachos listed in the 120 books of his *Pinakes*. Of the Greek literature created before 250 B.C. we have only a small, even though very valuable, part. We do not even have the complete works of those authors who were included in the lists of classics compiled by the Alexandrian philologists. Of all the works of pagan Greek literature perhaps only one percent has come down to us.[34] All others were in part already forgotten by the third century A.D., in part they perished later, either because they were not deemed worthy to be copied when a new book form, the bound book (codex), supplanted the traditional scroll in the fourth century A.D.,[35] or because they belonged to "undesirable literature" in the opinion of certain Christian groups.

8

Notes to Chapter 1

1) Blum (1959) p. 9. – The complete titles of works cited by name of author and year are listed in the chronological bibliography at the end (p. 248).

2) This work is the starting point of all historians of bibliography, with the exception of Besterman (1940) who mentions on pp. 2-6 also some biographies and biobibliographies from Antiquity and the Middle Ages. The others treat only the period after the invention of printing.

3) Besterman (1940) p. 4.

4) Modern researchers of Antiquity like to use the term "pinakography" for the listing of ancient authors, irrespective of whether or not a list contains both biographical data and lists of works. The term is not documented; Stephanos of Byzantium (6th century A.D.) once mentions in his *Ethnika* under the heading Abdera the *pinakographoi* (authors of lists); perhaps he refers to Hesychios of Miletos, who called his *Onomatologos* a *pinax* of persons known in fields of learning. See Wentzel (1898) p. 309 f.

5) See Pfeiffer (1968) pp. 127-134. The older works are listed in Pfeiffer, pp. viii-ix, while those that deal specifically with the history of philology in Antiquity are listed in Gudeman (1909) pp. 13 and 19.

6) Pfeiffer (1968) p. 3.

7) The term "classical philology" is sometimes used in a wider sense for all studies of Classical Antiquity; see Gudeman (1909) p. 8.

8) The first Roman philologists appeared towards the end of the 2nd century B.C. Both Greek and Roman philologists (with only a few exceptions) treated only the literature of their own nation.

9) The scholia from Antiquity exist partly as anonymous notes to the respective works, partly also as commentaries by Greek or Roman scholars, mainly from late Antiquity. Because of the valuable data contained in them they will frequently be cited in the following.

10) Pfeiffer (1968) pp. 66-67 and 158; Pfeiffer p. 43, note 7, disapproves of the use of the term philology for the works of pre-Alexandrian scholars. This is in line with his conception of the origin of philology in Alexandria. Since I cannot agree with him on this point, I have no qualms to call those ancient studies that belong, according to our conception, to philology "philological" ones.

11) Both Kallimachos and Erathosthenes who was probably his successor as director of the library used, as already noticed by ancient philologers, the noun *gramma* in the sense of *syngramma*. See Hilgard (1901) p. 160, 10-18, also Pfeiffer (1968) p. 162 and also pp. 3 and 66. The Romans adopted the Greek term and called the art *grammatica* (sc. *ars*).

12) Hilgard (1901) pp. 12, 3-13; 115, 8 f.; 123, 13-15; 164, 9 f.; 452, 34-36; Diomedes (1857) p. 426, 21-31 with reference to Varro; Quintilianus (1959) I 4, 3. The purported author of the *Technē*, Dionysius Thrax, was an Alexandrian philologist of the second half of the 2nd century B.C., a pupil of Aristarchos of Samothrake, mainly working on the island of Rhodos. Already in Antiquity there were doubts about the authenticity of the work, but German philologers of the 19th century defended it; Di Benedetto (1958) again doubted its authenticity. Pfeiffer (1968) pp. 267-272 finds that Di Benedetto's arguments are not convincing, I am of a different opinion. On one point, I would go even farther than Di Benedetto: he ascribes paragraph 1-5 of the *Technē* to Dionysios Thrax, while ascribing the main part, paragraphs 6-20 to an anonymous author of the 4th century A.D. In paragraph 1 the author defines *grammatikē* (philology) and enumerates its six parts; incidentally, the ancient commentators of the *Technē* linked their account of an "old" division of the discipline into four parts to this sixfold division. A division into six parts was however criticized already in Antiquity, e.g. by Sextus Empiricus (1954) I 250, and Usener (1892) p. 588 found fault with its "gross logical flaws". Even more serious is the fact that the *diorthōsis* (correction, textual criticism), a main concern of the Alexandrian philologists, is neither mentioned nor is it contained in a generic term (as in the threefold division of Asklepiades of Myrlea (see below, note 24). I doubt therefore whether the traditional division into six parts originated with the pupil of Aristarchos, even though Sextus Empiricus ascribes it to Dionysius Thrax. On Varro and Quintilianus, see Usener (1892) pp. 597-601, who assumed that the division of philology into four parts had its origin in a theory of the discipline proposed by the Greek philologist Tyrannion who taught in Rome since 67 B.C. This assumption was disputed by Wendel (1948) column 1818. At any rate, the ancient commentators of Dionysius Thrax held that the sixfold division of philology existing under his name was younger than the old fourfold division. Neither one nor the other has however been dated with certainty so far.

13) The accents and spiritus which were later inserted served also for the meaningful division of continually written sentences (*scriptio continua*); see Erbse (1961) p. 224.

14) Diomedes (1857) p. 426, 28 (after Varro): *emendatio est . . . recorrectio errorum qui per scripturam dictationemve fiunt.* On this see Usener (1892) p. 599 f. The *diorthotikon* appears in the scholia also in the first or second place; see Hilgard (1901) pp. 12, 4 and 115, 8. But this is unimportant, because a correction of the copy of a work may become necessary at various stages, as the understanding of the text gradually improves. In the first citation, p. 12, 4, where the *diorthōtikon* precedes the other parts of philology, it is assumed that the teacher will check the copy to be studied by his pupil, and will, if necessary, correct it before he lets the student read it.

15) Quintilianus (1959) I 4, 3 who combines the first and the third "part" of grammar (*lectio* and *emendatio*) writes: *enarrationem praecedit emendata lectio et mixtum his omnibus indicium est, quo quidem ita severe sunt usi veteres grammatici, ut non versus modo censoria quadam virgula notare*

et libros, qui falso viderentur inscripti, tamquam subditos submovere familia permiserint sibi, sed auctores alios in ordinem redegerint, alios omnino exegerint numero. (The explanation is preceded by the reading and correction, and the critical evaluation is mixed with all three. The old grammarians were so severe in their critique that they did not only permit to mark verses [which they thought to be not authentic] with a critical mark, and to expel from the family books that appeared under a false title, as if they had been changelings, but they also included some authors in the list [of classics] while excluding others altogether.) See Usener (1892) pp. 605 and 584, 8. Radermacher, the editor of Quintilianus, retained the traditional but incomprehensible word *narrationem* (instead of *enarrationem*), whereas Colson (1924), a commentator of Quintilianus, rejected without justification Usener's interpretation of *emendata lectio.*

16) Dionysius Thrax (1883) paragraph 1; Hilgard (1901) p. 170, 7-9.

17) Hilgard (1901) pp. 3, 24 f.; 304, 7 f. The grammarians of Pergamon of the 2nd century B.C. preferred to call themselves critics, in contra-distinction to their colleagues at Alexandria. Their most important representative, Krates of Mallos, said that grammarians dealt with lower tasks, but critics with the higher ones. See Gudeman (1909) pp. 3-5; Pfeiffer (1968) p. 158.

18) Hilgard (1901) p. 12, 19-23.

19) Hilgard (1901) pp. 170, 2-5; 304, 2-3; 471, 32-472, 2.

20) Hilgard (1901) pp. 471, 32-472, 2 and 568, 27. The doubts about the authenticity of Sophokles's *Antigonē* which are not voiced anywhere else, are generally considered to be unfounded. On the other hand, it was well known that Iophon accepted his father's help, cf. Aristophanes, *Batrachoi* (Frogs), v. 73 f.

21) Cf. the quotation from Quintilianus in note 15, also Pfeiffer (1968) pp. 204-207. According to Quintilianus X 1, 54, the selected lists of Greek classics originated with Aristophanes of Byzantium and Aristarchos of Samothrake.

22) The verb will be translated in the following as "to correct" as a *terminus technicus.*

23) The text was also called *ekdosis* (edition); it served generally as a model for other copies. See Pfeiffer (1968) p. 215.

24) Hilgard (1901) pp. 123, 13 f.; 164, 10 f.; also Usener (1892) p. 587 f. The sceptic Sextus Empiricus (second half of the 2nd century A.D.) reports a tripartition of the art, including the "tools" of grammar, in the first book of his work against the grammarians, *Pros mathēmatikus* (Against the scholars); this tripartition had been advocated by Asklepiades, a grammarian from Myrlea (first half of the 1st century B.C.). He taught that the discipline consisted of a grammatical part (*technikon* sc. *meros*), a historical part (*historikon*) and a special "grammatic" part (*idiaiteron, grammatikon*). The first and second of these three parts are equivalent to the third and fourth "tools" of grammar, the third is grammar itself. It comprised, according to Sextus Empiricus, the explanation of works of literature as well as their

evaluation, i.e. critical evaluation of its aesthetics and its authenticity, as Sextus explicitly states. For Asklepiades this meant certainly also the reading and correction of texts. See Sextus Empiricus (1954) I 91-93 and 252 f.

25)   A comprehensive term, comparable to our "literary history" did not exist at all. This was probably because authors of poetical and other literary works were not dealt with jointly, other than in dictionaries. An exception was Damastes of Sigeion. In Imperial times there appeared some voluminous works whose titles we know from a few citations, e.g. *Theatrikē historia* and *Musikē historia*. The *Theatrikē historia* of the learned King Juba II of Mauretania (under Augustus) was a history (and study) of the Greek theater and dramatical literature in at least 17 books; the *Musikē historia* of a younger author, Dionysios of Halikarnassos, known as "the musician" (under Hadrian) was a history (and study) of Greek music and musical-poetical literature in 36 books. As to the titles of these works, it is well to remember that the Greek word *historia* meant originally "inquiry, study", and so also the Latin *historia*, as used in *historia naturalis*.

26)   The *historikon organon* had to explain, among other things, the identity of the mythical and historical persons mentioned in literary works. Since there were also literary authors among these, they became also objects of study.

27)   This pertains for example to the *historiai* of King Juba II of Mauretania, and those of the younger Dionysios of Halkarnassos, "The musician", cited in note 25. We can form an impression of the *Chrēstomathia grammatike*, a work compiled entirely from secondary sources and ascribed to Proklos (5th century A.D.) only on the strength of a summary included by Photios (9th century) in his *Bibliothēkē*, cod. 239. The title *Chrēstomathia* is misleading: this work is not a literary chrestomathy, a collection of excerpts from literary works, but a condensation of noteworthy issues in the fields of literary scholarship and philology, limited to Greek poetry, its types and its main representatives. The so-called anonymous *Peri kōmōdias* has left us an excerpt from an outline of the history of comedies from late Antiquity; text in Kaibel (1899) pp. 6-10, cf. on this Körte (1921) column 1213. — Cicero's *Brutus* constitutes a history of Greek and especially Roman oratory demonstrated by the characteristics of its principal representatives in chronological order; cf. Leo (1901) pp. 219-223. In *De oratore* II 51-58 Cicero gives an outline of Greek historiography. — On the overview of Greek literature in Quintilianus X 6, 46-84 see Steinmetz (1964).

28)   Leo (1901) p. 322. Incidentally, only the 19th century made any substantial progress on literary history beyond what had been achieved in antiquity.

29)   Leo (1901) p. 318, and Pfeiffer (1968) p. 3. It is not clear whether Pfeiffer's definition of philology includes literary history. However, as his subsequent discussion shows, he counts the studies of older Greek scholars on literary history among those scholarly activities which coalesced in the 3rd century B.C. into Alexandrian philology.

30)   For particulars see the next chapter, especially on Theagenes, Stesimbrotos and Antimachos.

31) He lists on the average 5-6 homonyms, in one case 14 (Herakleides) in two cases 20 each (Demetrios and Theodoros).

32) E.g. in the fifth century B.C. there were two Attic tragic poets by the name of Euripides other than the famous one.

33) Despite the more precise Roman system of naming persons (*praenomen, nomen gentile, cognomen*) there were many homonyms, although relatively few among authors, because there were fewer of them than in Greece.

34) According to Gerstinger (1948) p. 10, about 2000 Greek authors were known by name before the discovery of papyri. But the complete works of only 136 (6.8%) fragments of another 127 (6.3%) were preserved. Gerstinger counted, however, only authors whose names were known, not works known by their titles. The numerical relation between these and the works that are preserved wholly or partially would certainly be even much worse. Whether a count of known titles would serve any purpose remains to be seen. The main sources would be the biobibliographic articles in the *Suda*, but even the authority on which it is based, the epitomator of the *Onomatologos* by Hesychios of Miletos (6th century A.D.) no longer listed many authors which e.g. Diogenes Laertios (3rd century A.D.) had still named in his work.

35) Widmann (1967) column 586-603.

2. Forerunners: Aristotle, His Predecessors and Pupils

2.1 The Beginnings of Greek Philology and Literary History

IT IS NOT my intention to repeat here the entire prehistory and early history of philology, since Pfeiffer has dealt with it extensively. But in order to clarify the situation of those Alexandrian scholars to whom the Ptolemies entrusted the care of the book treasures which they had collected, I must nevertheless begin fairly much at the beginning. Kallimachos was one of these scholars, and the result of his work as a librarian was his great bibliography of Greek authors, the *Pinakes*. Thus, we are going to deal here with the conditions of historical scholarship under which the work came into being that started the line of national biographical dictionaries which continues to this day.

Greek philology grew out of scholarly inquiry into the life and works of Homer. What the Greeks had learnt from this endeavor, they applied to other poets and finally also to prose authors. The philology of Homer was, as it were, the model for philology as such. The process is not surprising, because the study of Homer constituted in Greece at all times and despite all political, economic, and cultural changes, the foundation of higher learning, the *paideia* which gave the Greeks a feeling of superiority over the surrounding peoples, the barbarians.

In the 5th century B.C., when books had become more widespread, teachers put on the desks of their pupils "the poetic works", i.e. the works of the great epic and lyric poets, and later on also those of the tragic poets, but above all Homer's works; the pupils had to read them and to learn them by heart, as Plato tells us in the words of the sophist Protagoras.[1] What they hoped to achieve by this for the education of young people, their mental and moral development, need not be discussed here. At any rate, many Greeks thought that Homer had educated Greece, as Plato relates elsewhere.[2] The epic poetry of Homer was however already at that time no longer easily understood, not even by the teachers of young people. For example, the obsolete words used by the poet and the unusual customs which he mentioned needed some explanation. This led to the first lexical and antiquarian research. Other problems followed. It was found that Homer seemed to contradict himself quite often, and attempts were made to explain those contradictions. But above all people took offense at scenes that seemed to be irreconcilable with moral principles or with the dignity of gods and heroes. In order to defend Homer against critics such as Xenophanes of Kolophon (second half of the 6th century B.C.), Theagenes of Rhegion (late 6th century B.C.) resorted to an allegorical interpretation of offending scenes. He was presumably one of those itinerant bards who not only recited the Homeric epics at festivals but also interpreted them.[3] Others adopted his method of interpretation. In the era of the sophists, the Greek age of enlightenment (5th century B.C.), Homeric problems of all kinds formed a popular theme for discussions, and this continued until the era of the Roman emperors. The proposed solutions were at first, and to some extent even later on, entirely devoid of scholarship, but just because they were so unsatisfactory they provoked a scholarly interpretation, the very core of philology.

When the epic works of Homer were written down, many educated Greeks were unpleasantly surprised. If, for example, a man who knew his Homer well visited a friend, and happened to take a look at his host's copy, he would notice immediately that the text he read there differed in certain respects from the one with which he was familiar. This was due to the rhapsodes who had spread Homer's works but had taken liberties with the wording of the text. Thus, the copies made in various cities contained not only different variants of single verses but also interpolations, omissions and inversions of entire verses and groups of verses. The copies of Homer's epics which were in use in the Greek colonies in Egypt until the middle of the 2nd century B.C. differed in part considerably from each other, as is evident from papyrus fragments.[4] The same was true of the copies which were compared by the Alexandrian philologists of the third and second century B.C. in their critical studies of the texts. The ancient scholia to the *Iliad* and the *Odyssey* contain much information on this, most of which goes back to the works of Aristarchos of Samothrake (1st half of the 2nd century B.C.). Evidently, the Alexandrian textual critics had before them widely varying editions (*ekdoseis*) of the *Iliad* and the *Odyssey*. They called some of these "common" or "commoner" (*koinai*, *koinoterai*), others were called "finer" or "finest" (*chariesterai*, *chariestatai*), some were named after a man (*kat' andra*) or after cities (*kata poleis*), and after regions or islands. The following editions (except those of the Alexandrian textual critics Zenodotos, Aristophanes and Aristarchos) are randomly listed in the scholia because of variant readings or (more seldom) because there are too many or too few verses: that of Antimachos of Kolophon, an epic poet and writer of elegies who was esteemed by Plato (late 5th century B.C.), that of Massilia (Marseille) and of Sinope (a city on the Black Sea), also those of the regions of Argolis and Aiolis, and those of the islands of Chios, Cyprus and Crete.[5] The *Suda* (10th-11th century) and the Byzantine commentator of Homer, Eustathios (12th century), also cited an edition of Euripides, an Attic tragic poet (5th century B.C.) who is however not the same as the famous poet,[6] and the author of the so-called *Vita Marciana* of Aristotle mentions an edition of the *Iliad* edited by the philosopher, which is referred to as a *diorthōsis* by other authors.

An *ekdosis* (edition) meant primarily the publication of a new work by an author. This was generally done in the following manner: the author had one or more copies made from his original manuscript for his friends and patrons, and undertook or permitted the preparation of further copies from those copies. Sometimes a bookseller intervened and had copies made either from an original or from another copy in order to sell them. But the edition of an old work by a scholar was also called an *ekdosis*.[7] All modern philologists are of the opinion that the pre-Alexandrian *ekdoseis* of the *Iliad* and the *Odyssey* were not editions based on textual criticism, and thus not *diorthōseis* in the sense of the Alexandrian philologists. This is certainly correct. Although Eustathios refers to the editions of Massilia and Sinope, and to that of Aristotle, as *diorthōseis*,[8] the concept of *diorthōsis* (correction) was a fairly broad one: it included anything from simple correction of copying errors to philological textual criticism. It is therefore not possible to say what exactly was done by the men who edited Homer's work before or at the same time as the first Alexandrian philologists.

At least some of them had presumably realized that the copies of the version of the *Iliad* and the *Odyssey* which were circulating in their city were incorrect, and they had tried to produce a correct copy of that version of the Homeric epics which they held to be authentic, in order to make a model from which copies for teaching and for other purposes could be made.[9] The correction of the copy on which the editor based himself included perhaps sometimes primitive textual criticism on a small scale, because if he occasionally found a different reading or an additional verse in a copy of the same version, he had to make a philological decision.[10]

At any rate, towards the end of the fourth century lovers of literature were aware that the copies of Homer's epics which circulated within the realm of Greek culture, including those that had been made from specially prepared editions, diverged considerably from each other, and that all of them presented a doubtful text. This is apparent from an anecdote by Diogenes Laertios (3rd century A.D.) to whom we owe many items of information that are important for our investigation; in his work on the lives and opinions of famous philosophers he says that the epic poet Aratos (who himself later corrected and edited the text of the *Iliad* and/or that of the *Odyssey*[11]) once, when he was still a young man, asked the philosopher Timon of Phleius, a follower of the skeptic Pyrrhon, how he could obtain a reliable text of Homer. He received the mocking advice to stick to the old copies rather than to those that had already been corrected. Evidently, Timon did not have a high opinion of the achievements of those who had up to then corrected or edited Homer's epics.[12]

By this time (beginning of the 3rd century B.C.) it had also long since been noticed that not all poetic works ascribed to Homer bore his name legitimately. Our oldest witness for the doubts about the authenticity of certain works in the epic cycle of myths known as *Kyklos* is Herodotos (ca. 444 B.C.). It seemed questionable to him whether the *Kypria* had been written by Homer, because of the description of the itinerary of Paris and Helen from Sparta to Troy in this work differed from that in the *Iliad*.[13] The scholars of the 4th century B.C. went much further in their critical evaluation of authenticity. It seems that Plato considered as authentic works of Homer only the *Iliad* and the *Odyssey* as well as the *Margitēs*, a comical epic poem which has not come down to us, and whose hero was the blockhead Margites.[14]

There were also attempts to discover the real authors of the works which had been falsely attributed to Homer and other bards of ancient times. Some scholars thought that the epos on the conquest of Oichalias by Herakles *Oichalias halōsis* which was known to them as a Homeric work and which has not come down to us, had in reality been written by Kreophylos of Samos, one of the hosts of the blind bard.[15] But because the poem now bore Homer's name, it was thought that it must have been designated as such by Kreophylos. Others maintained, in order to salvage the epos for Homer, that he had left it to Kreophylos as a token of his thanks for the latter's hospitality, but that the Samian had published it as his own work.[16] The bibliographic controversy caused Kallimachos to write a satiric epigram; he held that Kreophylos was the real author of the epos, and thought that it was too great an honor for him to declare the work to be one by Homer.[17]

The case is significant. Since the Greeks had not yet understood why works of different authors were ascribed to Homer and other ancient poets, they usually suspected fraud. Therefore, to discover the real author was for them tantamount to the unmasking of a forger. Some incidents reinforced this conception.[18]

Thus, Herodotos relates that Onomakritos who lived at the court of the Peisistratides at Athens (second half of the 6th century B.C.) had been found guilty of splicing into his collection of prophecies of Musaios an oracle that he had fabricated himself. It seems that it was for this reason that Aristotle later suspected him of having written the poems that were known under the name of Orpheus.[19]

The determination of Homer's genuine works belonged already to the problems of his biography, because for an author the bibliography, the listing of his works, constitutes indeed a part of his biography. In view of the role which Homer played as the educator of Greece it was being asked already at an early stage who this man had been. Although the biographies under the title *Bios Homēru* (Life of Homer) which have come down to us under the names of Herodotos and Plutarch as well as anonymously, were put into the form in which we know them only in the era of the Roman Emperors, the data contained in them are much older; they can be traced in part back to the 6th century B.C.[20] The same is true for the *Agōn Homēru kai Hēsiodu* (The contest between Homer and Hesiod).

The first "biographer" of Homer was apparently that Theagenes of Rhegion who began, towards the end of the 6th century B.C., the allegorical interpretation of the *Iliad*. He appears in the first place among the older "scholars" listed by the Christian Tatianos (second half of the 2nd century A.D.) who dealt with Homer's poetry, his origin and his period of flourishing.[21] The second place in the list is occupied by Stesimbrotos of Thasos (second half of the 5th century B.C.) of whom we also have opinions on some problems in Homer, and the third place is held by his pupil Antimachos of Kolophon (end of the 5th century B.C.) whom we already met as editor of the *Iliad* and the *Odyssey*. Pfeiffer conjectures (on the basis of later Alexandrian practices) that Antimachos wrote a biography of Homer as an introduction to his edition;[22] this is plausible. At any rate, all three Homer scholars named as the earliest ones by Tatianos dealt demonstrably both with the works of the poet (interpretation, edition) and with his life. They combined therefore, to put it in modern terms, philology in the narrower sense and literary history. In the scholia to the *Technē* of Dionysios it is therefore said that philology in the broader sense began with Theagenes and was perfected by Aristotle and the Peripatetic Praxiphanes.[23]

We may assume that the early biographers of Homer used the same methods as the more recent ones. Since they did not have any documentary evidence for his life and work, they tried to utilize any hints which they found in the works ascribed to him and his contemporaries for his biography and bibliography. In addition, they drew on popular tradition, the stories and anecdotes that were told about the blind bard.

It is likewise probably that they already dealt with the same problem as their successors. Tatianos's words indicate that they discussed the two main questions which all biographers sought to answer: one pertained to Homer's origin, his *genos*, the other concerned his prime or period of flourishing, his *akme*, which was later established as his fortieth year. It was natural that people wanted to know who were the parents and even the grandparents of the poet—Homer's family tree was even traced back to Orpheus—and where he had seen the light of day. As is well known, seven cities claimed the honor of having been Homer's birthplace. Naturally, Stesimbrotos pleaded for the island of Thasos, Antimachos for Kolophon. One's father and place of birth were indeed the most important marks of identification by which a person was distinguished from other bearers of the same name.

Just as difficult as the identification of the place of birth was that of his lifetime. Attempts were made to relate it to a generally known "dated" event, the Trojan War. People also looked for a contemporary whose known period of flourishing could serve as a point of reference for Homer's *akmē*. Thus a synchrony was constructed with Hesiod, the other great epic poet of the archaic period, and a literary contest between the two rivals was supposed to have taken place. Later on, famous teachers or pupils of a poet or scholar were accorded precedence among Homer's contemporaries. But of Homer's teachers it could only be said that he had immortalized one of them in the person of Phemios, the bard of Odysseus and of Penelope's suitors. But neither the early biographers of Homer nor their successors limited themselves to a discussion of his origin and period of flourishing; following the popular tradition, they also told about the peculiar fate of the blind bard who had had no "permanent home" but had led a wandering life. Neither would they have refrained from telling of his death and grave. One cannot tell whether they dealt with bibliographic questions as did many later biographers, namely contesting or defending the authenticity of certain epics. At the time of Antimachos of Kolophon, for example, it had long since been doubtful that the *Kypria* were genuine.

Homeric studies were, as mentioned, the paradigm for similar studies on other poets, especially on those who were dealt with by teachers in higher education, namely Hesiod and the great lyric and tragic poets of the sixth and fifth century. For those too it was primarily a matter of the interpretation of their works, but they probably also treated questions of textual criticism, and those pertaining to biography and bibliography. Although results of biographical and bibliographical research of the fifth century have come down to us only in fragments and indirectly, it is evident that as early as ca. 400 B.C Greek scholars had a not insignificant knowledge of the lives and works of the early poets of their nation, because soon thereafter the first comprehensive works of literary history were published.[24] The dating of poets was still largely uncertain, but even for Greek history in general it was only then that a reliable chronological framework, based on documentary material began to be erected.

The historian Hellanikos of Lesbos (second half of the 5th century B.C.) started this work. He compiled, probably based in part on archival documents, *Hiereiai tēs Hēras hai en Argei,* a list of the mythical and historical priestesses of Hera in Argos, the main site of the Hera cult; he inserted into this framework a general chronicle of Greece, half of which extended, however, into the mythical period.[25] He also compiled a list of the *Karneonikai,* the victors in the Karneian contests at Sparta, a festival devoted to Apollo which comprised not only athletics but after a certain point also poetical and musical contests, artistic competitions (solo and chorus songs accompanied by a string or wind instrument). Because of the connection between poetry, especially lyric poetry, and music (the authors of lyric poems also composed the musical accompaniment) the list of Hellanikos (which was certainly based on archival studies) provided also reference points for the chronology of some early lyric poets-composers. For example, at the first artistic Karneian contest (26th Olympiad or 676/673 B.C.)

18

one of Hellanikos's compatriots, the lyric poet and kitharode Terpandros of Lesbos, had been the winner, and thus his *akmē* could be dated. Hellanikos also expressed his views on a question of Greek musical history in his *Karneonikai*, namely on the introduction of cyclic choruses (dithyrambs recited by a chorus standing in a ring around the altar) by Arion, another of his compatriots; he probably had a good reason for this. But one should not conclude from this that he enlarged his list to make it a "musical history of Hellas", as Jacoby thought.[26]

With his *Karneonikai* Hellanikos laid the foundations for a typically Greek form of literature (in the widest sense), akin to chronicles, whose form was the *pinax* (literally tablet, list): the list of victors. This expressed, quite apart from parochial pride, the passion of all Greeks for games (first observed by Jacob Burckhardt),[27] a passion so strong that they wanted to preserve the memory of the great games and their victorious participants for eternity.

Following the model of Hellanikos his somewhat younger contemporary Hippias of Elis created an *Olympionikōn anagraphē*, a list of victors in the games at Olympia, the most important national ("Panhellenic") games.[28]

Among the sophists of the second generation who were led towards scholarly research by their endeavors for enlightenment, Hippias was outstanding by virtue of his versatility. He also devoted himself to philological and literary studies, but above all to antiquarian research and studies of cultural history. If we read today that Aristotle and his pupils who conducted similar studies, continued the sophistic tradition,[29] we ought to think primarily of Hippias. Initially, he wanted perhaps to collect only material for his lectures, arguments for his assertions. He was the first to expound a thesis which characterizes the men of enlightenment of the fifth century and which was the foundation of their critique of society, namely the thesis of the difference between that which has been ordained by nature (*physei*) and what is only stipulated by human statute (*nomo*) and is therefore not eternal and immutable, but transitory and changeable.[30] But in the course of time the same thing happened to him which, for example, also happened to Aristotle's pupils: he often lost sight of the original goal of his research, and the scholarly research became an end in itself.[31] This is particularly obvious in his list of victors at the Olympic contests which was also certainly based on archival studies. The general importance of this *anagraphē* for the chronology by Olympiads is not our subject here. Although it did not yield any data for the history of Greek literature and music (in Olympia there were no artistic contests), with its help and indirectly, as it were, it was possible to date exactly the victory odes which had been written by Simonides, Pindar and Bakchylides in honor of the Olympic victors, among which were some of the outstanding creations of Greek choral lyric poetry of the fifth century.[32] In Delphi, at the Pythian games, however, the artistic contests took pride of place. We shall deal below with the list of *Pythionikai* compiled by Aristotle.

The authors of the oldest works on literary history, probably written in the first decades of the fourth century, are held to be Glaukos of Rhegion, a compatriot of Theagenes, although separated from him by a century, and Damastes of Sigeion who is named as a pupil of Hellanikos. The former wrote *Peri archaion poiētōn te kai musikōn* (On early poets and composers), the latter wrote *Peri poiētōn kai sophistōn* (On poets and sophists). While we know only very little about the work of Damastes,[33] we are somewhat better informed about that by

Glaukos, because later scholars used it more than the other. Thus, some of the information in the work *Peri musikēs* (On music), falsely attributed to Plutarch, can be traced back to Glaukos.[34]

What has come down to us of the contents of his book pertains only to earlier Greek composers and lyric poets-composers; it seems that Glaukos did not deal with other poets. He was apparently mainly concerned to establish the relative chronology of early composers and lyric poets; he wanted to show, without distinguishing between mythical and historical persons, who was the first to appear with a new art or art form, and who imitated him, that is to say, who were the first, second, third, etc., representatives of the respective art or art form. These were already the aspects under which later on the history of all arts and sciences was presented: invention (*heurēma*) and succession (*diadochē*). The representatives of individual literary genres seemed to the Greek scholars to be either "inventors" (*heuretai*) of artistic or scholarly innovations or "successors" (*diadochoi*) of these inventors, or their pupils, and pupils of pupils, etc., who in turn had sometimes distinguished themselves by their own "inventions".[35] Glaukos was certainly not the first to think in these categories, but he is the earliest author for whom this can be documented.[36]

Somewhat younger is perhaps a work preserved and stored in Sikyon (west of Korinth, north of Argos) which was also in the form of a list, an *anagraphē*. It listed the poets and composers according to the periods of office of the priestesses of Hera at Argos (apparently following Hellanikos),[37] starting with Amphion, the mythical inventor of kitharody and of kitharodic poetry,[38] a son of Zeus and a Theban princess who married the ruler of Sikyon. Presumably, this *anagraphē* was inscribed in stone, which would not have been unusual.[39] Its unknown author had perhaps used the work of Glaukos, but improved on the chronology by relating the lifetime of the poets and composers to the period of office of the priestesses of Hera at Argos. A pupil of Aristotle, Herakleides Pontikos, used this list as the basis for a work on music and composers which, though it has not come down to us, was used by pseudo-Plutarch in his work on music.[40] We do not know whether the works of poets and composers were mentioned or even listed in the Sikyonic *anagraphē* or in the works of Glaukos and Damastes, but it is not very likely.

Thus, there were already certain preliminary studies, when two younger scholars who were prominent among Plato's pupils, Aristotle and Herakleides Pontikos, began to devote themselves to research in philology and the history of literature. Plato himself did not concern himself with such studies, but neither did he prevent his pupils from pursuing them.

2.2 The Works of Aristotle on Philology and Literary History

Aristotle was born in 384/383 B.C. and entered Plato's Academy in Athens when he was about seventeen years old.[41] He came from the city of Stageiros on the Thracian Chalkidike not far from the Macedonian border. His father had been an outstanding physician who had been consulted by the Macedonian king. Aristotle stayed with the Academy, first as a pupil, then as a teacher until 347 when Plato died. The next twelve or thirteen years he spent teaching and doing research in various places. For a few years, beginning in 343/343, he taught the

Macedonian crown prince Alexander, a son of Philip II. When he returned to Athens in 335/334, accompanied by his oldest pupil, Theophrastos of Eresos (Lesbos), he had conceived his own philosophy in constant spiritual controversy with Plato, and had also done research in the most variegated branches of science and learning, among which were some, such as dialectics and zoology, which had until then been neglected. In his research he was constantly concerned about three things: first, finding out what existed, then, understanding and explaining why and for what purpose it existed, and finally, determining what was its essence. Thus, he actually created the method of scientific research. So much separated him now from the Academy that he did not reenter it, but gathered pupils around himself at the other end of the city, initially in and later near the gymnasium called the "Lykeion". In this circle he conducted during the last twelve or thirteen years of his life extremely versatile activities centered on teaching and research. In this, he was obviously aided by his older students; this was a usual practice. They helped him also to develop his large collections of materials which were characteristic for his method, and to assemble new ones. He left, among other things, a collection of 158 city constitutions which had been intended as background material for political studies.[42] His school became famous under the name *Peripatos* (walkway); through the last will of Theophrastos, who succeeded him as head of the school, it became a community (perhaps a society for the cult of the muses?) with its own plot of land on which a sanctuary for the muses, the *Museion*, was erected. As a foreigner, Aristotle had not been able to buy real estate in Athens. Even Theophrastos could do this only with the help of one of his students, Demetrios of Phaleron who ruled Athens from 317 until 307 as procurator of Kassandros of Macedonia.[43]

Although the philological and literary studies of Aristotle take up only a relatively small part of his huge works, they were nevertheless not insignificant, and partly even fundamental, pointing the way for future studies. Unfortunately, we have only fragments of these. Their exact dating is therefore difficult. Also, Aristotle discussed certain questions several times during his lifetime. Naturally, he often continued where earlier scholars had left off. Thus, he dealt with controversial points in the *Iliad* and *Odyssey*, continuing the traditional interpretation of Homer. Once there existed ten books by him on *Aporēmata Homērika* (Homer problems). The new scholarly spirit that imbued him manifested itself here in historical explanations, for example in the following one, which was later accepted by Kallimachos. While Plato had stated that it could not be true that Achilles (a Thessalian) had dragged the body of Hektor round the grave of Patroklos (that is, Homer must have lied), Aristotle pointed out that it was still customary in Thessalia to drag the body of a murderer round the grave of his victim.[44]

When Aristotle became the teacher of Alexander of Macedonia, he made a corrected copy of the *Iliad* which he studied with his pupil and which he finally gave to him. Alexander took this copy with him on his campaigns in Asia. His biographers reported this because of special circumstances. Later on, it was lost. It has been the subject of speculation why the Alexandrian philologists did not cite Aristotle's *diorthōsis* of the *Iliad* which is once also designated as an *ekdosis*.[45] They probably did not have a copy of this edition, or perhaps it was never copied. The teachers who wanted to give young people a higher education corrected of course their copies of the *Iliad* before they gave it to their pupils,[46] although it is not known how far they went in doing so. Perhaps Aristotle did more than other teachers or earlier correctors of the Homeric text. As a reader and collector of books he was unequalled. Already in Plato's Academy he had the nickname *anagnōstēs* (reader) and he left the largest library that had until then been collected by a Greek.[47] We may therefore assume that he was familiar not only with the Attic version of the *Iliad* and the *Odyssey*, and one cannot exclude the possibility that he owned also copies with divergent wordings and verses, and that he used these in his *diorthōsis* of the *Iliad*, so that he performed also textual criticism to an unknown extent. He was surely aware of the uncertainties surrounding Homer's text, with which the above-mentioned Aratos-Timon anecdote deals.[48]

It is certain that he occupied himself with questions concerning authenticity. He was explicitly of the opinion (already held by Plato) that of the "Homeric" epics only the *Iliad*, the *Odyssey* and the *Margitēs* were genuine. He substantiated his opinion by aesthetic criteria, i.e. by the superiority of the three works from which he had derived his conception of epic perfection.[49] When he separated the genuine works of Homer from the multitude of those that circulated under Homer's name, he did already the same as Kallimachos and all other later bibliographers who sought to establish the literary property of individual authors.

Aristotle dealt also with specifics in Homer's biography. Contrary to earlier scholars, he thought the poet had been born on the island of Ios.[50] (A grave of Homer was displayed there.)

It is self-evident that he also dealt with other poets. Among his works were, besides the already mentioned *Aporēmata Homērika*, also similar writings on the interpretation of Hesiod, Archilochos (one of the earliest and most important lyric poets), Euripides, Choirilos (one of Aischylos's predecessors) and other poets.[51] There was also a dialog *Peri poiētōn* (On the poets) which he had written quite early, at any rate before his famous work on literary aesthetics, the *Peri poiētikēs*, generally known as his *Poetics*.[52] We know the dialog only from a few quotations by later authors; Rostagni tried to deduce his train of thought.[53] One of the few passages which can be somewhat reconstructed deserves to be mentioned here. Since Aristotle was primarily concerned to determine the character of poetry, he rejected already in the first chapter of his later work, the *Poetics*, the prevalent idea that poetry was different from prose only by the meter of the verses. He declared summarily, that Empedokles had nothing in common with Homer except the *metron*; the latter should be named a *poiētēs* (poet), the former however a *physiologos* (natural scientist). Aristotle referred here to the main work by Empedokles, a didactic poem later called *Peri physeōs* (On nature). But in the dialog "On the poets" he dealt at greater length with Empedokles. This is known from details cited by Diogenes Laertios in his chapter on Empedokles. Aristotle discussed in that dialog not only the origin and lifetime of Empedokles but also praised him as "Homerical" (*homērikos*) extolled his poetic language and stylistic skill, and mentions that he had written, besides the *Peri physeōs*, also other poems, among them an unfinished epos on the Persian wars and a hymn to Apollo (which was burned by his sister), and also tragedies and political works.[54] Some modern researchers thought that there was a contradiction between the passage in the *Poetics* and the statements of Diogenes Laertios. Rostagni was right to reject this.[55] In the *Poetics* Aristotle refers only to one work by Empedokles, his didactic poem, but in the dialog he considers his entire output. It even seems to me that the statements of Diogenes Laertios are taken from an answer to an assertion that relates to a sentence in the *Poetics*. One of the partners in the dialog had probably claimed in relation to the epos *Peri physeōs* that Empedokles was not really a poet but a natural scientist who wrote in verses. Another speaker, however, pointed to the poetic language of the Sicilian and to his genuine poetic works. Moreover, he or a third one reminded the others that Empedokles had also written political works. In this manner Aristotle managed to work into the dialog a mini-bibliography of Empedokles which was, to be sure, quite brief but cited also two unpublished works.[56] Such a thing is not attested for any of Aristotle's predecessors. This cannot be mere chance, if one considers that Aristotle was a peerless reader and collector of books.

Four works of Aristotle are of particular interest for our investigation. All had the form of lists, *pinakes*, and all were probably also produced shortly before or soon after his return to Athens, and they were based on archival studies. In the list of Aristotle's works transmitted by Diogenes Laertios (3rd century A.D.) and by Hesychios of Miletos (6th century A.D.) they appear under the following titles:[57] *Olympionikai* (Victors at the Olympic games); *Pythionikai* (Victors at the Pythian games) [which took place near Delphi]; *Nikai Dionysiakai* [Hesychios adds: *astikai kai lēnaikai*] (Victories [in the dramatic contests] of the City and Lenaean Dionysia); *Didaskaliai* (Performances [of plays at the City and Lenaean Dionysia]); thus in Diogenes. Hesychios has: *Peri didaskalion* (On the performances [of plays]).

The four lists have not come down to us, but they are more or less well known from quotations by later scholars, the last two also from inscriptions which were derived from them. Evidently, they belonged to the type of lists of victors which had been started by Hellanikos with his *Karneonikai*. As we shall see, however, the *Didaskaliai* went considerably beyond those. The *Olympionikai* on the other hand were presumably nothing more than a revised and enlarged new edition of the *Olympionikon anagraphē* by the sophist Hippias, which had been updated until the thirties of the fourth century B.C.[58] But about his list we know least.

The *Pythionikai* were probably commissioned by the Amphiktyones, the association of inhabitants in the vicinity of the temple of Apollo in Delphi. The list was perhaps preceded by an introduction on the history of the Pythian games. Aristotle was aided in his studies of the documents in the archives of the priests of Delphi by Kallisthenes, a nephew or grandnephew whom he had raised in his house and who had already worked in the same archives on a history of the (third) Holy War (356-346). Kallisthenes followed Alexander in 334 B.C. to Asia in order to record the achievements of the king in his battles with the Persians.[59] The list of the *Pythionikai* must have been largely completed by that time. The two editors were highly honored by the Amphiktyones, and the list which they had compiled were carved in stone around 331 B.C.[60]

A list of *Pythionikai* was —contrary to a list of *Karneonikai* or *Olympionikai* — a productive source for the chronology of literary history, both directly and indirectly. It listed under the respective dates 1) the lyric poets who had won at the artistic competitions, the most important of the Pythic games, and from this one could deduce their period of flourishing; 2) together with successful athletic contestants also those in whose honor victory odes had been written and set to music. Thus it was possible for the Alexandrian grammarians to date the Pythian odes of Pindar, as documented in one case.[61]

2.3 Aristotle's List of Performances of Plays in Athens (Didaskaliai)

While the *Olympionikai* and the *Pythionikai* of Aristotle provided much useful information for the scholars who dealt with older lyric works, his *Didaskaliai* were of extraordinary value for the history of Attic drama, because they listed all tragedies, satyr plays and comedies that had been staged in the fifth and fourth century in Athens at the most important Dionysian festivals, namely the Great or City Dionysia and the Lenaean Dionysia, in the following called Dionysia and Lenaea for short. About fifty or sixty years after the compilation of the Aristotelian *Didaskaliai* Kallimachos revised them, so that the list of performances of plays became one of the dramatic poets and their plays, under the (abbreviated) title *Pinax tōn didaskalōn* (List of dramatic poets), the first list of authors of a certain literary genre and their works. We must therefore get as exact an idea as possible of the Aristotelian *Didaskaliai*. (The *Nikai Dionysiakai* of Aristotle, his fourth list, were probably only an appendix based on the *Didaskaliai*, as we shall see later.)

In order to understand the Aristotelian *Didaskaliai* and its problems, it is necessary to begin with some facts on the history of the theater.[62] The performance of plays at the Dionysia and Lenaea were not the only ones that took place in Attica at that time, but they were superior by far to all others that were performed at Dionysian festivals in Athens and elsewhere. One can trace them back to various years, the oldest ones to the end of the sixth century. In the course of time, they all assumed the character of artistic contests, the last one being the performance of tragedies at the Lenaea (ca. 432 B.C.). Since then, contests of both tragedies and comedies took place regularly at the Lenaea (in January) and at the Dionysia (in March).[63] The officials in charge, the *Archōn epōnymos* (the archon after whom the year was named) who was responsible for the Dionysia and the *Archon basileus* (king) who oversaw the Lenaea, admitted, however, only a limited number of poets and new plays: in regular years of the classic period they allowed three tragic poets with three tragedies and one satyr play each for the Dionysia, and two tragic poets with two tragedies each for the Lenaea, and for both festivals five comic poets with one comedy each.[64] In order to be admitted, a poet probably had to submit his manuscript to the archon, and had "to ask for a chorus" as the saying went, because the chorus was since ancient times the main factor in the performance of a tragedy or comedy. It was then entirely up to the archon to assign a chorus to a poet or to deny it to him. Until the end of the fourth century it was also the archon who decided on the *chorēgoi*, literally the "leaders of the chorus". Those were rich citizens who, taking turns, paid the chorus and provided its costumes. The success of a play depended to a high degree on the interest and generosity of a choregos. All other costs of the performances, such as the actors' salaries, were paid by the state. Since ca. 309 B.C., when Demetrios of Phaleron ruled Athens, the state paid also the salary and costumes of the chorus. A state official, the *agōnothetēs* (manager of contests) took the place of the choregoi; we owe the larger part of our information on Aristotle's *Didaskaliai* to the official who performed this duty in the year 279/278.[65]

In addition to plays, the Dionysian festivals featured also dithyrambs, chorus songs that dealt with single episodes of the heroic sagas, and which, similar to plays, also had their own titles. At the Dionysian festivals in Athens, dithyrambic contests took place together with dramatic contests already in the first quarter of the fifth century,[66] and all ten Attic *phylai* (literally "tribes", i.e., local groups of citizens) took part in that contest. Five of them provided a chorus of boys, five others of men, who recited a new dithyramb. The choregoi were not appointed by the archon, but were nominated by each phylos from their members. Today it is generally assumed that Aristotle listed in his *Didaskaliai* also the performance of the dithyrambs, but it must be admitted that one can find only the faintest traces of the respective parts of his works, while those that deal with the performance of plays are more evident. I shall return to this issue later on.

It was customary that the poets produced and directed their new plays and dithyrambs themselves. This was called *didaskein* (literally "teaching"), and the authors of plays and dithyrambs were specifically called *didaskaloi* (literally "teachers"), as the lexicographer Harpokration (2nd century A.D.) explains.[67] Thus the peculiar term *didaskaliai*, "rehearsals, productions" which was used by Aristotle as the title of his list. It needed however a more precise designation which made it clear that it dealt with the production of such and such works at such and such a festival, because plays were produced not only at the Dionysia and the Lenaea, and it was not only plays that were produced. But because there was no other such list, the one by Aristotle was simply cited as "the" *Didaskaliai*.[68] Kallimachos evidently linked the title of his *Pinax tōn didaskalōn* to the *Didaskaliai*.

Exceptions to that rule, namely the production of plays by persons commissioned by the author, are known only since the last third of the fifth century. It is questionable whether they were rare. Our knowledge of Attic theatrical practices is limited. It is mainly based on information on the works of the "classics", Aischylos, Sophokles, Euripides, and Aristophanes which were preserved through the Byzantine tradition. The three tragic poets directed their own plays. The works left by Sophokles and Euripides were produced by their relatives. Aristophanes, however, preferred to have his comedies produced by other persons who were experienced directors. By chance we know also that a comedy by Eupolis, one of Aristophanes's rivals, and plays by Antiphanes and Anaxandrides, poets of the so-called lesser comedies (second and third quarter of the fourth century) were produced by other people. Other than that, it is only known that Aphareus, a tragic poet of the fourth century who was also known as an orator, a son of the sophist Hippias and a stepson of Isokrates, had his plays produced by a certain Dionysios and others.[69] The author remained however even in these cases the *didaskalos* in the broader sense. The director who was commissioned and of course paid by the author was called a *hypodidaskalos* (literally "sub-teacher") in the fourth century.[70]

At the end of a performance a jury decided who had won and who placed second and third; at the contests for comedies they also decided who had won the fourth and fifth place. The victors were crowned with a wreath and received a prize. Those who had won the second place were also considered winners. All poets who participated in a contest received an honorarium.[71] Aristophanes deplores in the *Batrachoi* (Frogs), verse 367, the reduction of the "poet's remuneration." The "victorious" choregoi and the best principal actors also received prizes.

When the state began to arrange performances and contests, i.e. since ca. 500 B.C., the responsible archons kept records of the events and preserved them in their archives.[72] They did this not out of an interest in literary history but mainly in order to document their expenses for the festive performances (honoraria for poets, the actors' salaries, etc.). Although the costs were covered only partially by the state, they had to record the names of the choregoi, because the citizens who defrayed the costs of the choruses paid thereby also a special tax (*leiturgia*) and had then the right to be excepted for some time from such levies. Since the archons were also responsible for the integrity of the contests and the allocation of prizes, they also had to record the names of the competing poets, the titles of the plays and the names of the principal actors, and finally they had to record the decisions of the jury. This can be inferred from the fact that Aristotle was still able to establish, about one hundred and fifty years later, who had placed fifth (!) in the contest of comedy writers held at the Dionysia in 485 B.C., what had been the title of his play and the name of the principal actor.

The *Didaskaliai* of Aristotle are being cited by later, mainly anonymous, scholars who got their information primarily from the Alexandrian philologists, e.g. the authors of scholia to the classical plays and the other works; five times they are cited as a work of Aristotle and eight times without giving the name of the author.[73] Thus, in a scholium to Plato's *Apology of Socrates* we read that in the same year in which the comedy *Pelargoi* (Storks) by Aristophanes had been performed, the *Oidipus* trilogy by Meletos had also been produced, "as Aristotle relates in the *Didaskaliai*".[74] (The son of that tragic poet who had been ridiculed by Aristophanes was one of the accusers of Socrates.) Eleven citations deal with Attic dramatic poets and with plays of the classical period, and they pertain explicitly to a list of premieres of these works. The wording is either "Aristotle lists in the *Didaskaliai*" or "as listed in the *Didaskaliai*".[75] Since, as already mentioned, there was no other list of performances of plays in Athens during the fifth and fourth century B.C., one may identify the *Didaskaliai* which are cited anonymously with those written by Aristotle,[76] and one can also deduce from them all other detailed informations on those performances. This pertains especially to the learned notes known (incorrectly) as *hypothēseis* (summaries of contents) which introduced twenty plays in the manuscripts of Aischylos, Sophokles, Euripides, and Aristophanes; of these, we have fragments on papyrus copies of the tragedies of Aischylos and Menander. Those are partly mutilated data on the content and the premiere of the respective play, sometimes also on other related facts of interest for the history of literature and theater, e.g. on the loss of certain plays. They originated with the great Alexandrian philologist Aristophanes of Byzantium, a namesake of the famous author of comedies (second half of the 3rd century B.C.).[77] According to Choiroboskos, a Byzantine scholar of the 6th century A.D., Aristophanes of Byzantium used the list of dramatic poets and their plays which Kallimachos had compiled from the Aristotelian *Didaskaliai* for his own *hypothēseis* with which he introduced the respective works in his edition of the classics.[78] Aristophanes may indeed have taken the data on the loss of certain plays from that list. But the *Pinax* of Kallimachos may have served him primarily as an index to the Aristotelian list of performances of plays, because there he could find in one place all the particulars which he recorded (names, plays and successful competitors).[79]

Two examples, in English translation, with brief explanations (in brackets) will make this clear. The learned *hypothēsis* to the *Nephelai* (The clouds) of Aristophanes which has been transmitted to us in a second version—the first one was a failure and was rewritten by the author—begins as follows:

> The first *Clouds* were performed in the city [at
> the City Dionysia] under the archon Isarchos
> [423 B.C.], when Kartinos won with *Pytine*, and
> Ameipsias with *Konnos*.

(Thus, Aristophanes won at best the third place.)

Similarly, but with an unusual addition pertaining to the principal actor, we read in the *hypothēsis* to *Eirēnē* (Peace) of Aristophanes:

> But the victor [more precisely: the runner-up] was the
> poet with his play under the archon Aikaios [421 B.C.] in
> the city [at the city Dionysia]. The first was Eupolis with
> his *Kolakes*, second was Euripides with *Eirēnē*, third
> Leukon with *Phratores*. Apollodoros acted in the play.

(Then follow 20 incomprehensible letters.)[80]

When a poet had not produced his own play but had had it directed by somebody else, this was recorded in the *hypothēsis*: ("it was directed by so-and-so" e.g. the *Acharnians* of Aristophanes were directed by a certain Kallistratos who had been entrusted by the poet with the production of several plays. Aside from the *hypothēseis*, but in documents which are based on them or on their source, we find also the active form: "he [the author] produced it [the play] by so-and-so".[81]

Our knowledge of Aristotle's *Didaskaliai* has been considerably broadened and at the same time ascertained through fragments of Athenian inscriptions found during the last one hundred years. In addition, we have the fragments of a Roman inscription which is derived from the *Pinax tōn didaskalōn* of Kallimachos, in turn based on Aristotle's *Didaskaliai*. Ever since Wilhelm published a new edition of the entire material of inscriptions (1906) there has been much debate on these "documents of dramatic performances in Athens", because they are of great importance for research into the history of Attic drama. Reisch called them once "true monuments of Greek literary history".[82] But they are also very important for the understanding of the beginnings of Greek biobibliography.

Fragments of an inscription were found on the southern slope of the Acropolis in the late 1870s; they contain a list of dramatic performances whose parts show the same structure as the data on the *Didaskalia* in the *hypothēseis* which originated with Aristophanes of Byzantium. The inscription was placed soon after 278 B.C. on the three walls of an open-fronted hall which had probably been donated by the agonothete of the year 279/278, and it was continued long into the second century B.C.[83] It listed year after year, divided by festivals and genres, the tragedies (with the satyr plays) and the comedies which were performed at the Dionysia and the Lenaea.[84] Under each *archōn epōnymos* three tragic poets and five comic poets were listed with their plays and the principal actors, beginning with the first winner, the runner-up, etc., and at the end the victorious actor. The entry for the tragedies and satyr plays performed at the Dionysia in the year 340 may serve as an example. (At that time, a new satyr play and an old tragedy were performed in the beginning under the direction of the principal actor. In the year 340, the tragic poets produced—for unknown reasons—only two plays each.) The entry, one of those that has been best preserved, consists of three sections, divided by short dashes in the margin: satyr play, old tragedy, new tragedy. The English translation follows:[85]

> Under [the archon] Nikomachos [won] with a satyr play
> Timokles with the Lykurgos—
> with an old [tragedy] Neoptolemos
> with the Orestes of Euripides—
> as a poet [won with new tragedies]
> Astydamas
> with the Parthenopaios, played by Thettalos
> [and] with the Lykaon, played by Neoptolemos
> second Timokles with the Phrixos
> played by Thettalos
> [and] the Oidipus, played by Neoptolemos
> third Euaretos
> with Alkmeon, played by Thettalos
> [and] the . . . , played by Neoptolemos
> as actor, Thettalos won—

The text of this inscription is evidently derived from the same source as the data in the *hypothēseis* of Aristophanes of Byzantium, i.e. from the *Didaskaliai* of Aristotle; all experts agree on this. But Aristotle could carry his list of dramatic performances at most until the year 323 B.C., in which he left Athens after Alexander's death because of the hostile stance of many anti-Macedonian Athenians; he went to Chalkis where he died the next year. We may assume, however, that the persons who continued his list—presumably his students—followed the pattern set by him. One may therefore infer the structure of earlier parts of the list from the fragments of the inscription that pertain to the performance of plays after 323 B.C.

If we summarize all the data on the Aristotelian *Didaskaliai* which have been transmitted to us in manuscripts or inscriptions, including those that come from Kallimachos's *Pinax tōn didaskalōn*, the following picture emerges. Aristotle listed the poets, their plays and their principal actors probably in the same manner in which we read them in the inscription on satyr plays and tragedies performed at the Dionysia in 340 B.C.[86] But he made also a note a) when a poet had not produced his play himself but had had it directed by someone else (*dia tu deinos*, "by so-and-so"), as, for example, Aristophanes had his *Acharnians* produced by Kallistratos, or when a play had been produced after its author's death by one of his relatives, as for example the *Bacchae* of Euripides which were produced by the son or nephew of the same name; and b) when a poet produced an unsuccessful play in a revised version (*anedidaxe*)[87] which for example, Aristophanes contemplated for his *Clouds* but then decided not to do. When the three plays written by a tragic poet formed a unit, a trilogy, he added their collective title, e.g. the *Oresteia* of Aischylos.[88] He distinguished between contemporary poets and actors of the same name by adding "the elder" or "the younger", but it seems that these distinguishing characteristics were now and then left out when the text was carved in stone.[89] Perhaps he also added occasionally annotations, as did one of his successors who explained that the comic poet Ameinias who placed third in the Dionysia of 311 B.C. had still been an ephebe, that is, he was not yet twenty years old.[90]

Some researchers think that Aristotle listed in his *Didaskaliai* also the choregoi,[91] but this is improbable. Although the name of a choregos, Xenokles of Aphidnai, is listed in the *hypothēsis* to the *Oresteia* (more specifically to the *Agamemnon*) by Aristophanes of Byzantium, this is an exception which Aristophanes probably made because he dealt with the most famous of all premieres in the history of Athenian theater.[92] He might have taken the name of the choregos not from the *Didaskaliai* of Aristotle but from another source; it appears also in an Athenian inscription from the fourth century, known as *Fasti*, with which we will deal later.[93] There is no other passage from which it could be inferred that Aristotle listed also the choregoi, who were, with very few exceptions, entirely without interest for the history of literature and theater.[94]

Aristotle's *Didaskaliai* were doubtless based on the documents in the archives of the archons, because only there could he find the countless details that he included in his list. Other sources, such as oral traditions, inscriptions of votive offerings by victorious choregoi, editions of plays by famous poets, or information from chroniclers, were only taken into account where official documents were lacking.

Aristotle probably wrote an introduction to his *Didaskaliai* (as he did in his *Pythionikai*) in which he dealt with the origin and development of dramatic performances and contests in Athens. The list of Aristotle's works, transmitted by Hesychios of Miletos, has *Peri didaskaliōn* (On the performances), not *Didaskaliai* as in Diogenes; this could have been the heading of the introduction.[95]

Since the origin of Aristotle's *Didaskaliai* is similar to that of his *Pythionikai*, completed around 334 B.C., (both resulting from archival research) they are rightly thought to belong to the same period in his life. They were probably compiled soon after his return to Athens in 335 B.C. This is also likely because the so-called reform of the theater by Lykurgos took place at that time, so that the intellectual climate was favorable for the compilation of a list of theatrical performances.

Regarding the period dealt with in the Aristotelian *Didaskaliai*, one must consider that Kallimachos in his *Pinax tōn didaskalōn* listed the Attic dramatic poets who had appeared from the beginning (*ex archēs*) of Athenian dramatic performances. It is therefore likely that Aristotle went back in his *Didaskaliai* to the very beginning, or at least as far as there were documents on performances of plays, that is, until about 500 B.C., as he had done in his *Pythionikai*. Perhaps he dealt with older performances, on which accurate information did not exist any more, in his introduction. Whether he carried the list forward until his own time, i.e. the years between 335 and 323 B.C., or broke it off at an earlier point in the hope that his students would continue the list, is impossible to say.[96]

If the *Didaskaliai* which he personally compiled ran until the year 335 B.C., they may have contained the premieres of about 1580 tragedies and 970 comedies.[97] The number of tragic poets named in the list is difficult to estimate. There might have been about a hundred poets of the Old and Middle Comedies, taking into account that some of the poets of the Middle Comedies were extraordinarily productive.

Another inscription, also found at the same place as that of the *Didaskaliai* on the southern slope of the Acropolis, is closely connected with it. It was once carved on the inside of the architrave of the hall donated by the agonothete of the year 279/278, the three inner walls of which bore the *Didaskaliai* inscription; it was also carved soon after 278 B.C. and was continued until the second half of the second century B.C.[98] This inscription listed the successful poets and actors with the number of their victories which they had won at the dramatic contests of the Dionysia and the Lenaea. There were eight parts: A. Winners at the Dionysia. 1. Tragic poets. 2. Tragic actors. 3. Comic poets. 4. Comic actors. B. Winners at the Lenaea. 1. Comic poets. 2. Tragic poets. 3. Tragic actors. 4. Comic actors. The sequence of poets and actors in each part was not alphabetical but according to the (undefined) year in which they had won their first victory at the respective festival. Those who had won prizes at both the Dionysia and the Lenaea were listed twice. Thus we learn, for example, that Sophokles won eighteen times in the tragedy contest at the Dionysia. Since, according to the *Suda*, he won altogether twenty-four times, he must have won the first prize at the Lenaea six times.[99]

This list is usually known as the "List of victors". But the title of a certain section which has been reconstructed by Wilhelm with almost complete certainty was: [*Nikai*] *lēnaika poētōn kōmikōn* (Victories of comic poets at the Lenaea). The title of the entire list was probably: *Nikai Dionysiakai astikai kai lēnaikai* (Victories at the Dionysia and Lenaea [namely those of tragic and comic poets and actors]). Thus, according to the intention of its author, the inscription was not a list of victors, but one of victories.

The inscription does not contain anything that may not have been in the *Didaskaliai*. As Wilamowitz and Reisch have emphasized, it is nothing but an excerpt from that list,[100] or, more exactly, its exemplar was an excerpt from the exemplar of the *Didaskaliai* inscription, i.e. from the *Didaskaliai* of Aristotle. In order to compile a list of victorious poets and actors it was not necessary to rely on the documents of the archons, one needed only to exploit the list of Aristotle. This was not a difficult task. One prepared eight sheets, one for each part, then went through the *Didaskaliai* from beginning to end, and wrote down each victorious poet or actor on the respective sheet, followed by a stroke, e.g. Dionysia, tragic poets: Sophokles /. When the same poet or actor was listed a second time, a second stroke was added, and so on. This "stroke statistic" explains that the poets and actors are arranged in each part in the sequence of their first victories. This made it also convenient to continue the list.

It is likely that the "List of victors" was compiled by Aristotle or by one of his students as a kind of appendix to his *Didaskaliai*.[101] A survey of victorious poets and actors and the number of their victories was certainly very welcome not only for Athenians but also for all other Greeks with their keen interest in contests. This follows from the fact that the numerical data were included in the biographies of poets and in the articles of author dictionaries. We can still read them in the *Suda*. The agonothete of the year 2798/278 B.C. who erected that hall in which the inscription gave a survey over the dramatic performances at the Dionysia and at the Lenaea, probably found the "List of victors" already as an appendix to Aristotle's *Didaskaliai*. He therefore had the hall built in such a manner that the lists of performances and those of the victors could be engraved on the inner walls and on the inner side of the architrave respectively.

According to a conjecture by Körte, with whom most researchers concur, the "List of victors" (which is actually a list of victories) can be traced to the work which is named in the list of Aristotle's works by Diogenes Laertios (and Hesychios of Miletos) not far from the *Didaskaliai* under the title *Nikai Dionysiakai (astikai kai lēnaikai.)*[102] Surprisingly, these "victories at the City and Lenaean Dionysia" are not cited by any later scholar, contrary to the citations of the *Didaskaliai*. Thus, we do not know what they contained, but their title corresponds exactly to the conjectured title of the "List of victors". Although Körte did not take into consideration that its exemplar was not one of Aristotle's independent works but only an appendix to his *Didaskaliai*, this does not invalidate their identification with the *Nikai Dionysiakai* in the list of Aristotle's works. Their text was probably on a separate scroll, which was included separately in the list of Aristotle's works; the entry followed originally that of the main work and was only later separated from it, so that it precedes it in Diogenes Laertios together with a likewise lost work *Peri tragōdiōn* (On the tragedies). Such things happened quite often in the list of Aristotle's works. If the *Nikai* were an appendix to the *Didaskaliai* it would explain why they were never cited.

The exemplar of the "List of victors" is of interest for our investigation primarily as the result of a utilization of Aristotle's *Didaskaliai*, and because of the method of its compilation, since Kallimachos too made use of the *Didaskaliai*. Although he pursued a different goal, a bibliographical one, he proceeded, as we shall see, exactly like the author of the "List of victors" when he cataloged the Alexandrian library. We encounter here questions of ancient techniques of intellectual work which have so far scarcely been considered.

In this context, we must mention a third inscription, the oldest and most voluminous of the "documents on dramatic performances in Athens". According to Wilamowitz, they are called *Fasti* (annual lists, namely of the winners at the contests of dithyrambs and plays at the Dionysia).[103] The fragments, which were mostly found on the Akropolis, show that the following were listed under the name of each *archōn epōnymos*: 1) the *phylē* whose chorus of boys had won a victory with a new dithyramb; and 2) the same for its chorus of men, as well as the *choregoi* who had paid the two choruses; 3) the *chorēgos* and 4) the *didaskalos*, the author of the winning comedy who was generally also its director; 5) the *chorēgos* and 6) the *didaskalos* of the three winning tragedies; in addition, beginning with a certain year before 447 B.C., the victorious principal actor of tragedies.[104] The records originally extended until a year sometime between 346 and 342 B.C. They were soon thereafter carved in stone and were then continued. It is noteworthy that the authors of the dithyrambs recited by the choruses of boys and men are not mentioned, and that only the names of the victorious tragic and comic poets are given but not the titles of their plays.[105] The inscription was apparently not designed to give information of a literary character but was, in the style of older lists of victors, intended to herald the fame of groups and persons who had won prizes in the artistic contests at the City (and Lenaean?) Dionysia.

Wilhelm thought initially that the inscription reproduced the *Nikai Dionysiakai* of the list of Aristotle's works, but later he sided with Körte (1906) who had rejected the idea that the original copy for the inscription could have been compiled by Aristotle because he had left Athens already in 347, whereas the inscription had been carved between 346 and 342 B.C. Wilamowitz was also of the same opinion (1906). But Reisch (1907) thought that the inscription called *Fasti* by Wilamowitz had only been made around 329 B.C., when Aristotle dwelt again in Athens. He therefore did not hesitate to trace them to Aristotle's *Nikai Dionysiakai*. Jachmann (1909) wanted to find an answer through a comprehensive hypothesis. He assumed that after his return to Athens Aristotle collected all data on the performance of dithyrambs and plays which he could find in the archives of the respective archons in his *Didaskaliai*, and that these were then twice excerpted, first for the exemplar of the *Fasti* inscription, and then for the *Didaskaliai* inscription. Although Körte (1911) doubted that the *Fasti* could be traced to Aristotle's *Didaskaliai*, oddly enough he nevertheless approved Jachmann's hypothesis which was based on this assumption.

Since then, so far as I can see, researchers of Classical Antiquity did not deal any more with the three inscriptions and their sources, but only with the data that they contain which are of interest for literary history. The tracing of the *Fasti* to the *Didaskaliai* (as Jachmann thought) or to any other work by Aristotle has now generally been rejected,[106] but the *Didaskaliai* inscription is held to be an excerpt from the Aristotelian list of performances. Pfeiffer also thinks that the *Fasti* did not originate with Aristotle, but he says nevertheless that Jachmann's reconstruction of the *Didaskaliai* "has not been superseded".[107]

I have no doubt that Körte was right when he said that the *Fasti* could not be traced back to Aristotle because of the period of their origin. The inscription was carved without interruption until it covered a year between 346 and 342 (between those there is a gap). The following entries are not only in a somewhat different script but more importantly, they show also a different arrangement of lines. It is therefore implausible that the second stone carver relieved the first one immediately (thus Reisch). Rather, the part carved by the second hand is a later edition. Thus, the main part of the inscription listed only the victors of performances that had taken place until a year between 346 and 342. When its exemplar was completed, Aristotle was no longer in the city which he had left soon after Plato's death (347). Apart from that, it is neither attested nor is it likely in the light of Aristotle's intellectual development that he conducted archival studies while still being a member of Plato's Academy, in order to compile lists of victors, much less of all participants in contests.

But if the exemplar of the *Fasti* is not traceable to Aristotle, then the hypotheses of Reisch and Jachmann become invalid. One must then assume that somebody before Aristotle scanned the archives of the archons in order to collect material for an inscription which would immortalize the names of groups and persons who had won victories in the Dionysian contests. This would not have been an unusual undertaking, since fifty years earlier Hellanikos had already listed the victors of the Karneian contests at Sparta, using archival records.

The comparison with the work of his predecessor throws into relief the specific nature of Aristotle's *Didaskaliai*. Contrary to the former, he extracted from the records not only the names of the victors, but also those of all poets and actors who had produced new and old plays at both Dionysian festivals. He was concerned not with the fame of the prize winners but with information concerning literary history.[108] His *Didaskaliai*, being a complete chronicle of performances of plays at the Dionysia and Lenaea, went far beyond the customary lists of victors, including his own *Pythionikai*. For this reason, they were not immediately carved in stone as had been done with the latter. That this was still done, albeit many years after his death, was due only to the interest of the agonothete for the year 279/278 who built the hall on whose walls and architrave the list and its appendix were inscribed.

But if the *Fasti*, in which also the victors in the contests of dithyrambs were listed, cannot be traced to any of Aristotle's works, one would have to rely only on some oblique notes by two later scholars[109] in order to prove that Aristotle had listed also the performances of dithyrambs in his *Didaskaliai*, and that therefore the exemplar for the *Didaskaliai* inscription had only been an extract from his work.

The lexicographer Harpokration who says that the term *didaskaloi* meant specifically the authors of dithyrambs, comedies and tragedies, documents this as follows: the orator Antiphon (5th century) calls Pantakles (who had rehearsed a dithyramb with a boys' chorus) in one passage a *didaskalos*; Aristotle's *Didaskaliai* show that Pantakles was a poet (of dithyrambs?). Moreover, a scholium to the *Ornithes* (Birds) of Aristophanes says that Aristotle stated in the *Didaskaliai* that there had not been only one Kinesias (a poet of dithyrambs who had once been highly regarded but had been ridiculed by Aristophanes) but that there had been two persons by this name (both poets of dithyrambs?). In neither of these two passages is it stated that Pantakles or Kinesias were listed (*anagegraptai* or *pheretai*) as poets of dithyrambs in Aristotle's *Didaskaliai*. Any conclusion drawn from these two passages is therefore uncertain. Aristotle may have mentioned Pantakles and Kinesias also as tragic poets, because some dithyrambic poets wrote also tragedies.[110] There is yet another fact. According to Choiroboskos, the only scholar who indicates the contents of the *Pinax tōn didaskalōn* by Kallimachos, it listed the authors of ancient plays. In my opinion, this indicates that Kallimachos's source, the *Didaskaliai* of Aristotle which he merely reorganized, were only a list of performances of plays. The term *Didaskaliai*, as pointed out above, was merely a citation title.[111] If so, the work of Aristotle which can be inferred from the inscription of the agonothete in 279/278 and from other sources would not be an excerpt but would have been inscribed in stone in its entirety, as were his *Pythionikai*.[112]

Aristotle could have had a good reason for not listing the performance of dithyrambs. For him, as a literary historian, only the dithyrambs performed by choruses and their authors were of interest.[113] He would even have to list, analogous to the performances of plays, all authors and titles of the songs performed by the choruses of boys and men from each of the ten *phylai*. However, it is odd that the *Fasti* inscription does not even list the authors of the winning dithyrambs performed by the choruses, much less their titles. Although many authors of dithyrambs were not Athenians, I doubt that they were not mentioned for that reason. It is more likely that the names of dithyrambic poets were not listed in the records. The contest of dithyrambs unlike that of plays, was not a competition of individuals, poets and actors, but one of collective bodies, the *phylai* and their choruses. Prizes were awarded to the *choregoi* as representatives of those *phylai* whose choruses had won. Reisch thought that the state must have paid a honorarium to the authors of dithyrambs as well as to those of plays. But there is no evidence for this, not even for older times. The contests of dithyrambs were organized differently from those of plays.[114] Everything depended on the *choregoi* of the *phylai*: they cast lots for the poets and probably also paid them. The poets in turn paid the flute players. Later on, it was the other way around: the *choregoi* cast lots for the flute players and those paid the poets, whose names are listed after those of the former in votive inscriptions of victorious *choregoi* from the fourth century. According to Pseudo-Plutarch's *Peri musikēs* (On music) the change occurred already in the times of Melanippides, i.e. in the second half of the fifth century, when the performances of dithyrambs lost their literary importance and became musical events.[115] But if the archon did not have to pay an honorarium to the authors of dithyrambs, nor to award them a prize, he was also under no obligation to list their names in his records, and a list of performances of dithyrambs in which poets were not named because they could not be named was of no value for Aristotle. For this reason I do not assume that the *Didaskaliai* also contained performances of dithyrambs.

The data that can be traced back to Aristotle's *Didaskaliai* are generally thought to be reliable.[116] Only regarding the authors of plays which had been produced by directors has the reliability of Aristotle's data been questioned by many researchers, albeit without saying so expressly. The discussion of this problem started with the comedies of Aristophanes.[117] Aristophanes, who wrote at least forty plays, eleven of which have come down to us, was probably not the first poet who had his plays produced by men who had proven themselves as directors, but he is the earliest one of whom this is reported in the *hypothēseis* to his comedies and elsewhere.[118] Three of his early comedies, the *Daitalēs* (Banqueters), his first work (427 B.C., festival?, second place), the *Babylōnioi* (426, Dionysia, first or second place), and the *Archarnians*, his earliest extant play (425, Lenaea, first place) were produced by Kallistratos, and a fourth whose title is unknown (426, Lenaea, place?) was probably produced by Philonides.[119] The latter apparently wrote also comedies himself, unlike Kallistratos. The first play produced by Aristophanes himself was the *Hippēs* (Knights, 424, Lenaea, first place). In the two biographies of Aristophanes written in Antiquity it is said that he had his early plays produced by Kallistratos and Philonides, but some of his later comedies were also produced by other people, among the extant ones the *Ornithēs* (Birds) and the *Lysistratē* by Kallistratos (414 and 411 respectively), perhaps the *Sphēkēs* (Wasps) and certainly the *Batrachoi* (Frogs) by Philonides (422 and 405 respectively), also the *Plutos* by his son Araros (388). The lost *Amphiaraos* was produced by Philonides in the same year as the *Birds* by Kallistratos (414), though not like those at the Dionysia but at the Lenaea.

The parabasis of the *Knights* says that many people wondered why the poet had not long since asked for a chorus for himself, and that they had questioned him why he had failed to do so.[120] Most experts relate this remark to the fact that Aristophanes had had his earlier plays produced by Kallistratos and Philonides, and they conclude from this that it was the director's task to ask the archon for a chorus when the author of a play did not want to produce it himself. Consequently, they think that in such cases only the name of the director and not that of the author were entered in the records. This opinion was presented at the beginning of the 20th century especially by Reisch and Wilhelm, following some 19th century researchers.[121] Subsequently, all other researchers agreed, except Capps, and it has not been refuted until now.[122] It was even thought that it had been confirmed by a fragment found later by Wilhelm, in which Araros, Aristophanes's son, is named as the victor in the comedy contest at the Dionysia of the year 387. There is indeed evidence that Aristophanes wrote two further plays after the *Plutos* (performed in 388), namely the *Kōkalos* and a second *Aiolosikōn*, but that he did not produce them, leaving this to his son Araros. We may furthermore assume that Araros who, according to the *Suda*, produced a comedy of his own for the first time in a year of the 101st Olympiad (376/373) won at the Dionysia of the year 397 with the *Kōkalos* or the *Aiolosikōn* of his father. It was therefore thought to be evident that a director who had successfully produced somebody else's play, was also recorded as a victorious *didaskalos*.[123]

Körte thinks that the director received in that case even the honorarium of the author, because, according to his ancient biographers, Aristophanes was ridiculed by three rivals, Aristonymos, Ameipsias and Sannarion, as one who had been born, like Herakles, on the fourth of the month (*tetradi gegonōs*), since his first plays had been produced by Kallistratos and Philonides. (This proverbial saying was used for persons who toiled for others, like Herakles for Eurystheus.)[124] Therefore, there would not have been any administrative need for the archon to list the name of the author in his records.

But there can be no doubt that Aristotle named in his *Didaskaliai* the authors of the plays, more exactly, that he thought he could name them, even if they had not produced their plays themselves; this follows unmistakably from the inscriptions which are based on his work and from the *hypothēseis*.[125] In the inscription of the "List of victors" which reproduced an appendix to the *Didaskaliai* there appears among the tragic poets who had won their first victories soon after 372 at the Dionysia that Aphareus who had had his successful plays produced by a certain Dionysios.[126] And the *hypothēseis* contain evidence that Aristotle named not only the author but also the director who had been commissioned, if such was the case. It is however, questionable (and that is the crucial question) whether Aristotle found the name of both in the records of the archons. If these contained only the names of directors but not those of authors, as Reisch and Wilhelm thought, where did he get the names of the respective authors? Among all researchers who followed Reisch and Wilhelm, only Oellacher posed this question, but gave a facile answer. He explained that Aristotle could have found the names of authors in the manuscripts which had been submitted to the archons and preserved in their archives.[127] The archons however, as we shall presently see, did not collect manuscripts in their archives. Now, did Aristotle add the names of authors just based on literary knowledge or on random information? Certainly he would have known that the *Birds*, produced in 414, were the famous comedy by Aristophanes, even if this had not been noted in the records. But he dealt not only with the plays of the few important authors, but also with those of all other playwrights, with many hundreds of unsuccessful tragedies and comedies which were probably never published in book form. Did he therefore list the man named in the records as author when he did not realize that the name pertained not to the author but only to the director? If so, the history of bibliography would have begun with quite a few false author

35

attributions. According to Mensching, this is exactly what happened.[128] Although there is no hard evidence for this, there is a case that would justify Mensching's apprehensions, and even worse ones. Modern classical philologists are agreed that the data in the *hypothēseis* to the *Wasps* which are traceable to Aristotle's *Didaskaliai* contain a false indication of an author. It says there that at the Lenaea of 422 the *Wasps* of Aristophanes were produced by Philonides, and that the *Proagōn* of Philonides and the *Presbeis* of Leukon were also produced.[129] Although there was a lost but often cited comedy *Proagōn* by Aristophanes, nothing is known about a play with the same title by Philonides. It is therefore assumed that the comedy *Proagōn* which was produced in 422 had been the one by Aristophanes. He had commissioned Philonides to produce not only the *Wasps*, but also to announce the *Proagōn* as his own work. In this manner, Aristophanes could stage two new plays at the same time, which was actually not permitted. If this had been the case, then Aristotle could not have noticed that the *Proagōn* of 422 was the well-known comedy by Aristophanes, and would have named Philonides erroneously because his name appeared in the records. He would have, to put it bluntly, "nodded". (*Quandoque bonus dormitat Homerus* [Sometimes even good old Homer nods].)

This prevailing opinion is however not so well founded as it may seem. If we interpret the verse in the parabasis of the *Knights* of 424, from which we started, in a wider context, we arrive at a different conclusion. In order to explain why he had not long since asked for a chorus (verse 513) Aristophanes gives the following reasons: 1) the writing of comedies *kōmōdodidaskalia*[130] is very difficult and only few succeed; 2) the public is fickle, it will drop an author who was extolled only yesterday (he gives a few examples); 3) one must have been first an oarsman, then a helmsman's assistant on the fore-deck before taking the helm of a ship himself.[131] Aristophanes distinguishes here between three stages in his career, metaphorically as an oarsman, helmsman's assistant and helmsman. But if he acted as director (helmsman) for the first time in the *Knights*, while being only a director's assistant (or helmsman's assistant) in his earlier plays, directed by Kallistratos and Philonides, there were only two stages. What was the comparison with an oarsman aimed at? The answer is in the parabasis of his next but one play, the *Wasps* of 422. The *Clouds*, performed in 423, which Aristophanes held to be his best work, had been a failure. The poet was deeply hurt by this misfortune. Therefore, the chorus in the *Wasps* explains:[132]

> You have wronged him much, he protests, a bard
> who have served you often and well before;
> Partly, indeed, himself unseen,
> assisting others to please you more;
> With the art of a Eurycles, weird and wild,
> he loved to dive in a stranger's breast,
> And pour from thence through a stranger's lips
> full many a sparkling comical jest;
> And partly at length in his own true form,
> as he challenged his fate by himself alone.
> And the Muses whose bridled mouths he drave,
> were never another's, were all his own.

It is unmistakably clear from these verses that Aristophanes had not published
his first comedies openly, that is, under his own name. The poet refers to this in
the parabasis to the revised version of the *Clouds*, written between 420 and 417,
which is the one that has come down to us (verses 528-532). There he recalls the
friendly reception of his first play, the *Daitalēs*, produced in 427 (here personified
by the two principal characters:[133]

> No! for ever since from judges
>   unto whom 'tis joy to speak,
> Brothers Profligate and Modest
>   gained the praise we fondly seek,
> When, for I was yet a Virgin,
>   and it was not right to bear,
> I exposed it, and Another
>   did the foundling nurse with care,
> But 'twas ye who nobly nurtured,
>   ye who brought it up with skill.

All of Aristophanes's comedies that were performed before the *Knights* (424,
Lenaea) were produced by other persons, as we know, but it did not occur to the
poet to compare himself with an unwed mother ("a virgin") who abandons her child
to be raised by another woman, just because he had commissioned Kallistratos to
direct the *Acharnians* (425, Lenaea). Therefore, the case of the *Daitalēs* cannot
have been the same as that of the *Acharnians*: Kallistratos did not only direct
Aristophanes's first play, but must also have produced it under his own name.
The same is true for the comedy by Aristophanes which was produced by Philonides
at the Lenaea of 426, and whose title we do not know. At this stage of his career
he was, in the metaphor of the parabasis to the *Knights*, like an oarsman. (The two
lowest rows of oarsmen were not visible in the classical trireme.) Looking back on
this period, he could also depict himself as an imitator of the prophet Eurykles who
seemingly let his thoughts be uttered by others, until he was unmasked as a
ventriloquist.

Based on the cited passages, and following some earlier researchers Zacher
explained in 1890 that the first plays of Aristophanes had been performed by
Kallistratos and Philonides under their own names. But his conception was not
accepted, and it seems that Russo, who suggested it anew in 1962, did not succeed
either.[134] All other researchers are still of the opinion that the first plays of
Aristophanes were performed by Kallistratos and Philonides in the name of the
author. Zacher and Russo made, however, a mistake which led their critics to reject
their conception altogether. They maintained that the "secret" career of
Aristophanes as a playwright had lasted until the *Acharnians*, and that the *Knights*
had been not only the first comedy directed by himself, but also the first to appear
under Aristophanes's own name. That is certainly not quite plausible, because
Aristophanes spoke already earlier through the mouth of the chorus. In the
parabasis to the *Acharnians* which had been directed by Kallistratos, he recalled
proudly the success of the *Babylonians* in 426 which had also been directed by
Kallistratos. He said that his fame as a poet had thereafter even reached the court
of the Persian king (verses 646-649). In another passage of the *Acharnians* (verse
377 f.) he complains that he alone knew what he had to suffer from the mighty
demagogue Kleon, because he had criticized in last year's comedy (the *Babylonians*)

the brutal policy of Athens towards her confederates in the presence of their representatives, a policy instigated by Kleon. (Kleon had summoned him before the Council.) Aristophanes appeared therefore already in the *Babylonians* as their author, and began his public career as a playwright with that play. If he perhaps won the first prize at the Dionysia with the *Babylonians*, which is quite probable, then this was an extraordinary event: the first victory of a new poet since many years.[135] At any rate, the year 426, in which he appeared as the author of a successful comedy, meant much more for his career than the year 424, in which he himself produced a play for the first time. It was, in my opinion, not that important (as all other researchers think) whether Aristophanes produced a comedy himself or had this task performed by someone else, which indeed he did also after 424, probably more frequently than we know. What mattered was whether a play was produced as his work, not whether it had been produced by him or another person.

When the success of the *Babylonians* had been repeated or even heightened with the *Acharnians*, it was widely rumored that the poet had already produced two plays before these comedies, albeit not under his own name. Aristophanes himself, gratified by the victories he had won, had probably revealed his "pseudonym". Now we should not think that his fellow-citizens, not to speak of the authorities, were very pleased with this revelation, because the young man had deceived them. The consternation, even of those among his audience who were sympathetic to him, must have been the more painful for Aristophanes, since it coincided with the indignation which his political critique had evoked in Kleon's party. He therefore endeavored to give extensive reasons for his conduct in the parabasis to the *Knights*, and even in the parabasis to the *Wasps* and to the second *Clouds*, when he again spoke about his beginnings, he dropped some hints about extenuating circumstances or excused himself. But he did not think that he had to explain why he had commissioned Kallistratos and Philonides to produce the plays that were performed before his *Knights*. Apparently nobody had found fault with this procedure (which all researchers seem to find strange) and even later nobody did so. Aristophanes only alluded to it in the verse of the parabasis to the *Knights* (verse 543) in which he compared himself as assistant to the director with a helmsman's assistant. His only aim was to justify that he had concealed from both authorities and audience until the *Babylonians* that he was the author of the plays produced by Kallistratos and Philonides, and that he, as he says in the parabasis to the *Knights* (verse 513), had not long since asked for a chorus. In the comparisons which he makes in order to explain his peculiar procedure, two motives intersect: on the one hand, he wants to be recognized as the real author of the plays performed by Kallistratos and Philonides, on the other hand he wants to play the role of a mere co-author, an assistant of other poets (*Wasps*, verses 1028 and 1032), so that his deception would appear as laudable modesty.

If this interpretation is correct, then we may not conclude from the cited passages that the name of an author was not at all listed in the records if he had commissioned someone else to produce his play and that person then asked for a chorus and also received the honorarium. In my opinion, there is no reason to believe that this rather unlikely assumption is valid. When Kallistratos and Philonides asked for a chorus for the first two plays of Aristophanes they did so as their purported authors and as such they also received the honorarium. The archons did not have to investigate whether or not they were the real authors of the submitted plays; moreover, they could have been the authors. And if

Aristophanes's rivals ridiculed him, referring to his first plays which had been produced by Kallistratos and Philonides, and called him one that had been born on the fourth of a month like Herakles, who like that hero toiled for others, they could only have had in mind his first two plays. I am, however, not sure whether the ancient scholars were right in connecting the (not datable) ridicule of other poets with the relationship of Aristophanes to Kallistratos and Philonides. Aristophanes compared himself with Herakles in his struggle with Kleon, both in the *Wasps* of 422 (verses 1029-1045) and in the *Peace* of 421 (verses 748-758). Perhaps the ridicule of his dear colleagues was not so much aimed at the author Aristophanes who had hidden behind the directors and had yielded to them the prize and the honorarium, but rather at the poet who imagined himself to be Herakles in his theatrical attacks.

We may therefore assume without hesitation that also those (real or presumed) authors who had commissioned others to produce their plays were duly listed in the records by the responsible archons. The *Didaskaliai* of Aristotle which were based on those records contained therefore generally reliable data on authorship and deserved the confidence placed in them by his successors, among them Kallimachos.[136] It is highly likely that the archons also noted the names of the directors who had been commissioned by the authors. Although it was the duty of the authors to pay the directors, the archons probably had to announce who had produced the plays submitted to the contests. Had this not been recorded, even Aristotle would have found it difficult to get that information, because the pre-Alexandrian editions of plays did probably not contain information on the premieres, as later given by Aristophanes of Byzantium in his *hypothēseis*.

But the records did indeed not always show the real authors of performed plays. What did Aristotle do if he discovered a fraud, and did he discover it in every case? He certainly realized that the purported authors of Aristophanes's first two comedies had been in reality only the directors. As shown by the data in the *Didaskaliai* relating to the *Daitalēs*,[137] he substituted in the two plays for the purported authors Kallistratos and Philonides the real one, Aristophanes, while mentioning those two as directors. Thus, his procedure for Aristophanes's plays which had been produced by directors under their names was, despite the different circumstances, not different from that used for plays performed under the name of an author who had commissioned a director. This has confused most ancient and modern scholars, because it now looked as if there had been no difference in a performance of, say, the *Daitalēs* and the *Achamians*, both of which had been produced by Kallistratos.

A memory of the actual state of affairs has however been preserved in the anonymous *Peri kōmōdias*; the relevant passage says:[138] "Aristophanes produced for the first time under the archon Diotimos [427 B.C.] a comedy [the *Daitalēs*], directed by Kallistratos. It is said that he gave to him the political comedies, but those against Euripides and Socrates he gave to Philonides. When he had been judged to be a good poet by those two [comedies], he also owned up to the others and won. Then he gave his plays to his son." It seems to me that the anonymous author wanted to report that Aristophanes, from a certain date onwards, produced his comedies under his own name, or had them produced by others.[139] Because he linked this report to a (controversial) note on the distribution of the plays among Aristophanes's directors, the meaning of his words has been somewhat obscured. But there can be no doubt, in my opinion, that he also meant so say that Aristophanes had produced his comedies until a certain time under his own name, and that he gave his plays thereafter to his son (Araros). This is confirmed by a sentence in the *hypothēsis* to *Plutos* that goes back to Aristophanes of Byzantium but is abbreviated; *Plutos* is the last of Aristophanes's comedies that has come down to us. The sentence reads as follows:[140] "He produced this comedy as the last one under his own name and wanted thereby to recommend his son Araros to the audience; the last two, the *Kōkalos* and the *Aiolosikōn*, were staged by him [his son]." Both ancient biographers of Aristophanes also mention that the poet wanted to recommend his son Araros to the audience through the *Plutos*; one of them says in addition, that Aristophanes had *Plutos* produced by Araros, the other emphasizes that *Plutos* was the last comedy produced by Aristophanes.[141] What was meant by that recommendation is probably impossible to explain.[142] On the other hand, I think we may deduce from the cited sentence that the performance of the *Plutos* was considered as a turning point in Aristophanes's career, as seen in the learned tradition from which those data are derived. But that would not have been the case if Araros had only produced the *Kōkalos* and the *Aiolosikōn*, as he had produced the *Plutos* (388) and as Philonides had produced the *Frogs* (405) and Kallistratos the *Lysistratē* (411) and many other plays. Therefore we must interpret the remark in the *hypothēsis* to *Plutos*, that this play had been the last one produced under Aristophanes's own name (here expressly so stated), in the sense that Araros produced the *Kōkalos* and the *Aiolosikōn* under *his* name.[143]

But if *Plutos* was equivalent to the *Babylonians* as a milestone in Aristophanes's career, and the poet's plays that followed, like those that preceded the *Babylonians*, were not produced as his own works, then Araros was listed in the records as the (purported) author. The fact that his name appears in the *Fasti* (Dionysia 387) does therefore not provide evidence that only the name of a director was listed in the records if an author had commissioned him with the production of a play.

Aristotle certainly knew that Araros had not written the comedy which he produced at the Dionysia in 387.[144] He would therefore have listed Aristophanes as the author (*poētēs Aristophanēs*) but Araros as the director (*dia Ararotos*) by whom the play had been staged. As the real author of a comedy Araros appeared probably in Aristotle's *Didaskaliai* under a later date. This would also be the explanation for the statement in the *Suda*, according to which Araros produced a comedy written by himself for the first time in a year of the 101st Olympiad (376/373). Capps wanted to change the date transmitted in the *Suda*, so as to make it compatible with the one in the *Fasti*. But such a change would imply that Aristotle did not notice who was the real author of the comedy produced at the Dionysia of 387 by Araros.[145]

But did not Aristotle "nod" when listing the comedy *Proagōn* of Aristophanes, produced at the Lenaea of 422 under the name of Philonides? In the parabasis to the *Wasps*, produced at the same festival, Aristophanes once again said that he had produced his first plays under his own name. He tried to whitewash his deception of authorities and audience by describing his role as that of an assistant to other poets. I think therefore that it is untenable to believe that he at the same time tried again to deceive the archon and the audience.[146] The *Proagōn* mentioned in the *hypothēsis* to the *Wasps* was, in my opinion, indeed a work by Philonides.[147] Aristotle certainly listed Aristophanes's play with the same title under a different date. It happened frequently that two or even three comedies had the same title.[148] It is irrelevant that we know nothing about the *Proagōn* by Philonides, because even of some plays by the most important poets of the Old Comedy, Aristophanes and Kratinos, we know only the title.[149]

The authenticity of the author listing in Aristotle's *Didaskaliai* pertaining to the *Proagōn* by Philonides, performed at the Lenaea in 422, is thus beyond doubt. This does not preclude, however, that Aristotle was indeed deceived in other cases. The poet Plato, a younger contemporary of Aristophanes, confessed in his lost comedy *Peisandros* that he sold plays because of poverty. The buyers who eagerly sought literary fame, even if it was faked, produced of course these comedies under their own names.[150] Whether Aristotle always detected such frauds, which were certainly not frequent, must remain unresolved.

The importance of Aristotle's *Didaskaliai* for the scholarly analysis of Attic plays can hardly be overestimated, because they contained an almost unbelievable mass of information on literary history. Although only a small part of it has come down to us, all that we know about the chronology of performances of plays in Athens can ultimately be traced back to Aristotle's work. The *Didaskaliai* made it possible for Greek scholars, especially for those in Alexandria, not only to date the individual plays but also to draw far-reaching conclusions about the lives and works of their authors. For example, the period of flourishing of a poet could be determined more exactly with the aid of data on his first and last appearance.[151] From the titles of his performed plays one could compile a chronological list of his works, even though it was sometimes necessary to supplement it. At any rate, Aristotle's *Didaskaliai* constituted a safe foundation for the biography and bibliography of Attic tragic and comic poets of the fifth and fourth century B.C. When a play traditionally ascribed to a famous poet was not listed in the *Didaskaliai*, this raised doubts about its authenticity. Such doubts had of course to be reinforced by other facts, because the *Andromachē* of Euripides, for example, was not listed in the *Didaskaliai*, because it had not been performed in Athens. Conversely, if a play that existed under the name of a famous poet was also listed in the *Didaskaliai* as his work, such as the *Rhēsos* of Euripides, it provided a quite respectable argument for those scholars who defended its authenticity against those who denied it on stylistic grounds.[152] The *Didaskaliai* were certainly also useful for the identification of plays without indication of authorship, or those that went under the names of several authors, and without a title or under several different titles. With the help of the Aristotelian list it was possible to find the real author and the real title of a play, provided it fulfilled other necessary conditions, such as being from the same period, linguistic criteria, and so on.[153] To be sure, because of its arrangement it was unwieldy to use for certain investigations. That was the reason for Kallimachos's revision.

Whether Aristotle utilized the biographical and bibliographical information which he had gathered in the compilation of the *Didaskaliai* in his work *Peri tragōdiōn* (On the tragedies) is impossible to say, because nothing is known about it other than its title which appears in the lists of the philosopher's works. We may however assume that he assisted the Athenians with his informations when, at the request of Lykurgos, they wanted to produce an "official copy" of the tragedies of Aischylos, Sophokles and Euripides. The orator and politician Lykurgos, who had been his classmate in Plato's Academy, sought to improve the status of the theater in Athens during the latter half of the thirties. It is even customary to call this the "theater reform" by Lykurgos.[154] As director of the finance department of the state which he led with great skill from 338-326, he built the theater of Dionysos in stone. On his request, the Assembly decided to erect statues of Aischylos, Sophokles and Euripides, and to make official copies of their tragedies, and actors were pledged to stick strictly to the wording of those texts. It seems that the actors changed the text of plays at will, as the rhapsodes had once done with the epic poems. It was Lykurgos "wish" that at least the plays of the three great tragic poets should be performed again in their original form. The decision of the Assembly was indeed executed. The "official copy" which was thus created was however not one single gigantic scroll (as one may think when hearing the modern expression "official copy") but it consisted of many scrolls. About a century later, King Ptolemaios Euergetes of Egypt borrowed those scrolls against a very high security (15 talents) in order to have them copied in Alexandria; however, he forfeited the security, kept the scrolls, which were certainly deposited in the library of the Museion, and returned instead the copies made in Alexandria to Athens.[155]

The request of Lykurgos shows that the archons did not preserve in their archives the manuscripts submitted by playwrights. For the creation of an "official copy" of the tragedies of Aischylos, Sophokles and Euripides it was therefore necessary first to obtain copies of the plays which were as faithful as possible, that is to say, copies which were not based on those kept by actors, but reproductions of the original text. It is probable that Aristotle, the great book collector, helped his former classmate Lykurgos to achieve this. Textual criticism was probably not performed when the "official copy" was made, but it was inevitable, in my opinion, to submit the plays which circulated under the names of the three tragedians to a test of authenticity, to segregate those which were actually not written by them, or if they were included in the collection, to mark them as spurious. So far as I can see, this has not yet been noticed. Regarding the authenticity of individual plays which had purportedly been written by famous poets, and which were subsequently declared to be spurious by the Alexandrian scholars, there had certainly been some doubts for some time. According to the ancient biographers, the authenticity of five plays by Aischylos was disputed, and seventeen tragedies by Sophokles and three by Euripides (not including the *Rhēsos*) were considered to be spurious. Some even thought that there had been outright forgeries. Herakleides Pontikos, who had also been a member of Plato's Academy, was accused by Aristoxenos, one of Aristotle's pupils, of having published tragedies under the name of Thespis. But no one was better equipped than Aristotle to judge which of the plays that existed under the names of Aischylos, Sophokles and Euripides were really their work, because he had conducted studies in literary history and his list was based on archival material. I presume therefore that he collaborated decisively in the first critical edition of the collected dramatic works. If such was the case, then the list of officially copied plays constituted a reliable bibliography of the three tragedians.

If we consider the manner in which Aristotle worked, we shall not be surprised that he made a list of performances of plays that had taken place at the Athenian Dionysos festivals for his studies in literary history. Here we can even see clearly how his specific research and general conception were connected.[156] As a natural scientist, Aristotle was convinced that all biological processes occurred according to the same pattern: birth—growth—fulfillment—decay—death. Human beings, animals and plants develop up to a certain point. When the goal (*telos*) of ascent is reached, the descent begins, but the ascent is a gradual perfection (*teleiōsis*). If one wants to understand and to define the essence of an animal (and that is, after all, the task of the scholar) one must start with its finished form. Aristotle saw historical processes in the fields of politics and culture in the same light. The development of an artistic genre, such as the tragedy, which he held to be the highest form of the art of poetry, seemed to him to be analogous to that of a living being. He therefore formulated in his *Poetics* the terse sentence: "After going through many changes, tragedy stopped when it had found its own natural form"[157] (*physis*, here the same as *telos*, "goal"). He thought that it had reached its goal with Sophokles, and that it had realized its true essence in his masterworks, especially the *Oidipus*. Aristotle wanted not only to state a fact of literary history but desired also and above all to point the way to a definition of tragedy; he was primarily concerned with the definition of its essence. The essence of tragedy could be seen in a perfect work such as the *Oidipus* of Sophokles.

The teleological conception of Aristotle depended entirely on the chronology of tragedy. Therefore he did not spare any pains to make a list of all dramatic performances according to the records of the archons, because this provided him and anybody else who wanted to research the development of tragedy and comedy with a stable chronological framework. The efforts of his friend Lykurgos (the "theatrical reform") made it probably easier to execute this enterprise, but they were not the cause of it. This is proven by the late publication of the *Didaskaliai* in the form of an inscription, which was due to a private initiative.

This work by Aristotle is one of the many in which his scientific attitude demonstrated its value also in practice. In one of his zoological works we read what he told his pupils about the meaning of specific and minute zoological research. His words are a "praise of devotion to small things", as Jaeger says.[158] The same is true, *mutatis mutandis*, also for work in literary history.

His pupils who continued his list were only concerned about fixing the chronology but not about establishing a theory. As in so many other areas, the Peripatetics did not pursue the superior conceptions of the founder of their school any further.

2.4 The Doxographic Works of Aristotle and His Pupils

Aristotle also laid the foundations for a history, or more precisely, a history of dogmas of philosophy and the sciences. Already in an early work, the *Peri philosophias* (On philosophy) which was once held in high esteem but has nevertheless not been preserved, he described the history of culture, particularly that of philosophy from the beginnings to Plato.[159] Among the few details that are known to us from quotations, one is of special interest for our investigation. Aristotle stated, when speaking about the Orphic teachings, that the poems ascribed to Orpheus had not been written by him, but by Onomakritos who lived at the court of the Peisistratides in Athens, and who had become known as a collector (and forger) of the oracles of Musaios.[160] However, he did not deny that they contained Orphic teachings, that is, he distinguished not only between authentic writings and forgeries, but also between the old religious content and the more recent poetic form.

Instead of the usual argumentation with his predecessors, Aristotle sometimes gave an overview of the historical development of problems — of course as seen from his own position — concerning the opinions (*doxai*) which they had held, that is a doxography.[161] Thus, in the work transmitted to us as Book Alpha of his *Metaphysics* he gave an outline of the opinion of earlier thinkers on the first causes, the principles.[162] Following this example, and partially overlapping with the sketch of his master, Theophrastos described the teachings of the old "physicists" (natural philosophers) extensively. Other pupils of Aristotle described in a similar manner the teachings of some representatives of the sciences: Eudemos treated the mathematicians and astronomers, Aristoxenos wrote about the theoreticians of music, Menon on the physicians.[163]

Doxography entailed knowledge of the lives and writings of authors. Aristotle had the necessary knowledge, and he was also aware of the biographical and bibliographical problems. We need only to recall his remarks on Empedokles (in *Peri poiētōn*) and on Orpheus (in *Peri philosophias*).[164] However, in the first book of *Metaphysics* he was very parsimonious with biographical or bibliographical data. He called the philosophers quite simply by their first names, added the place of birth only for Hippasos, Herakleitos, Anaxagoras and Alkmaion, did not mention their teachers (except for Parmenides, Demokritos and Plato), and noted only in two instances the chronological relation between one philosopher and another who was not his pupil: in one passage he stated that even though Anaxagoras was older than Empedokles, the former had been active at a later time than the latter; in another passage he says that Alkmaion lived at a time when Pythagoras was already an old man.[165] On Empedokles (who had expounded his philosophical conceptions in the form of poems) he mentioned that one could deduce his teachings from his poem, referring to Empedokles's didactic poem *Peri physeōs* (On nature).[166] He did not cite the work of other philosophers. Within the framework of the first book of the *Metaphysics* he evidently wanted to give only a survey of the historical development of the theory of principles, without any biographical or bibliographical details. According to the customary principle to name the "inventors", he emphasized, where appropriate, who had been the first to hold a certain opinion, but did not hesitate to say that in two cases it had not yet been established whether it had been this or that philosopher.[167]

Theophrastos, on the other hand, listed biographical data in his description of the teachings of natural philosophers (*Physikōn doxai*) which were probably drawn from the most diverse sources. These data were certainly most welcome to the Alexandrian librarians and bibliographers, especially to Kallimachos. This work, consisting of 16 books, was the most important product of philosophical doxography which served later generations of scholars as an example; it has not come down to us, but we can deduce from quotations that Theophrastos introduced the "physicists" with their full names (personal name, father's name in the genitive case and place of birth in adjectival form) and also used to name their teachers. Thus he indicated, for example that Anaximenes, the son of Eurystratos of Miletos, had been a pupil of Anaximandros. By means of these personal data it was possible to identify these persons and to indicate their chronological as well as their intellectual relationships. In other cases he indicated the relative chronology, like Aristotle, by stating, for example, that Empedokles had been younger than Anaxagoras. Occasionally he even noticed contradictions in the biographical tradition: thus he reported that the birth place of Leukippos, the teacher of Demokritos, had been variously given as Elea or Miletos.[168]

But Theophrastos, like Aristotle, generally refrained from giving quotations from the works of philosophers, even though his exposition was based on their teachings. If he reported that Leukippos had held such and such an opinion in his work *Peri nu* (On the mind) it was one of the few exceptions.[169] Aristotle's other pupils who were active as doxographers (and whose works are also lost) did apparently as Theophrastos had done: they gave some biographical data for each author but did not quote his works. This limited the value of their doxographic compilations for library or bibliographic purposes. Their practices were strange by our own standards. But many ancient scholars evidently thought that it would be pedantic to quote an author with a reference to the cited work or even a chapter in that work, and we must consider that the Peripatetics wanted to describe not so much the contents of individual works, but the teachings of each author as reflected in his works, classified with those of others by topics.[170] It would have been cumbersome to cite all references in each case. In addition, for some authors it was questionable whether some works had perhaps been ascribed to them which originated with their pupils, their teachers or with another scholar in the same field. This was not seldom the case under the conditions of schools and traditions at that time. Thus it was doubtful whether Pythagoras had written anything at all or whether the so-called Pythagorean writings were perhaps altogether the work of his pupils. It was also questionable whether the writings of Leukippos, the teacher of Demokritos, which had become known under the latter's name, had been written by Leukippos or by Demokritos. Theophrastos assigned two works to Leukippos, but Epikuros, who was thirty years younger, declared that Leukippos had never existed.[171] If the Peripatetics avoided under these circumstances quoting individual works we cannot blame them. It also seems that they did not make any efforts to solve bibliographic problems (and that was, after all, not their aim) if they thought that they were sufficiently acquainted with the teachings of an author, based on his works which were considered to be authentic. To be sure, this practice was not without risk. Thus, for example, Aristotle and his pupil Menon who, on Aristotle's initiative, described the teachings of physicians based on a group of works known to them under the name of Hippokrates, had formed a certain opinion about these theories. According to a papyrus from the 2nd century A.D., acquired by the British Museum in 1892, they were therefore sharply criticized by an unknown scholar of the 1st century A.D., the so-called Anonymus Londinensis, because their opinion on Hippokrates, to which the Anonymus refers by a quotation from Menon's work, was at that time—and even until the end of the 19th century— diametrically opposed to the prevalent view. Modern experts were faced by a dilemma caused by the comments of the Anonymus which had come to light: if his assertions were correct, then Aristotle and Menon had committed an "horrendous error" (Diels) by ascribing to Hippokrates works which he had not written at all; if not, the traditional view of Hippokrates was false.[172] We need not pursue the controversy on this problem which has not yet been settled. The example shows only how questionable were the reconstructions of literary history and the history of scholarship as long as the literary property of authors had not yet been ascertained, and no firm bibliographic foundation had been laid.

Aristotle and his oldest listeners, especially Herakleides Pontikos and Theophrastos, wrote, according to the lists of their works, also on and against the teachings of many other philosophers. But they did not deal with specifics on the lives and individual works of the respective thinkers, to judge from the existing fragments in the Corpus Aristotelicum.[173]

The doxographic works of Aristotle and his pupils deserve our attention also because of a special reason. Let us consider how the great work of Theophrastos, the *Physikōn doxai* in 16 books may have been compiled. We may assume that he had at his disposal an almost complete collection of relevant literature, and that he used as far as possible primary sources.

His method was probably not different from the one still used today: he made excerpts from the scrolls according to certain topics which resulted from the subjects dealt with by the ancient natural philosophers; he then arranged the excerpts according to some classification system by topics in chronological order, and finally edited them for publication. Aristotle had advised his pupils to write down the opinions of the older philosophers from their works.[174] The technique employed by Theophrastos, who followed the example of his teacher, made it impossible to collect and to classify large quantities of literary material. Kallimachos proceeded similarly.

Related to doxography was a work of Aristotle, the results of which were contained in a book described by Cicero, who held it in high esteem but did not cite its title. In this work, Aristotle reported the contents of all writings on rhetoric (there were at least forty of them) in chronological sequence and with commentaries.[175] According to Cicero, he did that so well that interested readers preferred his annotated abstracts to the original texts. These abstracts were introduced and perhaps also connected by notes on the history and teaching of rhetoric. Aristotle apparently indicated the place of birth and the teacher of each author,[176] and probably also the title, but in this case this was not important because almost all these works had the title *Technē (rhetorikē*, "The art of rhetoric") or similar titles.

The work praised by Cicero has been correctly identified with the *Technōn synagōgē* which is named in the lists of Aristotle's works before his *Technē rhētorikē* (Rhetoric); its title means presumably, according to its contents, "Summary of theories on the art [of rhetoric]".[177] This peculiar compilation, the oldest collection of abstracts known to us, was probably a preliminary work of Aristotle for his own *Rhetoric*, but it contained also the beginnings of a history of the theory and practice of rhetoric.[178] It was therefore largely comparable with the description of medical theories by Menon,[179] cited by Galen as *Iatrikē synagōgē* (literally: "Medical summary"). But while Menon reported the teachings and opinions of the authors – in many instances certainly based on several works – Aristotle dealt with specific works. The Alexandrian librarians and bibliographers relied therefore probably on the *Technōn synagōgē* when they had to catalog older works of rhetoric about whose authors they were in doubt, or when they had to compile lists of authors who had written on rhetoric.

If we try to characterize these scholarly endeavors of Aristotle by one single concept, the term *Historia litteraria* (once known to all educated people, but today only seldom used) is most appropriate. This term means not only the history of *litterae* but also their knowledge, according to the original meaning of *historia*; the translation "literary history" is therefore only an incomplete rendering of the concept. *Litterae* meant the entire field known to us as the realm of arts and sciences, including the art of poetry, rhetoric and music.[180] Since Aristotle sought to encompass the development of various sciences and arts, we may consider him as the ancestor of all scholars who sought to explore and to describe the *Historia litteraria*.

2.5 The Works of the Peripatetics on Philology, Literary History and Biography until the Middle of the Third Century B.C.

Many of Aristotle's pupils and their own pupils shared his interest in philology and literary history. In some of them these interests were even more pronounced than they were in Aristotle himself. This pertains to the following scholars of the last third of the fourth and the first third of the third century B.C.:

1) Herakleides Pontikos, that respected pupil of Plato, had also heard Aristotle in the Academy (!) but he had returned to his hometown Herakleia on the Pontos when Aristotle reappeared in Athens (335 B.C.). Although he may be counted among Aristotle's pupils, he does not belong to the Peripatetics, but is generally dealt with together with them. His works, which cannot be dated, belong however more to the pre- and exoperipatetic researches in fields that were also investigated by the Peripatetics.

2) Theophrastos of Eresos on Lesbos, Aristotle's versatile successor, who was, however, more interested in other disciplines. We have already made his acquaintance as a doxographer of natural philosophy.

3) Phainias of Eresos, a fellow countryman of Theophrastos and of about the same age as he, who had heard Aristotle when he taught in Mytilene on Lesbos (345-343 B.C.) and remained there.

4) Aristoxenos of Tarentum, nicknamed "the musician", a rival of Theophrastos, who had hoped to become Aristotle's successor. Even today he is highly regarded as a theoretician of music, and we met him already as a doxographer of musicology.

5) Dikaiarchos of Messene (Messina).

6) Chamaileon of Herakleia on the Pontos, a somewhat younger fellow countryman of Herakleides, who apparently returned to his home town after studying in the Peripatos.

7) Demetrius of Phaleron, a pupil of Theophrastos, who switched from science to politics, ruled Athens under Macedonian sovereignty from 317 till 307, had to flee, and lived since 297 in Alexandria at the court of Ptolemaios I.

8) Praxiphanes of Mytilene on Lesbos, also a pupil of Theophrastos. He taught on Rhodos. Eudemos, a pupil of Aristotle who hailed from the island, and had worked meritoriously on mathematical and astronomical doxography, taught also there during the last period of his life. It is said that Praxiphanes,

purportedly the teacher of Kallimachos, was the first to be named a grammarian in the later Alexandrian sense.[181]

9) Hieronymos of Rhodos, probably a pupil of Praxiphanes.[182] The relevant writings of these scholars are lost, but we know the titles of many of their works, and we also know a little more about some of them because they were used by later authors. Thus, it is possible to indicate at least approximately which subjects were dealt with by the pupils of Aristotle and by their own pupils. It is much more difficult to say what they did not deal with, because so little has come down to us.

The exegesis of Homer, the germ cell of philology, was very popular with them, which is not surprising, seeing that the Greeks now as ever attached the greatest importance to the study of Homer as an educational tool. Herakleides, Dikaiarchos, Chamaileon, Demetrios and Praxiphanes left works on problems in the *Iliad* and the *Odyssey*, as Aristotle had done. Whether their solutions approached a scholarly interpretation is a moot questions. Of course they dealt also with the interpretation of other poets. This transpires from their biographical works on individual authors. In their attempts at exegesis they encountered of course here and there verses that were differently worded in the existing copies, so they had to ask themselves which version was the original one.[183] But none of them undertook a *diorthōsis* (correction) of a version of the *Iliad*, the *Odyssey* or any other epic, as Aristotle had done. At least, the Alexandrian grammarians did not know of any textual criticism of a poetic work that originated with the Peripatos.

On the other hand, quotations from their works show that the Peripatetics dealt with questions of authenticity. Since this occurred partially within the framework of their writings on literary history and bibliography, I shall first deal with those.

The following summary shows the subjects dealt with by the Peripatetics:

Poetry, general:	Herakleides, Theophrastos, Praxiphanes
Poets, general:	Herakleides, Phainias, Praxiphanes
Epic poets	
Homer:	Herakleides, Chamaileon, Praxiphanes (?)
Hesiod:	Herakleides, Chamaileon
Lyric contests:	Dikaiarchos
Lyric poets	
Archilochos:	Herakleides
Telestes:	Aristoxenos
Alkaios:	Dikaiarchos
Sappho:	Chamaileon
Stesichoros:	Chamaileon
Lasos:	Chamaileon
Pindar:	Chamaileon
Simonides:	Chamaileon
Anakreon:	Chamaileon
Alkman (?):	Chamaileon
Drama	
Choruses:	Aristoxenos
Dances:	Aristoxenos
Contests:	Dikaiarchos

Tragic poets, general:	Aristoxenos, Hieronymos
Thespis:	Chamaileon
Aischylos:	Herakleides, Theophrastos (?), Chamaileon
Sophokles:	Herakleides, Dikaiarchos
Euripides:	Herakleides, Dikaiarachos
Comedy, general:	Theophrastos, Chamaileon
Comic poets	
Antiphanes:	Demetrios
Satyr plays, general:	Chamaileon
Music, general:	Herakleides, Theophrastos, Aristoxenos
Contests:	Dikaiarchos
Musicians, general:	Herakleides
Flutists:	Aristoxenos
Kitharists:	Hieronymos
Philosophers	
Pythagoreans:	Herakleides
Socratics:	Phainias
Empedokles:	Theophrastos
Pythagoras:	Aristoxenos
Archytas:	Aristoxenos
Socrates:	Aristoxenos
Plato:	Aristoxenos
Oratory, general:	Theophrastos, Demetrios, Hieronymos
History, general:	Theophrastos, Praxiphanes

This summary contains also general works on the arts and their representatives, because most of these probably contained both systematic and historical discourses (e.g. on the sequence of poets and composers and their inventions).[184]

Dikaiarchos's work *Peri musikōn agōnōn* (On the artistic contests, i.e. the lyric and dramatic contests which were also musical ones) which was based on Aristotle's *Didaskaliai*, was, if we may judge from the quotations, a valuable product of research on literary history.[185] Dikaiarchos also wrote summaries of contents of plays by Euripides and Sophokles. These *hypothēseis*, which were later used by Aristophanes of Byzantium, appeared perhaps in the work on the contests, and they contained at any rate notes on literary history. Probably related to these was a treatise by Herakleides Pontikos on the myths in the plays of Euripides and Sophokles.[186]

But more than anything else, the pupils of Aristotle and their pupils contributed to the elucidation of literary history through their monographs on individual poets. Aristotle himself had not written such a work which could have served them as an example. The oldest monograph on a poet that emanated from this circle was the treatise of Herakleides Pontikos on Homer.[187] But before Herakleides, Antisthenes, a pupil of Socrates, had written on Homer, and earlier still Theagenes of Rhegion and some of this successors that are listed by Tatianos.[188]

The authors of monographs on poets (except Aristoxenos) entitled their works *Peri* ... (On ...). Thus, they were to some extent free to choose the points they wanted to discuss, but in a biographical work they could not avoid giving certain indispensable data and answering a few obvious questions. This was in the nature of things, and led in Hellenistic times even to the formulation of a fixed scheme for biographies of writers. We may therefore assume that they mentioned in each case the place of birth and the father of a poet (his *genos*), if necessary also his teacher (if he was known) and his main place of activity (if this was not his place of birth), even if there is by chance no actual evidence for such data.[189] We do have evidence that they described the period of flourishing (*akmē*) of a writer, reported his special experiences, his relations with his contemporaries, especially with other poets or rulers, (which were also important for the chronology), listed his inventions and other achievements, and mentioned remarkable character traits.[190] It is debatable whether they already recorded the namesakes of poets and their distinguishing characteristics, as was usually done in later periods.[191]

Since generally no original documents on the lives and works of the poets existed, the authors of monographs had to rely on data and hints found in the works of those poets and their contemporaries. They sought therefore to extract as much as possible from these sources. It is certain that they sometimes arrived at false conclusions. Since their works were not intended for any subject experts (which at that time did not yet exist) but for the interested general public, they did not hesitate to draw upon popular traditions of famous poets, on stories, anecdotes, aphorisms and the like, and they also utilized the representations and remarks of the Attic comic poets who had often made prominent writers the butt of their jokes. Peripatetic biography assumed thereby an almost belletristic character which formed a peculiar contrast to its name. But the authors of these works on individual poets wanted, like the poets themselves, not only to please but also to teach, to spread knowledge about men who, with few exceptions, were considered as the educators of the nation.[192] Certainly the Alexandrian grammarians found in these works many useful informations, although it may not always have been easy even for them to distinguish between reliable informations and arbitrary conjectures made by the authors.

A similar case was that of the works on groups of philosophers and on individual philosophers, written by Aristotle's pupils. Those works dealt less with the teachings of the respective thinkers – that was the task of doxography – but rather with their lives. These informations were obtained almost exclusively second-hand because the works of the philosophers were poorer in personal data than those of the poets, and neither Pythagoras nor Socrates had left any written notes.

The monographs of Aristoxenos on Pythagoras, Archytas, Socrates and Plato differed from others in their title: they were not entitled *Peri Pythagoru* (On Pythagoras) etc., but *Pythagoru bios* (Life of Pythagoras) etc.[193] Aristoxenos evidently wanted to show that he had more to offer than the authors of works entitled *Peri* . . . The fragments indicated indeed that he did not only report what had been found in the works of others on poets, but that he also and above all delineated the character of the man; there is also evidence that he indicated the origins of Pythagoras and the teachers of Socrates.[194] However, he let himself be guided entirely by his prejudices. For example, while he admired Archytas, a pupil of Pythagoras who excelled as mathematician and as strategist, he was not well disposed toward Socrates. Sympathy and antipathy dominate therefore his description of their personalities: Archytas appears as the incarnation of self-restraint, whereas Socrates personifies lack of restraint. Incidentally, the study of moral types conducted in the Peripatos showed its influence here. Aristoxenos's example had a bad influence on the biographers among the younger Peripatetics and their successors (scholars who never belonged to the Peripatos but who had conducted studies in literary history and biography like the Peripatetics were later also called Peripatetics);[195] they were thereby led to make infamous conjectures such as those in which Aristoxenos had vilified Socrates as well as Plato whom he also disliked.[196]

According to our modern conception, works on persons who had written important poetic, scholarly or philosophical books should have listed them in one consecutive sequence or should at least have mentioned them in the course of the narrative, and they should have distinguished them from those works that had been falsely ascribed to the authors. But no trace can be found in the works that have come down to us which would suggest that Aristotle's pupils and their pupils had done so in their monographs on poets and philosophers. Later on, after Kallimachos, biographies of persons who had been prominent as writers were often but not always connected with bibliographies of their works. Did the older scholars feel unable to produce a reliable survey on the production of the authors about whom they wrote? Or did they think, as did some of their younger successors, that a bibliography of generally known works of a famous author would go beyond the framework of a biographical work with literary claims? I dare not decide that.

Aristotle's pupils dealt of course in their biographical writings with specific works written by the respective authors, if these works were interesting from a biographical point of view or were in need of an explanation.[197] But Aristoxenos in his *Life of Plato* mentioned the *Republic* apparently only in order to claim that this work had been copied almost entirely from the *Antilogika* of Protagoras.[198] That was characteristic for him. But other scholars were also quick to accuse an author who had been influenced by another or who had been impressed by another writer's work of (intellectual) theft (*klopē*). Thus Dikaiarchos stated, for example, that Euripides had plagiarized a tragedy by Neophron in his *Mēdeia*.[199] It is evident that Aristoxenos wanted to defame Plato. Other scholars used the word "theft" only as a primitive but not vindictive term for a complex situation in literary history.[200]

As already mentioned, there is evidence that the Peripatetics sometimes dealt with questions of authenticity and ascription of individual works and parts of works, mostly relying on older scholars. To be sure, only one of the relevant references comes from a biographical work: Chamaileon discussed in his dissertation on Stesichoros, whether he or Lamprokles had written the famous hymn to Athene *Pallada Persepolin* (Pallas the destroyer of cities) which had been cited by Aristophanes in the *Clouds* (verse 967), and which the school children of Athens had to learn by heart.[201] He decided in favor of Lamprokles, apparently because the comic poet Phrynichos, a contemporary of Aristophanes, had named him as author.

Dikaiarchos would have had to give reasons in his *hypothēseis* to plays by Euripides and Sophokles why he thought that *Rhēsos* had been written by Euripides, if its authenticity had been disputed already in his own time; but this is questionable.[202] On the other hand, it is not impossible that he already knew that in addition to the prologue to *Rhēsus*, which he held to be authentic, there was yet another one, as was known to the later Alexandrian grammarians. It seems that even at that time it was doubtful whether Nikostratos or, as Dikaiarchos thought, Philetairos was the author of *Antyllos* (and of other comedies).[203] Since the author had claimed to be the son of Aristophanes, Dikaiarchos concluded from the attribution that Aristophanes's third son was called Philetairos.

Aristoxenos stated that the comedy *Politeia*, which went under the name of the famous Sicilian poet Epicharmos, was actually a work by the flutist Chrysogonos.[204] He also claimed, that some of the tragedies purportedly written by Thespis were actually forgeries by Herakleides Pontikos.[205] In another passage, he pointed out that there existed copies of the *Iliad* with a proem different from the traditional one.[206]

Praxiphanes was the first to hold the opinion, later shared by Aristarchos of Samothrake and by Krates of Mallos (the Pergamenian rival of the Alexandrian), that the traditional proem to the *Erga kai hēmērai* (Works and days) of Hesiod was spurious; he asserted that he had seen a copy of the epic without the proem.[207]

Finally, a particular work, written by a Peripatetic probably in the Peripatos, should be mentioned, namely the *Archontōn anagraphē* (List of archons) by Demetrios of Phaleron who, as already mentioned, lived in Alexandria since 297 B.C.[208] Demetrios included in his list of Athenian high officials not only events of general history (as Hellanikos had done in his list of Argivian priestesses of Hera) but also those of literary history, especially the history of philosophy.[209]

2.6 The Library of Aristotle

The library of Aristotle which is mentioned by several ancient authors must have been a very plentiful collection of Greek literature, and it was also at the disposal of his pupils. The works of Aristotle and his pupils, especially those mentioned above, show a comprehensive knowledge of literature and could not have been written at all without such a library. Public libraries, where scholars could study works of interest to them or where they could even borrow them, did not exist at that time, neither in Athens nor anywhere else. But Aristotle had the necessary means to acquire the books which he needed from booksellers or other people. Thus, after the death of Speusippos, Plato's successor, he bought his books (library?) (there were only a few of them) for the sum of three talents (18,000 drachmas).[210] The geographer Strabo (d. A.D. 20) claims in a passage that Aristotle had been the first man, so far as known, to collect books; that, to be sure, is an exaggeration, because Euripides (485-406 B.C), for example, already had a library. But if that statement is limited to the systematic organization of a research library, then it is correct.

The nickname *anagnōstēs* (reader) which Aristotle acquired in Plato's Academy, seems to indicate that he had a library already at that time. He was also a new type of philosopher in that he, unlike those of an earlier period and quite like those of a modern scholar, perused the literature and made excerpts.[211]

During this lifetime, this became the custom of all scholars, largely thanks to his own example, but in his youth, immediately before this change, it still made him the butt of jokes on the part of his school mates who were listeners rather than readers. Euripides, a reader and collector of books, had also been ridiculed by his contemporaries, especially by Aristophanes.[212] Plato himself declared in the *Phaedrus* that written notes served not for the communication of knowledge but only as memory aids for the knowledgeable.[213] Basically, Aristotle shared this opinion. During his time in the Academy he, like his teacher, published works (mostly in the form of dialogs) that were intended for a larger public, but as head of a school he acted through talks, lectures and didactic writings which grew out of his lectures and were intended only for the school itself.[214] Nevertheless, he thought it indispensable to complement the oral transmission of knowledge by the study of literature. His method demanded to begin every inquiry with the collection of material. This included also the perusal and evaluation of the relevant literature.[215]

The fate of Aristotle's library is a very remarkable chapter of ancient library history, and it is also important for our present investigation. His collection contained three parts: 1. the copies of works by other authors which he had bought, that is, his library proper; 2. the personal copies of his own works, written by himself or by others, both those that were intended for a larger public, the more polished "exoteric" works, and those that were aimed only at his pupils, the "acroamatic" works which resulted from his lecture notes (literally: only intended to be heard); 3. his written legacy (in the archival sense), consisting of notes (*hypomnēmata*) of all kinds (annotations, excerpts, lecture notes and the like),[216] letters and personal papers. Well-known scholars of Antiquity as well as modern researchers identified, however, Aristotle's works which formed part of his library with that library itself, as if it had contained only his works and his literary legacy. The term *ta Aristotelus biblia* (Aristotle's books) which occurs in addition to *hē Aristotelus bibliothēkē* (Aristotle's library), is admittedly ambiguous: it means both the books acquired by Aristotle and those written by him. Even those researchers who distinguished between these kinds of books did generally not consider that the books written by Aristotle himself constituted, despite their large number, only a very small part of his library; strictly speaking, they were even no more than an annex to that collection of books which surpassed all earlier ones in scope and importance. This is so because researchers devoted to Aristotle tried to elucidate the fate of the philosopher's library with regard to the history of transmission of his works. Gottschalk and Moraux treated the problem also from that point of view.[217] Since I cannot agree with them on some important points, I must here deal with the fate of Aristotle's library, limiting myself to questions that are relevant for my investigations.

Thanks to Diogenes Laertios we know the provisions of the last wills of Aristotle and his first three successors.[218] While the latter indicated who should inherit their books, Aristotle did not mention his library even with a single word in his testament, dictated in Chalkis shortly before his death. There can be no doubt, however, that it became the property of his successor Theophrastos, as Strabo and other authors report. Aristotle perhaps transferred it to him when he retired to Chalkis where he died a few months later (322 B.C.).[219] Theophrastos bequeathed (287 B.C.) his library together with that of Aristotle to his pupil Neleus of Skepsis who had still heard Aristotle and was the oldest among the ten

Peripatetics to whom he left the school. Gottschalk assumes, contrary to his predecessors, that Theophrastos had made this decision so that Neleus could edit his unpublished works.[220] (The last will of the fourth head of the school, Lykon, contains such a provision.) However, if that was the purpose, there was no need for Theophrastos to bequeath the entire collection. The older explanations, namely that Theophrastos in making such a provision had thought that the future owners of the school would elect Neleus as its head, or wanted to achieve just that, also leave some questions unanswered. But when Straton, a younger man and an excellent natural scientist, was elected as head of the school instead of Neleus, the latter returned to his hometown together with the library bequeathed to him by Theophrastos. At least, that is what Strabo and other authors say. The geographer writes in connection with the city of Skepsis in the Troas:[221]

> From Skepsis came the Socratic philosophers Erastos
> and Koriskos and Neleus the son of Koriskos, this last
> a man who not only was a pupil of Aristotle and
> Theophrastos, but also inherited the library of
> Theophrastos, which included that of Aristotle. At
> any rate, Aristotle bequeathed his own library to
> Theophrastos, to whom he also left his school; and
> he is the first man so far as I know, to have
> collected books and to have taught the kings in
> Egypt how to arrange a library. Theophrastos be-
> queathed it to Neleus; and Neleus took it to Skepsis
> and bequeathed it to his heirs, ordinary people, who
> kept the books locked up and not even carefully
> stored. But when they heard how zealously the Attalic
> kings to whom the city was subject were searching
> for books to build up the library in Pergamon, they
> hid their books underground in a kind of trench. But
> much later, when the books had been damaged by
> moisture and moths, their descendants sold them to
> Apellikon of Teos for a large sum of money, both the
> books of Aristotle and those of Theophrastos. But
> Apellikon was a bibliophile rather than a philosopher;
> and therefore, seeking a restoration of the parts that
> had been eaten through, he made new copies of the text,
> filling up the gaps incorrectly, and published the
> books full of errors.

In the following passages Strabo explains the philosophical decline of the Peripatos after the death of Theophrastos: since the Peripatetics lacked Aristotle's works due to the removal of his library by Neleus, they could no longer philosophize in the manner of their master; the situation improved when his works came to light again in Skepsis, so that the Peripatetics could now again philosophize in the Aristotelian manner, but because of the mistakes in Apellikon's copies they were still in many cases reduced to conjectures.[222] Strabo also reports that Sulla seized the library of Apellikon who had died shortly before the capture of Athens (88 B.C.) and that he had it shipped to Rome. The Greek philologist Tyrannion of Amisos who lived in Rome since about 68 B.C. and who was interested in Aristotle, had later dealt with the library (had scanned it for works of the philosopher), and booksellers had made copies of the extant works of Aristotle, but they had employed bad copyists and had not checked the copies for accuracy. So far Strabo.[223] In Rhodos, the geographer had heard Boethos of Sidon, a Peripatetic who was later elected head of the school, and he had been a pupil of the philologist Tyrannion of Amisos in Rome.[224] Both were certainly well informed about the fate of Aristotle's and Theophrastos's library, and about the purchase of the books by Apellikon in Skepsis. But did Strabo report exactly whatever he had heard from them or from others? Among other peculiarities, the commentators have noticed that he speaks in the first part about the library of Aristotle and Theophrastos, but in the second part he speaks only of the works of the two philosophers. Furthermore, so far as we know, neither the removal of the library of Neleus nor the purchase of the books by Apellikon in Skepsis had the philosophical consequences claimed by Strabo. Should we assume nevertheless that Apellikon bought there the entire library of Aristotle and Theophrastos?

Plutarch relates in his biography of Sulla briefly the same as Strabo when he speaks of the seizure of Apellikon's library, probably using Strabo's report;[225] he adds, however, that Tyrannion had made copies of Aristotle's and Theophrastos's works contained in the library, and that he had given them to the Peripatetic Andronikos who edited them and compiled the current lists (*pinakes*) of works by Aristotle and Theophrastos.[226]

Here we meet for the first time the name of the scholar who served so well as the editor of Aristotle and Theophrastos: Andronikos of Rhodos. Unfortunately, we do not know exactly when and where this Peripatetic lived and worked. Some commentators on Aristotle in late Antiquity claimed that he had been the eleventh head of the school, the predecessor of his pupil Boethos of Sidon who was Strabo's teacher; if so, he would have lived in the first half of the first century B.C., mostly in Athens. This conception was lately again defended on good grounds by Moraux.[227] It is at any rate certain that he had a strong influence on the transmission of Aristotle's work. According to Porphyrios, the editor of Plotinos, who took him as his model, it was he who collected the works of Aristotle which had a common subject (that is, the acroamatic writings which were intended only for his pupils) and edited them as the so-called *pragmateiai* (didactic writings). (The Corpus Aristotelicum that has come down to us is probably based on this edition.) Furthermore, as also mentioned by Plutarch, he compiled a comprehensive list of the works of Aristotle and Theophrastos. This *Pinax* was probably among the most important achievements of Antiquity in the field of author bibliography. Even though this bibliography together with a commentary in five books is lost, it is still possible to discern some of its characteristics. I shall return to this later in section 5.4.

The *Pinax* of Andronikos was used by the author of a shorter list of Aristotelian works, a certain Ptolemaios who is now being identified with a Platonic by that name (circa A.D. 300?).[228] His *Pinax* formed part of a biographical work on Aristotle which is also lost. But we still have two Arabic translations made in the 13th century (not directly from the Greek but from the Syriac, but partially with Greek titles).[229] At the end there is a note: "Here ends the list of his [Aristotle's] works which I have seen. There are people who know [yet] a number of other books." Presumably, Ptolemaios copied these words from Andronikos, because it is unlikely that he himself had seen all of Aristotle's works listed by him; part of these probably did not exist any more in this time.

The last section of his list runs as follows:[230]

(92.) The books that were contained in the library of Apellikon.
(93.) The letters collected by Artemon, eight books.
(94.) Other notes.
(95.) State [constitutions?], two books.
(96.) Other letters found by Andronikos, ten books.
(97.) Notes. The number of lines and the beginnings are found in the
fifth book of Andronikos's work on the *Pinax* of Aristotle's works.
(98.) Problems in Homer, ten books.
(99.) On the art of healing.

Some scholars thought that the first entry was a heading and that the following numbers (with a few exceptions) constitute the works of Aristotle bought by Apellikon in Skepsis. It is, however, likely that the works collectively listed at no. 92 (these were perhaps *hypomnēmata*, i.e. notes, sketches, etc.) were listed separately in the *Pinax* of Andronikos, like the *hypomnēmata* mentioned in no. 97. In any case, we can draw the following conclusion from this report: if those were all the books which Apellikon had discovered in Skepsis, then he had not found and bought "the" works of Aristotle and Theophrastos, but only remnants of their literary remains.[231] (Other important *hypomnēmata* are entered in earlier parts of the list.) Strabo's report is therefore questionable.

Another report which partially contradicts the one by Strabo on the fate of Aristotle's and Theophrastos's library was once contained in a work by Athenaios. This polyhistor, born in Naukratis, Egypt, wrote about A.D. 200 a work in 15 books entitled *Deipnosophistai* (The Banquet of the Learned) which contains discussions on culinary, cultural, historical and literary questions in the form of a discourse among the participants in a banquet. The work is highly regarded by scholars of Classical Antiquity as a reservoir of the choicest erudition, because Athenaios could still see and copy many important works which have not been preserved (as, for example, the *Pinakes* of Kallimachos). In the first book, which has come down to us not in its original form but only in a epitome by an unknown author, Athenaios praises the erudition of the host, named Larensios, and his extensive collection of books.[232] The author of the epitome writes:[233]

He [Athenaios] says that he [Larensios] owned so many ancient
Greek books that he surpassed all who had been celebrated for
their large libraries, Polykrates of Samos, Peisistratos, the
tyrant of Athens, Euklides, likewise an Athenian, and Nikokrates
of Cyprus, the kings of Pergamon, Euripides the poet, the
philosopher Aristotle [and Theophrastos[234]] and Neleus, who
preserved the books of the last two named. From Neleus, he says,
our king Ptolemaios surnamed Philadelphos, purchased them all and
transferred them with those which he had procured at Athens and
Rhodos to his beautiful Alexandria.

Gottschalk supposes that Athenaios's remark was perhaps aimed against Strabo's description of the fate of Aristotle's and Theophrastos's library.[235] In any case, in the *Deipnosophistai* he spoke not only about the works of the two philosophers, as Regenbogen thought,[236] but he dealt with their entire library.

56

Even the epitome of this passage leaves no doubt on this point. Aristotle and Theophrastos are not mentioned as writers of books but as collectors, together with Polykrates, Peisistratos, the kings of Pergamon and other famous book collectors, and the host Larensios is being placed above all these. Athenaios had added with patriotic zeal that our king Ptolemaios Philadelphos (or rather, his agent) had brought the books that had been bought from Neleus and which had once been the property of Aristotle and Theophrastos, together with those acquired in Athens and Rhodos to beautiful Alexandria. But he did not say that together with the library of Neleus other books by Aristotle and Theophrastos which the king's agents had bought in Athens and Rhodos had also been brought to Alexandria. His remarks pertained to works by other authors which had been acquired for the Museion in the two most important centers of book trade in the eastern Mediterranean. It follows also from the passage that according to the reporter, Neleus had transferred his library to the king not in Athens but in Skepsis.[237]

But Athenaios also writes in another passage, in the fifth book, that Apellikon of Teos had bought the library of Aristotle. He quotes there a section from a lost historical work by Poseidonios in which Apellikon is mentioned, because towards the end of his life he was active politically and militarily, though with little success.[238] Poseidonios described this remarkable and very rich man who had studied in the Peripatos and had become an Athenian citizen, as a passionate collector of books, historical documents and the like. According to him, Apellikon had bought Aristotle's library and had even stolen old documents from the Athenian state archives in order to enrich his own collection. Athenaios accepted this unthinkingly, as is the custom of polyhistors, without noticing that he himself had reported in the first book that Ptolemaios II Philadelphos had bought the library of Aristotle and Theophrastos.

These documents from Antiquity have been variously evaluated and combined by modern researchers.[239] I mention here only two diametrically opposed hypotheses. Wendel declared that it is possible to combine Strabo's report with that of Athenaios, if we assume that Neleus transferred the library proper of Aristotle and Theophrastos, that is, the works of other authors bought by them, to Ptolemaios II, but that he had kept the works of the two philosophers for himself and bequeathed them to his heirs who finally sold them to Apellikon.[240] But according to the list of Aristotle's works compiled by the Platonic Ptolemaios, Apellikon bought in Skepsis not "the" works of Aristotle but only remnants of his literary legacy. Wendel's hypothesis is therefore untenable as far as Aristotle's works are concerned, if the remarks in the Pinax of Ptolemaios, which are based on Andronikos, are correct. In my opinion, this is the only reliable information which we have on Apellikon's purchase of the books. Either Apellikon himself or others vastly exaggerated the scope and importance of his purchase.[241] Nevertheless, most scholars agree with Wendel's hypothesis.[242]

Wendel and his followers started from the assumption that the library of Aristotle and Theophrastos had been removed from Athens.[243] But this has been contested lately. Pfeiffer and Gottschalk claimed that Neleus had left it to the Peripatos; Gottschalk thinks (as does apparently also Pfeiffer) that not only the works of other authors acquired by Aristotle and Theophrastos but also the works written by the two philosophers themselves and their scientific remains were left in Athens.[244] He supposes that Apellikon owned some manuscripts of Aristotle and

Theophrastos, though he had not bought the scrolls in Skepsis but had stolen them from the Peripatos. (Remember that he had stolen documents from the state archives!) In order to conceal this theft, he had invented the story of his book purchase in Skepsis. He also thinks that Athenaios's report is unhistorical. Due to the large number of works by Aristotle and Theophrastos which Ptolemaios II Philadelphus had bought for the Alexandrian library—copies bought by him or made for him, perhaps also a few originals presented to him by the Peripatetics—it had been falsely assumed that the king had bought the entire library of Aristotle and Theophrastos.[245]

Moraux on the other hand does not doubt that the library of Aristotle and Theophrastos had been removed from Athens. But regarding the clarification of its further fate he is skeptical. He thinks that there were two contradictory ancient traditions on this matter.[246] According to one (that of Athenaios), Ptolemaios II Philadelphos had bought the library, according to the other (Strabo, Poseidonios) Apellikon had bought it. Which of these traditions was the correct one is, according to Moraux, no longer possible to ascertain. But in my opinion there is no reason to give up. Strabo and Poseidonios do not attest to a tradition according to which Apellikon had bought the library. According to Strabo, he had only bought the works that had been written by Aristotle and Theophrastos. But if Poseidonios claims that Apellikon had bought the library of Aristotle, he almost certainly misunderstood his authority who had spoken about the books of the philosopher but had meant only his own writings (the double meaning of biblia). That Apellikon did not even buy the writings of Aristotle from Neleus's heirs, is shown by the Pinax of Ptolemaios.

Regarding the fate of the library of Aristotle and Theophrastos as such, there was, in my opinion, only one single ancient tradition, namely the one reported by Athenaios. According to this, Ptolemaios II Philadelphos (that is, an agent of the king) bought from Neleus all the books which he had inherited from Theophrastos, both the works of other authors that had been bought by his two teachers and the books written by the two themselves. (The only issue not considered in this view is the fact that a small part of the literary remains was left in Skepsis, where Apellikon found it later.) It is unlikely that the information reported by Athenaios was a Ptolemaic court legend. It was hardly possible for someone to claim, just for the sake of praising the king, that he had bought the books left by Aristotle and Theophrastos, if those had remained then as always in the Peripatos, which could not have been a secret. One may not reckon with a fabrication which could easily be refuted. Also, nobody would have concluded solely from the large number of copies of works by Aristotle and Theophrastos in the Alexandrian library that Ptolemaios II Philadelphos had bought their entire library. The Ptolemies certainly owned also copies of many works by Euripides, but nobody concluded from that they had bought the poet's library.

In the fifth book, Athenaios reverts once more to the mass of books collected by Ptolemaios II Philadelphos; he cites them there as an additional proof for the immense riches of the royal house, but does not elaborate because, as he says, these things were commonly known.[247] This remark occurs in the section that connects two longer excerpts from a lost work by Kallixeinos of Rhodos, Peri Alexandreias (On Alexandria). One of these describes a magnificent parade held by Ptolemaios II Philadelphos, the other is on the immense shipbuilding enterprise of Ptolemaios IV.[248] In this work, which consisted of at least four books, Kallixeinos must have dealt also with the library of the Museion. Even though he was not a contemporary of Ptolemaios II, (he lived at the earliest under the fourth one, that is, around 210.) he was still so close to his era that he had exact information on it, as is shown by his description of the parade. If Athenaios, as was no doubt the case, based his information also on the work by Kallixenios, his reports deserve to be believed.

This assumption is supported by the following consideration. An ancient scholar noted at the end of Theophrastos's *Metaphysics*, that this fragment did not appear in the *anagraphē* (list) of the works of the philosopher compiled by Hermippos, nor did it appear in the one written by Andronikos. Thus, Hermippos (the reference is obviously to the Kallimachean) had compiled a bibliography of Theophrastos which should have been complete; presumably, it was connected with his biography of Theophrastos which is sometimes cited.[249] Now it is true that Ptolemaios II Philadelphus and also his father had bought copies of Theophrastos's works before his library came to Alexandria (if indeed it was brought there). The two pupils of the philosopher who lived for some time at the Alexandrian court, namely Demetrios of Phaleron as counselor of the first Ptolemaios, and Straton of Lampsakos as teacher of physics for his son, had certainly aroused some interest in the works of their master and the Peripatetic philosophy in general, and the rulers could not foresee that the day would come when they would be able to buy the library of Theophrastos. But it is unlikely that an Alexandrian scholar would have undertaken to compile a bibliography of such a prolific author as Theophrastos only on the strength of the copies that had been bought earlier. Rather, the work of Hermippos presupposes that the complete works of the philosopher were available in Alexandria, which at that time was possible only after the library bequeathed by him to Neleus had been acquired.[250] Thanks to this acquisition, a catalog of the works of Theophrastos which were available in the library of the Museion was technically almost tantamount to a bibliography of his works. We may therefore assume that Hermippos compiled his *anagraphē* by using the library's catalog, or even that he himself cataloged the copies of works by Theophrastos which were held by the library.

Diogenes Laertios inserted in the Theophrastos chapter of his work an almost complete list of his writings, which was apparently also included by Hesychios of Miletos in his work, both using the same source.[251] It consists of four consecutive lists of titles without interposed headings which are (except for the third) arranged alphabetically by the first letter of the first principal word. The first (109 titles) lists the bulk of the exoteric and acroamatic works on logic, ethics, politics, and physics; the second (60 titles) other writings on these disciplines and works on rhetoric, poetry and music which are missing from the first list, as well as his letters and notes; the third (28 titles) and the fourth (22 titles), except for some addenda, mainly doubtful or spurious writings and such authentic ones which form parts of larger works mentioned in the two first lists. For each work, there is an annotation showing how many books (= scrolls) it contains, each book being counted separately, so that for a work consisting of three books the annotation does not say "3 [books]" but "[book] 1, 2, 3". Parallels to this are found in only a few of the bibliographies transmitted by Diogenes Laertios.[252] At the end, there is a note on the sum total of the standard lines (*stichoi*) in the works of Theophrastos, namely 230,808.[253]

The four lists, especially the two principal ones, are some of the most interesting relics of Greek bibliography, and we shall deal with them in more detail below. Almost all researchers, above all Regenbogen, the most eminent of all Theophrastos researchers of our time, assume that these bibliographies are ultimately based on the *anagraphē* of Hermippos, even though they went through several intermediate stages at which they were shortened and partially also distorted. If this is correct, they inform us about bibliographical work in the circle of Kallimachos, and they are among the important, even though only indirect, records of this work.

But is this assumption sufficiently justified? From the remark of that ancient scholar cited above concerning the fragment of Theophrastos's *Metaphysics* we may conclude that there were no more than two bibliographies of the philosopher's works in Antiquity. The question is thus only whether Hermippos or Andronikos was the source of Diogenes Laertios's work. The principal argument in favor of Hermippos, namely the alphabetical arrangement of the lists, so typical for the practice of the Alexandrian library, must, however, be qualified. As we shall see, the Alexandrian librarians alphabetized the names of authors of individual classes, and also the titles of certain works of the same kind (e.g. plays), but the titles of works which dealt with various parts of philosophy (logic, ethics, etc.) were generally not confounded in a single alphabet. The bibliographies of Theophrastos's works are an exemption, but it can be explained by the moves toward alphabetization made in the library of the Museion, and as an attempt which Hermippos dared to make after the alphabetization of authors' names in individual classes and that of titles of works of the same kind. (This attempt was apparently not approved, it was not fully executed and was not repeated.)

On the other hand, it is virtually impossible that the titles of all works in the Theophrastos bibliography of Andronikos were arranged alphabetically. Unlike Hermippos, the Rhodian was a genuine Peripatetic; as already mentioned, he combined the acroamatic writings of Aristotle and Theophrastos which dealt with the same subjects to form the collections that have come down to us. Although the alphabetization of titles was not unknown to him, he limited it in his bibliography of Aristotle, whose arrangement probably reflects that of Ptolemaios's list, to certain categories of writings and collections. (See section 5.4.) We may therefore assume that he listed also in his Theophrastos bibliography the titles of acroamatic principal works in classified order by subject, according to the subdisciplines of philosophy.

The Hermippos hypothesis is therefore no doubt supported by the alphabetical arrangement of the Theophrastos bibliographies. I also think that the introductory and concluding words of Diogenes, and the sum total of the standard lines reported by him indicate that his source or that of his authority was a complete list of Theophrastos's works, and that this list gave for each work, more precisely for each book of each work, the number of standard lines, that is, it was based on autopsy.[254] The summation of standard lines would be inexplicable if the list would just be one of the holdings of any collection. It made sense only if the listed holdings, according to the bibliographer's opinion, contained the complete works of Theophrastos, including his literary remains. It seems to me in this context especially remarkable that these holdings comprised indeed not only the exoteric and acroamatic writings of the philosopher but also material from his literary

60

remains, among other things six books of not specified *hypomnēmata* (no. 170) whose authors—Aristotle or Theophrastos—were disputed; probably these were collections of all kinds of notes, excerpts, and sketches, perhaps started by Aristotle and continued by Theophrastos. In the list of Aristotle's works transmitted by Diogenes Laertios which is, apart from its arrangement, analogous, such materials are also listed, among others twelve books *atakta* (sc. *hypomnēmata*, "unordered notes", no. 127). Such incomplete *hypomnēmata* were hardly ever copied, and they were also generally not listed with the works of an author. The few exceptions indicate that the respective bibliography was based either on an inventory of the literary remains of an author or on a catalog of a library which had acquired such remains.[255]

On the strength of this circumstantial evidence we are justified in our assumption that the list of Theophrastos's works reported by Diogenes Laertios was based on the *anagraphe* of Hermippos, which in all probability was based on the literary remains of the philosopher.[256] This in turn corroborates the report of Athenaios, because if the works of Theophrastos were brought to Alexandria, then Ptolemaios II Philadelphus must have bought the library of Theophrastos (including that of Aristotle) from Neleus in Skepsis, except for that part of the *hypomnēmata* of the two scholars which remained for unknown reasons in Skepsis and which were there rediscovered and purchased by Apellikon. Incidentally, Ptolemaios II was known as such a passionate collector of Aristotle's works that he was even offered faked "Aristotelian" works—and that he bought them.[257]

There can thus be no doubt that Neleus removed from Athens the library of Aristotle and Theophrastos which he had inherited. That was of course a loss for the Peripatos but not a catastrophe, because the members of the school certainly had copies of at least the most important works of the first two heads of the school, and it was not difficult for them to acquire the works of other authors in which they were interested. The decline of the school in the latter part of the third century B.C. was not at all due to the removal of the library of its founder and his first successor, as Strabo and Plutarch thought.[258] Neleus's act was probably not just a senseless revenge by a man embittered by the election of Straton. Perhaps he wanted to found a school himself in his homeland, in Skepsis or in the city of Assos on the coast, where once two pupils of Plato from Skepsis, namely Neleus's father Koriskos and Erastos, had taught together with Aristotle and Xenokrates, who later became the head of the Academy. To be sure, Skepsis was no longer the same.[259] Therefore, the aging Neleus was soon led to transfer his library to Ptolemaios II. The library of the Museion was thereby augmented by the largest and most precious treasure of books which existed at that time outside of Alexandria. After having received all works by other authors acquired by Aristotle and Theophrastos, the library constituted such a rich collection of Greek literature that Kallimachos could compile the first national author dictionary on the strength of its holdings.

It is self-evident that not only the writings of Theophrastos but also those of Aristotle came to Alexandria with Neleus's library. This if of crucial importance for a controversy that touches also on the theme of our investigation. Diogenes Laertios inserted a list of works also in the chapter on Aristotle, as he had done in his chapter of Theophrastos; this list, expanded by an appendix, appeared also in the work of Hesychios of Miletos.[260] Since Hermippos also wrote a biographical work on Aristotle, it was generally assumed until 1951 that he included in this book also a bibliography, as he had done in his work on Theophrastos, and that the list of works that has come down to us through Diogenes and Hesychios was based on the one compiled by Hermippos. But Moraux refuted this idea. He sought to prove that the transmitted Greek bibliographies of Aristotle were based on one by Ariston of Keos, the fifth head of the Peripatos, and a contemporary of Hermippos. Some experts adopted this conception; others, especially Düring, still ascribe that bibliography to Hermippos.[261] All agree, however, that the bibliography must have been compiled by a predecessor of Andronikos, because the didactic writings compiled by the latter and listed in the Arabic lists of Aristotle's works are not yet mentioned in that bibliography.

Moraux argued against the Hermippos hypothesis mainly because of the arrangement and the incompleteness of the bibliography transmitted by Diogenes and Hesychios. The titles are there not arranged alphabetically, as in the bibliography of Theophrastos, but they are roughly arranged by form and content. Their conjectured grouping was, however, often destroyed in the course of time or it was perhaps never executed in its entirety. In the beginning, the exoteric works of Aristotle are listed, almost all in the form of dialogs, at the end are his collections of notes and excerpts (*hypomnēmata*) and the results of his archival studies in tabulated form (*pinakes*) as well as the compendium of 158 *politeiai* (constitutions), and his letters and poems. In between, one can discern groups of acroamatic works on logic, ethics, politics, rhetoric, poetry and physics (in the large sense used in Antiquity), but only here and there, because the respective titles are partially mixed up. Several works are listed twice, as Moraux himself has stressed,[262] but under different titles, without the author of the bibliography having noticed this. For that reason alone we must hesitate to ascribe the bibliography to a head of the Peripatetics.

The arrangement of the list is not unusual. Most lists of works transmitted by Diogenes Laertios convey the same picture. The alphabetical arrangement of Theophrastos's works on logic, ethics, politics, physics, etc. is an exception. The arrangement of Aristotle's bibliography may therefore not be used as an argument against its origin in Alexandria.

The same is true for its incompleteness. Most of Aristotle's writings on physics and metaphysics are indeed missing. Moraux denies that their titles were ever listed. But the introductory and concluding words of Diogenes and the sum total of the standard lines reported by him allow us to conclude for the bibliography of Aristotle as well as for that of Theophrastos that the source used by Diogenes and Hesychios or their authority listed (according to the bibliographers' opinion) the complete works of the philosophers.[263] Neither does the sum total prove, as Moraux thinks, that no titles were omitted.[264] The lack of works on natural science and other writings may have its cause in the vicissitudes of the transmission, the accidents of which always endangered especially the preservation of such lists, as Moraux himself has shown in an example.[265] All missing titles may have been written in a single column. Both in the bibliography of Theophrastos and in that of Aristotle there is also, in addition to the exoteric and acroamatic works, a listing of unspecified *hypomnēmata*, e.g. twelve books *atakta* (sc. *hypomnēmata*, i.e. unordered notes, no.)[266] which were certainly never copied, but reached the bibliographer through the literary remains of the philosopher (together with the personal copies of their works). No one, not even the king of Egypt, could have come into the possession of such *hypomnēmata* in any other manner. It is also doubtful whether a "layman" like Ptolemaios II Philadelphos who collected the works of Aristotle had copies made specially also of the many other collections of materials which were listed by the authority on whom Diogenes and Hesychius relied.[267] This pertains likewise to the collections of materials listed in the bibliography of Theophrastos. We are therefore justified in considering the bibliography of Aristotle (from which those of Diogenes and Hesychius are derived) as well as the bibliography of Theophrastos as the product of Alexandria from the 3rd century B.C. Their compilation was made possible by the transfer of the library of Aristotle-Theophrastos-Neleus to Alexandria. It is also not unlikely that Hermippos himself compiled this bibliography too.

It should be mentioned already at this point that among the bibliographies transmitted by Diogenes Laertios there are three which are rather similar to those of Aristotle and, except for the arrangement, to that of Theophrastos, namely the lists of works by Speusippos, Xenokrates and Straton.[268] (Speusippos and Xenokrates were former schoolmates and rivals of Aristotle, Speusippos became the first, Xenokrates the second successor of Plato; Straton was a pupil of Theophrastos and became his successor.) In the beginning, the dialogs are listed, at the end the *hypomnēmata* and the letters. The principle according to which the titles of other works are arranged, if there was such a principle at all, cannot be discerned. Unspecified *hypomnēmata* are listed among them, and the books of larger works are separately specified. At the bottom of each list the sum total of standard lines is given. In the list of works by Xenokrates there are also still remnants of a count of lines in individual works based on the sum of standard lines.[269] The analogies are remarkable because Aristotle bought the books of Speusippos after his death; they shared therefore the fate of his library, and were also brought to Alexandria. We do not know what happened to the books of Xenokrates and Straton. Perhaps the Ptolemies acquired these too.[270] Ptolemaios II Philadelphos had indeed once been taught by Straton. In any case, the bibliographies of these two philosophers were probably also of Alexandrian origin.[271] Even the bibliography and edition of Aristotle's works by Andronikos originated, in my opinion, not in Athens, much less in Rome, but in Alexandria, of course before 47 B.C., in which year the library of the Museion was destroyed by fire.[272] Only there could Andronikos find a complete collection of the documents that he needed. The same is true for his bibliography and edition of Theophrastos's works.[273]

Strabo says in the passage cited above that Aristotle was not only the first to collect books but that he also taught the Ptolemies how to set up a library. This may only mean that the Ptolemies were induced by his example to build the great Alexandrian library. Wendel supposed more than that: the Ptolemies received perhaps with the library of Neleus, i.e. with that of Aristotle and Theophrastos, also its technical arrangement.[274] But did the technical arrangement of Aristotle's library go beyond a reasonable shelving of scrolls according to their title tags (*sillyboi*)?[275] Wendel presupposes apparently that the library was cataloged, because he assumes that the Alexandrian technique of book description (which can be deduced from Kallimachos's *Pinakes*, and which he traces to ancient Oriental examples) was transmitted to the scholars of the Museion through Aristotle's library.[276] Based on this assumption, Regenbogen writes: "There can be no doubt that such larger private or school libraries already had their catalogs, i.e. their *pinakes*, even though nothing of this kind has actually

63

come down to us."[277] Contrary to this conclusion we must remember that it was very difficult to catalog, in the strict sense of that word, an ancient library as wide in scope and as rich as the one owned by Aristotle.[278] It is therefore unlikely that such a task had been undertaken before the Alexandrian scholars had completed their great work, the cataloging of the library of the Museion, on which the *Pinakes* of Kallimachos were based. Only thereafter, by means of these lists, was it easy, or at least easier, to catalog a large library.

Aristotle was probably content to arrange his books by authors of works, such that the authors of individual literary genres and scientific disciplines formed separate classes, and were arranged within each class by age. Such an arrangement must have seemed natural to him, because it corresponded to the facts of literary history. He may have disregarded the many bibliographical problems that arose in some cases, because their solution—which would have been indispensable in the cataloging of a library—would have entailed protracted investigations. As we shall see, the Alexandrian librarians presumably worked to begin with in a similar manner. Incidentally, even in large public libraries of modern times, let alone in private libraries, it was until the end of the 18th century quite customary to think that one could do without any catalog at all, if only the books were arranged in a detailed systematic and chronological sequence, although a catalog would have made it that much easier to survey the collection and to use it.[279]

Notes to Chapter 2

1) Plato, *Protagoras* 325 A.

2) According to Plato, *Republic* 606 A. See Jaeger (1933) vol. 1, pp. 63-88 ("Homer as educator").

3) Pfeiffer (1968) pp. 9-11.

4) Pasquali (1952) p. 214 f.

5) Ludewich (1884) pp. 3-8; Wendel (1949) p. 59 f.; Pfeiffer (1968) pp. 94-95.

6) Eustathios (1827) p. 297, 4; Pfeiffer (1968) p. 72, note 4. The *Suda* mentions among the works of that Euripides (no. 3694) the Homer edition with the addition: *unless it originated perhaps with another* [Euripides?]. It is deplorable that we know so little about the Homer edition of Euripides, because the Athenian version of the Homeric epics was apparently of great importance for their textual history.

7) A later meaning of *ekdosis* (interpretation) which has been dealt with by Erbse (1959) need not be considered in this context.

8) Eustathios (1827) p. 6, 41-43. Gräfenhan (1843) vol. 1, p. 276 pointed this out.

9) Lesky (1968) column 834.

10) Although the so-called city editions are never designated in the scholia as *diorthōseis* (as mentioned by Erbse (1959) p. 289), Eustathios nevertheless called them by that name; see above, note 8. Pfeiffer (1968) p. 94 is also right when he says that the edition of Antimachos was never called a *diorthōsis*. Nevertheless one must consider that all older Homer editions, including those edited by the predecessors of Aristarchos in Alexandria itself, Zenodotos and Aristophanes of Byzantium, are cited in the scholia without any designation. Generally (and if there are exceptions they are very rare) they are there indicated by *hē Antimachu* or *hē Zēnodotu* (the one by Antimachos or by Zenodotos) and *hē Massiliōtikē* or *hē Sinopikē* (the one from Massilia or from Sinope); one had to complete the phrase by *ekdosis* or *diorthōsis*. This was practically the same, because in my opinion there was no *ekdosis* without *diorthōsis*, there were only different degrees of *diorthōsis*. But perhaps the editions (or at least some of them) which were named after cities, regions or islands were not really editions at all, but copies that had been bought in those places. But that also designations by names of a person were only indications of provenance, as conjectured by Haeberlin (1889) p. 497 f., is precluded by the formulation *kata* (e.g. *Antimachon*), "according to Antimachon"; cf. *kata Markon*, (Gospel) "according to Mark". It is questionable whether diacritical marks (*sēmeia*) were occasionally inserted already in pre-Alexandrian Homer

editions; cf. Jachmann (1949) p. 223 and Pfeiffer (1968) p. 180, note 5. The marks used by Alexander the Great in his personal copy of Homer, as related by Strabo XIII 594, were apparently not *sēmeia* in the philological sense. Pfeiffer (1968) p. 71 explains them as notes; see also note 45 below.

11) Pfeiffer (1968) pp. 120-121.

12) Diogenes Laertios (1964) IX 113. Aratos's question, which is more interesting than Timon's often cited answer, was: how could he obtain Homer's genuine epic? It is generally assumed that Timon's answer was aimed at Zenodotos, the first Alexandrian philologist who dealt with Homer; see Pfeiffer (1968) pp. 97 and 121. But it does not contain a direct reference to Zenodotos. He was indeed the first corrector of Homer's text in the narrower sense, but in the larger, traditional, sense all earlier editors of Homers epics were also correctors of those works; see above, note 10. At most, Timon might have included Zenodotos in his remark, if he had already seen his *diorthōsis* of Homer's text.

13) Herodotos II 116; on this Pfeiffer (1968) p. 44.

14) Pfeiffer (1968) p. 73.

15) Rzach (1913) column 2150-52.

16) A similar story was told of Thestorides of Phokaia; see Homerus (1912) vol. 5, pp. 201-203.

17) Callimachus (1949) Ep. 6 (purporting to be the title of a book; the book itself speaks) in A. W. Mair's translation (Callimachus, 1921) [listed as Ep. 7 in that edition]):

> I am the work of the Samian who once received the
> divine singer in his home; and I celebrate the
> sufferings of Eurytos and of fair-haired Ioleia;
> but I am called the writing of Homer. Dear
> Zeus, for Creophylus this is a great thing.

18) On literary forgeries in Antiquity and on ancient criticism of authenticity see Speyer (1971), especially pp. 111-131.

19) Herodotos VII 6; Aristotle, *Fragmenta* (1886) no. 7; on these Jaeger (1955) pp. 131 and 133.

20) Pfeiffer (1968) p. 11. The texts of the biographies can also be found in Allen's Homer edition, vol. 5 (Oxford 1912).

21) Tatianos, *Pro Hellēnas*, ch. 31. The English translation of this passage, which is of interest for the history of scholarship and is therefore cited, follows: "The poetry of Homer, his origin and the period during which he flourished were first investigated by Theagenes of Rhegion who lived in the times of Kambyses, by Stesimbrotos of Thasos, by Antimachos of Kolophon, by Herodotos of Halikarnassos, and by Dionysios of Olynthos; after those,

by Ephoros of Kyme and Philochoros of Athens, and by the Peripatetics Megakleides and Chamaileon, and then by the grammarians Zenodotos and Aristophanes, Kallimachos, Krates, Eratosthenes, Aristarchos and Apollodoros." Theagenes was also interested in Homer's usage of language and in textual criticism of his epics; see Pfeiffer (1968) p. 11.

22) Pfeiffer (1968) p. 94.

23) Hilgard (1901) pp. 164, 26-28 and 488, 12-14; Pfeiffer (1968) p. 158.

24) The works mentioned in the following cannot be exactly dated. The period in which their authors lived is also not exactly known, except in a few cases. The scholars who flourished in the second half of the 5th century B.C. witnessed the Peloponnesian war, the struggle between Athens and Sparta on supremacy in Greece (431-404 B.C.); those who flourished in the first half of the 4th century B.C. were witnesses to the squabbles among the Greeks which came to an end only after the victory of Philipp II of Macedonia over the Greeks at Chaironeia (338 B.C.) which laid the foundation for Macedonian rule over Greece.

25) Jacoby (1957) no. 4, fragment 74-84 with commentary, and also Regenbogen (1950) column 1413 f.

26) Jacoby (1912) column 143 and (1957) no. 4, fragment 85-86 with commentary, and (1949) p. 58 f.; thereafter Regenbogen (1950) column 1414.

27) Jacob Burckhardt, *Griechische Kulturgeschichte* (Basel 1957) vol. 4, pp. 84-90 (first published posthumously 1904).

28) Jacoby (1957) no. 6, fragment 2 with commentary; Pfeiffer (1968) p. 51.

29) Thus, for example, Wehrli (1967) Heft 7, p. 122 with reference to Herakleides Pontikos.

30) Vorländer (1963) vol. 2, p. 58 — The antithesis *physei* : *nomo* appears several times in the biobibliographic articles of the *Suda* where it has a special significance. For example, it says there that the philologist Aristarchos had been from Samothrake *physei*, i.e. by birth, but *nomo*, by citizenship, he had been an Alexandrian.

31) Pfeiffer (1968) p. 52 is, in my opinion, not quite fair to Hippias when he writes that behind the scholarly endeavors of the sophist were the practical needs of his profession. Too many of Hippias's manifold enterprises went far beyond that and can only be explained by a genuine scholarly interest.

32) It has been established that the ancient philologists dated the victory odes with the aid of lists of victors. Besides, the lists of victors could be exploited not only for literary but also for artistic purposes, because they made it possible to date the statues erected in honor of the victors; see Robert (1900).

33) Jacoby (1957) no. 5, fragment 11 a-b (Homer's origin and period). Damastes, as also later Aristotle, *Fragmenta* (1886), no. 5, referred by the term "sophists" probably to the old teachers of wisdom, especially the Seven Sages who recited their thoughts mostly in verses. Poets and prose writers were not treated together in later works, except in dictionaries.

34) Hiller (1886); Leo (1901) p. 101; Jacoby (1912); Wehrli (1967), Heft 7, p. 112. Pfeiffer (1968) did not deal with the work of Glaukos. In the pseudo-Plutarchian book *Peri musikēs* the work is indicated in ch. 4 (1132 E) as *syngramma* (writing), in ch. 7 (1133 F) as *anagraphē*. One may, however, not conclude from the second citation that it had the form of a list: there, *anagraphē* does not mean list but record; likewise in Plutarch, *Perikles* 2.

35) Leo (1901) pp. 46-49; 74-83; 100 f.

36) Plato's remarks, *Phaedrus* 267 A and B, cited by Leo (1901) p. 49, note 1, are probably of a more recent date.

37) Pseudo-Plutarch, *Peri musikēs* ch. 3 (1132 A); Jacoby (1949) p. 58; Regenbogen (1950) column 1414; Wehrli (1967) Heft 7, p. 112. Wehrli conjectures without giving his reasons that the *Anagraphē* of Sikyon was a list of prize-winners at the agones of the muses held at Sikyon. What little is known of it does not, however, justify this opinion.

38) This was the singing of songs with accompaniment by kithara, and the writing and setting to music of the recited texts.

39) One ought to compare it especially with the so-called *Marmor Parium*, a chronological inscription made about the middle of the 3rd century B.C. and found on Paros, which lists not only political but also cultural and literary events; see *Lexikon der Alten Welt* (1965) s.v. "Marmor Parium". See also the Roman inscription of Kallimachos's *Pinax* of Attic dramatic poets (section 4.2 below). Furthermore, the inscriptions carved in stone of lists of victors in contests that were held at a particular place, e.g. the Pythian contests in Delphi.

40) Wehrli (1967) Heft 7, fragment 157. Perhaps Menaichmos of Sikyon also referred to the Sikyonic *Anagraphē*. According to the *Suda*, this Menaichmos lived "under the diadochs" and wrote a book *Peri technitōn* (On the artists), a local history of Sikyon, and a biography of Alexander the Great. The first work is cited four times by Athenaios (late 2nd century A.D.). It dealt with poets, musicians and inventors of musical instruments; Susemihl (1891) p. 532 f.; Pfister (1913) p. 535 f.; Laqueur (1931). Pfister supposes that Menaichmos got the idea for his book *Peri technitōn* and some material for it from the Sikyonic *Anagraphē*. Despite certain chronological difficulties it might also be possible to identify him with the Menaichmos who wrote a *Pythikos* (sc. *logos*) before 335 B.C.; see note 60, below.

41) On the life and work of Aristotle see Düring (1966), especially pp. 1-52, often contrary to Jaeger (1955); on his role in the history of philology, see Pfeiffer (1968) pp. 67-84. — For events that cannot be dated to a month but

only to a year, it is necessary to give two dates (e.g. 384/3), because the Attic year began in July of our calendar.

42) The historical and systematic description of the Athenian constitution *Athēnaiōn politeia* which has come to light again on papyrus is generally ascribed to Aristotle. However, Düring (1966) p. 476 doubts on noteworthy grounds that it is his work.

43) Wilamowitz (1881) pp. 263-269 after Diogenes Laertios V 39, and Brink (1940) p. 905. Wehrli (1967) Heft 4, fragment 5, commentary, emphasizes that special permission was often given, but since Aristotle neither asked for nor received one, we must assume, contrary to Wehrli, that Theophrastos could buy the plot only under the rule of Demetrios of Phaleron. On Demetrios and his role in the foundation of the Museion at Alexandria and the establishment of the library of the Museion see section 3.2 below. – On the legal position of the Peripatos see Lynch (1972) pp. 106-127, contrary to Wilamowitz. On the pursuit of scholarly studies in the Peripatos see Jaeger (1955) pp. 331-365. Düring (1966) p. 351, note 47 is, however, of the opinion that the situation as depicted by Jaeger obtained only at the time of Theophrastos, after 318 B.C. But the collections of material organized by Aristotle confirm in my opinion the conception of Jaeger. There is also nothing to indicate that only the settlement of the legal issues related to the acquisition of the plot led to a substantial expansion of research and teaching in the Peripatos.

44) Plato, *Republic* 391 B; Aristotle, *Fragmenta* (1886) no. 166. On these, Hintenlang (1961) p. 22 f. and Pfeiffer (1968) p. 69.

45) Pfeiffer (1968) p. 71 f. On the designation of *diorthōsis* as *ekdosis* see note 11. The *Aporēmata Homērika* of Aristotle were, however, often used by the philologists of Homer in Alexandria; see Aristotle, *Fragmenta* (1886) no. 142-179. Incidentally, the edition by Euripides is never mentioned either in the scholia to Homer. The only pre-Alexandrian editor of Homer who is mentioned by name in the scholia is Antimachos. – The fate of Aristotle's copy of Homer explains also why no list of Aristotle's works mentions his *diorthōsis* of the *Iliad*, except the list that has been inserted into the Vita Marciana; see Gigon (1962) p. 1. The statement found there, "the edition of the *Iliad* which he presented to Alexander" is evidently not taken from a catalog of Aristotle's works but from a biography of Alexander. I see no reason to doubt the statement transmitted by Alexander's biographers, as Gigon (1962) p. 36 and Pfeiffer (1968) p. 71 do, because it seems not unlikely that Alexander carried with him on his campaign a copy of the *Iliad* that had been corrected by Aristotle, that he kept it under his pillow together with his dagger, that he read it at times with certain scholars in his entourage, that he made signs and notes in it (see above, note 10), and that he finally, after the battle of Issos, gave an order to put it into the box (*narthēx*) that had contained the ointment vessels of Darius, the most valuable piece of the Persian loot. Thus it became famous as the *Iliad* "out of the box" (*hē ek tu narthēkos*). Incidentally, the *narthēx* of Darius was not an ointment pot (Gigon p. 36). For the storage of a very large scroll or more likely of several somewhat smaller scrolls containing the text of the

Iliad a container of at least 40 x 30 x 25 cm. was needed. The anecdote of the storage of the *Iliad* in that *narthēx* (Plutarch, *Alexander* 26) is not meant to illustrate the contrast between Oriental *tryphē* (effeminacy) and Hellenic *arētē* (valour, heroism, glorified in the *Iliad*) (Gigon p. 36 f.) but it demonstrated, in my opinion, the unusually high esteem in which a bellicose king held that work of poetry, to be sure a heroic poem, but after all only a work of literature. According to a conjecture by Wendel (1949) pp. 63-65, the *"Iliad* out of the box" found its way into the library of the Macedonian royal palace at Pella, was seen there by Aratos and was introduced by him into the literature on Homer; see Wendel-Göber (1955) p. 90 f. The Alexandrian philologists of Homer, however, as pointed out, did not pay any attention to the Aristotelian *diorthōsis* of the *Iliad*.

46) In an anecdote told by Plutarch, *Alkibiades* 7, and said to have occurred around 435 B.C., an Athenian teacher claims to own a copy of Homer which he himself had corrected; see Wendel-Göber (1955) p. 55.

47) Aristotle's nickname is given in the Vita Marciana; see Aristotle, *Fragmenta* (1886) p. 428, 2 and Gigon (1962) p. 2, 41 and 43; also Düring (1966) p. 8. In order to understand the joke one must remember that in Antiquity people read aloud, but that well-to-do gentlemen had slaves read aloud to them. Some (perhaps Plato?) compared Aristotle who read aloud but of course for himself with such an *anagnōstēs*.

48) It is therefore quite unlikely that he only had a beautiful copy of the *Iliad* made, and then corrected only the copying errors in it, as Düring (1966) p. 125 supposes. In view of the differing verses in various versions it is altogether impossible to speak about "the" *Iliad*.

49) Aristotle, *Poetics* ch. 4; 8; 23; 24. Pfeiffer (1968) p. 73.

50) Aristotle, *Fragmenta* (1886) no. 76.

51) Aristotle, *Fragmenta* (1886) p. 16, line 143-145. Moraux (1951) p. 272 f. thinks that the problems of Archilochos, Euripides and Choirilos are identical with those of *Kyklos peri poiētōn* in line 115.

52) According to Rostagni (1926) p. 448, Aristotle wrote the dialog on the poets for his pupil Alexander around 343 B.C. But if his *Poetics* were already written in the academy, as Jaeger (1955) p. 348 and Düring (1966) p. 163 presume, then the dialog must also be dated before 347 B.C. Incidentally, the work reflected the literary discussions which had become popular with the appearance of the sophists.

53) Aristotle, *Fragmenta* (1886) no. 70-74; Rostagni (1926).

54) Diogenes Laertios VIII 51; 57; 74 = Aristotle, *Fragmenta* (1886) no. 70 and 71. In another lost dialog, the *Sophistēs*, Empedokles is named as the inventor of rhetoric; see Diogenes Laertios VIII 57 = Aristotle, *Fragmenta* (1886) no. 65.

55) Rostagni (1926) pp. 450 and 435, note 2.

56) According to Hieronymos of Rhodos, the two poems were burned not by Empedokles's sister but by his daughter; see Wehrli (1967) Heft 10, fragment 30 with commentary. In this context, it does not matter whether this information is credible; what matters is that Aristotle included it in his survey of Empedokles's works.

57) On the lists of Aristotelian works see Moraux (1951). The list of Diogenes (V 22-27) is printed in the editions of Diogenes and also, together with that of Hesychios, in Aristotle, *Fragmenta* (1886) pp. 3-18, and in Moraux (but there the list of Hesychios only partially).

58) Rostagni (1926) p. 405; Pfeiffer (1968) p. 80, note 7. The list of Olympic victors, the remains of which were found in Athens on the Lykabettos—see Dittenberger (1915) no. 1056—contained perhaps the list of Aristotle; see Reisch (1907) p. 314, note 2. – The reliability of Aristotle's list of Olympic victors is, according to Hester (1941), shown in his remark on the very small number of young Olympic victors who went on to win at Olympia also as adults (*Politics* VIII 4), a fact which has been confirmed by the inscriptions.

59) On Kallisthenes see Jacoby (1919, Kallisthenes) and (1957) no. 124.

60) Quotations from the *Pythionikai*, see *Aristoteles pseudepigraphus* (1863) pp. 545-550 and Aristotle, *Fragmenta* (1886) no. 615-617. On the confused and probably partly corrupt data in the lists of Aristotle's works, see Moraux (1951) p. 125 f.; text of the Delphian honorific decree for Aristotle and Kallisthenes in Dittenberger (1915) no. 275. In the decree, the list compiled by the two scholars is called "List of those who were victorious at the Pythian contests, beginning with Gylidas, and a list of those who organized the contest". See Regenbogen (1950) column 1414; Jaeger (1955) p. 347 f.; Düring (1966) p. 126; Pfeiffer (1968) p. 80 – In the list of works given by Diogenes Laertios there is also in addition to the *Pythionikai* in line 133 a (not preserved) *Pythikos* (sc. *logos*), presumably a speech honoring Apollo and his Delphic temple, with a history of the Pythian contests. Perhaps this *Pythikos* preceded the *Pythionikai* as an introduction. In the list of works written by Hesychios of Miletos the *Pythikos* does not appear; instead, in line 123 there is an addition to *Pythionikai*: "Pythionikai, a book with which he defeated Menaichmos". The note is unusual and enigmatic. A Menaichmos who might be identical with the one from Sikyon also wrote a *Pythikos*; see Laqueur (1931) column 698 f. with an addition by Fiehn; Jacoby (1957) no. 131, fragment 2 with a commentary. Rose thought therefore that the word *Pythikon* in the list may have been left out immediately before the note "with which he defeated Menaichmos", which is plausible, so that the (corrupt) text had originally been "which is ascribed by some to Menaichmos"; see *Aristoteles pseudepigraphus* (1863) p. 547 and Aristotle, *Fragmenta* (1886) p. 15 (with corrected data on the tradition). Although this is a bold assumption, only a bibliographic note of this kind was suitable in a list of works; see notes to lines 168 and 169. What could it have meant that Aristotle defeated Menaichmos with his *Pythikos* in a contest? The explanation given by Brinkmann (1915) p. 627, and repeated by Moreaux (1951) p. 125, that the compilation of a list of winners at the Pythian contests had itself been the object of a contest in which Aristotle

71

won over Menaichmos, is not plausible. The exploitation of documents does not lend itself to a fair contest. Whether there was an earlier list of winners in the Pythian contests which had been destroyed by wars, as had been conjectured, seems questionable to me. The information taken from a pre-Aristotelian work on the Pythic victories of Terpandros and Sakados in the pseudo-Plutarchian work *Peri musikēs*, ch. 4 (1132 F) and ch. 8 (1134 A) could also have been drawn from another source.

61) See Aristotle, *Fragmenta* (1886) no. 617.

62) On the following, see especially Reisch (1903); Körte (1921), pp. 1229-31; Mensching (1964); Pickard-Cambridge (1968) passim; on the explanation of the name of the Lenaean festival (from *lēnos* "wine-press" or *lēnai* "Bacchantic women") see Pickard-Cambridge p. 29; on performances of plays at the so-called rural Dionysian festivals, see Pickard-Cambridge pp. 45-52.

63) Pickard-Cambridge (1968) p. 124 f. (chronological summary). Conjectural beginning of the contests: A. Dionysian festivals. 1. Tragedies 534 (?); 2. Comedies 486. B. Lenaean festivals. 1. Comedies ca. 442; 2. Tragedies ca. 432 B.C.

64) Pickard-Cambridge (1968) pp. 79-84.

65) Reisch (1907) p. 302 f.; Pickard-Cambridge (1968) p. 107 f.

66) At the Lenaean festivals apparently first in Hellenistic times; see Pickard-Cambridge (1968) p. 41 f.

67) Reisch (1903); Pickard-Cambridge (1968) pp. 71 and 84-86.

68) The complete title of the list would have been, analogous to the *Nikai* listed in the bibliographies of Aristotle (Diogenes, line 135, Hesychios, line 125) something like: "Performances of tragedies, satyr plays and comedies at the City and Lenaean Dionysia".

69) Pickard-Cambridge (1968) pp. 84-86. The evidence for Antiphanes (not mentioned by Pickard-Cambridge) is in the anonymous *Peri komodias*; see Kaibel (1899) p. 9, 60 f.

70) Zacher (1890) p. 331 f.; Reisch (1903) column 404 f.; Oellacher (1916) p. 121 f.; Pickard-Cambridge (1968) p. 91. It has unfortunately become a custom in the more recent professional literature to call the person who directed a play a *didaskalos*, whether he was the author or a director commissioned by the author. Since. so far as I can see, the director who had been commissioned by the author was never expressly called *didaskalos* in the fifth and fourth century, I prefer to distinguish between author and director.

71) Pickard-Cambridge (1968) p. 90.

72) Reisch (1903) column 395 f.

73) *Aristoteles pseudepigraphus* (1863) pp. 550-561; Aristotle, *Fragmenta* (1886) no. 618-630. On the following, see Reisch (1903), especially column 396-399; Regenbogen (1950) column 1415-17; Moraux (1951) pp. 126-138; Pickard-Cambridge (1968) pp. 70-74 and 124 f.; Pfeiffer (1968) p. 81.

74) Aristotle, *Fragmenta* (1886) no. 628.

75) E.g. Aristotle, *Fragmenta* (1886) no. 619 and 629.

76) The frequent lack of author indication may also have been caused by the fact that other persons continued it, beginning in an unknown year, but not later than 322 B.C.

77) Achelis (1913); Pfeiffer (1968) pp. 192-196. The learned *hypothēseis* must be distinguished from adaptations of the content which have been transmitted to us and which are also called *hypothēseis*.

78) Callimachus (1949), fragment 456; on this Pfeiffer (1968) p. 195; also Achelis (1913) pp. 418-423. The information given by Choiroboskos, which has been only indirectly transmitted in *Etymologicum genuinum* and *Etymologicum magnum* s.v. *pinax*, has come down to us in distorted form. According to the quotation, the scholar mentioned "tables containing the list of plays"; further, we read there that Kallimachos made "tables containing the lists of the old ones" (*para tōn archaiōn*). Bernhardy substituted for *para tōn* ("of the") the word *poiētōn* (poets), i.e. "lists of old poets"; see Achelis (1913) p. 419. I think this is correct: *poiētōn archaiōn* corresponds to *didaskalōn*; however, nobody, not even Achelis, has so far explained the sense of *para tōn archaiōn*. On the other hand, Achelis doubted, without giving valid reasons, that the information on Kallimachos's list of plays came from Choiroboskos. These *pinakes* cannot refer to Kallimachos's catalog of all Greek authors, because it did not contain the chronological data given by Aristophanes of Byzantium.

79) In the *Pinax* of Kallimachos he found the names of poets arranged in chronological order, with the titles of their plays and the dates of their premieres (this is a somewhat simplified description).

80) *Hypothesis* V of the *Clouds* and *hypothesis* I of the *Peace*. In other *hypothēseis* of the *Peace* the chronology according to years of archons is supplemented by the one according to Olympiads which had been coordinated with the former by Erathosthenes (Alexandria, second half of the 3rd century B.C.). The name of the principal actor does not appear in any of the other *hypothēseis* which have been transmitted to us in medieval manuscripts; but it is listed in the data that precede the *Dyskolos* by Menander which are also based on Aristophanes of Byzantium, and which are preserved on papyrus. See Pfeiffer (1968) p. 192, text in Menander (1953) pt. 2, T. no. 28. The corrupt sequence of letters *hēnikahermēnloiokrotes* at the end has been interpreted in various ways, none of which is as yet convincing. The editors mention an amendment proposed by Richter (in his 1860 edition): *enika Eirēnē Leokratēs* (Leokrates won with the *Peace*). This would be an addition concerning another performance of the play, but without any motivation. Rose

suggested *enika Hermōn ho hypokritēs* (the actor Hermon [who was known as a contemporary of Aristophanes] won); see his *Aristoteles pseudepigraphus* (1863) p. 554 f. But Hermon did not play in the *Peace*, and there was no reason to mention the principal actor who had won in the contest of actors. Besides it seems that at that time there were as yet no contests of comic actors at the Dionysia, as Körte (1897) p. 172 pointed out; see also Pickard-Cambridge (1968) p. 124. Körte's own explanation is not convincing either: he presumed that this was a note concerning the second performance of the *Peace* at the Lenaea which had erroneously been written here. But the victory of an actor who used to appear in several plays was not connected with a particular play.

81) Achelis (1913) p. 540. All data concerning the *Didaskaliai* which were then known were published in *Aristoteles pseudepigraphus* (1863) pp. 559-561. The active form *edidaxe* see there, no. 8, 15, and 17.

82) Reisch (1907) p. 290.

83) For the text of the inscription see Wilhelm (1906) pp. 34-88; *Inscriptiones Graecae*, editio minor II/III 2,2 (1931) no. 2319-23 (formerly 972-975) and Pickard-Cambridge (1968) pp. 107-111. On the archeological report see Reisch (1912); the name of the agonothete, who belonged to the community of the Phrearrioi, has not been preserved. In addition to the literature mentioned in note 73, see Wilamowitz (1906); Capps (1906 and 1907); Reisch (1907); Preuner (1924) pp. 110-112; Snell (1966) pp. 27-33; Pickard-Cambridge (1968) p. 72 f. According to Reisch, the votive inscription of the agonothete of 279/278 (*Inscriptiones Graecae* II 1193) relates to the building; Preuner argued, however, that there already was a votive inscription on the building (*I.G.* II 1264); see Snell (1966) p. 27. I do not think that this objection is valid, because that inscription does not pertain to a votive offering by the agonothete but to the victories at the contests on dithyrambs which were won during his period of office. The fragments contain data on the performances from the following periods: Dionysia, tragedies: 341-349; Dionysia, comedies: 312-141; Lenaea, tragedies: 420-417; Lenaea, comedies: 289-288.

84) At the Lenaea, the comedies are listed before the tragedies, because initially only comedies were performed there.

85) Greek text in *Inscriptiones Graecae*, editio minor II/III 2, 2 (1931) no. 2320, and in Pickard-Cambridge (1968) p. 109:

'Επὶ Νικομάχου σατυρι
Τιμοκλῆς Λυκούργωι
παλαιᾶι: Νεοπτόλεμ[ος
'Ορέστηι Εὐριπίδο
ποη: 'Αστυδάμας
Παρθενοπαίωι ὑπε: Θετ[ταλός
Λυκά]ονι ὑπε: Νεοπτόλε[μος
Τιμο]κλῆς δεύ: Φρίξωι
ὑπε:] Θετταλός
Οἰδί]ποδι ὑπε: Νεοπτόλ[εμος
Εὐ[άρ]ετος τρί
'Αλκ]μέ[ω]νι ὑπε: Θεττα[λός
....]ηι ὑπε: Νεοπτό[λεμος
ὑπο: Θ]εττταλὸς ἐνίκα

In the first and third line the word *enika* (won) must be supplied, but
because no competitors are named, the verb must be understood to mean
only "appeared". Pickard-Cambridge does not comment on this directly but
he thinks that at that time only one new satyr play and one old tragedy were
performed; contests with individual new satyr plays and old tragedies were
only held in the 3rd century B.C.; see Pickard-Cambridge (1968) pp. 72-74.
Later on, the word *enika* was evidently used in a figurative sense; see
Pickard-Cambridge (1st ed., 1953) p. 75.

86) So also Pickard-Cambridge (1968) p. 108. In the Roman inscription two old
comedies (plays by Kallias of 434 and 440 B.C.) are simply indicated as
kōmōdiai; cf. Pickard-Cambridge (1968) p. 121, no. 1097, line 2 and 3.
Either these plays had as yet no titles, or they were not listed in the records.

87) Evidence in the data from the *Didaskaliai*, transmitted by manuscripts; see
Aristoteles pseudepigraphus (1863) pp. 559-561, passim, and Aristotle,
Fragmenta (1886) no. 618-630, passim. Evidence from fragments of
inscriptions: performance of a new play by another man, see Pickard-
Cambridge (1968) p. 122, no. 1098, line 9 (probably complement);
performance of a play by a deceased poet, see ibid., p. 110, no. 2323, column
II 3, line 3; renewed performance of a failed play in a new version, see ibid.
p. 121, no. 1098a, line 5, and p. 121, no. 1097, line 12.

88) Aristotle, *Fragmenta* (1886), no. 618, 619 and 628.

89) Manuscripts: Aristotle, *Fragmenta* (1886) no. 629. Inscriptions: "the older
[poet]", see Pickard-Cambridge (1968) p. 110, no. 2323, column II 3, line 3;
"the older and the younger [actor]", see ibid., p. 109, no. 2323a, line 3 f. In
the above-mentioned section from fragment no. 2320 the tragedian
Astydamas is named. There were two famous poets by that name; the
younger one is probably referred to here, and the appropriate addition was
left out when Aristotle's text was transcribed in stone. In another much-
discussed passage (see Pickard-Cambridge (1968) p. 109, column I, line 8
and 10) a comic poet Diodoros appears both in the second and third place.
These were probably two different poets (if it was not an error made by the
stone carver) and only the distinguishing addition was omitted. It has not
been proved with certainty that a poet was permitted to participate in a
contest with two plays. On the case of the comic poet Anaxandrides who
purportedly won first and third place at the Dionysia of 375 B.C., see
Dittmer (1923) pp. 21-33.; Pickard-Cambridge (1968) p. 82 f.

90) Pickard-Cambridge (1968) p. 110, no. 2323a, line 13. This is said of
Menander (321 B.C.) already in the manuscripts; cf. Pickard-Cambridge
(1968) p. 84; it could also have been in Aristotle's *Didaskaliai*.

91) Jachmann (1909) p. 40 f.; Regenbogen (1950) column 1415.

92) The *hypothēsis* is printed in the Aischylos edition by Page (Oxford 1972),
also in *Aristoteles pseudepigraphus* (1863) p. 559. The premiere of the
Oresteia took place in 458 B.C. Shortly after that, Aischylos went to Sicily,
where he died in 456. The people of Athens probably still remembered the

performance of the *Oresteia* when they decided to perform his plays again, which was unusual; cf. Pickard-Cambridge (1968) p. 86.

93) Reisch (1903) column 398. The entry for the premiere of the *Oresteia* has been preserved by chance; cf. Pickard-Cambridge (1968) p. 104, no. 2318, column II, line 17.

94) Jachmann provides as proof for his assumption besides the *hypothēsis* of *Agamemnon* only that of the *Alkēstis* by Euripides. But the choregos who is purportedly named there owes his existence solely to a conjecture by Wilamowitz, which has not been accepted by others. On the corrupt passage see Murray in his Euripides edition (Oxford, 1963). Since Euripides did not win with his *Alkēstis* and the other tragedies performed at the same time, Jachmann thought that Aristotle had listed not only the victorious choregoi, such as Xenokles of Aphidnai, but all of them. One cannot infer this even from the learned *hypothēsis* to the *Hippēs* (Knights) of Aristophanes, first produced in 424 B.C. There it is stated that the cost of the chorus was paid from public funds (*demōsis*) and not by a private individual. But that was a different thing.

95) Reisch (1907) p. 311.

96) In view of the amount of data in the *Didaskaliai* it is doubtful (see Mensching (1964) p. 16, note 3) whether the *Didaskaliai* really continued until 335 B.C., seeing that they consisted of one single book, that is, they were written on a single scroll. This would have been a very large scroll.

97) A. Tragedies. 1. Dionysia. Contests from 500 to 335 B.C. = 165 years, minus ca. 15% nonperformances through war, epidemics, etc. (in the *Didaskaliai* there were indications to that effect for the respective years); that leaves about 140 normal years with nine performances each, thus 1260 tragedies. 2. Lenaea. Contests from 430 to 335 B.C. = 95 years, minus 15%; that leaves about 80 normal years with four performances each, thus 320 tragedies. Total: 1580 tragedies. B. Comedies. 1. Dionysia. Contests from 485 to 335 B.C. = 150 years, minus 15%; that leaves 127 years, of these 100 with five performances each, i.e., 500 plays, and about 25 years (Peloponnesian War) with three performances each, i.e. 75 plays. Total: about 575 comedies. 2. Lenaea. Contests from 440 to 335 B.C. = 105 years, minus 15%; that leaves 89 years, of these 64 with five performances each, i.e. 320 plays, and about 25 years with three performances each, i.e. 75 plays, together about 395 comedies. Total: 970 comedies. The number of satyr plays cannot be estimated, because it seems that in the classical era only one satyr play was produced with three tragedies. For the comedies, Körte (1921) column 1237 and 1265 f., and Mensching (1964) pp. 43-49 tried to compute the number of poets and their plays (not only those that were produced in Athens), and to compare it with the data in the anonymous *Peri kōmōdias* in Kaibel (1899) p. 9. According to Körte, we know 41 poets of the Old Comedy, and 51 for the Middle Comedy. (The New Comedy appeared in full-fledged form only after Aristotle's death.)

98) Text of the inscription in Wilhelm (1906) pp. 89-166; *Inscriptiones Graecae*, Editio minor II/III 2, 2 (1931) no. 2325 (formerly 977); Pickard-Cambridge

(1968) pp. 112-120. Cf. Reisch (1903) column 399; Körte (1906); Wilamowitz (1906) p. 615; Reisch (1907) p. 313 and (1912); Regenbogen (1950) column 1416 f.; Snell (1966) pp. 21-27; Pickard-Cambridge (1968) p. 73; Pfeiffer (1968) p. 81.

99) Körte (1906) p. 396.

100) Wilamowitz (1906) p. 615; Reisch (1907) p. 313.

101) This was already admitted by Reisch (1907) p. 313.

102) Körte (1906) pp. 395-398. His conception was accepted by Wilhelm (1906) p. 257, but was rejected by Reisch (1907) p. 313. Moraux (1951) p. 126 f., Pickard-Cambridge (1968) p. 103 f. and Pfeiffer (1968) p. 81 agree with Körte, Regenbogen (1950) column 1416 f. and Jaeger (1955) p. 349, note 1 do not mention it.

103) Text of the inscription in Wilhelm (1906) pp. 6-33 and 257; on this, Wilhelm (1907). Only one fragment was found on the northern and southern slope of the Acropolis, respectively. Such displacement of fragments from large monuments is not a rare occurrence, as Wilhelm (1906) p. 8 points out. On the text, see Dittenberger (1915) III 1078; *Inscriptiones Graecae*, Editio minor II/III 2,2 (1931) no. 2318 (formerly 971); Pickard-Cambridge (1968) pp. 101-107. Cf. Reisch (1903) column 398 f.; Körte (1906) pp. 392-395; Wilamowitz (1906) p. 614; Reisch (1907); Jachmann (1909), especially p. 45 f.; Körte (1911) pp. 223 and 226 f.; Regenbogen (1950) column 1415 and 1417; Moraux (1951) p. 127, note 24; Jaeger (1955) p. 349, note 1; Pickard-Cambridge (1968) p. 71 f.; Pfeiffer (1968) p. 81, notes 3 and 5. The fragments contain data on the performances in the years between 472 and 328.

104) It was also mentioned from which year onwards the actors performed an old tragedy or comedy in addition (*paredidaxan*).

105) In this inscription there are only three data on each tragedy contest in the classical era: the choregos, the poet of the victorious tragedies, and the prize-winning principal actor. But in the *Didaskaliai* inscription there are 22, namely the poets of all performed tragedies, their titles, their principal actors and the prize-winning actors.

106) In the new edition of Jaeger's *Aristotle* (1955) p. 349, note 1, the *Fasti* inscription is still considered as a likeness of Aristotle's *Nikai*.

107) Pfeiffer (1968) p. 81.

108) Therefore, he did not consider the choregoi which had been listed by his precedessor.

109) Aristotle, *Fragmenta* (1886) no. 624 and 629.

110) Crusius (1905) column 1220.

111) Callimachus (1949) fragment 456.

112) Whereas we have a fairly good idea of Aristotle's work, it is of course impossible to say what the entries in his sources, the records of the archons, looked like.

113) Aristotle even thought that the tragedy had partly evolved from the dithyrambos.

114) Reisch (1903) pp. 402-404; Pickard-Cambridge (1968) pp. 74-79.

115) Pseudo-Plutarch, *Peri musikēs*, ch. 30 (1141 D); on this Crusius (1905) column 1223 f.

116) Capps (1904) p. 63 f. emphasized that the dates of performances of more than fifty tragedies and comedies, as given in the scholia that are based on the *Didaskaliai*, turned out to be correct. An accusation made against the *Didaskaliai* by Kallimachos, of all people, was dismissed as unjustified by Eratosthenes; cf. Callimachus (1949), fragment 454.

117) On the following, see Zacher (1890); Reisch (1903) column 404-406; Wilhelm (1906) pp. 111-115; Capps (1907) pp. 187-193; Wilhelm (1907); Jachmann (1909) pp. 7-9 and 20-25; Lipsius (1910); Oellacher (1916) pp. 120-131; Körte (1921) column 1231 F.; Dittmer (1923) pp. 44-46; Geissler (1925) pp. 2-10; Russo (1962) pp. 25-49; Pickard-Cambridge (1968) pp. 84-86; Gelzer (1970) column 1404-08. All data pertaining to Aristophanes can also be found in Cantarella's edition of his comedies, vol. 1 (Milano, 1953).

118) *Aristoteles pseudepigraphus* (1893) pp. 559-561; Westermann (1845) p. 155, 8-156, 2; 162, 44-163, 49 = Kaibel (1899) p. 8, 43-48.

119) On the chronology of Aristophanes's early plays see Russo (1962) pp. 25-49, summary p. 41, and Gelzer (1970) column 1407 f. The performance of a comedy at the Lenaea of 426 can be deduced from the vilification of the avaricious choregos Antimachos in verses 1050-52 of the *Archarnians*, performed at the Lenaea of 425. (Antimachos dismissed the chorus after the performance without a banquet.) It cannot be proved that this was the comedy *Dramata ē Kentauros*; see Russo (1962) pp. 26-29 and Gelzer (1970) column 1409. Russo doubts without a valid reason that this comedy had been produced by Philonides who, according to ancient biographers, produced some early plays by Aristophanes as also Kallistratos had done.

120) The parabasis was an integral part of the Old Comedy. It contained personal explanations by the author which he let the chorus express in his own name. To these passages, which are outside the dramatic context, posterity owes valuable information on Aristophanes and his works.

121) Reisch (1903) column 404-406; Wilhelm (1906) pp. 111-115. According to this conception Wilhelm completed the mutilated names of two persons who are named in the inscription as victors among the comic poets which won their first victories between 430 and 420; Ari[stomenes] and Ka[llistratos]; thus, he substituted instead of Ari[stophanes] one of his younger rivals and instead of a second author the director of Aristophanes's comedies. But these names cannot serve as evidence for Wilhelm's hypothesis. The list

probably contained not the names of Aristomenes and Kallistratos but those of Aristophanes and Kantharos, another of his younger rivals; see Geissler (1925) pp. 2-10. It is indeed unlikely that among the authors (poētai) a director of Aristophanes's comedies would be listed. Likewise, we may not rely (as Wilhelm did) on the "conspicuously high" number (seven) of the victories of the comic actor Philippos, one of Aristophanes's sons, which might include those which he had won as a director of comedies by Eubulos. Quite apart from the fact that the "insignificant" Philippos could indeed have won seven victories, the numerals have been substituted: their sum was perhaps not seven, but three or two.

122) Wilhelm (1907); Capps (1907) pp. 187-198; Jachmann (1909) pp. 7-9; Pickard-Cambridge (1968) p. 85 claims that it is now evident that the inscriptions which were based on records named the real author, not the director who had been commissioned. But this is not generally accepted and does not address the real problem.

123) The expression edidaske (he produced) commonly used in the Fasti could be used both by an author who produced a play himself or had it produced by a director, and by the director who produced it.

124) Körte (1921) column 1231 f.; Russo (1962) p. 44; Gelzer (1970) column 1396 f. On the biographic tradition see Dübner (1877) Proleg. no. XII, 8-12 and XIII, 9-14. The comic actor Sannarion also used this comparison referring to Aristophanes. All references in Kock (1880), pp. 669; 677; 794.

125) Contrary to the Fasti in which the ambiguous term edidaske (he produced) is used (see note 123), the inscription of the Didaskaliai always says enika poētēs ho deina (as poet won so and so).

126) Geissler (1925) p. 7. Wilhelm and Jachmann assumed therefore that a change had taken place about 380 B.C.: before that time, only the director of a play not produced by an author himself had been listed, but afterwards also the author was named in the records. Geissler indicated that this hypothesis is difficult to defend.

127) Oellacher (1916) p. 126.

128) Mensching (1964) p. 17.

129) Gelzer (1970) column 1403 and 1405 f. The title of the comedy alluded to the ceremony which took place before the contest (agōn) and which was therefore called proagōn, in this ceremony, the poets and actors announced to the audience the plays that would be performed. Cf. Pickard-Cambridge (1968) p. 67.

130) The word is generally translated as "comedy performance". But since in Aristophanes didaskalos "master" is equivalent to poiētēs "poet", and kōmōdodidaskalos is equivalent to kōmōdopoiētēs (Peace, verses 734 and 737), as well as tragōdodidaskalos being equivalent to tragōdopoios (Thesmophoriazusae, verses 30 and 88), the term kōmōdiodidaskalia can here only mean comic poetry. Subsequently he only mentions comic poets. Cf. Russo (1962) p. 45.

131) Aristophanes (1924) *Knights*, verses 541-544, translated by B. B. Rogers:

"So in fear of the dangers he lingered; besides, a sailor,
he thought, should abide
And tug at the oar for a season, before he attempted the vessel to
guide;
And next should be stationed awhile at the prow, the winds and the
weather to scan;
And then to be pilot, himself for himself."

It was the task of the *propatēs*, the pilot's assistant, to serve on the foredeck and to observe the winds. See also Plutarch, *Agis* I.

132) Aristophanes (1924), *Wasps*, verses 1017-1022, translated by B. B. Rogers.

133) Aristophanes (1924) *Clouds*, verses 528-532, translated by B. B. Rogers. The word *aneileto* in verse 531 is a pun: it means both "nurse [the child]" and "won a victory". On the interpretation of the second parabasis of the *Clouds* see Gelzer (1970) column 1434.

134) Zacher (1890), especially p. 324; Kaibel (1896) column 973 f.; Russo (1962) p. 41; Gelzer (1970) column 1399 f.

135) Gelzer (1970) column 1407 f., correctly against Russo (1962).

136) The doubts of Alexandrian philologists and librarians about the ascription of some plays had other reasons. See Kaibel (1889) pp. 42-49; Oellacher (1916) p. 123.

137) *Peri kōmōdias*, ch. 11 = Kaibel (1899) p. 8, 43:

ἐδίδαξε δὲ πρῶτον ἐπὶ ἄρχον-
τος Διοτίμου διὰ Καλλιστράτου· τὰς μὲν γὰρ πολιτικὰς τούτωι
φασὶν αὐτὸν διδόναι, τὰ δὲ κατ' Εὐριπίδου καὶ Σωκράτους
Φιλωνίδηι. διὰ δὲ τούτων νομισθεὶς ἀγαθὸς ποιητὴς τοῦ λοι-
ποῦ ⟨αὐτὸς⟩ ἐπιγραφόμενος ἐνίκα. ἔπειτα τῶι υἱῶι ἐδίδου τὰ
δράματα.

138) The passage quoted in note 137 is evidently corrupt. In the only extant manuscript it is given as *tus loipus epigraphomenos enika*. I think that the change made by Zacher, *tais loipais*, is more likely, but the addition *autos* is superfluous, because an object is necessary and the concept of *autos* is already contained in *epigraphesthai*. In order to understand the meaning of *epigraphesthai*, one must compare the scholium to verse 78 of the *Frogs* by Aristophanes which says that Sophokles's son Iophon was ridiculed "because he ascribed to himself the tragedies of his father", i.e. he declared himself to be the author of certain tragedies written by his father. In this context belongs also the scholium to Aristophanes's *Plutos*, verse 179: "he does not

mean the poet [Philonides] who is listed in the plays by Aristophanes". The sentence refers no doubt to the conditions known to us, but it is corrupt; the wording as transmitted to us can not be satisfactorily interpreted. Probably we should read, as suggested by Dobree, "who had appropriated for himself the plays by Aristophanes". Cf. Dübner (1877), *Adnotationes* p. 550; Zacher (1890) p. 316 f. differs. On the question of the distribution of Aristophanes's comedies among the directors Kallistratos and Philonides, see Russo (1962) p. 42 f.

139)   The difference was unimportant because Aristophanes had his plays performed by others even at the height of his career.

140)   *Hypothēsis* IV of *Plutos*:

'Εδιδάχθη ἐπὶ ἄρχοντος
'Αντιπάτρου, ἀνταγωνιζομένου αὐτῷ Νικοχάρους μὲν Λάκωσιν,
'Αριστομένους δὲ 'Αδμήτῳ, Νικοφῶντος δὲ 'Αδώνιδι, 'Αλκαίου
δὲ Πασιφάῃ. τελευταίαν δὲ διδάξας τὴν κωμῳδίαν ταύτην ἐπὶ
τῷ ἰδίῳ ὀνόματι, καὶ τὸν υἱὸν αὐτοῦ συστῆσαι 'Αραρότα δι'
αὐτῆς τοῖς θεαταῖς βουλόμενος, τὰ ὑπόλοιπα δύο δι' ἐκείνου
καθῆκε, Κώκαλον καὶ Αἰολοσίκωνα.

141)   Dübner (1877) Proleg. no. XI, 76-80 and no. XII, 36 f.

142)   Capps (1907) p. 192; Leo (1912) p. 72.

143)   Cantarella remarks correctly but without giving his reasons (and contrary to the prevalent opinion) on the performance of *Kōkalos* and the second *Aiolosikōn*: "sub nomine Ararotis". Cf. his *Aristofane* (1953) p. 165.

144)   It cannot be ascertained which of the two comedies left (or bequeathed) by Aristophanes to his son is meant here. Cf. Russo (1962) p. 48 f.

145)   Capps (1907) p. 189 f. It is not impossible that Araros produced a comedy of his own only in the seventies.

146)   It seems therefore doubtful to me whether he induced Araros to perform the *Kōkalos* and the *Aiolosikōn* under his own name. Aristophanes was probably already dead when his son produced the two comedies, and after the fraud had been discovered, Araros claimed that his father had "given" him the plays.

147)   The text of the *hypothēsis* to the *Wasps* is corrupt, but the corrupt passage does not pertain to the main issue. Cf. Gelzer (1970) who made the most important suggestions for improvement. Aristophanes was the first winner with his *Wasps*, Philonides was the runner-up with his *Proagōn*. It is questionable whether, as stated in the *hypothēsis*, Philonides produced the

81

Wasps, that is, whether Philonides produced beside his own play also the one by Aristophanes. Such a case would be unique. Several scholars simply deleted the words *dia Philōnidu* which are suspicious also because they appear between the date by archons and the one by Olympiads. I must leave this question unanswered.

148)   In a cursory survey of those plays of the old Comedy of which not only the title but at least one fragment (quotation) is known, as listed by Kock (1880), I found that 12 titles appear twice and two titles appear three times. Of these 14 titles seven were also used by Aristophanes. Under these circumstances I doubt also whether the comedy *Kōmastai*, performed under the name of Ameipsias at the Dionysia of 414, is the work with the same title by Phrynichos who produced at the same festival his *Monotropos*, not to mention the identification of *Konnos*, produced by Ameipsias at the Dionysia of 423, with the identically named play by Phrynichos. See the skeptical remarks by Körte (1941) column 919; also Mensching (1964) p. 35 f.

149)   Mensching (1964) p. 28 (Kratinos) and 42 (Aristophanes). That the *Proagōn* is not mentioned among the three plays by Philonides listed in the *Suda* is not a valid argument, because this Byzantine lexicon lists only seldom all works of an author.

150)   Kock (1880) p. 628; Körte (1950) column 2540; Pickard-Cambridge (1968) p. 85. The poet referred to himself with a proverbial saying as an imitator of the Arcadians; see fragment 100. The Arcadians were highly regarded as soldiers who fought successfully in foreign service but never won a battle for their own country. Therefore, those who toiled for others were also called *Arkadas minumenoi*. The comparison was apt if Plato had sold his own plays to other people. In this case one could call him too (and with more justification than Aristophanes) one who was born on the fourth of a month, like Herakles. See Kock (1880) fragment 99. But if, as Körte thinks, the comparison referred to the fact that Plato, like Aristophanes, had his plays produced by others, then it did not make sense.

151)   Thus Eratosthenes, Kallimachos's probable successor as director of the library who also wrote a large work on the Old Comedy, could prove by records that the poet Eupolis had not been thrown into the sea by Alkibiades during the crossing to Sicily because of personal revenge, as was claimed by some people. He could point out that comedies were produced by Eupolis, the most important rival of Aristophanes, after 415 B.C. (the year in which the Sicilian expedition of the Athenians began). See Cicero, *Epistulae ad Atticum* VI 1, 18; Strecker (1884) p. 38, no. 48.

152)   The *Rhēsos* which had been transmitted with Euripides's other plays is today generally thought to be the work of another poet. The philologists must therefore explain that the *Rhēsos* listed by Aristotle had soon become lost, and that another play by an unknown author, dealing with the same subject, had been falsely ascribed to Euripides already in ancient times.

153)   Kaibel (1889) pp. 42-46.

154)   Wilamowitz (1895) p. 132; Jaeger (1955) p. 349.

155) On the "official copies" of the tragedies by Aischylos, Sophokles and
Euripides which were made at the request of Lykurgos see Wilamowitz
(1875) p. 132 and 148; Ziegler (1937) column 2068-70; Wendel-Göber (1955)
p. 66; Erbse (1961) pp. 217 f. and 244; Pfeiffer (1968) pp. 82 and 192. The
passages containing the references (Pseudo-Plutarch, *Vitae X oratorum* 841 f.
on Lykurgos and Galen, *Comm. II in Hippocratis 1. III Epidemiarum* 239
(vol. XVII 1, p. 607 Kühn) on Ptolemaios) in Schmidt (1922) p. 5 f.; the
passage on Galen also in Wendel-Göber (1955). The passage on Lykurgos
in Pseudo-Plutarch runs as follows: "He also proposed laws . . . to erect
statues of the poets Aischylos, Sophokles and Euripides, and to copy their
tragedies all together to preserve them and that the city clerk . . . " The
following text is somewhat corrupt but the meaning is clear: that the city
clerk should tell the actors the official version of the tragedies from which
they may not deviate. The making and preservation of official copies of the
tragedies would have been unnecessary if the archons had preserved the
manuscripts of plays submitted by poets in their archives, as Erbse (1961)
p. 218 still assumed. The existence of such a collection is not documented
elsewhere either. The order to copy the plays "all together" does not mean
that the leaves on which the copies were made had to be glued together to
one giant scroll. On the contents of a normal scroll (three plays) see
Hemmerdinger (1951) p. 87. The passage on Galen is essentially not
problematic. It says there that king Ptolemaios III Euergetes borrowed the
scrolls of the three tragedians from "the" Athenians; those were therefore
the official copies, and Lykurgos's proposal, adopted by the people and
enacted as a law, was executed. The old *biblia* (scrolls), that is, those
borrowed by the king from Athens, are compared with the new ones, i.e. the
copies made in Alexandria. That means that the "official copy" consisted of
a number of scrolls. The security deposited by the king, 15 talents, was the
equivalent of 870 pounds of gold (1 talent = 58 lbs.). Ziegler (1937) column
2070 presumes that it was not Ptolemaios III Euergetes (246-221 B.C.), as
mentioned by Galen (Bd. XVII 1, p. 603 Kühn) but Ptolemaios II
Philadelphos (285-246 B.C.), the founder of the gymnasium "Ptolemaion" in
Athens, who had borrowed the scrolls; see also Wendel-Göber (1955) p. 66.
It is, however, not certain which Ptolemaios founded that gymnasium.
Pausanias, that ancient Baedeker, says only that Ptolemaios founded it.
According to Pasquali (1913) p. 209 it was probably built after 288 B.C., that
is, by the third Ptolemaios. The story is not incredible. It is only unclear
why the Athenians demanded such a high security and why the king was
willing to deposit it. Perhaps it was still possible at the time of Lykurgos
and Aristotle, around 335 B.C., to obtain in Athens and vicinity accurate
copies of all plays by the three great tragedians, not only those that were
performed in Athens. But a century later that was no longer so, because
Athens had in the meantime suffered much from wars, sieges and
occupations. Why Ptolemaios III forfeited the security is not known.
Perhaps he did it out of sheer vainglory which became fixed in people's
memory. After all, the new scrolls, if painstakingly collated and corrected,
were as good as the old ones (which were also only copies of copies).

156) On the following, see Fritz (1956) pp. 91-106; Düring (1966) pp. 27 and
169 f.; Pfeiffer (1968) pp. 68 and 83.

157) Aristotle, *Poetics* (1932) 1449 A, translated by W. H. Fyfe. On the identity of *physis* and *telos* see Pfeiffer (1968) p. 68. Perhaps Aristotle elaborated on this in his otherwise unknown work *Peri tragōdiōn* (On the tragedies).

158) Jaeger (1955) pp. 359-365 with a translation of *Peri zōōn moriōn* (On the parts of animals) A 5. Düring (1966) p. 515 f. also rendered the famous passage into German, with an important correction of Jaeger's translation; p. 516, note 49 and p. 460, note 171.

159) Jaeger (1955) pp. 125-170; Düring (1966) pp. 185-189.

160) Aristotle, *Fragmenta* (1886) no. 7; on this, Jaeger (1955) p. 131.

161) The term is modern; see Pfeiffer (1968) p. 84, note 6. On the doxographic works of Aristotle and his pupils see Praechter (1953) p. 23 f.; Jaeger (1955) p. 358 f. The sophist Hippias of Elis may be considered as his predecessor also in this field; his *Synagōgē* (collection) contained among other things a compilation of opinions on various problems by ancient poets and scholars; see Snell (1944); Pfeiffer (1968) p. 52.
It seems that Aristotle owed to him whatever he knew about Thales of whom he had no written works. It was even doubtful whether Thales had ever written anything; see Diogenes Laertios I 23. On beginnings of surveys on the history of problems in Plato's works see Düring (1966) p. 7, note 30 and p. 112, note 420.

162) Aristotle, *Metaphysics* A 983 b-988 a.

163) The works of Eudemus were, according to their titles, histories of sciences; they are cited as *Geometrikē historia, Arithmetikē historia* and *Astrologikē historia*. See Wehrli (1967), Heft 8, fragment 133-150 with commentary. Aristoxenos entitled his description which served as an introduction to his *Harmonika stoicheia* (Elements of harmony), following Theophrastos, *Doxai harmonikōn* (Teachings of the harmonicians); cf. Wehrli (1968) column 338. The work by Menon has the title *Iatrika* (Medical matters) or *Iatrikē synagōgē* (Medical summary); see Diels (1893) and below, note 179.

164) Aristotle indicated clearly that he had not seen a work by Thales; see also note 161 above.

165) Aristotle, *Metaphysics* A 984 a and 986 a.

166) Aristotle, *Metaphysics* A 985 b.

167) Aristotle, *Metaphysics* A 984 b (Anaxagoras and Hermotimos); 985 b (Alkmaion and the Pythagoreans).

168) Diels (1879) pp. 476, 16; 477, 17; 483, 11.

169) Diels (1879) p. 321 b 12; Diels-Kranz (1952) no. 67 B 2. There can hardly be any doubt that this statement by Stobaios (5th century A.D.) is ultimately based on Theophrastos.

170) On the arrangement of the work best known to us, the *Physikōn doxai* of Theophrastes, see Diels (1887, Leukippos) p. 7; Regenbogen (1940) column 1536 f.

171) Diels-Kranz (1952) no. 67 A 2 and B 1-2.

172) Diels (1893) pp. 433-433; Edelstein (1935) column 1322-31; Jaeger (1963) p. 234 f.

173) See the list of works in Diogenes Laertios V 22-27; 87-88; 42-46. In the Corpus Aristotelicum there are works on Xenophanes, Zeno (of Elea) and Gorgias which were not written by Aristotle himself but by the early Peripatetics; see Düring (1968) column 315 f.

174) Aristotle, *Topics* I ch. 17, 105 B.

175) Aristotle, *Fragmenta* (1886) no. 136 and 137; see also no. 138-141. Radermacher (1951) lists 38 authors of works on rhetoric before Aristotle. Several anonymous writers ought certainly to be added to that list.

176) No. 137; birthplace of Antiphon; no. 139: teacher of Isokrates.

177) See the lists of Aristotle's works in Aristotle, *Fragmenta* (1886) p. 6, line 77 (Diogenes); p. 13, line 71 (Hesychios); p. 20, line 24 (Ptolemaios); on these Moraux (1951), p. 97. According to Diogenes, the work consisted of two books, according to Hesychios and Ptolemaios only of one. In Diogenes, line 80 yet another *Technōn synagōgē* is listed. The noun *synagoge* means both "collection" and "summary"; with regard to books, it generally means "collection", but in this case "summary" is more appropriate. Diogenes calls the work in another passage (II 104 = Aristotle, *Fragmenta* no. 138) *epitomē tōn rhētorōn* (Summary of [the art of] the orators); see also note 202. This would indicate that *Technōn synagōgē* means a compendium of writings on rhetoric. In the lists of Aristotle's works we find soon thereafter another *synagōgē*, the *Technēs tēs Theodektu synagōgē*; see Aristotle, *Fragmenta* (1886) p. 6, line 82 (Diogenes) and p. 13, line 74 (Hesychios), according to Diogenes in one book, according to Hesychios in three books. The work of Theodektes, who was one of Aristotle's friends, consisted, according to the catalog of the library of the gymnasium in Rhodos, of four books. Solmsen (1932) pp. 144-151 and (1934) column 1733 tries to interpret *synagōgē* in the title of Aristotle's work as "collection". But here too the translation "summary" is simpler and also more likely, because *technē* was the title of Theodektes's work. See also Moraux (1951) pp. 98-101. Wehrli (1967) Heft 10, p. 127 thinks that the *Technōn synagōgē* was a collection of material on cultural history, not written by Aristotle himself but still compiled in the Peripatos, although he does not give a reason.

178) Leo (1901) p. 49 and 99 f. On p. 49 Leo declares that Aristotle had established the principle of research and description, observed by all his successors (i.e. the authors as *heuretai*, inventors); but in note 1 he contradicts himself when he says that Plato preceded Aristotle in this respect. The principle of *heurētēs* was probably even much older.

179) Aristotle, *Fragmenta* (1886) no. 373 and note 163 above.

180) The *Historia litteraria* was distinguished and described as a subfield of history only at the beginning of the 17th century by Francis Bacon. Until the 19th century, it was taught as a discipline in its own right at many schools and universities, especially in German-speaking countries, and many books were written about it. The history of poetry which later became the history of literature was at that time only a small part of the history of scholarship. See Blum (1980) pp. 39-40.

181) See note 23 above; see also Wehrli (1967) Heft 9, fragment 8-10 and 16-17, with commentary.

182) On the cited scholars and their works see the relevant fascicles (Hefte) of Wehrli's collection *Die Schule des Aristoteles. Texte und Kommentar* (2. Aufl. 1967-69), also his summary in Heft 10, pp. 95-128. Wehrli excluded Theophrastos, which is understandable because what has been preserved of his works would have been beyond the scope of the collection. Only five of the Peripatetics of the 4th and 3rd century B.C. dealt with by Wehrli did not pursue studies in the history of literature: Eudemos (except for the doxography), Klearchos, Straton, Lykon, and Ariston. It is remarkable that except for Demetrios, who had to leave the city, Herakleides, Phainias, Chamaileon, Praxiphanes, and Hieronymos did not live in Athens for the better part of their lives, but this fact is not quite clear. In addition to the Peripatetics dealt with by Wehrli there were of course at that time also others who were active in literature, e.g. the "Homer scholar" Megakleides named by Tatianos (see above, note 23) and Menon, the founder of medical doxography.

183) For example, Chamaileon, fragment 29 in Wehrli (1967), Heft 9.

184) Herakleides (Wehrli, Heft 7), fragment 157-163 and 166 with commentary; Phainias (Heft 9), fragment 32-33 with commentary; Hieronymos (Heft 9), fragment 29-33 with commentary.

185) Dikaiarchos (Wehrli, Heft 1), fragment 73-85 and 88-89 with commentary.

186) Fragments 79-82. On the work of Herakleides Pontikos see Wehrli (1967) Heft 7, fragment 180 with commentary.

187) Herakleides wrote also a special treatise on the age of Homer and Hesiod (the priority question), and a work on Homer and Archilochos, which may have been an early attempt at literary *synkrisis* (comparison), as in his work on the three tragic poets (Aischylos, Sophokles, Euripides). See Wehrli (1967) Heft 7, fragment 176-179 with commentary.

188) On Anthisthenes see the list of his works in Diogenes Laertios VI 17; according to VI 16 he had also written on the lyric poet Theognis.

189) Leo (1901) pp. 99-107. It seems unlikely to me, however, that in works with the title *Peri* . . . (On . . .) the customary personal data (origin, period of flourishing, teachers, and if necessary place of work) were missing. It might

be accidental that Chamaileon, whose monographs on poets were apparently typical, "is never cited for the *genos* or other main features in the biography [of a poet]" in contradistinction to Aristoxenos.

190) Examples from the works of Chamaileon, who wrote most of the monographs on poets, according to Wehrli (1967), Heft 9: fragment 32 a and b: Pindar's mission; fr. 26; Sappho's relation to Anakreon; fr. 33: Simonides's relations with Hieron, the tyrant of Syracuse; fr. 28: Stesichoros's musical setting of poems by Homer and others; fr. 41: Aischylos's choreographic achievements; fr. 30; Lasos's wit; fr. 33: Simonides's quickness of repartee; fr. 40 a and b: Aischylos's alcoholism (he wrote while being drunk).

191) Wehrli (1967) Heft 2 assumes in his commentary to fragment 66, that the custom of the younger biographers to compile lists of homonyms goes back to Aristoxenos, but I think that one cannot conclude this just because he mentioned in his *Life of Plato* an athletics teacher by the name of Aristoteles. Herakleides Pontikos distinguished perhaps between three mythical musicians by the name of Linos, if indeed the last sentence of fragment 160 in Wehrli (1967) Heft 7 can be traced to him.

192) Gudeman says in his article on Satyros (1921) column 320 that this so-called Peripatetic, one of the best-known Hellenistic (Alexandrian) biographers of writers, had wanted to achieve two things: *et prodesse et delectare* (to be useful and to please).

193) On the following see in addition to Leo (1901) pp. 102 f. and 118 also Wehrli (1967) Heft 2, fragments 11-25 (Pythagoras); 47-50 (Archytas); 51-60 (Sokrates); 61-68 (Plato) with commentary; Wehrli (1974), commentary to fragment 1.

194) Fragment 11 b; 47; 52 a.

195) Brink (1940), column 904. Aristoxenos also wrote a biography of a poet, the dithyrambic poet Telestes (see fragment 117), but we have no idea what it was like.

196) E.g. fragments 52 a and b, and 54 a and b: Socrates the lover of his teacher and husband of two wives; see also fragment 58; commentary to fragments 61-68: Plato a plagiarist of Protagoras and Pythagoras, but hardly one of Demokritos, as Wehrli p. 86 thinks about fragment 131.

197) E.g. Chamaileon in Wehrli (1967) Heft 9, fragment 31 (from his work on Pindar) and fragment 36 (on Anakreon).

198) Wehrli (1967) Heft 2, fragment 67. In another passage (see fragment 43 and commentary on fragment 61-68) Aristoxenos claimed that Plato had bought three works of the Pythagorean Philolaos, containing the until then secret teachings of Pythagoras for 100 minas (10,000 drachmas), evidently in order to acquire Pythagoras's wisdom. See also Wehrli (1974) commentary to fragment 40.

199) Wehrli (1967) Heft 1, fragment 63. There was also suspicion of fraud when works like the Homeric epics existed under different names.

200) It was of course a different matter when a pupil of Aristotle accused another one to have committed a literary theft: thus, Chamaileon claimed that the treatises of his older fellow countryman Herakleides Pontikos on Hesiod and Homer were plagiarisms of his own works. See Wehrli (1967) Heft 7, fragment 176, and Heft 9, fragment 46 with commentary. On plagiarism in Antiquity see Ziegler (1950).

201) Wehrli (1967) Heft 9, fragment 29 with commentary.

202) Wehrli (1967) Heft 1, fragment 81 with commentary. Against Wehrli's conclusions which are partially too far-reaching, see Ritchie (1964), pp. 4-44, especially p. 9 and 29-37.

203) Wehrli (1967) Heft 1, fragment 83 with commentary. Also Jachmann (1909) p. 24.

204) Wehrli (1967) Heft 2, fragment 45 with commentary.

205) Wehrli (1967) Heft 2, fragment 114 and Heft 7, fragment 181.

206) Wehrli (1967) Heft 2, fragment 91 I with commentary.

207) Wehrli (1967) Heft 9, fragment 22 a and b with commentary; Pfeiffer (1968) p. 220 and 241.

208) Wehrli (1967) Heft 4, fragments 149-154 with commentary.

209) E.g. on the appearance of Thales and Anaxagoras, and on the deaths of Socrates and of the orator Isokrates.

210) Gellius III 17, 3 and Diogenes Laertios IV 5. According to Wendel-Göber (1955) p. 60, note 3, Aristotle bought only the writings of Speusippos, according to Mensching (1963) p. 75, he bought all books that had been in his possession.

211) Düring (1966) p. 607, note 125.

212) Rohde (1951) p. 20; Wendel-Göber (1955) p. 56.

213) Plato, Phaedrus 274 C-277 A, especially the myth of Theuth. Plato argues that only knowledge taught orally by the teacher reaches exclusively those for whom it is intended, and that it can be further explained, if necessary, when pupils ask questions.

214) Brink (1940) column 907 f.

215) Similarly Wendel-Göber (1955) p. 59 f.

216) On these *hypomnēmata* see Moraux (1951) pp. 153-166; Bömer (1952) pp. 216-221.

217) Gottschalk (1972) pp. 335-342; Moraux (1973) pp. 3-31 with many references to works by earlier scholars, among which I mention only Brink (1940), especially column 939 f., Regenbogen (1940), column 1375-77, and Düring (1966), pp. 38-43 and (1968) column 184-200.

218) Gottschalk (1972). On Neleus see Fritz (1935) column 2280 f.

219) Thus also Stark (1972) p. 164. Aristotle left Athens when anti-Macedonian politicians after Alexander's death (323 B.C.) attacked him too, and accused him of blasphemy.

220) Gottschalk (1972) p. 326 f.

221) Strabo (1929) 13.1.54.

222) On Strabo's explanation, see Moraux (1973) pp. 23-26.

223) Strabo's text is unclear, perhaps incomplete. My paraphrase follows largely the interpretation of Regenbogen (1940) column 1376, and Moraux (1973) p. 33 f. On Tyrannion's work see Moraux (1973) pp. 33-44.

224) Gottschalk (1972) p. 338 f.

225) This opinion is also shared by Moraux (1973) pp. 21-23 and p. 48.

226) Plutarch, *Sulla* 26. On this passage see Moraux (1973) p. 34.

227) On Andronikos see Moraux (1973) pp. 45-94. Other scholars, especially Düring (1968) column 196-199, move Androniko's main activity to Rome and date it in the second half of the first century B.C. See also below, section 5.4.

228) Dihle (1957); Moraux (1973) p. 60, note 6 and p. 69 f.

229) Baumstark (1900) p. 54. Printed there, pp. 61-70 and (with back-translation into Greek) in Düring (1957) pp. 221-246. See on this Moraux (1951) pp. 288-309, especially p. 198, and Moraux (1973), especially pp. 64-66 and 85-89.

230) On this part of the list see Moraux (1973) pp. 88-91, partly differing from Düring (1957) pp. 230 f. and 245.

231) Moraux (1951) p. 198: "La bibliothèque d'Apellicon qu'Andronicus lui-même aurait utilisée (Strabo) ne devait pas contenir beaucoup d'ouvrages inconnus sauf peut-être quelques aide-mémoire ou papiers personnels; dans le cas contraire, le pinacographe lui aurait sûrement accordé plus qu'un simple mention à la fin."

232) The reference is probably to P. Livius Larensis; see Dessau (1890) p. 156.

233) Athenaeus (1927) I 3a.

234) [and Theophrastos] supplied by Wilamowitz, correctly according to the facts.

235) Gottschalk (1972) p. 339.

236) Regenbogen (1940) column 1377.

237) Wendel (1949) p. 105, note 112 explains that Athenaios erroneously named Ptolemaios II instead of the first who died in 283 B.C., but we need not assume that this was the case, because we do not know when Neleus sold his library.

238) Athenaios V 214 d; Jacoby (1957) no. 87, F 36, p. 247, 29-248 with commentary; Gottschalk (1972) p. 340 f.; Moraux (1973) pp. 28-30.

239) Moraux (1973) p. 13, note 29.

240) Wendel-Göber (1955) pp. 60 f. and 67, who do not mention Poseidonios's remark.

241) Apellikon could have told about his visit to Skepsis in his work on the friendship between Aristotle and Hermias, the ruler of Atarneus, on which he might have found material there, The two pupils of Plato who came from the same city, Koriskos, the father of Neleus, and Erastos had founded a school under the protectorate of Hermias in the city of Assos, situated about 30 miles southwest of Skepsis on the coast; Aristotle taught there between 347 and 345 B.C. See Susemihl (1891) vol. 2, pp. 296-299; Jaeger (1955) pp. 110-120.

242) Mainly Düring (1966) pp. 38-43 and (1968) column 190 and 195-200. He thinks that Neleus sold the library bequeathed to him by Theophrastos to Ptolemaios II while still in Athens, before he moved to Skepsis, excluding from it only the original manuscripts of Aristotle and Theophrastos which he took with him to his hometown out of reverence for his teachers. These manuscripts were subsequently found by Apellikon in Skepsis and were transferred to Rome by Sulla together with his entire library, and formed the basis of the Aristotle edition of Andronikos. (Contrary to this, Düring assumes in other passages, e.g. (1968) column 186, that the bibliography of Aristotle in Diogenes and Hesychios can be traced back to an inventory list compiled in Alexandria when the library of Aristotle-Theophrastos-Neleus had been brought there. But at this time, under Ptolemaios II, the original manuscripts were supposedly still in Skepsis.) Regarding the books mentioned in Ptolemaios's *Pinax* under no. 92, Düring (1968) column 190 thinks that these could have been other books which Andronikos had found in Apellikon's library. But he does not explain why these should have been listed in a bibliography of Aristotle. On Alexandria as the probable place of origin of the Aristotle edition by Andronikos see note 272 below.

243) Düring (1956) p. 13: "If we attach any importance to the ancient evidence, we must conclude that after the death of Theophrastos the Peripatos was not in the possession of Aristotle's and Theophrastos's library."

244) Pfeiffer (1968) p. 67; Gottschalk (1972) p. 342. Pfeiffer did not give reasons for his view; Düring, whom he cites in note 4, differs from him, as shown in the sentence cited in note 243. In another passage, p. 273, Pfeiffer assumes that the library of Theophrastos had been brought to Rome (perhaps with that of Apellikon?).

245) Moraux could refer to Gottschalk's article, published shortly before the publication of his book (1973) only in the notes; he says on p. 5 note 3 that he found him "very useful". If Gottschalk's assumption were right it would support Moraux's conjecture regarding the origin of the Aristotle bibliography as transmitted by Diogenes Laertios.

246) Moraux (1973) p. 28.

247) Athenaios V 203 e.

248) Athenaios V 196 a-203 b (parade of Ptolemaios II) and 203 e-206 c (shipbuilding of Ptolemaios IV) = Jacoby (1957) no. 627; also Jacoby (1919), (Kallixeinos).

249) Regenbogen (1940) column 1366 f.; Wehrli (1974) fragment 54 f. with commentary. Wehrli denies a connection between bibliography and biography, without saying, however, how to explain a bibliography of Theophrastos as a separate publication by Hermippos alongside the *Pinakes* of Kallimachos.

250) Wendel-Göber (1955) p. 71 came close to this conception, contrary to their hypothesis on the partition of Neleus's library, stated on p. 61.

251) Diogenes Laertios V 42-50; also Usener (1858) pp. 1-24; Schmidt (1922) p. 86-88; Regenbogen (1940) column 1363-70 and (1950) column 1422; Pfeiffer (1968) p. 131. Hesychios of Miletos's *Onomatologos* is lost. A short version (epitome) of this Greek author lexicon of the 6th century A.D. has been included in the *Suda*, but only the first five titles of the Theophrastos bibliography and those of four important other works are listed there.

252) Thus, for example, in the bibliographies of Speusippos, Xenokrates, Aristotle, and Straton.

253) A count of lines which actually filled a copy of a certain work, and its conversion into standard lines of the length of an epic hexameter (35 to 37 letters) was the form in which the size of literary works was measured (of course, only approximately) for commercial purposes such as the calculation of the copyist's pay and the price of a book.

254) Sums of standard lines of two separate works, in addition to the sum total of all works, are given in Diogenes's list of the works of Xenokrates. Did Diogenes list the number of standard lines for these two works only by chance, or was the number of standard lines always recorded but left out when the text was copied?

255) Unspecified *hypomnēmata* are found in Diogenes Laertios in the bibliographies of the following philosophers: Speusippos (IV 4 f.);

Xenokrates (IV 11-14); Aristotle (V 22-27); Theophrastos (V 42-50); Straton (V 59 f.); Kleanthes (VII 174 f.); Sphairos (VII 178); Demokritos (IX 46-49); for the first five the sum total of standard lines is also given.

256) It may not be argued against this conception that the Theophrastos bibliography of Andronikos was well known in the first century A.D., according to Plutarch. One can only make very vague assumptions about the immediate source of Diogenes Laertios and about his reasons to follow this authority who in turn depended on Hermippos. There is also no reason to assume with Regenbogen (1940) column 1368, and Pfeiffer (1968) p. 131 that the Theophrastos bibliography used by Diogenes Laertios or by his authority had been revised on the basis of the one compiled by Andronikos.

257) Moraux (1973) p. 15.

258) Moraux (1973) pp. 14-17.

259) Antigonos transplanted the inhabitants of the city which he had destroyed to Alexandria Troas, but Lysimachos permitted them after the defeat of Antigonos at Ipsos (391 B.C.) to return to the old place and to build a new city in the vicinity. Cf. Bürchner (1927) column 445. Lysimachos's rule ended in 281 B.C.

260) Diogenes Laertios V 22-46. The Aristotle bibliography included in Hesychios's *Onomatologos* has been transmitted to us through the *Vita Menagiana* of the philosopher. Both lists are printed in their entirety in Aristotle, *Fragmenta* (1886) pp. 3-18 and in Düring (1957) pp. 41-50 and 83-89.

261) Moraux (1951), especially pp. 211-247; Düring (1968) column 186 f.; Moraux (1973) p. 4, note 2. A few researchers, recently Stark (1972) pp. 172-174, ascribed to Aristotle himself the list of his works, but did not meet with approval. This hypothesis is indeed untenable because of the defects of the list. The autobibliographies of learned writers in Antiquity, e.g. Galen, are on a different level.

262) Moraux (1951) p. 242.

263) The sum total of standard lines presupposes of course data on the sum total of lines at the end of each scroll. It does not follow, however, as Moraux (1951) p. 242 says, that the bibliographers did not work from originals but only from copies made by hired copyists, in which the number of lines had been marked for the calculation of their pay. The number of lines was often given just to indicate the size of a work for bibliographic purposes.

264) Diogenes Laertios V 28 indicates the number of lines written by Aristotle as 445,270 *stichoi* (standard lines). If the bibliography transmitted by him contained originally 551 books (= scrolls), as assumed by Moraux (1951) p. 192, a single book consisted of an average of 808 lines. The individual books of the *Topics* had on the average 751 *stichoi* of 36 letters each, as Moraux has calculated by a conversion of lines in Bekker's edition. Moraux explains on p. 193: "Ce chiffre s'accorde assez bien avec ce que l'on peut tirer des indications données par Diogène. Le catalogue ne renferme donc

aucune lacune importante." Moraux's computation contains, however, too many uncertain factors to draw such a conclusion from it. Yet if we accept his data, but assume that the bibliography listed originally 580 books, that is, if the extant version omits the titles of works in 29 books, then we arrive at an average of 767 lines per book, which is much closer to the value calculated from the *Topics*.

265) Moraux (1951) pp. 186-191.

266) Moraux (1951) p. 122.

267) Düring (1966) p. 22, note 127 estimates that almost a third of the Aristotle bibliography compiled by the authority on which Diogenes and Hesychios relied, consisted of collections of materials.

268) Diogenes Laertios IV 4-5; IV 11-14; V 59-60.

269) Diogenes Laertios IV 13, p. 171, 13-15 Long. See note 254 above.

270) Dörrie assumes that the works of Xenokrates remained in the Academy. But they might also have been sold like those of his predecessor Speusippos.

271) Perhaps these and even the bibliography of Speusippos were also compiled by Hermippos. Only a few of his biographical works on members of the Academy and the Peripatos (which belong not to philosophy but to belles lettres) are cited only by chance; none of these is on Speusippos, Xenokrates or Straton. But it could very well be that Hermippos had written on, say, Xenokrates, because his notorious rivalry with Aristotle (see Wehrli (1974) p. 73 f.) would have been a suitable theme for his biographical activity.

272) This would support Moraux's recently established earlier dating of Andronikos. It is quite possible that Andronikos lived for some time in Alexandria before assuming the leadership of the Peripatos, and Tyrannion could have sent him copies of the Aristotle material which he had discovered in Apellikon's library. See on this point Moraux (1973) p. 52.

273) On the conjectural edition of Theophrastos by Andronikos see Regenbogen (1940) column 1378.

274) Wendel (1949) p. 18.

275) The *sillybos* was a strip of parchment (ca. 2 x 10 cm.) on which the contents of a scroll were briefly listed; it was glued onto the upper edge of a scroll, and was hanging down when the scroll was shelved. See Gardthausen (1922) p. 84 f.; Wendel (1949) p. 25; Schubart (1960) p. 73; Widmann (1967) column 567.

276) Wendel (1949) p. 76; Wendel-Göber (1955) p. 73.

277) Regenbogen (1950) p. 1419; likewise van Rooy (1958) p. 154 f.

278)   There was no reason to make an inventory of Aristotle's private library. On the difference between an inventory and a catalog see below, p. 229.

279)   See e.g. *Handbuch der Bibliothekswissenschaft*, 1. Aufl., Bd. 3.1 (Wiesbaden, 1955) pp. 578 and 691 (Bibliotheca Palatina, Heidelberg, 16th century; Bibliothèque Royale, Paris, 17th century) and Bd. 3.2 (Wiesbaden, 1957) p. 44 f. (Königliche öffentliche Bibliothek, Dresden, 18th century).

3. Preconditions: The Museion and Its Library

3.1 The Museion at Alexandria

VIEWED from our own vantage point, Aristotle and his pupils witnessed the end of an era in Greek history and the beginning of the era which has been known since Droysen as the "Hellenistic" period. Aristotle was 46 years old when Philip II, king of the Macedonians who had only recently been Hellenized, put an end to the freedom of the Greek tribes and cities in the battle of Chaironeia (338 B.C.). When the philosopher died (322 B.C.), his former pupil Alexander, Philip's son, had defeated the Persians and conquered an immense empire with the help of his Macedonians and the forcibly allied Greeks, an empire which now after his early death (323 B.C.) threatened to disintegrate. While Theophrastos headed the Peripatos, the three Hellenistic empires were founded on the soil of Alexander's realm in bloody fights between the conqueror's successors, the so-called Diadochi: in the Balkans the empire of the Antigonids, in Asia the realm of the Seleucids, and in Egypt the realm of the Ptolemies. Alexander's empire was partitioned, but the Macedonian-Greek rule over the conquered lands continued, and the culture of their rulers remained Greek.

Ptolemaios, the son of Lagos, one of the ablest among Alexander's generals, had been made governor of Egypt by Alexander. After Alexander's death, he made himself the absolute ruler of the country; in 305 B.C. he assumed the title "king". He ruled his territory with skill, and knew how to defend and even to expand it. Of course, it was easier for him than for the other Diadochi to prevail and to found a dynasty, because his territory had always had a strong administration, and the inhabitants were used to be exploited to the utmost by the king's officials.

The Ptolemies of the third century B.C., like the Seleucids, relied exclusively on the Macedonians and Greeks who had come to the country with the conqueror or after the conquest, lured by the prospects of getting rich quick.[1] Among the many immigrants, the Greeks outnumbered by far the Macedonians, but the old Greek colony of Naukratis became less important than the newly founded cities of Alexandria and Ptolemais. As mercenaries, officials, settlers, merchants, artisans, teachers, etc. the Greeks, together with the Macedonians, constituted the upper class favored by the kings. Their position was substantially different from that of their forefathers. While those had mostly been poor but free citizens of independent communities in their homeland, in the foreign country they lived as subjects of a monarch, but they enjoyed a certain affluence and belonged, as it were, to the ruling class.

What had been only wishful thinking on the part of the authors who had prepared Alexander's campaign with their publications had now not only come to pass, but their expectations had even been greatly surpassed. Ever since Philip II had begun to meddle in Greek affairs, the Greeks, and especially the Athenians, had been split into two parties. One party, for example Demosthenes in his *Philippics*, had fought the Macedonians because they saw in their advance a deadly danger for Greek liberty; the other party, as for example Isokrates in his *Philippos*, had urged him to unite the ever-quarreling Greeks and to fight together with them the Persian archenemy so as to wrest Asia Minor from them. Isokrates thought that the constant quarrels among Greeks were caused by the poverty of the country which could no longer feed its inhabitants; the Greeks needed additional living room for their growing population. In addition, only the conquest of Asia Minor would assure safety from Persian inroads. In his view, the Greeks had the right to rule over the "barbarians" because of their *paideia*; their cultural superiority justified in his opinion the subjugation of the peoples of Asia Minor.[2] Aristotle shared this opinion; he stated, for example, in the beginning of his *Politics* that it was only right that Greeks ruled over barbarians, relying on a quotation from Euripides.[3] All those who shared these views supported first Philip and then Alexander, who not only achieved what Isokrates had advised his father to do, but went far beyond. But they disapproved of the young king's endeavors who, when he had reached the zenith of his power, sought to reconcile victors and vanquished and to amalgamate them and ordered his friends and commanders as well as ten thousand of his soldiers to marry Persian women (the mass wedding at Susa, 324 B.C.).

The Diadochs did not continue this policy. They had no desire to see the descendants of Macedonians and Greeks, the pillars of their power, being absorbed by the indigenous population. Mixed marriages were therefore in Egypt an exception until the end of the third century B.C.[4] In the two empires of the Diadochi outside of Europe the Greeks kept to themselves, and they preserved their language as well as their life-style. Wherever Greeks lived there were not only Greek temples, but also theaters and gymnasiums which were unknown to the indigenous population. These were the very centers of Greek colonies, and they existed even in remote places. Societies of all kinds furthered solidarity among the Greeks. The largest societal role was played by "those from the gymnasium" (*hoi apo tu gymnasiu*); those were societies formed by each year's class of young men after they had finished their one-year education in a gymnasium. They constituted the elite among Greek colonists, because the gymnasiums admitted only young men of pure Greek descent whose fathers had also finished a gymnasium.[5]

The societies of Greeks were even more important in the empire of the Ptolemies because there, unlike in the empire of the Seleucids, only the three Greek cities mentioned above existed, whereas many other Greek colonies did not form administrative units. Moreover, the institutions in which the Greeks in Egypt preserved their Greek heritage were not founded by the state but were the fruit of their own initiative and the philanthropy of rich men who had themselves elected as gymnasiarchons and then provided the means for the maintenance of a gymnasium.

Whether the Egyptian gymnasia were engaged, in addition to the physical training of young people, also in their mental and artistic education is debatable. But the Greeks in the Ptolemaic empire were no doubt interested in giving their children not only the customary elementary education, but also, if they had the necessary talents, a higher education, the *paideia*, which elevated the Greeks above the barbarians. This was done everywhere through classical literature, as had been the case from time immemorial. The particulars are not known but the results are tangible.

Among the papyri found more or less accidentally in Egypt, where the sand in the ruins of Greek settlements covered and preserved them, there are surprisingly many fragments of scrolls with literary contents. These texts are works by classical and Hellenistic authors, poets and prose writers, and also writers on specific subjects. The literary papyri from the period of the Ptolemies are mostly from the third century B.C.[6] They show that literary education was much more widespread among Greeks in Egypt than had been thought before. Even in smaller places, people owned books, and in larger places, as in Oxyrhynchos, one of the principal sites at which papyri were found, they even possessed libraries. For the Greeks of the Ptolemaic empire (and certainly also for those in the Seleucid empire) the literature of their nation evidently represented the culture which legitimized their rule over the indigenous population. The study of their literature was, however, not only the basis for the self-confidence of Greeks in Egypt and in Asia, but it also united them against the Egyptians and Asians as an intellectual community on the basis of a common education. When we look at the actions of the Ptolemies in cultural matters we must always keep in mind the situation of the Macedonian-Greek upper class in Egypt.

Ptolemaios I was an educated man who, like Alexander, loved the company of scientists, poets and artists. Towards the end of his life (he died in 283 B.C.) he wrote a biography of Alexander which is lost but which was apparently quite accurate; it was the main source of the most important extant description of Alexander's campaign, the *Anabasis Alexandru* of Arrianos. Already in his own lifetime his capital Alexandria began to develop into the new spiritual center of the Greek world, challenging the position that Athens had occupied until then. Ptolemaios achieved this primarily by founding (probably around 295 B.C., when the tensions of foreign policy had eased somewhat) a museion for the cultivation of sciences and literature, which became "the" Museion in Greek cultural history.[7] The members of the Museion constituted (perhaps like those in the society of Peripatetics, founded by Theophrastos) a society for the cult of the muses, and a priest of the muses was its chief official. But while the society of Peripatetics had a private character and represented a certain school of thought, the Alexandrian Museion was a royal institution and was, despite the relations of the ruling dynasty to members of the Peripatos, not bound by any specific philosophy. It is therefore comparable to the academies of arts and sciences founded by the princes of the 18th century. In any event, it was extraordinarily well supported by Ptolemaios and his successors, especially by Ptolemaios II Philadelphos (co-regent since 285, sole regent since 283 B.C.). The members of the Museion, appointed by the king, were respected scholars, but not only men who dealt with philosophical questions in the narrower sense,[8] and famous poets, especially those who were also scholars; they were able to devote themselves to their work under the most favorable conditions — they could do research, they could do creative writing, and if they wished they could also teach. They were exempted from taxes, and received a salary as well as food and lodging in the palace quarter, the "Brucheion". There they had access to all necessary buildings and installations, among which was also a library. A part of the Brucheion was even called a Museion (in the larger sense). Since the members of the Museion made good use of the facilities at their disposal, Greek sciences and literature flourished for a long time in the residence of the Ptolemies. The scientists wrote fundamental works in the fields of chronology, geography, mathematics, astronomy, and medicine. No less important were their philological achievements and works on literary history with which we shall deal in more detail below. As already mentioned, philology (including literary history) became only then a discipline in its own right.

The poets appointed as members of the Museion by Ptolemaios and his successors were among the main representatives of Hellenistic poetry. It is not my task to describe the poetry of this new age — this has often been done[9] — but a specific type of poetry which flourished especially at the Ptolemaic court and which is therefore known as Alexandrian literature, must be emphasized here. The poets of this school were all very learned and tried in many cases to combine poetry and scholarship, by drawing on esoteric subjects, using unusual expressions, and displaying outlandish mythological, geographical and other knowledge. They were the first *poetae docti* of Greek literature, scholars who wrote only for a small circle of highly sophisticated listeners and readers. Kallimachos, who was most successful in this combination of poetry and scholarship, and his literary adherents loathed the popular contents and forms of poetry. Although they admired very much the works of the "classics," they did not wish to worship any classicism, because they knew that the age that had produced these works had long since come to an end.

The first great scholar-poet, Philitas of Kos, was appointed by Ptolemaios I as the literature teacher of his son, the later Ptolemaios II (perhaps on Kos?). One of his pupils, Zenodotos of Ephesos, relieved him at Alexandria. According to the *Suda*, Zenodotos was also an epic poet — in the lexicon he is mentioned as an "epic poet and philologist" — but, as we shall see, he became famous not as a poet but as librarian of the Museion and as a textual critic of Homer and other poets. Among the other learned poets who belonged for shorter or longer periods to the Museion under the first and second Ptolemaios, we shall name here only four, whom we shall also meet in the library of the Museion: Alexandros Aitolos, who was counted as one of the "Pleiades", the Seven Stars of Hellenistic tragic poets, whose works are all lost; Lykophron of Chalkis, of whom only one poem, the *Alexandra*, has been preserved, and which was notorious already in Antiquity for its obscurity; Apollonios Rhodios, famous as the author of an epic poem on the Argonauts, which has come down to us; and last but not least, Kallimachos. Theokritos of Syracuse, a great poet, but not a scholar, also lived for a time at the court of the Ptolemies.

If we ask why Ptolemaios I and his successor assembled so many scholars and poets at their court, it is not sufficient to point to the well-known motives of other monarchs who appeared as patrons of the arts and sciences, e.g. the wish to enhance thereby their own prestige and that of their court. We must also take into consideration that the superiority of Greek culture, intended to justify the Macedonian-Greek rule over Egypt, could not be better demonstrated than by the flowering of arts and sciences in Alexandria. This flowering proves also that Greek culture was alive and well, while the old Egyptian culture which had been admired by many educated Greeks had long since been dead. The Greeks did not care much for their Egyptian contemporaries.[10] Seen from this perspective, the foundation and support of the Alexandrian Museion was an act of cultural policy in the true sense of the word.

3.2 The Library of the Museion According to the Ancient Authors

Among the institutions of the Museion in Alexandria the library was no doubt the most important one. Many Greek and Roman authors praise the zeal of the Ptolemies in collecting books and the number of scrolls which they managed to assemble.[11] Although the relevant data vary considerably, it is a fact that the library of the Ptolemies was extraordinarily large. All ancient authors, with the sole exception of Irenaeus, name as its founder not the first but the second Ptolemaios, for example in the list of Greek rulers who founded libraries which begins with Peisistratos, the tyrant of Athens. On the beginnings of the library there existed two presumably Alexandrian traditions, on its downfall a Roman one. To begin with the latter: the philosopher Seneca (d. A.D. 65) mentions that 40,000 of the scrolls collected by the kings in Alexandria had gone up in flames, relying on Livius (50 B.C.-A.D. 17) who had written about this in one of the lost books of his historical work. We learn from later authors that the large library was annihilated by fire in the Alexandrian War (47 B.C.), when Caesar who had occupied the Brucheion was attacked by the Egyptians. The holdings of the library are said by Gellius to have been 700,000 scrolls, whereas Isidorus speaks of 70,000 scrolls.[12] According to Orosius, 400,000 scrolls were destroyed by the conflagration.[13] There is no doubt that either part or all of the library perished in the flames at that time.[14]

Regarding the two traditions on the beginnings of the library, one concerns the purchase of the library of Aristotle-Theophrastos-Neleus by Ptolemaios II, as reported by Athenaios, the other mentions the role played by Demetrios of Phaleron in the establishment of the library. This second tradition can be traced to the so-called Letter of Aristeas, in which the story of the translation of the Pentateuch into Greek by seventy-two Jewish scholars is reported.[15] The Septuagint, of which this was the oldest part, owed its origin actually to the needs of the Jewish communities in Egypt who did not know Hebrew any more. But the author of the Letter of Aristeas, a Jewish scholar who probably wrote in Egypt around 100 B.C., wanted to trace it to an initiative of king Ptolemaios (by which he meant Ptolemaios II Philadelphos)[16] in order to enhance its prestige. He therefore pretends to be a man at the court of the king by the name of Aristeas, and links his story with the foundation of the library in the Brucheion. He writes that Demetrios of Phaleron, the man in charge of the royal library, had been provided with much money in order to collect as far as possible all books in the world, and that he had executed the king's wish as far as this was within his power, through purchases or by making copies. When he was asked one day by the king in Aristeas's presence how many thousand books he had already collected, he answered that there were more than 200,000, but that he would make efforts to acquire up to 500,000 within a short time.[17] In this connection the author has Demetrios tell the king that it had been reported to him that the laws of the Jews (the Thora) were also worthy of a copy, to be added to the royal library. When asked what prevented him from having them copied, since he had the necessary means at his disposal, Demetrios explains to the king that a translation would be necessary, because the language and the script were Hebrew. The king then orders to write to the High Priest in Jerusalem regarding a translation of the Thora. We need not continue with this story in detail:[18] it ends with a description of the collective work of the scholars, organized by Demetrios on the island of Pharos (near Alexandria) whose result was the Septuagint.

Josephus and several Christian authors, among them Irenaeus (2nd century), Eusebios (3rd-4th century) and Epiphanios (4th century) retold the story, relaying directly or indirectly on Pseudo-Aristeas; most of them also mention the role purportedly played by Demetrios.[19] Almost all exaggerate the acquisition and translation of works in foreign languages brought about by Philadelphos II Ptolemaios in order to make the translation of the Thora more plausible. Epiphanios reports the number of books which Demetrios had already collected when asked by the king not as about 200,000 but only 54,800.[20] He mentions further that a second, smaller library had later been established in the temple of Serapis, the Serapeion, which had been known as the daughter of the library in the palace quarter, the Brucheion.[21] (In other passages, that library is also known as the first or great one, also the library of the king or of the Museion, or simply as the library in Alexandria.)[22]

What Pseudo-Aristeas tells about the origin of the Septuagint is of course fictional. But he would hardly have connected Ptolemaios and Demetrios with the translation of the Pentateuch if he had not read somewhere—perhaps in the work by Kallixeinos on Alexandria which was later also used by Athenaios—that the king had entrusted Demetrios with the organization of the library of the Museion, that he had put at his disposal large sums for the purchase or copying of Greek works and occasionally even for the acquisition and translation of important works in foreign languages. He made, however, a mistake: the king served by Demetrios was not the second but the first Ptolemaios. Apart from that, his report on the role played by Demetrios in the foundation of the great Alexandrian library may contain some historical kernel.

The former ruler of Athens had found refuge at the court of Ptolemaios I about ten years after his expulsion, ca. 297 B.C.[23] It seems that the experienced statesman who had also made a name for himself as a learned author, was very welcome there. Ptolemaios included him even among his immediate counselors, the so-called "First friends of the king".[24] But when Ptolemaios II became sole ruler (283 B.C.) he banished Demetrios to Upper Egypt, because he had advised his father against making him his successor. According to Diogenes Laertios who devoted a whole chapter (with bibliography) to the former pupil of Theophrastos,[25] Demetrios advised Ptolemaios I on political questions, but it is likely that he did so also on other issues. Thus he may have recommended his former class mate Straton of Lampsakos as physics teacher for his youngest son, the later Ptolemaios II.[26]

A few years after the arrival of Demetrios in Alexandria Ptolemaios I founded the Museion. The scholars appointed by the king as members needed of course books, at least the literature of their specialty, in order to be able to work. But the poets who belonged to the new school also needed works from which they could excerpt exotic subjects, unusual expressions, and all manner of out-of-the-way mythological and other information. Ptolemaios was also ready to put at their disposal a well-stocked library. Nobody could better assist him in this task by word and deed than Demetrios. Therefore it is not implausible that he, as reported by Pseudo-Aristeas, acquired by order of the king and for much money the books that formed the main stock of the great Alexandrian library.[27] We may assume that he sent agents to the booksellers and book owners of Athens and other cities, not only in order to buy individual books but also whole collections, and that he had copies made of books which were not for sale but in which Alexandria was interested. When it became widely known what Ptolemaios had ordered him to do, he was probably offered books from every quarter, including also forgeries.[28]

In this manner the Alexandrian library collected probably multiple copies of many works. The Homeric epics, for example, were evidently available in many copies. This neither could nor should be avoided. Demetrios had certainly instructed his agents to look not only for rare works but also for reliable copies of commonly available works. Considering the well-known faultiness of ordinary copies they always sought to obtain better copies than those which were already in the collection. The scrolls that had been acquired were probably only sorted somehow under Demetrios. A more precise order was only provided for by a curator of the collection who was appointed later on.

Wilamowitz and others assumed even that Demetrios had recommended to Ptolemaios I to found in Alexandria a museion after the example of the Peripatos.[29] This is possible, but the institution actually established by the king was not indebted to any particular school of philosophy, and was substantially different from its example; it fulfilled a function in Egypt, a country ruled by a thin Macedonian-Greek upper class, which the Peripatos in Athens did not have. But certainly the king did not need to be taught by Demetrios that such an institution needed a library, because even long before he had admitted him to his court he had probably heard how research was being done in the Peripatos and how useful the large library of the head of the school had been for this purpose.

On the other hand, one should not diminish the role of Demetrios in the foundation of the Alexandrian library, as Pfeiffer and others have done, because Ptolemaios I chose the literature teacher of the crown prince, Zenodotos of Ephesos (probably born ca. 335 B.C.) to be his librarian.[30] The article "Zenodotos" of the *Suda* on which these authors rely says:[31]

> Zenodotos of Ephesos, epic poet and philologist, pupil of Philitas, lived
> under Ptolemaios I. He was the first corrector of Homer and was in
> charge of the Alexandrian library and educated the children of Ptolemaios.

It does not say that he was the first head of the library, only that he was the head of it. It is not known when he was entrusted with this office. It is also not evident that he, as is generally assumed, was the head of the library and the teacher of prince Ptolemaios (II) and princess Arsinoe (II) at the same time. In the second half of the third century, when the large library was well arranged and cataloged and did not grow at such a rapid pace as in the first few decades of its existence, it may have been possible to combine the two offices. During the first half of the century this was in my opinion hardly possible. Zenodotos was probably appointed as head of the library only after he had completed his task as teacher, ca. 291 B.C., when the future Ptolemaios II was seventeen years old.[32] But at that time Demetrios of Phaleron, who according to Pseudo-Aristeas was in charge of the library, had already been busy acquiring books for the library in large quantities. Was he now perhaps relieved by Zenodotos, or should we discard the notion of his work for the library? It seems to me that neither of these conclusions would be justified. Demetrios relinquished only one of his tasks: he was still in charge of the acquisition funds and pursued the growth of the collection, but he left its administration to Zenodotos. The day came when the sheer quantity of the acquired scrolls required that a specially appointed full-time scholar would take them into his custody, and provided for their orderly arrangement, storage and description, but above all for the identification of the works that were contained in them. In the long run, this could not be a part-time job for one of the "First friends of the king". The *bibliophylax*, the keeper of the royal collection of books (literally the "guardian of books")[33] was responsible for the maintenance and utilization of the collection. On the other hand, he was apparently neither obligated nor empowered to pursue its growth. At any rate, there is no evidence that any of the Alexandrian librarians was concerned about acquisitions or that he had funds at his disposal for that purpose. The situation was probably the same in Alexandria as later in Imperial Rome, where a high official of the finance administration with the title *Procurator bibliothecarum Graecarum et Latinarum* (whose authority is not known in detail) was the superior of the learned directors of the various book collections. The heads of many libraries in early modern times and even those of some later ones were not responsible for the growth of their collections.[34]

Even though, as pointed out above, the *Suda* does not expressly say so, we may assume that Zenodotos was the first to assume the office of keeper of the royal book collection. His rank was lower than that of Demetrios and he was probably subordinated to him.[35] There is thus no reason to diminish the value of the services rendered by Demetrios to the establishment of the Alexandrian library because Zenodotos had been appointed as *bibliophylax*. It is not known who was responsible for the further growth of the library after Demetrios's banishment. Presumably, Ptolemaios II entrusted this task also to one of his "friends".[36] Perhaps he even dealt personally with an acquisition for the library, e.g. the purchase of the library which Neleus had inherited from Theophrastos and Aristotle. In any event, he supported the library during his forty years of government so lavishly that he was thought to have been its founder already in the second century B.C., and that people associated him with the unforgotten man who had begun the collection of literature on behalf of Ptolemaios I, and who had mightily advanced it, namely Demetrios of Phaleron.

According to Pseudo-Aristeas, Demetrios had been ordered to acquire all the world's books. That meant all Greek works, because Demetrios refrained from copying the Thora since its language and script was Hebrew. There are some indications that the Ptolemies endeavored not only to satisfy the (not always easily ascertainable) literary needs of all present or future members of the Museion, but that they aimed at a higher goal. Already in Kallimachos's time the Alexandrian library owned works whose acquisition can only be explained by the endeavor of the Ptolemies to assemble a complete collection of the entire Greek literature. As can be seen from quotations of later authors, he listed among others works by authors of cookbooks, among which were special cookbooks for cakes, as well as a "Law of banquets" which the Athenian courtesan Gnathaina wished to have observed by her lovers and those of her daughter.[37] Other ancient authors indicate that the Alexandrian library also had many works on magic and apparently also on fishing, of course in prose, because didactic poems on fishery belonged to literature in the narrower sense.[38] If Demetrios in Pseudo-Aristeas says that the laws of the Jews were also worthy of being copied for the royal library, we may not conclude from this that only those Greek works were included in the library which were found to be worthy. It seems rather that no work was excluded, and that even those books were admitted which according to our conception belonged to the curiosa.[39]

Galen reports that Ptolemaios III Euergetes went so far in his zeal to acquire all Greek books that he forced the passengers of ships which anchored in the harbor of Alexandria to relinquish to him all books that they carried and to accept instead copies which were hurriedly made. The confiscated books were marked with a note *ek ploiōn* (from the ships).[40] Galen's story may be an exaggerated generalization, but it presumably contains a memory of the illegal means sometimes employed by the king against travelers.

The interests of the Ptolemies were not at all limited to older works, but extended also to newer literature. It would have been rather curious if they had not included in their library the works of poetry written at their own court, the more so since the authors no doubt customarily presented copies of their creations to their royal patrons. Even the second version of the *Argonautika*, completed on Rhodos by Apollonios Rhodios who had left the court after a quarrel with Kallimachos who had criticized the first version, was acquired for the Alexandrian library. The consideration of contemporary authors is also evident from the fact (known to us by chance) that Kallimachos listed in his *Pinakes* a certain Lysimachos who had excessively flattered his pupil, king Attalos I of Pergamon (269-197 B.C.) in a work on his education, *Peri tēs Attalu paideias*.[41]

Although we have no direct evidence, there is no doubt that the Ptolemies included in their collection also works written by "barbarians" in Greek, e.g. the *History of Egypt* by the Egyptian priest Manetho which was even dedicated to Ptolemaios II Philadelphus. There is also evidence that they collected works that had been translated into Greek from foreign languages, e.g. the works known under the name of Zoroaster on magic which particularly interested Ptolemaios II, and which were later listed by the Kallimachean Hermippos. They probably also possessed Egyptian religious works and recreational literature that had been translated into Greek.[42] Finally, the Septuagint legend shows that they acquired important foreign works specifically for the purpose of having them translated into Greek. The history of libraries knows of similar enterprises by later monarchs.[43]

In their endeavor to encompass the Greek literature as completely as possible, the Ptolemies went far beyond all earlier Greek book collectors, even beyond Aristotle. However large his library was, it contained probably only works which were either objects of research themselves or constituted sources and aids for scientific investigations. For this reason, too, it is implausible that the collection of the entire Greek literature by the Ptolemies should have been based on the advice of Demetrios of Phaleron, a pupil of one of Aristotle's pupils. The idea originated probably with Ptolemaios I or with his successor. Be that as it may, it was a splendid thought to erect in the city that was not only the capital of the Ptolemaic empire but which was to become the new center of Greek culture, a monument to that culture built from the works of all Greek authors. It was, after all, the literature more than any other manifestation of the Greek spirit which represented the culture which united the Greeks in the areas of their settlements in which they had lived for centuries and in the territories conquered by Alexander, despite their political discord.[44] At the same time, a library of

Greek literature demonstrated the *paideia* thanks to which the Greeks felt justified to rule over other nations.

As a collection which was intended to contain the entire Greek literature and which indeed included already around 250 B.C. most works that then existed, the great Alexandrian library seems to us to be — contrary to the purely scientific library of Aristotle — a forerunner of those modern national libraries which collect not only works published in the territory of the respective country, but all works written in the language of that country wherever they are published, including translations from foreign languages. Like those, the Alexandrian library served also for the preservation of the national literature. The Alexandrian librarians observed quite soon that many literary creations of earlier centuries had already been lost. Even the Ptolemies, though they spared neither efforts nor money, did not succeed in finding copies of certain dramas even of famous poets such as Euripides and Kratinos.[45] The ancient scholars would certainly no longer have had some works at their disposal, had it not been for the Ptolemies who had bought a copy in good time. For whatever we still possess of Greek literature we are ultimately indebted to the Ptolemies and their Hellenistic, Roman and Byzantine followers.

3.3 The Library According to the Report of Ioannes Tzetzes

Further information on the early history of the great Alexandrian library can be gleaned from the prolegomena of Ioannes Tzetzes to his commentary on Aristophanes. This Byzantine scholar (ca. 1110-1180) mentions the beginnings of the library because Lykophron of Chalkis "corrected" (that is, he edited critically) the text of the comedies which had been acquired for the library by Ptolemaios II. In this connection, Tzetzes recorded also a few other data on the library which are valuable for us because most of the sources on which he relied are now lost.

The prolegomena exist in three versions which are designated according to the principal sources, a manuscript in Paris and two in Milan, as *Pb*, *Ma*, and *Mb* respectively. Only the later *Ma* and *Mb* versions bear the name of Tzetzes, but the earlier *Pb* version is also ascribed to him by Kaibel and Wendel. All three versions are largely consistent with each other in those parts that are of interest to us here; *Ma* is, however, much shorter, *Mb* is somewhat more extensive than *Pb*.[46] I am relying here on the earliest version, despite its considerable editorial shortcomings.

The relevant section runs as follows:[47]

> Alexandros of Aitolos and Lykophron of Chalkis
> corrected at the instance of Ptolemaios Philadelphos
> the dramatic books; Lykophron [corrected] the
> comedies, Alexandros the tragedies and the satyr
> plays. Ptolemaios, who was a patron of the arts and
> sciences, had collected the books with the aid of
> Demetrios of Phaleron and other scholars and with
> royal funds and had brought them from everywhere to
> Alexandria. He stored them in two libraries, of which

the one outside [of the palace] contained 42,800, the
other inside the palace 400,000 mixed and 90,000
unmixed and single books, whose lists were later compiled
by Kallimachos. The king entrusted this library to
Eratosthenes, a contemporary of Kallimachos. The books
that had been collected were not only those of the
Greeks but also of all other peoples, including the
Jews. The books of other peoples were submitted to
scholars of the respective people who were proficient in
Greek and in their own language and were translated into
Greek, and he [the king] had also the books of the
Jews translated by seventy [scholars]. Thus he had the
books of other peoples translated into Greek. As I
just said, the dramatic books were corrected by Alexandros
and Lykophron, but the poetic ones first by Zenodotos
and later by Aristarchos.

The data related by Tzetzes concern the following issues:

1. the correction (*diorthōsis*) of tragic and comic works;

2. the collection of books (*bibloi* or *biblia*), the two Alexandrian libraries and their holdings;

3. the compilation of lists of these books (*pinakes*);

4. the appointment of a chief librarian (*bibliophylax*);

5. the translation of foreign books, among which were also Jewish books;

6. once more the correction of dramatic writings as well as others, i.e. epic and lyric poems.

These are notes on the Alexandrian libraries which were arranged and
connected with each other as Tzetzes saw fit. In my opinion, all contain some
historical kernel, but the connections made by the Byzantine scholar must be viewed
with some circumspection. Tzetzes lists first the note that pertained directly to his
own subject, the comedies: the correction of tragic and comic works made by
Alexandros and Lykophron according to the copies in the library (item 1). At the
end (item 6) he reverts to the same issue with an addition relating to the corrections
of epic and lyric poems by Zenodotos. Regarding the sequence of these works,
Tzetzes indicates in version *Pb* only briefly, but in *Mb* expressly, that the
compilation of the *pinakes* (item 3) took place after the correction of the books, but
still during the reign of Ptolemaios II Philadelphos. In *Mb* he adds that
Kallimachos had been a young man at the court (*neaniskos tēs aulēs*)[48] when he
compiled the *pinakes*. Whatever this rank may have been (if indeed it was a rank),
the chronological relationship is correct inasmuch as Kallimachos was about twenty-
five years younger than Zenodotos.

It is odd that Tzetzes apparently thought that each of the three tasks mentioned
by him (the acquisition of books, the correction of writings, and the making of

the *Pinakes*) had been finished when the next was being undertaken, and that the third and last had been completed when king Ptolemaios II, under whom Kallimachos had started his work, was still alive. The Byzantine scholar thus did not consider at all that the successors of the king continued to acquire books, although this is exactly what they did. As we have seen, Ptolemaios III Euergetes even took some questionable actions in order to enrich his library. The library grew further when the Attalids, the rulers of Pergamon, also began to build up a large library in their capital (no later than in the beginning of the second century B.C.), which led to a famous and fierce competition on the acquisition of old books between them and the Ptolemies.[49]

What Tzetzes says on the collection of books (item 2) and the translation of works from foreign languages (item 5) is consistent with the data given by the successors of Pseudo-Aristeas on whom he no doubt relied. He writes however that in addition to Demetrios of Phaleron other scholars had also acquired books from everywhere by order of the king. These unnamed men were perhaps the "friends" of Ptolemaios II, who took Demetrios's place after his banishment.

Tzetzes claims also, contrary to Pseudo-Aristeas and his successors, that Ptolemaios II Philadelphos had erected a library not only within the palace quarter, the Brucheion, but also outside of it. This second library could only have been the one affiliated with the Serapeion, but according to Epiphanios this was erected at a later date. The records on the foundation of the Serapeion which were excavated in 1945 indicate indeed, as pointed out by Pfeiffer,[50] that this temple had been built only by Ptolemaios III Euergetes. Thus, Ptolemaios II Philadelphos could not have been the founder of the second library.

Tzetzes further indicates the holdings of the two Alexandrian libraries, purportedly founded by Ptolemaios II Philadelphos: the one in the Brucheion contained altogether 490,000 scrolls, the one in the Serapeion 42,800 scrolls. It is not clear whether he wants to say that Kallimachos had listed also the scrolls in the second library, whose foundation and growth he probably did not live to see.

Since the Byzantine scholar not only thought that Ptolemaios II had been the founder of the library in the Brucheion (as Pseudo-Aristeas had done) but ascribed to him also the foundation of the library in the Serapeion, I believe that he inserted the data on the holdings of the two libraries unthinkingly between his notes on the collection and the cataloging of the books in the Brucheion. He overlooked, however, that these data pertained not the era of Ptolemaios II, during which a second library did not exist, but to a later time, when the library at the Serapeion, which had been built up at the earliest by Ptolemaios III from duplicates in the "mother" library, already contained a sizable number of books. We cannot tell with certainty when this happened. But it is certain that at that time the library in the Brucheion had also grown considerably beyond the size which it had reached at the death of Ptolemaios II (246 B.C.). Perhaps the number mentioned by Tzetzes — 490,000 scrolls — were its purported holdings in 47 B.C. when it went up in flames.[51] We do not know how many scrolls it actually contained at that time, much less how many existed two hundred years earlier and how many were cataloged by Kallimachos.

If, however, the data on holdings which Tzetzes inserted in his report on the book collection and cataloging under Ptolemaios II Philadelphos pertain to a later period, it is out of the question that Kallimachos cataloged in the *Pinakes* mentioned by the Byzantine scholar 480,000 scrolls or even 532,800 scrolls, as is generally being assumed, or that those figures can be traced to him.[52] Tzetzes quite simply thought when he combined the notes which he had collected that Kallimachos must have cataloged 490,000 scrolls if the library in the Brucheion contained that number at the time of Ptolemaios II.

But it is also doubtful whether the great Alexandrian library ever grew to the size given by Tzetzes. The same is true for its "daughter". Even if we take into consideration that many works consisted of several books (generally equivalent to scrolls) and existed in several copies, the number of about 500,000 scrolls for the library in the Brucheion still remains inexplicable.[53] Although even some ancient authors mention numbers of this order of magnitude, those who report that the library possessed not several hundreds of thousands but "only" some tens of thousands of scrolls seem to me to be more trustworthy. Even a collection of 40,000-50,000 scrolls was an enormous one under the conditions of those times.

The data of Tzetzes on the holdings of the library in the Brucheion are different from those of all other authors in that they are differentiated. The library contained, according to versions *Pb* and *Mb* of his report (in *Ma* there are no numbers) 400,000 mixed (*symmigeis*) and 90,000 unmixed and single scrolls (*amigeis kai haplai bibloi*). What exactly that means is in dispute. The mixed scrolls can only mean, analogous to the medieval *codices miscellanei* (miscellaneous manuscripts), those that contained several works by one or more authors, while the unmixed ones contained only one work or a chapter of a work (a "book"). Minor works, such as some early dialogs of Plato, were generally written on one scroll together with others. In commercial production of books shorter works by the same author or those on related subjects were combined on one standard scroll of 6-7 meters length and a height of 25-30 centimeters.[54] In privately made copies there occurred, however, also combinations on scrolls of larger or smaller length or height. 90,000 scrolls of the library were not only unmixed but also single. The 400,000 mixed scrolls are not said to have had this property. But from this it does not follow, as is generally assumed,[55] that "single" and "unmixed" mean the same, but only that the 400,000 scrolls were partly single and partly non-single.

Some scholars thought that single scrolls were the opposite of doubles, and interpreted the words of Tzetzes to mean that the Alexandrian library held 400,000 scrolls, including all doubles, but that there had been only 90,000 scrolls excluding all doubles — this also because of the larger number of mixed scrolls which seemed to be implausible. This conception, based on the identification of "unmixed" and "single", was also shared by Wendel, although with some misgivings on linguistic grounds.[56] But the words of the Byzantine scholar do not admit of such an interpretation. The term "single scrolls" appears ostensibly only once more: Plutarch tells us that Marc Anthony was reproached because he had given the library of Pergamon, 200,000 single scrolls, to Cleopatra to make up for the loss of the scrolls of the great Alexandrian library in the conflagration of 47 B.C.[57] Here, as also in Tzetzes, the term "single" indicated apparently a property of each individual scroll, not a condition which resulted only from a comparison with other scrolls, such as the one that each scroll contained a different work, so that there were no doubles but 200,000 (!) different works.

Scrolls were probably called "single" if they were inscribed only on the obverse, the so-called recto side, which was done for more valuable scrolls, whereas scrolls inscribed on both sides were called *opistographoi* (written on the back side, or more precisely, also on the back side).[58] A term for the other papyri which were inscribed only on the recto side has so far not been found. A papyrus leaf or a papyrus scroll was normally inscribed only on one side, namely where the fibers ran parallel to the lines, but exceptions were not rare. I think that it is worth mentioning in this context that a library catalog from the third century A.D., preserved on papyrus fragments, indicates in each case after the number of scrolls taken up by an individual work how many of those were *opistographoi* — and there were quite a number of them.[59]

Now if "single" scrolls cannot be equated with "unmixed" ones, then we must conclude that the "mixed" scrolls were collective ones.[60] Thus, the Alexandrian library possessed so and so many collective scrolls, and so and so many scrolls inscribed on one side only which contained in each case only one work or one chapter; the numbers are a matter of conjecture. The collective scrolls were certainly inscribed partly on one side only, partly on both sides. The "library statistics" reported by Tzetzes are therefore incomplete. But the number of doubles was hardly included in them, because it could not be given in terms of scrolls (and only those were counted in his report) since minor works which existed in several copies, in each case together with other works, did not fill an entire scroll.

The distinction attested to by Tzetzes, namely between mixed and unmixed, and perhaps also between scrolls inscribed on one or both sides, is important. The cataloging of a collective scroll, containing, say, five minor works demanded as much work of the librarian as that of five scrolls, each containing the text of one work.[61] Therefore, there can be no doubt that the counting (not the number!) of scrolls by mixed and unmixed, and those inscribed on one or both sides originated at the time when Kallimachos cataloged the scrolls, and that the number of mixed scrolls was very large; otherwise there would have been no reason to list them separately.

The *pinakes* which Kallimachos compiled, according to Tzetzes, when he was still a young man, were, as I shall show below, catalogs of the books acquired by the kings. At this point, I only wish to indicate that they should not simply be identified with his famous *Pinakes* of persons who had been outstanding in a cultural field and their works, as is generally done. To be sure, those *Pinakes* were based on the earlier ones, and — as we shall see later — they depended so much on them that they would hardly have been called the *Pinakes* of Kallimachos if he had not already compiled the lists that formed their basis. On this point, the report by Tzetzes makes sense.

The compilation of those *pinakes* were preceded, according to Tzetzes, by a correction of the works. In the earlier version of his report (*Pb*) the Byzantine scholar writes simply that Alexandros Aitolos and Lykophron of Chalkis had corrected the dramatic books at the instance (*protrapentes*) of Ptolemaios Philadelphos, but in the later versions he says that they had done this because of great royal gifts (*megalodōriais basilikais protrapentes*) or prodded by the king (*synōthētentes basilikōs*). At the end of the paragraph he repeats that Alexandros and Lykophron corrected the dramatic works, but adds that first

Zenodotos and later on Aristarchos (of Samothrake) had corrected the poetic (i.e. the epic and lyric) works. The abridged later version *Ma* is here consistent with *Pb*. In the enlarged version *Mb* Tzetzes adds the note on Zenodotos not only to the last but also to the first sentence and makes it more specific: the three scholars, prodded by Ptolemaios II Philadelphos in a royal manner, had corrected the works, Alexandros doing the tragedies, Lykophron the comedies, and Zenodotos mainly the works of Homer and other (epic and lyric) poets. Neither here nor there does he mention Aristarchos, but a few lines further on he reverts once more to the Homer correction by Zenodotos and says that Aristarchos (who lived in the first half of the second century B.C. and who was made director of the Alexandrian library around 180 B.C.) had been the fourth or fifth corrector of Homer after Zenodotos.

The verb *diorthun* (to correct) used by Tzetzes was a technical term. It meant, as already explained, the textual criticism by philologists, their attempts to restore on the basis of extant copies the original wording of a work which had been distorted, enlarged or abridged in the course of time.

The *Suda* names Zenodotos (not quite correctly) as the first corrector (*diorthōtēs*) of Homer. Aristarchos is considered as the most eminent philologist of Homer in Antiquity. In the scholia to the *Iliad* and the *Odyssey* which are based on the works of this scholar and his pupils, the Homer text of Zenodotos, his correction (*diorthōsis*) or edition (*ekdosis*) of the two epics, is often cited.[62] There was once also an edition of Hesiod and Pindar and perhaps one of Anakreon by him.[63] However, no traces of the textual criticism by Alexandros and Lykophron have been found. Nevertheless, there can be no doubt that Tzetzes thinks that the three scholars performed textual criticism on the epic, lyric and dramatic works. But it was only Pfeiffer who first objected to the interpretation of Tzetzes's words which had been customary until then. Before that, all modern researchers stated, as Schmidt had done, that the verb *diorthun* in that passage of Tzetzes did not indicate a philological activity but a bibliothecal one: it did not mean to correct distorted texts but to arrange the acquired books in the right order. Schmidt had written:[64] "General considerations and the context in Tzetzes itself as well as the wording of that passage show that it does not refer to work on the texts but rather to work on the books, that is, it is not about editing but about ordering." The wording proves, however, just the opposite, nor does the context compel us to accept Schmidt's interpretation, because nothing else connects the notes of Tzetzes but the common subject, the Alexandrian library, whose collections provided the material for the work of the three correctors.

Regarding the general considerations to which Schmidt refers, it can indeed not be denied that it was the task of the *bibliophylax* to arrange the collection of books in his custody, but not to restore the original text of old poems. It is, however, not implausible that Zenodotos together with Alexandros and Lykophron undertook the task imposed on them by Ptolemaios II Philadelphos. As is well known, the customary copies of the *Iliad* and the *Odyssey* diverged considerably regarding the wording of the verses and the size of the books. This was clearly recognized when one compared the many copies which had been purchased for the library of the Museion in the hope to find some that were better than those already in the collection. Some scholars in other places had, of course, tried earlier to restore the original wording of the epics, but their basis had been too narrow. This was especially true for the teachers who corrected their copies before they studied them with their pupils, which is attested for Aristotle, the teacher of Alexander of Macedonia, and may be assumed also regarding Zenodotos, the teacher of the boy who became Ptolemaios II. Now for the first time a larger number of copies made in various places became available in Alexandria. Ptolemaios II evidently hoped that it would be possible to reconstruct from them the original text of the *Iliad* and the *Odyssey*. Considering the importance attached to the reading of Homer for the *paideia*, the uncertainty of the text of the *Iliad* and the *Odyssey*, which must have been recognized by the king as a pupil of Zenodotos, was very annoying. The situation was no better regarding the text of other works intended to confer upon young people that higher education which legitimized the rule of Greeks over Egyptians. It was probably for this reason in particular that Ptolemaios II wanted to restore the original form of the epic, lyric and dramatic works and to produce an authentic text from which copies could then be made for educational and other purposes. The first textual criticism on a broad basis would thus seem to have had its origin in considerations of cultural policy by one of the princes of the Diadochi. This assumption also seems to be supported by an analogy. The learned poet Aratos, who confirmed in the anecdote on Timon the uncertainty of Homer's text, was asked, according to the testimony of an ancient biographer of Antiochos I, the ruler of the Seleucid empire, to correct the *Iliad* "because it had been distorted by many".[65]

It is, however, out of the question that the three Alexandrian scholars corrected "the" epic, lyric and dramatic works, as Tzetzes claims. They probably dealt with the main works of the most famous authors; for Zenodotos this is even documented. Thus, the Byzantine scholar either exaggerated or, what is more likely, he confused two activities reported by the authorities on which he relied. Although the verb *diorthun* does not mean "to arrange", the scrolls acquired by the Ptolemies had to be arranged in some order. But before that could be done, their content had to be determined. This was the first task of Zenodotos when he was appointed director of the library. Of course he could not do this all alone: other scholars helped him to identify the works contained in the scrolls, and then to sort out the scrolls by literary genre, author and work. Alexandros and Lykophron did that for the poetic works together with Zenodotos before they began, by order of the king, to restore the corrupt wording of these masterworks with the aid of the extant copies, which was much more difficult. (There is evidence that Lykophron was interested in one of the main questions that occurred in the arrangement of the scrolls, namely the correct title of a work that was known under several different titles.[66] This would be an explanation for the implausible statement of Tzetzes.

But regarding Zenodotos, the Keeper of the royal book collection, we must ask whether the task of textual criticism on which he was now urged to embark, was compatible with his other duties in the library which he had not yet completed with the identification, arrangement and storage of the works. In order to assess this, one must first be clear about his work as a textual critic. Zenodotos based himself probably on a copy of a work, say the *Iliad*, which was considered to be reliable, compared the text with that of other copies and corrected it if he thought that those other texts were better. If he disapproved of the entire tradition, he may well have changed the text as he saw fit. He gave, however, no written reasons why he had chosen the variant reading preferred by him, or why he had inserted his own conjectures instead of traditional variants. He did not explain either why he thought that certain verses were undoubtedly spurious and why the authenticity of other verses seemed to be questionable to him, but he quite simply omitted the spurious ones, and indicated the questionable verses with a dash in the margin, the *obelos*. This is unmistakably clear from the scholia to the *Iliad* and the *Odyssey*, i.e. the remarks of later Alexandrian textual critics who often relied on the *diorthōsis* (correction) of Zenodotos.[67]

The indication of verses whose authenticity was doubted by the editor was a new feature. In this respect, the "edition" of Zenodotos, that is, the copy edited by him for further reproduction, constituted a milestone in the history of philological textual criticism. It did not, however, put an end to the uncertainties surrounding the text of Homer, as Ptolemaios II Philadelphos had desired—quite to the contrary, it displayed them even more vividly. But it constituted a foundation on which other scholars could build in their endeavor to reconstruct the original text.

It is likely that Zenodotos explained to his colleagues and pupils why he had decided for or against certain variants and verses, and that this led to discussions which were considerably different from the popular debates on moral and esthetic problems in Homer.[68] Now it became important to find arguments for or against the authenticity of disputed versions or verses. For this purpose it became necessary to thoroughly interpret the relevant passages, and this could only be done by someone who had special lexical, grammatical, mythological, antiquarian, and other knowledge. We know only very little about such studies by the colleagues and pupils of Zenodotos. His teacher Philitas has left unordered glosses (*ataktai glossai*) with explanations. (Glosses meant words that were not generally used, especially obsolete ones that had been used by poets of earlier centuries, and dialectal expressions.) The learned poet Simias of Rhodos, a contemporary of Philitas or Zenodotos, had collected glosses which purportedly filled three scrolls. These collections were intended as aids for the explanation of old poems, perhaps also as a source of information for new authors. Zenodotos's colleague Lykophron had mainly explained glosses in his work *Peri archaias kōmōdias* (On the Old Comedy) which contained at least nine books. Zenodotos himself dealt no doubt in his lectures with the meaning of obsolete words used by Homer and other poets, especially since their tradition was often disputed. It is even assumed that he compiled lists of glosses in alphabetical order (only by the first letter), but this is not certain. The Zenodotos who is named four times as the author of *Glossai* and *Ethnikai lexeis* (dialect words) was probably one of the younger namesakes of the Ephesian.[69] Agathokles, a pupil of Zenodotos, also dealt with Homeric glosses.[70] The explanation of obsolete words in old works certainly led not infrequently to considerations of textual criticism and subsequent decisions. But for a long time we hear nothing more of philological undertakings like the editions of poets by Zenodotos.

It seems that it was only Aristophanes of Byzantium (ca. 260-180 B.C., since ca. 200 B.C. director of the Alexandrian library) who resumed the work of Zenodotos, the reconstruction of the original text of the classics. Ancient biographers designated him therefore as a pupil of Zenodotos, but such a relationship is unlikely on chronological grounds.[71] Thanks to him and his pupil Aristarchos of Samothrake *grammatikē*, i.e. philology, now became an independent branch of scholarship and

111

experienced its first flowering. It can hardly be overestimated what the two scholars and their pupils accomplished for the text and interpretation of the great Greek authors by means of their editions and commentaries. But this does not belong to our subject. It should only be mentioned here that beginning with the middle of the second century B.C. one can observe a standardization of Homer texts on papyri, whereas earlier texts showed rather divergent numbers of verses.[72] It was apparently thought that thanks to Aristarchos an authentic text of Homer had now finally been edited, one which Zenodotos had been instructed to produce a hundred and fifty years earlier.

If we consider how large and difficult was the task of textual criticism undertaken by Zenodotos, and how much time and effort was needed for the necessary investigations and the subsequent discussions with other scholars, we must doubt that he also dealt with library-oriented tasks. But the identification, arrangement and cataloging of the books acquired by the kings did hardly come to a standstill when their Keeper began to devote himself to the task of reconstructing the original text of Homer at the behest of Ptolemaios II Philadelphos. Rather, we may assume that the king relieved Zenodotos of his library-oriented obligations, and appointed another scholar to the office of *bibliophylax*, because he was certainly no less eager to see that the books acquired by him and by his father for so much money should be put to good use.

It is plausible to assume that Kallimachos relieved Zenodotos. After all, it was he who, according to Tzetzes, compiled under Ptolemaios II Philadelphos the *pinakes* of the books that had been acquired, and who later also compiled *pinakes* of Greek authors and their works (which Tzetzes does not mention), that is, it was Kallimachos who performed the principal tasks in the library. But almost all experts have for a long time taken for granted that not he but Apollonios Rhodios (who is not mentioned at all by Tzetzes) became Zenodotos's successor. We shall examine their reasons in the following section. Tzetzes says that Eratosthenes, a contemporary of Kallimachos, was appointed as *bibliophylax*. This is again typical for the method of the Byzantine scholar. He had made a note that Eratosthenes (ca. 275-195 B.C.) had held the office of Keeper of the royal book collection, which was correct. According to the *Suda*, the scholar had been invited to come to Alexandria by Ptolemaios III Euergetes (246-222 B.C.). He, like Kallimachos and queen Berenike (II) was born in Kyrene, but he was at least 25 years younger than Kallimachos.[73] (It is said that Kallimachos was his teacher, and he perhaps recommended him for the job.) Now Tzetzes, in his endeavor to bring the chronological facts noted by him as close together as possible, since they could then more easily be connected, made Kallimachos's fellow countryman appear to be also his contemporary.[74] This is reminiscent of the false synchronism created by him when he combined the data on the holdings of the library with those of the cataloging of the books.

In summary, the following information can be gleaned from Tzetzes's report:

1. Ptolemaios II Philadelphos enlarged the library in the Brucheion (which had been founded by his father) on a grand scale, aided by scholars who took the place of Demetrios of Phaleron; he was also instrumental in having works in foreign languages translated into Greek.

2. The king requested the director of the library, Zenodotos (who had been appointed by his father), and two other members of the Museion, Alexandros Aitolos and Lykophron of Chalkis, to reconstruct critically the text of classical works on the basis of the acquired copies.

3. Kallimachos, while still a young man, compiled lists of the acquired books under the same king.

4. Eratosthenes of Kyrene (a compatriot of Kallimachos) was appointed Keeper of the royal book collection (under Ptolemaios III Euergetes).

5. The two Alexandrian libraries (purportedly) contained a total of 532,800 scrolls (before the burning of the larger one).

Notes to Chapter 3

1) On the following, see Rostovtzeff (1955) vol. 2, ch. viii, 1 and 2, especially pp. 835-874; Bengtson (1969), especially pp. 443-450 and 457-470.

2) Isokrates expounded his thoughts on the unification of all Greeks for the purpose of conquering Asia Minor already in his *Panēgyrikos* (380 B.C.). He assigned the leading roles to Athens and Sparta (at that time there was as yet no point in talking about Macedonia), but in his *Philippos* (346 B.C.) he assigned that role to the Macedonian king. On the *Panēgyrikos*, in which the subjugation of the peoples of Asis Minor is being justified by the cultural superiority of the Greeks, see Jaeger (1933) vol. 3, pp. 139-141. The propaganda of Isokrates is so similar to the modern one that the terms used in the text almost thrusted themselves upon me.

3) Aristotle, *Politics* 1252 b; Nissen (1892) p. 175 f.; Buchner (1954); Jaeger (1955) pp. 120-124.

4) Tarn (1966) p. 239; Schneider (1967) vol. 1, p. 497.

5) On this and the following see especially Nilsson (1955) pp. 85-98; also Schubart (1927) pp. 9-21; Zucker (1953) and Marrou (1957) p. 147 f.

6) Otto (1925) p. 98, note 197.

7) On the Alexandrian Museion in general see Müller-Graupa (1933) and Schneider (1967) vol. 1, pp. 547-551; Bengtson (1969) pp. 459-463; Pfeiffer (1968) pp. 96-104.

8) Theophrastos who was invited to come to Alexandria but declined, was thought to be a universal scholar.

9) Körte-Händel (1960) pp. 1-7; 337-344; Lesky (1963) pp. 744-750; Pfeiffer (1968) pp. 87-95. Among the older literature Bethe (1910) p. 312 f. is still to be considered. Kallimachos spoke about his poetic principles above all in the prologue to his *Aitia*; see Callimachus (1949) fragment 1, especially verses 25-28.

10) On the relationship of the Greeks to Egypt and the Egyptians see Zucker (1950) and Schneider (1967) vol. 1, pp. 30 and 496 f.

11) Schmidt (1922) p. 4 f. and pp. 8-15 listed all references and also printed most of them. In several passages the word *bibliothēkē* (literally depository of books) is used in the plural but in the sense of one library; that was not unusual, see Wendel-Göber (1955) p. 52. The literature on the library of the Museion cannot be separated from that on the *Pinakes* of Kallimachos (though the latter are here still excluded); here I cite therefore only Schmidt (1922) pp. 31-42; Gardthausen (1922); Wendel-Göber (1955) pp. 63-82; Pfeiffer (1968) pp. 98-104. A special case is that of Parson's book on the

Alexandrian library (1952). The author is neither a specialist nor a researcher but he reproduced the ancient documents in English translation and reported the opinions of modern scholars accurately. The works of de Vleeschauwer on the history of libraries, published in Pretoria (1955 and 1963) came to my attention only after I had finished the manuscript, but they did not cause me to make changes. His principal thesis, namely the dependency of the Alexandrian library on ancient Oriental examples, has been refuted already by van Rooy (1958). For an example of attempts at explanation by Parsons and de Vleeschauwer, see note 60 below.

12) Schmidt (1922) p. 4. T. 1; 2 a and b.

13) Schmidt (1922) p. 13 f., T. 32 a-e, and p. 4, T. 2a. Some Seneca manuscripts have 400,000, some Orosius manuscripts have 40,000.

14) Wendel-Göber (1955) pp. 75-77.

15) On the following see the edition and translation (1900) of the Letter of Aristeas by Wendland, Praefatio p. xxvi f. and Einleitung pp. 1-3; Christ-Schmid (1920) pp. 619-621; Michaelis (1957); Eissfeldt (1964) pp. 817-821. [For English editions and translations see *The Letter of Aristeas* (1913) and *Aristeas to Philocrates* (1951).]

16) Pfeiffer (1968) p. 100.

17) Aristeas, *Epistula* 9-11 = Schmidt (1922) p. 11, T. 27 a. The text of the Letter of Aristeas lacks final editing; remnants of an earlier version remained (see also next note) but Wendland did not deal with this. Section 10 of the Greek text is: *plerōsō d'en oligō chronō pros to plerōthenai pentekonta myriadas ta loipa.* Wendland substituted with Eusebius, who copied this passage, *spudasō* for *plerosō* and translated: "But I shall obtain shortly those that are still missing, so that 500,000 will be completed." But *spudazein* in the sense of "obtain" is not documented, not to speak of the peculiar *ta loipa* (those that are still missing?) at the end. The first version probably said something like: "But I shall shortly complete 500,000". This was then weakened to say "But I shall further try to complete the 500,000 in a short time." A mix-up of the two versions then resulted in the illogical text: "But I shall further try in a short time so that 500,000 will be completed." [The English translation of this passage by Andrews (1913) is: ". . . and I shall make endeavor in the immediate future to gather together the remainder also, so that the total of five hundred thousand may be reached." Hadas (1951) translates: ". . . and in a short while, I shall exert every effort for the remainder, to round out the number of half a million."]

18) Two versions of the text have been transmitted side by side. In section 11 Pseudo-Aristeas claims that the king immediately wrote to Eleazar. Then (Section 12-27) he reports that he had submitted a petition to the king regarding the release of Jewish prisoners of war. Thereupon (Section 28 ff.) he tells us that the king had ordered Demetrios to submit a petition on the translation of the Thora, according to his oral recommendation, and following the correct Ptolemaic administrative procedure, as Pseudo-Aristeas remarks. Demetrios had done so—Pseudo-Aristeas even reports the text of

the petition (Section 29-32) — and the king had then written to Eleazar, as petitioned by Demetrios, and had asked him to send to Alexandria seventy-two scholars who knew Greek in order to ascertain the writing of the Thora and to translate it.

19) Schmidt (1922) p. 11 f., T. 27 a-d and p. 4 f., T. 2 b. The information of the Byzantine historian Georgios Synkellos (not cited by Schmidt) in his *Chronographia* 273 B, namely that Ptolemaios II Philadelphos had founded the Alexandrian library in the 132nd Olympiad (252/248 B.C.) and that he had died thereafter, is based on an unexplained error. See Sitzler (1917) column 1089.

20) Epiphanios, *Peri metrōn kai stathmōn* 166 B = Schmidt (1922) p. 11, T. 27 b. Epiphanios goes beyond Pseudo-Aristeas in some details. Thus, he claims that Ptolemaios had written to all kings and governments and had asked them to send him works of their poets and writers. He reports further that Ptolemaios wrote twice to Eleazar, first regarding the text, then regarding the translation of the Thora.

21) On the library in the Serapeion see Wendel-Göber (1955) p. 68 and Pfeiffer (1968) pp. 101-102. This library had already been mentioned by Tertullian (2nd century A.D.); see Schmidt (1922) p. 12, T. 27 d.

22) Schmidt (1922) p. 32; also p. 15 (T. 36 and T. 38). The term often used today, "Library of the Museion", is documented only once, in the second *Bios* of Apollonios Rhodios. But it is likely that the library was situated in that part of the Brucheion which was known as the Museion (in the larger sense), as briefly described by Strabo XVII 793; this because Athenaios V 203 c says regarding the foundation of the library of Ptolemaios II Philadelphos that the books had been "assembled" in the Museion.

23) On Demetrios of Phaleron see the monograph by Bayer (1942); also Wilamowitz (1924) vol. 1, pp. 22 and 165, and Pfeiffer (1968) pp. 96 and 99-104.

24) Bayer (1942) p. 99; Pfeiffer (1968) p. 96, note 3. On the "friends" of the king in general, see Habicht (1958).

25) Diogenes Laertios V 75-85.

26) Diogenes Laertios V 58.

27) Contrary to all other authors who report the story of the origin of the Septuagint, Irenaeus and after him among others Eusebios indicate not the second but the first Ptolemaios as the king who founded the great Alexandrian library and had the Thora translated into Greek. See Irenaeus, *Adversus haereses* III 21, 2 and Eusebios *Historia ecclesiastica* V 8, 11, both cited in Schmidt (1922) p. 11, T. 27 a, but not printed. Pfeiffer (1968) p. 98 attaches a decisive importance to this passage; I doubt whether Irenaeus had any information on the strength of which he could correct the commonly held opinion. I think he only assumed that the king mentioned in

the Letter of Aristeas was Ptolemaios I. This was a mistake: the Letter of Aristeas refers to Ptolemaios II. The fact that Ptolemaios I was indeed the founder of the library is a different matter.

28) According to Galen, literary forgeries started to appear only when the rulers of Pergamon began to compete with the kings of Egypt regarding the acquisition of old books, that is, around ca. 200 B.C. See Schmidt (1922) p. 13, T. 29 and 30.

29) Wilamowitz (1924) vol. 1, pp. 22 and 165, also Pfeiffer (1968) p. 99.

30) On Zenodotos see Pfeiffer (1968) pp. 105-122. Nickau (1972) especially pp. 24-27.

31) Suidas (1928) vol. 2, p. 506, Zeta 74:

> Ζηνόδοτος, Ἐφέσιος, ἐποποιὸς καὶ γραμματικός, μα-
> θητὴς Φιλητᾶ, ἐπὶ Πτολεμαίου γεγονὼς τοῦ πρώτου, ὃς καὶ
> πρῶτος τῶν Ὁμήρου διορθωτὴς ἐγένετο καὶ τῶν ἐν Ἀλεξαν-
> δρείᾳ βιβλιοθηκῶν προῦστη καὶ τοὺς παῖδας Πτολεμαίου ἐπαί-
> δευσεν.

The only noun to which *prōtos* (the first) relates is *diorthōtēs* (corrector). This has also been observed by Nickau (1972), column 26. There are also other passages indicating that Zenodotos was the first corrector of Homer. On the use of the plural *bibliothēkai* for one library see above, note 11. It should not be concluded from this, as Nickau (1972) column 27 does, that already at that time two libraries existed in Alexandria.

32) It is of course not impossible that he was appointed only when his former pupil had come to power and had banished Demetrios (283 B.C.). If so, there would have been a gap between the end of his career as a teacher and his appointment as director of the library. I therefore prefer to assume that he became the director of the library immediately after his teaching career. This assumption is supported by the *Suda* which says that he had lived under Ptolemaios I. I think that the Byzantine lexicon lists the stages in Zenodotos's career in inverse order: first he was the teacher of the children of Ptolemaios I, then he became — still under the same ruler — director of the library, and finally he devoted himself on the order of Ptolemaios II to the correction of Homer.

33) This is the title of Eratosthenes in Tzetzes; see below, note 74. The Byzantine scholar sometimes also calls the library a *bibliophylakon* (book storage chamber).

34) On the *procuratores bibliothecarum* see Ihm (1893) pp. 522-524; Wendel-Göber (1955) p. 143 f. The first curator of the University of Göttingen (founded in 1737), the Hannoverian minister Gerlach Adolf Freiherr von Münchhausen still reserved for himself the privilege to decide on the

117

acquisition of books for the library of the university; see *Handbuch der Bibliothekswissenschaft*, 2. Aufl. v. 3, 2 (Wiesbaden, 1957) p. 119.

35) Bayer (1942) p. 94-98.

36) The other scholars who, according to Tzetzes, were engaged in acquiring books in addition to Demetrios were presumably such "friends".

37) Callimachus (1949), fragment 6; 7; 5.

38) On the writings about magic ascribed to Zoroaster see Wendel-Göber (1955) p. 71; Wehrli (1967) Heft 7, p. 83 and Wehrli (1974) fragment 2-4 with commentary; on books about fishing see Schmidt (1922) p. 62.

39) The remark of an ancient biographer that Apollonius Rhodios (or rather, the second version of his epic *Argonautika*, the first version of which had been sharply criticized by Kallimachos) had been found worthy to be included in the Alexandrian library, should not lead to conclusions beyond the immediate context; see Pfeiffer (1968) p. 142. If Apollonios had not revised his epic, no doubt his first version would have been acquired by the library.

40) Galen, *Commentarius II in Hippocratis librum VII Epidemiarium* 239 (XVII 1, 606 Kühn) = Schmidt (1922) p. 12, T. 28. See Wendel-Göber (1955) p. 66 f.; see also there on the production of copies at the request of the Ptolemies, which implies the existence of a scriptorium, as reported by Gellius, VII 17, 5.

41) Callimachus (1949) fragment 438; Wehrli (1974) fragment 56.

42) Otto (1925) p. 129 f.

43) I wish to recall here only the translation which Charles V of France had made for his library in the Tour de Louvre; see *Handbuch der Bibliothekswissenschaft*, 2. Aufl. vol. 3, 1 (Wiesbaden, 1955), p. 463. But we should not speak about a translations department in the Alexandrian library, as Schneider (1967) vol. 1, p. 536 does.

44) A practical demonstration of this solidarity among the Greeks was the relief work for Rhodos which was destroyed by an earthquake in 227 B.C.; see Bengtson (1969) p. 453.

45) *Aristoteles pseudepigraphus* (1863) p. 559, no. 6 and 10; also Pickard-Cambridge (1968) p. 120 f.

46) The relevant passages can be found in Kaibel (1899) p. 19 f. (*Pb*), p. 24 f. (*Ma*) and p. 31 f. (*Mb*); they are also reprinted in Schmidt (1922) p. 9 f., T. 24 a-d. On the commentary to Aristophanes by Tzetzes and the preceding Prolegomena see Wendel (1948) column 1972-77; also Pfeiffer (1968) p. 100, note 1. However, Cantarella ascribes *Pb* to an older anonymous author, without regard to Wendel's arguments; see *Aristofane* (1953) vol. 1, p. 38. Schmidt (loc. cit.) reproduced also the relevant passage from the so-called *Scholium Plautinum*, a partly free, partly faulty translation of the longer

later version (*Mb*), written on the margin of a Plautus-codex by an Italian humanist in the 15th century. Most experts agree today that this translation (which was once much quoted, even after the Greek original had been discovered) has only little value; see Pfeiffer (1968) pp. 100-101, and here below, note 52. On Tzetzes's remarks see Schmidt (1922) pp. 33-42; Wendel-Göber (1955) pp. 65-69; Pfeiffer (1968) pp. 102-104.

47) After Kaibel (1899) p. 19 f.

48) Herter (1931) column 389; (1937) pp. 86-88; (1973) column 186.

49) References in Schmidt (1922) p. 16, T. 48-50 and 53, and p. 43; Wendel-Göber (1955) p. 82 f., who assume correctly that already Attalos I (241-197 B.C.) had begun to collect books.

50) Pfeiffer (1968) p. 102.

51) It seems that around 100 B.C., when Pseudo-Aristeas wrote, it was believed that the library in the Brucheion contained about 500,000 scrolls. We may conclude this from Demetrios of Phaleron's reply (put into his mouth by Pseudo-Aristeas) that he would endeavor to complete within a short time the number of 500,000 scrolls.

52) The relevant passage has been much discussed, also in relation to Kallimachos. The *Pb* version says: *hōn tus pinakas hysteron Kallimachos apegrapsato* (whose lists were later compiled by Kallimachos), while the (*Mb*) version has: *hōs ho Kallimachos neaniskos hōn tēs aulēs hysterōs meta tēn anorthōsin tus pinakas autōn apegrapsato* (how Kallimachos, a young man at the court, after they [the works] had been corrected, compiled lists of the same). The passage in (*Mb*) is evidently corrupt. The author of the *Scholium Plautinum* translated it as follows: "*sicuti refert Callimachus aulicus regius bibliothecarius, qui etiam singulis voluminibus titulos inscripsit*" (as Kallimachos, the court librarian, reports, who also assigned titles to the individual scrolls). Dziatzko (1891), p. 350 assumed therefore that in the Greek text *istorei hos* should be read instead of *hysterōs* (as Kallimachos . . . reports, who . . .). This conjecture was considered to be valid until Pfeiffer (1968) p. 127 raised some justified doubts about it. Pfeiffer objected above all to the elimination of the adverb *hysterōs*, which is corroborated by *hysteron* in *Pb*. It also seems to me that the addition "a young man of the court" does not fit one who "reports" but rather one who "compiles". But above all I think it is inadmissable to rely on the author of the *Scholium Plautinum* who translated the not quite intelligible text freely and with his own explanations (on *sicuti: refert*, anticipating Dziatzko's conjecture; on *aulicus regius: bibliothecarius*, a conclusion drawn from Kallimachos's compilation of the *Pinakes*); sometimes he mistranslated: *singulis voluminibus titulos inscripsit*, because the manuscript which he translated had *epegrapsato* instead of *apegrapsato*, see Callimachus (1953) p. xcvii, T. 14a). The sentence in *Mb* was probably constructed like the one in *Pb*, i.e. it began with *hōn [tus pinakas]*. Because of a copying error that

he had either made or already found, namely *hōs* for *hōn*, a copyist inserted *autōn* after *tus pinakas*. The copying error is understandable, because *hōs ho deina* was a common form of citation, and Tzetzes had moved the noun *tus pinakas* which belong to *hōn* almost to the end of the sentence in its new version. The question mark put by Pfeiffer (loc. cit.) after *hōs* seems to indicate that he also surmised something like that. But Dziatzkos's conjecture must be rejected mainly because, as indicated above in the text, it is unlikely that the numbers reported by Tzetzes are based on Kallimachos. Rostagni (1914) p. 248 tried to support this hypothesis by an addition to the text of *Mb*, also found in the *Scholium Plautinum*, a sentence translated by the humanist as follows: *Fuit praeterea qui idem asseveret Eratosthenes non ita multo post eiusdem custos bibliothecae.* In *Mb* and similarly in *Pb* it says: *Eratosthenēs de ho helikiōtēs autu para tu basileōs to tosuton enepisteuthē bibliophylakion* (Eratosthenes, his contemporary, was appointed by the king as keeper of the library). According to Rostagni the passage ran originally as follows: *tauto martyrei Eratosthenēs ho helikiōtēs autu hos para tu basileōs . . .* (The same is witnessed by his contemporary Eratosthenes who was . . . by the king . . . etc.). Since there is nothing like it in *Pb*, this is probably an arbitrary addition by the humanist who failed to see a connection between this note and the previous one. But the notes of Tzetzes were connected only by their common subject, the Alexandrian library.

53) In order to arrive at about half a million scrolls one would have to assume that the 2,000 or so Greek authors wrote an average of ten works with twenty books each (or twenty works with ten books each), and that a copy of all these was held by the Alexandrian library; in addition, two further copies of about 5,000 works in ten books (or of 2,500 works in twenty books), thus altogether three copies.

54) Schubart (1960) pp. 52-59; Widmann (1967) column 560. A standard scroll contained about the text of Plato's *Symposium* (in the Loeb Classical Library edition: 82 pages of 30 lines, each 7.5 cm. long).

55) Also by Wendel-Göber (1955) p. 68 who write about "unmixed or single scrolls".

56) Wendel-Göber (1955) p. 68 f. The term "double" is not quite exact. What was meant were second and further copies of a work which were never altogether the same. Doubles in the strict sense of the word, i.e. copies of an exemplar, which are identical because they have been reproduced mechanically, exist only since the invention of printing, as has been stressed already by Haeberlin (1890) p. 8.

57) Plutarch, *Antonios* 58 = Schmidt (1922) p. 16, T. 51.

58) Birt (1882) pp. 177; 251; 321; Schubart (1960) pp. 16-18; Widmann (1967) column 572 f. The number of lines per scroll varied considerably. On the average there were 1,000 lines.

59) Manteuffel (1933), especially p. 369. Manteuffel estimates that 100 of 132 scrolls with philosophical works were written on both sides. One of the most important papyri found in recent times, the papyrus Bodmer with Menander's *Dyskolos*, is also written on both sides.

60) Haeberlin (1890) p. 16 f. already stressed that the interpretation of "unmixed" was an unassailable fact, and he doubted therefore the reliability of the traditional numerical data. But he too identified "unmixed" and "single". Following Parsons, de Vleeschauwer (1963) p. 65 thinks that the unmixed books were those that had already been inventoried, and that the mixed ones had not yet been inventoried. Earlier (1955) p. 25 he had assumed that the unmixed books referred to those works which had already undergone textual criticism.

61) The treatment of a "double", that is, a second copy of a work that had already been cataloged, was a purely technical task as seen from the point of view of a librarian but not from that of a philologist.

62) Ludwich (1884) pp. 3-6.

63) Pfeiffer (1968) pp. 116-118; Nickau (1972) column 38 f.

64) Schmidt (1922) p. 39 f.

65) Westermann (1845) p. 54. Aratos's purported *diorthōsis* of the *Odyssey* is also mentioned there; see also Pfeiffer (1968) p. 120, who assumes that the library whose director under Antiochos III (223-187 B.C.) was the poet Euphorion, existed already then in Antiochia at the court of the Seleucids; likewise Wendel-Göber (1955) p. 91 f.

66) According to Athenaios VII 278 a, Lykophron had said in his work on the Old Comedy that the epic by Archestratos (which was known under various titles) should be entitled *Gastrologia* similar to the *Astrologia* by Kleostratos of Tenedos; see Strecker (1884) p. 29.

67) On textual criticism by Zenodotos see Pfeiffer (1968) pp. 108-116; Nickau (1972) column 28-36; 43-45. Both mention, but do not stress, the difference between the omitted and the "obelized" verses reported several times in Scholia to Homer; Kroll (1909) already emphasized this difference. On the division of the *Iliad* and the *Odyssey* into 24 books (i.e. scrolls) ascribed to Zenodotos see Pfeiffer (1968) pp. 115-116; Nickau (1972) column 36.

68) Erbse (1961) p. 223 characterizes the issue precisely when he says: "Scientific philology developed from the discussion of their [the classical authors'] texts."

69) Latte (1925) pp. 154 and 162-171; Pfeiffer (1968) pp. 90-92, 146 f.; Nickau (1972) column 40-42. Nickau assumes that the *Glossai* and the

Ethnikai lexeis referred to the same work; this is indeed very likely because of the content of the quotations. In my opinion, the term *glossai* was used as a generic expression; the work was a list of dialect words. Nickau ascribes it to Zenodotos of Ephesos, the director of the Alexandrian library, but so far as we know he was not a collector of dialectal expressions. In support of his assumption Nickau, like others, cites a scholium on Homer which, however, does not seem to yield anything. In the *Odyssey* iii, 444 it says in the description of a sacrifice *Perseus d' amnion eiche* (Perseus held a bowl). The author of the scholium remarks that *amnion* is a vessel in which the blood of the sacrificial animal was collected, but that Zenodotos cites the word among the glosses beginning with the letter delta. The scholium is very much abridged. The omitted presupposition of the second sentence may have been: But Zenodotos (of Ephesos?) considered the letter sequence *damnion* as one unit and listed the word in his glosses under delta. Or it may have been: some scholars consider the letter sequence *damnion* to be one unit; the word *damnion* is listed in the glossary of Zenodotos (which one?) under delta. No matter who was the author of the glossary, the word *damnion* was there explained as a (dialectal?) expression for the sacrificial animal, according to that interpretation of the verse in the *Odyssey* which said that Perseus held a sacrificial animal; the same explanation is given in the lexicon by Hesychios of Alexandria, where the word appears in the plural. I cannot see any argument that would prove the authorship of Zenodotos of Ephesos.

70) Jacoby (1957) no. 472, fragment 8-11.

71) According to the *Suda* Aristophanes heard Zenodotos as a boy (*pais*), and Kallimachos as a youth (*veos*). Pfeiffer (1968) p. 171 and Nickau (1972) column 26 think that this was just about possible chronologically as far as Zenodotos is concerned. I do not wish to refute this, but I think nevertheless that this information is rather anecdotal. The Museion had the same rank as the Academy or the Peripatos. Its members did not give their pupils a high school education, as it were, but a higher education; their pupils were not boys but young men, such as Aristophanes, the pupil of Kallimachos. Aristoteles was about seventeen when he became Plato's pupil. An exception were the sons of princes who enjoyed an education by famous scholars. Alexander of Macedonia was about thirteen when Aristotle became his teacher at the age of forty-one.

72) Pasquali (1952) p. 214 f.

73) Pfeiffer (1968) pp. 153-154.

74) In the shortened later version of his report (*Ma*) Tzetzes claims also that the *bibliophylax* Eratosthenes collaborated in the task of correction with Zenodotos, Alexander and Lykophron. This might be a memory of the young Eratosthenes's sojourn in Alexandria.

4. Kallimachos and His Lists of Greek Authors and Their Works

4.1 The Life and Work of Kallimachos. His Work as a Librarian. His Scholarly Works (Except Lists of Authors)

ACCOUNTS of the life and work of Kallimachos are neither particularly extensive nor are they particularly sparse. Our main source is the article "Kallimachos" in the *Suda* which contains some biographical data and a selective bibliography of his works. The article is based on an epitome of the *Onomatologos* (Nomenclator), a lost bibliographic lexicon compiled from older reference books by Hesychios of Miletos in the 6th century A.D.[1] The abridgment of the *Onomatologos* affected also the article "Kallimachos". This explains some of its defects. Thus, we learn from it, for example, what was the name of Kallimachos's father-in-law, but we do not know what position he himself occupied at the court of the Ptolémies in Alexandria. Nevertheless, this article supplies interesting information not contained in any other source. The data of Hesychios which were incorporated in the *Suda* are corroborated and augmented only by some scattered notes of other ancient scholars. Kallimachos himself inserted into his extant works only a few personal remarks; the most important ones relate to the criticism to which his poetic works had been subjected.

The following is a translation of the article in the *Suda* (necessary or probable corrections suggested by earlier researchers are in brackets).[2]

> Kallimachos, son of Battos and Mesatma [Megatima], from Kyrene, grammarian, pupil of the grammarian Hermokrates of Iasos, married the daughter of Euphrates [Euphraios] of Syracuse. His sister's son was the younger Kallimachos who wrote about islands in verse. He was so zealous that he wrote poems in every meter and many books in prose. And he wrote more than eight hundred books. He lived in the time of Ptolemaios Philadelphos. Before he was introduced to the king, he was a teacher in an elementary school in Eleusis, a suburb of Alexandria. And he lived until the time of Ptolemaios Euergetes, the 127th [133rd] Olympiad, in the second year of which Ptolemaios Euergetes began his reign.[3]
>
> Among his books are the following: *The arrival of Io*; *Semele*; *The colony[?] of the Argonauts*; *Arcadia*; *Glaukos*; *Hopes*; satyr plays; tragedies; comedies; songs; *Ibis* (a poem on obscurity and slander against a certain Ibis, who had become the enemy of Kallimachos; that was Apollonios, the author of the *Argonautika*); *Museion*; *Lists of those who distinguished themselves in all branches of learning, and their writings*, in 120 books; *Table and register of playwrights, arranged chronologically*

from the beginning; A list of glosses and writings by
Demokrates [Demokritos]; *The names of months according*
to peoples and cities; Foundation of islands and
cities, and changes of their names; On the rivers of
Europe; On marvels and natural curiosities in the
Peloponnesos and in Italy; On changes of names [rather:
naming] *of fishes; On winds; On birds; On the rivers*
of the world; Collection of the marvels of the world
appearing in certain places.

According to this article, Kallimachos is classified as a grammarian (i.e. a
philologist) who wrote more than eight hundred works in verse and prose. The
selective bibliography lists, however, only a few poetic writings, in part even only the
kinds of such writings (which may have been headings of sections in the original)
and a few scholarly works;[4] none of his known poetic works is listed, except his
abusive poem against Apollonios Rhodios, *Ibis.* All other listed poems are
unknown. The first ones were perhaps parts of the famous *Aitia* (Causes), narrative
elegies on the mythical origin of worship rites and other customs. On the other
hand, the scholarly works of Kallimachos named in the list are sometimes also
mentioned by other authors. They begin with three *pinakes*: first, there are the
pinakes of Greek authors and their works.[5] The arrangement of the other titles is
mixed up. Among others there are collective titles and partial titles of two works,
and two partial titles of one work whose collective title is not mentioned, all of
which are separated from each other by other titles.

Only some of his poetic works have been preserved. Six hymns and 63
epigrams have come down to us in manuscripts from the 14th and 15th century.
Fragments of other poetic works by Kallimachos were found on papyri which were
discovered during the past decades in Egypt, among them fragments of his *Aitia.*
His scholarly works, however, which were used by several later authors are lost, and
we can only get a vague idea about some of them from quotations. The poems of
Kallimachos have often been dealt with, and they have been duly appreciated as
masterpieces of Alexandrian literature; for those, I therefore refer the reader to the
relevant literature. My investigation does not deal with the poet Kallimachos but
with his achievements as a scholar.[6]

The fame of Kallimachos as a poet is documented by many works; the Romans
also held him in high esteem. Kallimachos the scholar is relatively often quoted.[7]
Cicero once even put him on the same level as the most celebrated men of Greek
science: medicine is represented by Hippokrates, geometry by Euclid and
Archimedes, musical theory by Damon and Aristoxenos.[8] According to the *Suda*,
the lifetime of Kallimachos coincided nearly with that of his patron, king Ptolemaios
II Philadelphos (308-246 B.C.) under whose reign he lived. According to Gellius,
Kallimachos became a renowned poet at the court of that king shortly after the
outbreak of the first Punic War (264 B.C.), that is, he reached the highest point in
his career, his *akmē* (which is thought to have occurred in his fortieth year) around
263 B.C.[9] Accordingly, he was probably born in 303 B.C. Since he wrote a poem
that can be dated with certainty to the year 246/245 B.C., namely the elegy
Plokamos Berenikēs (The lock of Berenike [the wife of Ptolemaios III]),[10] he
outlived Ptolemaios II, but probably only by a few years. It is therefore true, as the
Suda says, that his lifetime extended into the era of Ptolemaios III.

He was born in Kyrene, an old Greek (Doric) colony situated not far from the coast in that part of Libya still named Cyrenaica after that city. The city was under the rule of Ptolemaios I since 322 B.C. Kallimachos came from a noble family; his grandfather, after whom he was named, had held the position of a *stratēgos* (army commander), as the poet says in an epitaph for the grave of his father.[11] The name of his father was Battos, the name of the founder and first king of Kyrene. According to Strabo, Kallimachos claimed to have been descended from that first Battos.[12] In an epitaph for his own grave he referred to himself as a Battiad,[13] and later poets, especially Roman ones, also called him by that name. The term is, however, ambiguous.[14] But no doubt the family of Kallimachos belonged to a group of Greeks who ruled over a north African region long before Alexander conquered Egypt. Kallimachos himself also lived always among Greeks. As far as he was concerned, Alexandria as well as Kyrene belonged to Hellas. Hellas was everywhere where Hellenic settlements and culture existed.[15] Even in Alexandria Kallimachos was not noticeably touched by Egyptian culture.

The *Suda* names as teacher of Kallimachos the grammarian Hermokrates of Iasos, of whom it is only known that he wrote about the theory of accents (prosody).[16] But the tradition that he studied in Rhodos together with Aratos under the Peripatetic Praxiphanes, whose ideas on literary esthetics he later attacked in a special work, is not trustworthy.[17] A sojourn of the young poet and scholar in Athens has also not been established. It seems that Kallimachos was largely self-educated. He was evidently an avid reader, like Aristotle, but he was also an attentive listener who, as he once said, lent his ear to those who wanted to tell a story.[18] Already in Kyrene there was much to read and to hear;[19] in Alexandria there was, of course, that much more.

We do not know when he moved to the capital. In an epigram he says that his hands "are empty of wealth."[20] His family was probably impoverished. In a suburb of Alexandria he worked, according to the *Suda*, as a teacher in an elementary school, until he was introduced to king Ptolemaios II Philadelphos, who was sole ruler since 283/282 B.C. The lexicon is silent about his further career. But in his notes on the beginnings of the Alexandrian library Tzetzes says that Kallimachos, a young man at the court, compiled the *pinakes* of the books acquired by the king. Accordingly, Kallimachos was called to the court of the king, who presumably liked the poems of the young teacher, around 280 B.C. There he worked in the library. In the course of time he certainly became a member of the Museion. At any rate, he stayed at the court until his death.

We may believe Tzetzes that Kallimachos began already as a young man to compile *pinakes* of the books acquired by the kings, that is, catalogs of the library in the Museion. But these were by no means a youthful work, as the Byzantine scholar seems to think: rather, they were the work of a lifetime, because the library was already at that time quite large and grew constantly. The *Pinakes* of Greek authors which evolved from the *pinakes* of the library and filled 120 books, according to the *Suda*, were therefore not of an even quality throughout, as the critical remarks of Dionysius of Halikarnassos show. But this was not because Kallimachos lacked help. Quite to the contrary: seven scholars, some of which were quite well known, are indicated as pupils of Kallimachos, and it is unlikely that all of them worked together with Kallimachos in the library.[21] This seems to me to be important. We do not know of so many pupils of any other

Alexandrian grammarians of the third and second century B.C., except for
Aristarchos of Samothrake, who was the director of the library under Ptolemaios VI
Philometor (180-145 B.C.).

According to Athenaios, Kallimachos once said that a big book is a big evil.[22]
Unfortunately we do not know in what context he made that remark. Perhaps he
did not speak as a librarian or generally as a scholar, and did not mean scrolls but
works, and not just any works, but only poetical ones.

Whether Kallimachos wrote his other scholarly works before or at the same
time as the *Pinakes*, or perhaps in part before and in part at the same time is
impossible to say. Some interpreters concluded from the last verse of the *Aitia* that
Kallimachos intended to devote himself in the future only to the compilation of the
pinakes; the verse is, however, ambiguous.[23] No doubt Kallimachos wrote poetry
until the end of his life. This is attested to not only by the *Lock of Berenike* but
also by the (afterwards inserted) prologue to *Aitia* in which he deplores the burden
of old age.[24] He has even been described as poet laureate,[25] because he wrote a
poem on the occasion of the marriage of Ptolemaios II with his sister Arsinoe
(276/275 B.C.), and dealt in another poem with the deification of the queen who
had died after only a few years (270 B.C.),[26] and of course also because of the *Lock
of Berenike*. It seems to me that this designation is inappropriate. Kallimachos was
honored by the Ptolemies, as Strabo says;[27] he enjoyed their patronage and
reciprocated with proofs of his devotion.

Whether he became the director of the royal library is in dispute. This question
has often been discussed.[28] But in my opinion, some important facts have been
neglected or have been misinterpreted. As indicated above, Zenodotos, the
literature teacher of the future Ptolemaios II, was appointed as director of the royal
library by Ptolemaios I after the end of his teaching career. Demetrios of Phaleron
continued, however, to devote himself to the development of the collection, which
was not the task of the *bibliophylax*, the Keeper of the library. After he had been
banished from the court by Ptolemaios II, the "friends" of the king acquired books
for the library. Zenodotos was probably relieved of his official duties when the king,
his former pupil, asked him to reconstruct, together with Alexandros Aitolos and
Lykophron, the text of the classical works with the aid of the copies available in the
library. The books were at that time probably already arranged by literary genres,
authors, and works. When Kallimachos now began to compile lists of those books,
he performed exactly the duty of a library director.[29] No one can say what he would
have had to do if somebody else had cataloged the collection. The scholars who are
named as his pupils also make it seem as if he had been the head of a school. But
such a position belonged only to the director of a library. All Alexandrian
grammarians of the third century and the first half of the second century B.C. who
are named as teachers of other grammarians, beginning with Zenodotos, of whom
three pupils are known,[30] were also directors of the royal library. But most modern
experts think that, according to the sources, Kallimachos had not been appointed to
the position of library director as Zenodotos's successor and as teacher of the crown
prince, the future Ptolemaios III Euergetes (born ca. 284 B.C.), because these two
positions were linked to each other. They assume either that Kallimachos himself
renounced the office of library director in order to avoid having to teach the crown
prince, or else, that the king himself found Kallimachos to be unfit for that task,
although he was otherwise favorably inclined towards him. Instead, the king

appointed one of his pupils, namely Apollonios, born ca. 300 B.C. in Alexandria, who was named the Rhodian after his adopted country, and who was the author of the *Argonautika*. When Apollonios had recited this epic for the first time, Kallimachos had criticized it sharply. This led to a bitter dispute between them which spilled over from the literary to the personal domain, and was the cause for a defamatory poem (now lost but mentioned in the *Suda*) against his former pupil, entitled *Ibis* (after the dirty bird).[31] Apollonios ultimately relinquished his post or was forced to resign, and moved to Rhodos. Ptolemaios III Euergetes (246-222) appointed as his successor a younger compatriot of Kallimachos and queen Berenike, namely Eratosthenes of Kyrene, one of the greatest scholars of the third century. Kallimachos and Apollonios were, by the way, not the only members of the court who quarreled with each other; it was notorious that not everything in the Museion was sweet harmony.[32] But the quarrel between the two famous poets has always been of particular interest to scholars. However, in the framework of the present investigation we are concerned only to find out whether Kallimachos cataloged the library in his capacity as its director or whether he merely participated in this work as "one of the scientific assistants under the direction of Apollonios" as Schmidt presumes.[33]

Neither the article in the *Suda* nor any other source indicates that Kallimachos was the director of the library and the teacher of the crown prince,[34] but that does not mean very much, because the information on his career is incomplete. In the article of the *Suda* on Eratosthenes there is no hint either that he was director of the library; we know that only from the article on Apollonios and from the notes of Tzetzes on the beginnings of the library.[35] Apollonios does not appear in those notes at all. His two *bioi* which have come down to us together with his *Argonautika* do not indicate either that he was director of the library and teacher of the crown prince. The first one says[36] that he was born in Alexandria, lived under the Ptolemies (which is certainly corrupted),[37] was a pupil of Kallimachos (the second *bios* says "of the grammarian Kallimachos") and lived first with his teacher.[38] It should be noted that Apollonios also wrote scholarly works: he wrote against Zenodotos (because of his version of the text of Homer) on Hesiod (defending the authenticity of the *Aspis*) and on Archilochos.[39] The author of the first *bios* then continues:[40] Apollonios had begun to write poems only at a late time, but others had claimed that he had recited his *Argonautika* when he was still an ephebe but had not been successful. Because of this humiliation and the criticism by other poets he had left his home town Alexandria and had moved to Rhodos. There he had rewritten his epic, had become famous and honored as a teacher and had even been made a citizen. The author of the second *bios* adds that some people say that Apollonios had returned to Alexandria, and that he had recited his *Argonautika* there with great success, had been found worthy of the library of the Museion, and had finally been buried alongside Kallimachos. In the past, these words were interpreted to mean that Apollonios had been appointed as director of the Alexandrian library after his return from Rhodos. Only Pfeiffer recognized that the expression "he had been found worthy of the library of the Museion" referred to Apollonios as an author, and did not mean more than that his *Argonautika* had been found worthy of inclusion in the library, as shown by parallel cases.[41] But this statement was probably misunderstood already in Antiquity. It is also unhistorical, because the Ptolemies sought to include in their collection all books written in Greek, including cookbooks, and did not make any selection.

The whole story of Apollonios's return to Alexandria is implausible, as Herter and others have stressed.[42]

The brief article "Apollonios" in the *Suda* mentions, however, his library post:[43]

Apollonios of Alexandria, epic poet, dwelt in Rhodos,
was the son of Silleus, pupil of Kallimachos, contemporary
of Eratosthenes, Euphorion and Timarchos, lived under
Ptolemaios Euergetes, and became the successor of
Eratosthenes as director of the Alexandrian library.

The lifetime of Apollonios Rhodios is here indicated in the traditional manner, first, by the synchronism with Eratosthenes and the poet and scholar Euphorion, whose birth occurred, according to the relevant articles in the *Suda*, during the 126th Olympiad (276/272 B.C.)[44] (it is not known who was Timarchos);[45] secondly, by the *akmē* under Ptolemaios III, who ruled from 246-222 B.C. For a contemporaneity in the narrower sense one would assume that Apollonios Rhodios was also born during the 126th Olympiad, and that was probably indeed the intention of Hesychios or the authority on whom he relied. If so, the learned poet would have reached his *akmē* about ten years after the beginning of Ptolemaios III's reign.[46] These data are compatible with each other, but they yield only approximate dates.

The article says in the beginning that Apollonios, who was born in Alexandria, dwelt in Rhodos, that is, he lived there after he left Alexandria. The last sentence presupposes, however, his return to Alexandria because it says that he became the successor of Eratosthenes as director of the library. According to the *Suda*, Eratosthenes had been called to Alexandria by Ptolemaios III (after 246). We do not know how long he held the office of library director; he reached the age of eighty. But it is unlikely that he was succeeded by a man his own age.

An explanation of this peculiar statement comes from a papyrus fragment from the first half of the second century B.C., found in Oxyrhynchos, which contains, among other things, a list of directors of the great Alexandrian library.[47] In order to evaluate and reconstruct this important document, it is necessary to know certain facts. The fragment consists of six columns: the first one is destroyed, except for a few remnants; the second, third, fourth, and fifth are for the most part well preserved (each has 36 lines with an average of 22 letters); of the sixth only about half still exists. The text of the fragment was part of an anthology compiled in the first century B.C. or A.D., a collection of all kinds of interesting facts in the form of lists or abstracts. In column one, lines 1-5, some famous sculptors and painters are listed (only the ends of lines have been preserved). On a scrap of papyrus which apparently belongs to the same column (according to Hunt, one of the editors, it contained lines 14-17, but there too only the ends of the lines remain) one can read *grammati[koi]* and *[Phila]delphu*. That is all that remains of this column. It certainly contained a new section dealing with famous grammarians, but apparently only the Alexandrian ones which were indeed the oldest (except for their precursor Praxiphanes). Since the most important among them were also directors of the Alexandrian library, I presume that the list stated first and foremost that it had been founded by Ptolemaios II Philadelphos (with the help of Demetrios of Phaleron?). The column had enough space for this. Furthermore, the grammarians who had been entrusted with the administration of the royal book collection were listed with annotations, certainly first Zenodotos, then perhaps Kallimachos, but none of this has been preserved.[48] Our text starts only in column two, lines 1-21:[49]

> [Apollo]nios, son of Silleus, of Alexandria, named the Rhodian,
> pupil of Kallimachos. He was also the teacher of the first king.
> He was succeeded by Erathosthenes. Thereafter, [came] Aristophanes,
> son of Apelles, of Byzantium, and Aristarchos, then Apollonios of
> Alexandria, named the Eidographer, after him Aristarchos, son of
> Aristarchos who was from Samothrake. He was also the teacher of the
> children of Philopator. After him Kydas of the lance bearers. But
> under the ninth king flourished the grammarians Ammonios and
> Zeno[dotos] and Diokles and Apollodoros.

This is the end of that section. The next one deals with inventors in the field of warfare. The former section contains a regular list of successors in the office of library director, as Hunt already recognized.[50] It extends to an officer in the royal guard by the name of Kydas who apparently took over the office of Aristarchos when he, together with many other scholars, left Alexandria in 145 B.C. because they feared the ruthless Ptolemaios VIII.[51] It seems that the four last-named grammarians never became directors of the library.[52]

The list contains three obvious mistakes, besides mentioning Aristarchos two times, which is odd: 1. Apollonios Rhodios cannot have been the teacher of the first king; the editor therefore changed *prōtu* (first) to *tritu* (third), which was approved by all other researchers. Apollonios, who according to the *Suda* was about ten years younger than Ptolemaios III (born ca. 284 B.C.) became thus his teacher; therefore, he must have been born at least 15 years earlier, that is, ca. 300 B.C. 2. Aristarchos did not teach the children of Ptolemaios IV Philopator but, according to the *Suda*, those of Ptolemaios VI Philometor; Hunt corrected the papyrus also in this passage accordingly.[53] 3. Ammonios and Apollodoros — assuming that these are the famous pupils of Aristarchos, which can hardly be doubted — flourished not under the ninth but under the eighth Ptolemaios.

All researchers were surprised to find in the list besides Apollonios Rhodios a second Apollonios with the epithet *eidographos* (classifier). This man was until then only known from two remarks of ancient and Byzantine scholars who had said that he was a talented librarian and dealt with the classification of old lyric poems.[54] But it had not been known that he came from Alexandria and that he had been the director of the library.

The list also mentions Aristarchos both before the second Apollonios (only by his name) and after him (by his name and with other data). The original sequence of library directors is here evidently disrupted. The report can be interpreted in various ways. The most likely interpretation is, that Apollonios the Eidographer was originally listed before Aristophanes, but was first omitted from the exemplar from which the Oxyrhynchos papyrus was made, was then added in the margin and was finally inserted by the copyist of this papyrus who had already begun with the

130

Aristarchos entry, after its beginning (which was to be erased), i.e. after Aristophanes. The following reasons support his assumption: 1. In the article "Aristophanes Byzantios" in the *Suda* an Apollonios is mentioned as his predecessor.[55] 2. In the article "Apollonios Alexandreios" of the *Suda* he — apparently the later Rhodian — is listed as the successor of Eratosthenes and therefore also as predecessor of Aristophanes. 3. The most famous pupil of Aristophanes, Aristarchos of Samothrake, was most probably his immediate successor in the office of library director. But if this office was held by an Apollonios after Eratosthenes, and then by Aristophanes and Aristarchos, the Apollonios named in the *Suda* as successor of Eratosthenes cannot have been the Alexandrian scholar who emigrated to Rhodos, but his namesake who was also from Alexandria, Apollonios the Eidographer.[56] But it seems to me that there was not only a mix-up of two men born in the same city and bearing the same name, but that even parts of the articles dealing with the two homonymous persons were confounded. Such confusions of articles in the lexicon have already been found in several instances. They are generally not to be blamed on the editor of the lexicon nor on his authority Hesychios (or his epitomator) but they were caused by the reference works used by Hesychios, and are only seldom due to copyist's errors but rather to conjectures of scholars. The Hellenistic biographers and bibliographers had great difficulties distinguishing among the many bearers of the same name; sometimes, they made one person out of two homonymous ones, but the opposite also happened.[57]

In the case of the two men named Apollonios the following reasons support my conjecture: 1. The original article "Apollonios I" probably contained, like many other articles, at the end a summary of the works of that author who was an eminent scholar as well as a poet. But the extant article does not mention any of the works of Apollonios, not even his most famous one, the preserved epic on the Argonauts. The last sentence says instead that Apollonios became the successor in office (*diadochos*) of Eratosthenes, his purported contemporary, whereas in reality he was succeeded by Apollonios II (the Eidographer). This sentence, with the *diadochē* statement came therefore most likely from the article "Apollonios II". 2. In the *Suda* a statement about the *akmē* (So-and-so lived under . . .) generally precedes that of a *synchronismos* (So-and-so was a contemporary of . . .) which makes sense.[58] In the "Apollonios" article it is the other way around: the *akmē* follows the *synchronismos*. This is easiest to explain by the assumption that not only the last sentence (the statement of the *diadochē*) but also the last but one sentence (the *akmē* statement) came from the article "Apollonios II". The antepenultimate sentence, however, (the *synchronismos* statement) relates to Apollonios I, because a man the same age as Eratosthenes would hardly have become his successor. The seam between the two parts of the confounded Apollonios articles would therefore lie between the *synchronismos* and the *akmē*. But there was probably also an *akmē* statement in the "Apollonios I" article — before the *synchronismos* statement — namely the same as the one in the "Apollonios II" article. Although the second Apollonios was somewhat younger than the first one, the two namesakes from Alexandria could nevertheless have had their *akmē* in the same era, under Ptolemaios III Euergetes, say, the first ca. 235 and the second ca. 225 B.C. I think that this is the reason why they were, according to a particular biographic tradition, erroneously thought to be the same person. When the two Apollonios articles were confounded, the first *akmē* statement before the *synchronismos* was omitted and the last two sentences in the article "Apollonios II" were substituted for the list of works.[59]

Thus, according to the papyrus, Apollonios was born ca. 300 B.C., i.e. soon after Kallimachos, but according to the *Suda* he was born ca. 275 B.C. Here we have two opposing statements.[60] The question is, which one is more reliable? The answer will decide not only how to reconstruct the career of Apollonios but also that of Kallimachos. The list in the papyrus is said to be based on a reliable tradition,[61] and this is certainly true for most of the entries—we must here disregard the mistakes of the copyists—but we are by no means forced to accept everything in it. The data in the *Suda* which are summarily dismissed by some are generally also based on sound tradition; this is evident from the data in the article "Kallimachos". The currently accepted opinion, according to which Apollonios was almost the same age as Kallimachos, is supported solely by the remark in the papyrus "he was also the teacher of the first [rather: the third] king". But is this remark so reliable that we should dismiss the chronological data in the *Suda* which are doubly corroborated by the *synchronismos* and the *akmē*, according to which Apollonios was at best of the same age as the future Ptolemaios III? Apollonios was not at all the teacher of the third king, but possibly the teacher of the son of the second king. A later passage in the list says: "Aristarchos was the teacher of Philopator's children" [rather: Philometor's]. This is correct. Should now the text for Apollonios be amended accordingly, or is that only an incorrect wording?[62] It seems to me that a third explanation is more likely. Towards the end of the third century, when the second Apollonios was very likely in charge of the Alexandrian library, a boy was king, namely Ptolemaios V Epiphanes, born 210 B.C., who reigned from 204-180 B.C. The library director who educated him was indeed the teacher of a king, namely the fifth one. One cannot dismiss the suspicion that the source of the papyrus had instead of *prōtu* (first) not *tritu* (third), as Hunt thought, but *pemptu* (fifth). Thus, Apollonios Rhodios may have owed his title as teacher of a king to his namesake, the Eidographer.[63] Under these circumstances I think that one must rely on the data of the *Suda*.

Although it is therefore likely that Apollonios Rhodios taught the future Ptolemaios III, who was the same age, he may still have been the director of the Alexandrian library before Eratosthenes, as indicated in the papyrus.[64] According to the prevalent opinion, there would then indeed be no room in the list of Alexandrian library directors for Kallimachos because, according to Tzetzes, Aristarchos was the fourth or fifth (not the fifth or sixth) director after Zenodotos.[65] The Byzantine scholar refers, however, in those passages no doubt not to the library directors but to the textual critics of Homer's epics. In his opinion, Zenodotos was the first corrector of Homer, Aristarchos the fourth or fifth. He does not say who were the others. Among those, there were presumably also scholars from places other than Alexandria, for example, Aratos or the Cretan Rhianos.[66]

It is therefore entirely possible that Kallimachos was mentioned in the list of Alexandrian library directors before the first Apollonios.[67] The designation of the Rhodian as a pupil of Kallimachos would even indicate that he had been named in the list,[68] because if a grammarian followed his teacher immediately in the office of library director, this was a special case of *diadochē* (succession) which may perhaps have been unique in the third century.[69] This does not prove, of course, that Apollonios was indeed the successor of Kallimachos.

The researchers who determined the birthdate of Apollonios at ca. 300 B.C. had to explain why he was preferred over his teacher Kallimachos when Zenodotos had to be relieved as library director. They always presupposed that the office of library director was linked to that of the teacher, or more precisely, the literature teacher of the crown prince. But if Apollonios was born only in ca. 280 B.C. or even later, he was not a competitor of Kallimachos. It is therefore quite possible that he taught literature to the crown prince; after all, he had once been a school teacher. But he did not have to teach in order to become, or to remain library director, because it is very doubtful whether the two offices were then indeed linked to each other, as is always claimed.[70] When Philitas taught the future Ptolemaios II there was presumably as yet no library to speak of in the Brucheion. But his successor Zenodotos was probably entrusted with the administration of the royal book collection only after he had finished his career as a teacher ca. 291 B.C. We do not know when he was relieved of his office as *bibliophylax,* in order to devote himself to textual criticism of Homeric and other poems. Assuming even that the crown prince had at that time already needed a literature teacher, it is not evident that a scholar was then expected to deal both with the cataloging of innumerable scrolls and with the literary education of a royal prince. Ptolemaios II was also not bound to appoint the library director as teacher of his son, or to make the teacher a library director, much less did he need to fill the two offices with a man who was able to carry out both tasks, just because his father had appointed the scholar who had been his own teacher to the post of library director. No tradition existed as yet at that time which would have recommended to the king to link the two offices. Was there such a tradition later on? There is no evidence that the library director Eratosthenes also taught the future Ptolemaios IV Philopator.[71] His successor Apollonios the Eidographer was perhaps the teacher of Ptolemaios V Epiphanes. It is not known whether his successor Aristophanes also held this office. It is only documented that Aristarchos as library director also taught the children of the fifth and sixth Ptolemaios.[72] It should therefore not be taken for granted that the office of library director was linked to that of the literature teacher of the crown prince.

There is thus no valid reason not to assume that Kallimachos, who performed the duties of a library director at least during the second quarter of the third century, was indeed appointed as director of the library. It is unlikely that Zenodotos, who had reached the midpoint of his life already in 295, when he became the teacher of the future Ptolemaios II, remained nominally the library director until the appointment of Eratosthenes (after 246 B.C.). His successor could only be Kallimachos, because Apollonios was born only ca. 275 B.C. It is possible that Apollonios relieved Kallimachos when he had become weary of his office, and that he served for a few years as library director until he quarreled with his former teacher and moved to Rhodos.[73] But it is not impossible that he was included in the list of the Alexandrian library directors only as a pupil of Kallimachos because he had been mistaken for the other Apollonios, the Eidographer. What happened to the facts in the process of being transmitted to us is no longer possible to reconstruct, but this is immaterial for our present investigation.

From the *Suda* and other works we know the titles of fifteen scholarly works by Kallimachos.[74] All of these are lost, but a few can be reconstructed in outline with the aid of later authors who had used them. Thus we may get an approximate idea of Kallimachos as a scholar.

Even in his poetic works it is sometimes possible to discern some scholarly character traits. The Alexandrian *poetae docti* sought to give artistic expression to subjects which had never or seldom been dealt with, as is well known. Kallimachos used his studies in the libraries also in order to collect material for his poetic production. Thus, he may have encountered some peculiar customs whose mythical origin he later retold in his *Aitia*. In one known case he said so expressly. After having told the story of Akontios of Keos and Kydippe of Naxos, the most famous part of the *Aitia*, he says that he found the subject in an old (and not fictitious) author by the name of Xenomedes who had written the history of Keos.[75] He then relates in broad outline the contents of Xenomedes's work. Among other things, one could read there that Keos has originally been called Hydrussa, and how it had acquired its later name, an information that interested Kallimachos very much, as we shall see. To us it seems peculiar that the poet wished to document, as it were, a harmless love story with a happy ending (a well-known family of Keos claimed to have been descended from Akontios and Kydippe), but that was quite in tune with his maxim, transmitted to us out of context: *amartyron uden aeidō* (I sing of nothing that has not been witnessed).[76]

We would assume that he did the same in his scholarly works and particularly in those, even if the 44 excerpts made by a certain Antigonos of Karystos from Kallimachos's collection of marvelous and unusual natural phenomena would not show this quite clearly. This collection is cited as *Eklogē tōn paradoxōn* (Selection of natural curiosities) and as *Thaumasia* (Marvelous things) by Stephanos of Byzantium. In the Kallimachos article of the *Suda* we find (a) *Thaumatōn tōn eis hapasan tēn gēn kata topus ontōn synagōgē* (Collection of the marvels of the world appearing in certain places) and (b) separated from the first by several other titles, a specific title *Peri tōn en Peloponnēsō kai Italia thaumasiōn kai paradoxōn* (On marvels and natural curiosities in the Peoloponnesos and in Italy).[77] In the list of works by Kallimachos at least a second work on the *thaumasia* and *paradoxa* was probably also named. We do not know whether Kallimachos published these writings as parts of one work, or whether they were combined to a larger unit at a later time. The cumbersome title given in the *Suda* was hardly the one assigned by Kallimachos.[78]

If we did not know the name and the position of the author we would have to conclude from the work alone that he had a very large collection of books at his disposal. It is obvious that Kallimachos perused the relevant departments of the Alexandrian library, noted on sheets unusual local curiosities reported in the books (trees that grow in the sea, mice that live in springs, and the like) with an indication of the author's name, and then arranged those sheets geographically.[79] With the publication of his collection he started a long line of paradoxographers, whose works were very popular in Antiquity and in the Middle Ages. Two things are noteworthy: 1. Kallimachos did not list observations which he himself had made in nature, but only descriptions of curiosities which he had found in the literature. 2. He conscientiously listed the authors from whose works he had excerpted his notes. Among those were famous natural scientists such as Aristotle and Theophrastos, whose works are partially still extant, but most of these authors are merely names for us.

His collection was almost a documentation of curiosities with one restriction: he mentioned the titles of works from which he had taken his statements only in some exceptional cases, as for example when he indicated a certain Megasthenes as the author of *Indika*, and a certain Philon as the author of *Aithiopika*.[80] He never criticized the sources from which he took his material, nor did he try to discover the causes (*aitiai*) of the curiosities. He was not a scientist like Aristotle, but was he really a courtier with a penchant for oddities, a collector in the grand manner, driven by refined curiosity, as Howald and with him most later literary historians thought?[81] Körte-Händel hesitated, however, to agree with Howald; according to them, we are still uncertain about the nature of Kallimachos's scholarship.[82] I think that this is correct. But we can obtain a better insight only through a more detailed investigation of Kallimachos's scholarly endeavors, including his achievements in library-related and bibliographic fields.

The quotations from other works of Kallimachos are unfortunately far less numerous and extensive than those from his collection of curiosities. Not all works listed in the *Suda* are quoted by ancient or Byzantine authors, and conversely, not all quoted works appear in the incomplete bibliography transmitted to us by the *Suda*. The titles of works known to us are as follows:

Peri tōn en tē oikumenē potamōn (On the rivers of the world). As in the case of the collection of curiosities, the *Suda* lists in addition a part of this work which was also arranged geographically: *Peri tōn en Europē potamōn* (On the rivers of Europe). An author of a scholium cites another part: *Peri tōn kata tēn Asian potamōn* (On the rivers of Asia).[83]

Peri orneōn (On birds). This work in several books, frequently quoted by later scholars, was compiled from the works of Aristotle and other scientists and arranged by species.[84]

Peri agōnōn (On contests). *Nomina barbarika* (Customs of the barbarians). *Peri nymphōn* (On nymphs). On the subjects of these three works, which are not listed in the *Suda*, there were also works by earlier scholars. Hellanikos had already compiled *Nomina barbarika*, and so had Aristotle.[85]

Ktiseis nēsōn kai poleōn kai metonomasiai (Foundation of islands and cities and changes of their names.)[86] Kallimachos was very much interested in the subject of this work which is listed only in the *Suda*, and he dealt with it also in his poems whenever there was an opportunity.[87] Since changes in the names of places were often connected with their colonization, he dealt also with this issue. His predecessors, among whom was again Hellanikos, had done the same.[88]

Ethnikai onomasiai (Designations according to peoples) [i.e. the inhabitants of regions, islands and cities]). This collective title is cited by Athenaios. The *Suda* does not list it but mentions two titles which were apparently parts of this work: *Peri onomasias ichthyōn* (On the names of fishes), also cited by Athenaios, and *Mēnōn prosēgoriai kata ethnē kai poleis* (The names of months according to peoples and cities).[89] Perhaps *Peri anēmon* (On winds) was also part of this work.[90] The *Ethnikai onomasiai* listed dialectal names of fishes, months and winds. Thus, Kallimachos was interested not only in the various names that a place had had in the course of time, but also in different designations for the same concept which were in use in the Greek language community. He probably took the dialectal terms mainly from the lists of glosses compiled by scholars such as Philitas and Simias (and perhaps also Zenodotos). But his work was apparently the first *onomastikon* (vocabulary) arranged by subject groups.[91]

We may assume that Kallimachos used in all the works mentioned here the material collected by his predecessors and that he added notes which he had made while reading the works.[92] But it is not impossible that he also used oral information in his works on changes in place names and dialectal names of fishes, etc.

In addition to these works, ancient and Byzantine scholars mention four times the *hypomnēmata* of Kallimachos, which are not listed in the *Suda*.[93] Modern researchers are unsure about the character of these *hypomnēmata*. But there is no reason to assume that they were different from the *hypomnēmata* bequeathed by Aristotle to Theophrastos and continued by the latter, so that it was later not known whether they should be ascribed to him or to his teacher. These were collections of notes, excerpts, sketches and the like.[94] The lexicon of Harpokration (2nd century A.D.) has an entry for *Akē* which says that Kallimachos had explained in his *hypomnēmata* that this was the city now named Ptolemais.[95] This note was probably found in Kallimachos's work on the foundation of islands and cities and the changes of their names. The indication of this work as a *hypomnēma* is not dubious, rather the opposite. The work on marvelous and unusual natural curiosities partially reported by Antigonos was certainly a *hypomnēma* in the same sense then used, because it contained nothing but excerpts from various authors. His work on birds, of which we have a somewhat more precise idea than of his other scholarly works thanks to some quotations, was also based on excerpts from Aristotle and other natural scientists. It is likely that all of Kallimachos's works listed above were thought to be *hypomnēmata* because they only presented the material that he had found in the library, sometimes with an indication of authors,[96] but in an unpretentious literary form, and they displayed neither a scientific conception nor did they establish a theory. Incidentally, Istros and Philostephanos, who were pupils of Kallimachos, also compiled *hypomnēmata*.[97]

Nevertheless, Kallimachos was not just a collector, much less was he a hunter of curiosities. It was not enough just to collect, to find and note down interesting information from the literature. The notes had to be filed according to their purpose and had to be arranged by some rational principles. This was not so easy, especially since Kallimachos certainly took notes for several different collections while perusing the literature. Evidently, he knew not only how to collect but also how to classify scientific material. Even if he had not compiled the *Pinakes* of Greek authors, we could imagine him only as a scholar surrounded by many boxes full of sheets with notes.[98] Since then, there have been innumerable scholars of this kind. Among the ancient ones, the best known is Plinius. The author of the *Naturalis historia* excerpted, as he assures us in his foreword, more than 2,000 scrolls, and he began his work with long lists of the Latin and Greek authors on which he had relied for each chapter, among whom was also our Kallimachos and a physician by the same name from the second century B.C.[99]

What was the purpose of Kallimachos's collections? Philitas and Simias probably intended their glossaries as aids for the explanation of old poetic works, perhaps also as a mine of information for new poets. Was this also the intention of Kallimachos? The ancient commentators on the *Birds* of Aristophanes relied on Kallimachos's work on birds when they did not know which birds had been meant by Aristophanes. Kallimachos had indeed written about some but not all birds mentioned in the comedy.[100] It was thus not his intention to explain the relevant passages in the *Birds*. On the other hand, his collections went much further than necessary for the explanation of old poets and for the creation of new poetic works. Since Kallimachos collected material from many fields and certainly compiled also collections other than those of which we know by chance, we may presume that he as director of the royal library intended to compile the knowledge on diverse subjects contained in the books, first of all those in which he himself was most interested, and to present it to the world of scholarship in an orderly fashion. Thus, his *hypomnēmata* are different from those seemingly similar writings of other scholars. Because of their strict adherence to the literature they are to be considered as attempts by a librarian to utilize the collection of books in his care, and to exploit its riches through compilations. Thus, his compendium on birds may have had a purpose that was not the same but similar to that of a modern librarian who compiles a special catalog of the ornithological literature in his library.

It will be easier to understand the main work of Kallimachos, the compilation of the *Pinakes* of Greek authors, if we conclude from his *hypomnēmata* that he was capable to peruse and utilize large masses of literature, and that he has mastered the techniques of collection and classification of scientific material which had been developed by Aristotle and Theophrastos.

The pamphlet of Kallimachos against Praxiphanes which was substantially different from his other scholarly works—he probably attacked the literary and esthetic views of the Peripatetic—need not be considered in this context.

4.2 His List of Attic Playwrights

Among the scholarly works of Kallimachos his lists of literature (*pinakes*) are of special importance. The *Suda* article lists three of them sequentially: 1. The list of all Greek authors and their works, often cited as "the" *Pinakes* of Kallimachos; 2. a list of (Attic) playwrights; and 3. a list of glosses and writings of Demokritos. Postponing for the time being a discussion of the first one, I shall now deal with the second and third list.

The title of the second list, which was probably not formulated by Kallimachos, or at least not in that form, is recorded in the *Suda* as *Pinax kai anagraphē tōn kata chronus kai ap' archēs genomenōn didaskalōn*. (Table and register of playwrights, arranged chronologically from the beginning [viz. of the performances].)[101] Only a single Greek scholar, a philologist of the 6th century A.D., mentions this list in a passage that has survived by chance: Choiroboskos says that Aristophanes of Byzantium had used it when writing his *hypothēseis*.[102] But three fragments of a huge inscription from the first or second century A.D. which in all probability was based on a copy of Kallimachos's list have been found in Rome.[103] The inscription probably adorned the walls of a large public library, consisting of a Greek and Latin department, which held many works by Attic playwrights. At any rate, the inscription bespeaks a great admiration for these

137

poets and their extraordinary creativity. I presume that it was carved in stone under Hadrian. Kallimachos was highly regarded in Rome not only as a poet but also as a scholar and literary historian, as witnessed by Cicero who puts him on the same level as the most celebrated men of Greek scholarship.[104]

Even though the three fragments of the inscription are rather narrow, one can clearly recognize that in the part of the inscription to which they belong there was a list of Attic comedy writers with their plays that had been performed in Athens as the Dionysia and the Lenaea. The oldest performance mentioned in the fragments took place in 440 B.C., the latest one in 349 B.C. But I think it unlikely that the inscription listed only the writers of comedies, as most researchers assume, because it is impossible to understand what would have induced the owner of the building to omit the writers of tragedies which are included in all similar inscriptions.

Moretti investigated the whereabouts of the three fragments, and indicated also three others which probably belong to the same inscriptions; they are however, so small that one cannot deduce from them very much.[105] He also inquired into the seven fragments of a Greek, purportedly Rhodian, inscription, first published by Kaibel after notes by Filippo Buonarroti (1661-1733), because he assumed a connection between those fragments and the three others. He found out that Buonarroti had seen the stones in S. Paolo in Rome; although they were no longer there, Moretti found there an eighth fragment of the same inscription. It listed the victories which Greek actors had won in tragedies and satyr plays in Athens and Rhodos. The eight fragments pertain to victories in the first half of the fourth century B.C. According to Moretti, the inscription was made in Rome during the first or second century A.D., similar to the one which is based on Kallimachos's *pinax* of playwrights, which is however not mentioned by Moretti. He dates both inscriptions to the Augustean era, but does not preclude a later date. He thinks that it is certain that they belong together, and Snell shares his opinion.[106] But nothing seems to indicate that these are two parts of a larger entity. Although both inscriptions originated in the same place (Rome) and in the same period (1st or 2nd century A.D.), and have related contents, the differences between them, which were stressed by Moretti as well as by Snell, preclude the assumption that they were originally connected with each other. Contrary to the inscription on playwrights which was based on an interest in literary history, the list of actors owed its origin only to professional interests. Its originator was, as Moretti himself said, almost quite certainly the Roman theater guild, the local *synodos* of Dionysian *technites*, the artists who took part in theatrical and musical performances. At any rate, nothing can be gained from it for the reconstruction of Kallimachos's *Pinax tōn didaskalōn*. It shows, however, that the inscription of playwrights in Rome was not something unique.

Judging from the three fragments, the playwrights were listed chronologically according to their first performance.[107] Among their plays those that had won a first prize were named first, then those which had won the second prize, etc., and those that had been victorious at the Dionysia were listed before those that had won at the Lenaea. Plays in the same rank and kind of festival were arranged chronologically by years of performance according to the names of archons. A fictitious example may illustrate this scheme which looks somewhat odd to us. If a poet had scored the following:

Year B.C.	Festival	Rank	Play
384	Lenaea	2	A
383	Dionysia	3	B
382	Dionysia	2	C
381	Lenaea	1	D
380	Dionysia	1	E
379	Lenaea	1	F
378	Dionysia	2	G
377	Dionysia	1	H

then the entry read as follows:

...[name of poet] won in the City [i.e. at the City Dionysia] under ... [name of the archon in 380 B.C.] with the play E, under ... [377] with the play H; at the Lenaea under [381] with the play D, under ... [379] with the play F; he won second place in the City under ... [382] with the play C, under ...[378] with the play G; at the Lenaea under ... [384] with the play A; he won third place in the City under ... [383] with the play B.[108]

The chronology relevant to the arrangement of the authors was thus subordinated to the principle of contests: plays that had won a higher prize at the more important festival, the Dionysia, preceded the others. If a poet had never won any prize this was also noted. It was also listed which plays still existed: this was done by a note after the title, which took the following form in one of the fragments: *hautai monai sōi[ai]* (these only are preserved [i.e. the *Bakchai* by Lysippos]).[109] Not many of the older plays had been salvaged, but apparently most of the more recent ones still existed, so that only those were indicated which had been lost.[110]

Körte stated already in 1905 that the Roman inscription had probably been a reproduction of the text of the *Pinax tōn didaskalōn* of Kallimachos, and at that an unabridged one, because it listed long forgotten poets and plays that had long since been lost, both of which would certainly have been omitted in an excerpt from the list. He gave the following reasons for his assumption: the master copy for the inscription could have had the same title as Kallimachos's *Pinax kai anagraphē*, etc., because it listed the Attic playwrights who appeared in the course of time every since theatrical performances began, but it was hardly likely that a second scholar would have undertaken the same work; the author of the text could only have been an Alexandrian librarian because of the notes on the salvage or loss of certain plays. Since the Ptolemies sought to collect the entire Greek literature without regard to cost, the Alexandrian librarians could declare as lost all Attic plays of which the Ptolemies had not been able to secure a copy. I think that this was already permitted in Kallimachos's time;[111] later amendments were probably rather rare.[112]

The exemplar of the Roman inscription was based in turn on Aristotle's *Didaskaliai*, as already recognized by Körte. Its author had only rearranged that list, by putting the plays which had been performed in Athens at the Dionysia and the Lenaea under the names of their authors. This too points to the fact that the text of the inscription goes back to Kallimachos, because the archaic term used by him for the playwrights, namely *didaskalioi*, probably alludes to a connection between his *Pinax* and the *Didaskaliai*.

The experts agreed with Körte on all points mentioned here, and there is indeed nothing to object to.[113] But there were objections to his dating of the *Pinax* by Kallimachos. He had stated, without giving his own reasons, that Kallimachos had compiled the *Pinax* of Attic playwrights before his *Pinakes* of Greek authors, the former being a preliminary study for the latter. Other researchers were and still are of the opinion that the *Pinax* could only have been compiled after the catalogs of the royal library and the *Pinakes* based on those, because of the notes on the preservation of individual plays.[114] I shall revert to this question later on. The compilation of the *Pinax* is consistent with our image of Kallimachos as a scholar. Aristotle himself or one of his pupils had already compiled lists of the poets and actors who had won victories at the Dionysia and Lenaea, with the number of their victories in chronological sequence – in each case by the first victory; these lists had been based on Aristotle's *Didaskaliai*. The work undertaken by Kallimachos was similar but demanded a more detailed differentiation. It is not difficult to imagine how he proceeded when he perused the *Didaskaliai*, beginning with the tragedies performed at the Dionysia. When the name of a poet appeared for the first time, he probably wrote it on top of a sheet, then divided that sheet according to the number of prizes into three rows for the tragic poets, and into five rows for the comic poets; then, he listed the prize won by the poet, the festival and the archon under which the play had been performed, and the title of the drama. Thus, he noted, say, for the poet X that he had won second prize at the Dionysia under archon Y with the tragedy Z. If the poet appeared a second, third, etc. time, Kallimachos entered the data in the respective columns and rows. (Of course, he could also have arranged them chronologically or alphabetically by the first letter of the title.) He could not change the sequence of sheets, because it was the same as that in which the poets had appeared. He listed, of course, also repeat performances because those were generally for plays which had not met with approval, and were performed once more after having been revised by their authors. It seems also that he listed the names of directors who had staged plays instead of their authors. He did, however, not mention the principal actors.

When he had transferred the relevant data about the last performance of a comedy at the Lenaea mentioned in the *Didaskaliai*, the planned compilation of Attic playwrights and their dramas performed in Athens at the Dionysia and the Lenaea was virtually complete.[115] Kallimachos made only additional remarks for those poets who had never won the first, second or third prize (for comedies also the fourth and fifth), which indicates a conscientiousness bordering on pedantry. The additions by Kallimachos about the preservation of the plays must be distinguished from the list of Attic playwrights and their works, the *Pinax tōn didaskalōn* "proper", so I will not deal with them here as yet.

The *Pinax* "proper" owed its origin to the fact that Aristotle's *Didaskaliai* were cumbersome to use for most research. It was much more often asked which plays a certain author had produced in the course of time, than which plays had been performed at a particular festival by various poets.[116] The revision of Aristotle's list of performances of plays (the *Didaskaliai*) by Kallimachos resulted in a survey of the plays performed in Athens by individual poets (*didaskaloi*), the dates of their performances and the prizes that they had won. Of course, neither the extent nor the opening lines of plays were mentioned, because they were not listed in the *Didaskaliai*; Aristotle had not listed plays based on their manuscripts, but performances of plays, based on official records.

The primary arrangement of titles by the results of contests was consistent with tradition and the still lively general interest in contests of playwrights.[117] We moderns may be puzzled by this. But to the learned contemporaries of Kallimachos the list—which was indirectly based on the records of the responsible archons—may have been a valuable aid for studies in literary history, although or perhaps just because it emphasized the successful plays of the individual authors.

The experts knew, of course, also that neither the *Pinax* nor the *Didaskaliai* contained the entire production of the Attic playwrights, because Aristotle had not included plays, such as the *Andromachē* of Euripides, which had not been performed in Athens or had not been put on stage at all.[118]

When the plays in scrolls acquired for the Museion had to be identified and cataloged, Kallimachos's revision of Aristotle's *Didaskaliai* were certainly very useful. We must assume that the scrolls contained many texts with incorrect, incomplete or even missing data for author and title, or that they appeared in other scrolls under different names or titles. This is true also for the dramatic works, but for these it was often possible to find out the real author or the correct title with the aid of data in Aristotle's *Didaskaliai*. Ever since it became possible to find them also in Kallimachos's *Pinax* under the name of their authors, it was relatively easy to utilize those data. (It would, however, have been still easier if Kallimachos had arranged the titles not in chronological order by contests but alphabetically.) I presume therefore that the revision of Aristotle's *Didaskaliai* was the first assignment which Kallimachos carried out at the library. He probably undertook to do it as one of the tasks that the librarian and his assistants were expected to carry out.

But the remarks of Kallimachos regarding the preservation of individual plays presuppose that it was known which of the plays performed in Athens had already been collected in the library of the Museion. (As pointed out before, one could be reasonably sure that all plays not available in the library had been lost.) However, Kallimachos need not have made those remarks immediately when he compiled his *Pinax*; he could have added them later on, because they were indeed additions to the *Pinax tōn didaskalōn* "proper" which had been compiled from the data in Aristotle's *Didaskaliai*. An early compilation of Kallimachos's list seems to be indicated above all by the arrangement of the plays according to the contests which made it difficult to find a specific title. The scrolls in the library were, as we shall see, arranged first by authors of plays and then alphabetically by the titles of their plays, because it was easier to find them that way. After he had gained experience in the library, Kallimachos would hardly have thought to arrange his *Pinax tōn didaskalōn* in the manner described above. This is unlikely also for another reason. When the scrolls were cataloged it was found that the library possessed not only the *Andromachē* of Euripides but also other plays by Attic playwrights which Aristotle had not included because they had not been performed in Athens or even not at all. But it was impossible for Kallimachos to add the relevant titles to those listed by Aristotle because his *Pinax*, which was arranged by performances and results of contests, did not provide places for plays that had not been performed in Athens.

It therefore stands to reason that Kallimachos compiled his *Pinax* of Attic playwrights before his entirely different *Pinakes*, but that he noted in his own copy during the cataloging of scrolls which plays did or did not exist in the library as soon as it became clear what were the holdings of the library regarding a particular playwright and his plays that had been performed at Athens. This was practical, because the catalogs listed all acquired copies of works by Attic playwrights and could therefore not be used as easily for a quick survey. Thus, the Roman inscription may have reproduced the text of a copy made from Kallimachos's own private copy.

Now if Kallimachos's *Pinax* preceded his *Pinakes*, it was the oldest list of authors of a literary genre and their works. The arrangement of their titles according to the principle of contests still recalls the arrangement of authors and their plays in Aristotle's *Didaskaliai* according to their success in the dramatic contests, and the fact that Aristotle as well as his predecessors had still compiled lists of victors. The *Pinax* listed many more Attic plays than had been preserved; on the other hand, it omitted some of them, even some still extant works, nor did it contain data on opening lines or the extent of the plays. But even the older printed lists of authors and works are incomplete and lack data on the extent of works, and they are nevertheless called bibliographies; incidentally, they also cite not infrequently works and editions which are no longer extant. But Kallimachos showed in the compilation of the *Pinax* that he possessed the qualities that a librarian must have, namely the ability and willingness to create aids for scholarly work. This qualified him for a larger bibliographic task.

It should be mentioned that Kallimachos occasionally criticized Aristotle's *Didaskaliai*. In a scholium to Aristophanes's *Clouds*, verse 553, it is said that Kallimachos had objected to the fact that the *Didaskaliai* listed the comedy *Marikas* by Eupolis, one of Aristophanes's competitors, two years after the *Clouds*, although its was clear from that work that *Marikas* had been produced two years before the *Clouds*.[119] (In verse 553 the play by Eupolis is mentioned.) The author of the scholium adds, however, that Eratosthenes had declared Kallimachos's objection to be unfounded: the *Clouds* had indeed been produced before the *Marikas* (423 B.C.); the passage on which Kallimachos had relied had come from the second version of the play and had been written after the performance of *Marikas* (421 B.C.). According to this, Kallimachos had not noticed that the parabasis of the *Clouds*, in which Eupolis's play is mentioned, was not the original one, even though Aristophanes airs his disappointment over the failure of the premiere (423 B.C.) right at the beginning. This is odd, but one must consider that Kallimachos dealt with many more plays than we do. It is not known where Kallimachos criticized the *Didaskaliai*. Perhaps in a note to his article on Aristophanes in the *Pinax tōn didaskalōn*? Or in the preface to that list?

4.3 His List of the Works of Demokritos

The other specialized list compiled by Kallimachos according to the *Suda*, his *Pinax* of works by Demokritos,[120] is even more difficult to deal with than the *Pinax* of Attic playwrights and their works. The researcher is here confronted with a task not unlike that of an archeologist who wishes to reconstruct an ancient building on the strength of a brief literary hint and a few almost obliterated material traces. But researchers of Classical Antiquity are used to this kind of thing.

The *Pinax* is listed in the Byzantine lexicon as follows: *Pinax tōn Dēmokratus glōssōn kai syntagmatōn* (List of glosses and writings of Demokrates). The man with whom Kallimachos dealt so extensively must have been a famous author of many works. For this reason, all researchers agree that this could not have been a Demokrates (such as the Attic orator of Aphidnai who lived in the fourth century B.C.) but only Demokritos of Abdera, the main protagonist of ancient atomism (ca. 460-370 B.C.).[121] His name has been misspelled by so many copyists as Demokrates that a correction of the *Suda* text from *Dēmokratus* to *Dēmokritu* is unobjectionable.[122] Thus, the *Pinax* of Kallimachos would have been a bibliography of the philosopher, coupled with a glossary of Demokritos. This opinion was held especially by Diels-Kranz.[123]

But other researchers objected also to other parts of the title as given in the *Suda*, and recommended a rearrangement of the wording, without, however, changing the meaning.[124] Pfeiffer remarked that the *Pinax* was evidently a glossary but that its connection with a bibliography of Demokritos was strange. For this reason it seemed to him not quite evident that the word *syntagmata* in the title really meant "writings". He also took into account that Demokritos was a bold innovator of philosophical terminology who, although he wrote on Homer's glosses, did not use obsolete words himself.[125]

Pfeiffer himself did not make any suggestions for a change, but because of his reasons West proposed to write *gnōmōn* (maxims, epigrams) instead of *glōssōn*. He explained that Demokritos had once been famous for his maxims. Already in Hellenistic times a collection of authentic and spurious maxims of the Abderite had been compiled. The independently transmitted maxims ascribed to a certain Demokrates as well as those of Demokritos contained in the anthology by Ioannes Stobaios (5th century A.D.) were based on that collection.[126] Thus, Kallimachos had compiled a collection of Demokritos's maxims, perhaps the basic one. But so far as I can see, a collection of maxims, proverbs and the like were never called a *pinax*. A *pinax* of an author's works was a list of their titles, and what a *pinax* of his maxims was is impossible to say just by analogy.[127]

The reservations about the transmitted title of Kallimachos's list seem not to be convincing. Pfeiffer himself stresses that Kallimachos as a glossographer had predecessors (Philitas, Simias, perhaps also Zenodotos). But above all we must remember that he himself compiled dialectal terms at least for fishes and months. Just why he collected and explained glosses by Demokritos is, however, not quite clear. But it should be pointed out that the Peripatetics, who were remarkably well represented at the court of the Ptolemies by Demetrios of Phaleron and Straton of Lampsakos, had dealt extensively with the works of the Abderite. Aristotle and Theophrastos, as well as Herakleides Pontikos and apparently also

Straton had published works on or against Demokritos,[128] from which the glossographer Kallimachos could certainly have learned many things. Demetrios and Straton probably aroused the Alexandrians' interest in Demokritos, and saw to it that his works were acquired for the library of the Museion. Perhaps the library's rich holdings of works by the Abderite induced Kallimachos to deal with him more extensively. Although Demokritos had not used obsolete words, so far as this can be judged from the fragments of his works which have perished altogether (and Pfeiffer was indeed right on this point), glosses do occur not infrequently in his works, if the term is taken to mean, in the sense of Aristotle, all words not commonly in use.[129] A number of these were still included by Hesychios of Alexandria (5th-6th century A.D.)[130] in his lexicon. It is thus not improbable that Kallimachos compiled a glossary of Demokritos.

But regarding the designation of the Abderite's works as *syntagmata*, the composition of writings used to be called *syntattein*. Demokritos himself used that verb to indicate his activity as a writer.[131] The noun *syntagmata*, in the sense of "written works" is, however, not so common, compared with *syngrammata*. In one of the few passages in which it is used in this sense, it means just the written works of Demokritos.[132] It is possible that he himself designated his works in this manner.

At any rate, there can be no doubt that Kallimachos compiled a bibliography of Demokritos's works. Nor is it peculiar—even though there is no parallel—that a scholar who had both bibliographic and glossographic interests combined a glossary of an author with a list of his works. Might it not have seemed indispensable to a man whose correctness we have observed several times to list the writings of an author whose glosses he had compiled from those works?

The combination with the glossary also justified the separation of the Demokritos bibliography from those of all other Greek authors. Some researchers thought that the *Pinax* of Demokritos which is listed in the *Suda* as an independent work was actually a part of the general *Pinakes* of Kallimachos. But this is out of the question because of the glossary that it contains.[133] Rather, it is more likely that the *pinax* of Demokritos was written before the general *Pinakes*, because if the latter had already existed Kallimachos could have dispensed with adding to his glossary of Demokritos a bibliography of the philosopher's works.

The Demokritos bibliography of Kallimachos is not mentioned by any later scholar except by the editor of the *Suda*. Although Diogenes Laertios included in his chapter on Demokritos a bibliography, this had not been compiled by Kallimachos but (according to Diogenes) by a certain Thrasyllos, mentioned several times as a Platonic, who is perhaps the same as Emperor Tiberius's court astrologer.[134] But since Thrasyllos had in all probability used the Demokritos *pinax* by Kallimachos (as already Diels conjectured)[135] the bibliography reproduced (probably with abbreviations) by Diogenes deserves special attention. This list may have been part of the introductory essay which, according to Diogenes, Thrasyllos had written as a preparation for the reading of Demokritos, perhaps related to an edition of Demokritos that he had brought out.[136] In this edition, the scholar had described the life and work of Demokritos, and had listed his works, arranged in five classes, namely *ēthika, physika, mathēmatika, musika* and *technika* (sc. *syngrammata*), i.e. writings on ethics, natural science, mathematics (including astronomy and geography), music (including linguistics and literature), and on several "arts" (medicine, agriculture, painting, warfare).[137] He also combined four works each—after the example of the tetralogies of Plato's works, as Diogenes explains—to thirteen tetralogies.[138] (A work consisting of two or more books counted sometimes as one unit, sometimes as two.) This arrangement was intended to make the study of Demokritos easier, and it reflected the introductory nature of Thrasyllos's work.

In the appendix to the second class (*physika*) nine *asyntakta* (not combined works, that is, not combined into tetralogies) are listed, namely eight series of *Aitiai* (Causes), such as *Heavenly causes, Causes of seeds, plants, and fruits, Miscellaneous causes,*[139] and a work on magnets. After the last tetralogy, the thirteenth, Diogenes says, following Thrasyllos, that some also listed separately the following works from Demokritos's *hypomnēmata*.[140] These are nine works; the first has the title *Peri tōn en Babylōni hierōn grammatōn* (On the holy letters [writings?] in Babylon). In conclusion Diogenes states that the other writings which some ascribe to Demokritos were in part adapted from his works, in part (as generally acknowledged) not written by him.[141]

It is evident that Thrasyllos rearranged an older list of Demokritos's works by the principle of tetralogies. The separate listing of eight series of scientific *Aitiai* and the extra work on magnets does not indicate that he doubted their authenticity;[142] rather, he listed the *Aitiai* separately because of their form, since they were, strictly speaking, not "published" works (*syntagmata*), but were more like unpublished notes (*hypomnēmata*). Nevertheless, he included a series of medical *Aitiai* in the twelfth tetralogy because a fourth work was lacking there. For the same reason he included Demokritos's ethical *hypomnēmata* (unpublished notes on ethics) in the fourth place of the second tetralogy. The nine works listed by him after the thirteenth tetralogy which are said to have come from Demokritos's *hypomnēmata* he did not consider to be spurious. Works which were generally thought to be spurious he did not mention at all.

In the introduction to the appendix Diogenes (that is, Thrasyllos) explains that some people also listed such and such works. But because he speaks of "some" one should not conclude that he had at hand several different bibliographies of Demokritos's works. It was usual to say "some" even if there was only one predecessor, and Thrasyllos probably had only one, namely Kallimachos. He was certainly the first bibliographer of Demokritos, because if those works had already been listed by another scholar, say an Abderite, Kallimachos could have saved his efforts. Such a list, like the bibliographies of Aristotle and Theophrastos, could only be compiled at a place where it was thought that the complete works of the philosopher were available, that is, at that time only in Abdera and in Alexandria. Copies of all works by Demokritos which could still be obtained had certainly been acquired for the library of the Museion. It is even not unlikely that the Ptolemies had one day purchased the entire literary remains of the philosopher—as they had done with those of Aristotle and Theophrastos—in addition to the copies of his works which had been acquired earlier, because among the writings of the philosopher mentioned by Thrasyllus and probably already listed by Kallimachos were also *hypomnēmata* and similar notes (*aitiai* and *aporēmata*, i.e. problems) which had hardly been "published" by him.[143]

It is probably not an accident that we do not know of any Demokritos bibliographer between Kallimachos and Thrasyllos. After the publication of Kallimachos's list of Demokritos's works a scholar would have to have a special reason to compile a new bibliography of the philosopher. It seems that nobody had any cause to do this before Thrasyllos, who wanted to arrange the titles of Demokritos's works — and probably also the works themselves — by tetralogies for the reasons mentioned above. Thus, Andronikos also compiled a new *pinax* of Aristotle's works, when he thought that it would be useful to combine his acroamatic writings into larger units and to arrange them better than in the old Alexandrian *pinax*.

We may therefore assume that Thrasyllos started from the Demokritos bibliography of Kallimachos, but that this had been augmented in the course of time by titles of works which had probably not been written by Demokritos. It was usual in Hellenistic times and even later, to ascribe to the famous Abderite all manner of spurious writings, especially on magic and astrology. Thus, for example, works on magic written about 200 B.C. by a certain Bolos of Mendes, said to be a Demokritean, circulated under the name of Demokritos. Even though it is very difficult to judge the authenticity of works that are lost, many researchers think — contrary to Thrasyllos — that the nine works listed in his appendix were forgeries, and ascribe them to Bolos.[144] Some researchers also think that several of the works combined into tetralogies by Thrasyllos had been falsely attributed to Demokritos after the compilation of the *Pinax* by Kallimachos. But only the two last ones in the last tetralogy can be said to be spurious on good grounds: *Taktikon kai Hoplomachikon* (On tactics and On combat with heavy weapons). Their real author was probably that Damokritos who, according to the *Suda*, had published two books under the title *Taktikon*.[145] Most of the works in the tetralogies combined by Thrasyllos were certainly already listed by Kallimachos. But he may, of course, also have listed works not written by Demokritos; I shall return to this question later on.

We do not know how the Demokritos bibliography by Kallimachos was arranged. It is possible that Thrasyllos received the division of the Abderite's works into five classes from Kallimachos.[146] Schmidt pointed out that the titles of the second (ethical) and those of the third and fourth (scientific) tetralogy are alphabetically arranged.[147] I am, however, not sure whether the alphabetization of the few titles in the three tetralogies of the Demokritos bibliography was a purposive one; their sequence may have been determined by some special considerations of Thrasyllos or even by pure chance.

Kallimachos probably indicated in his Demokritos *pinax* the opening words of the listed works as well as their exact extent (i.e. not only the number of books but also the number of lines), as he also did in his general *Pinakes*. However, nothing of this remains, except for a few numbers of books.

It is noteworthy that among the 52 works combined into tetralogies at least nine (17.3%), probably even ten (19.2%) have so-called double titles, that is, two titles joined together by the word *ē* (or), e.g.

II 1: *Peri andragathias ē Peri aretēs* (On bravery, or On virtue [in the Greek sense, equivalent to prowess]);
III 1: *Peri diaphorēs goniēs ē Peri psausios kyklu kai sphairēs*

146

(On the difference of the angle, or On the touching of the circle and the sphere [according to Demokritos a sphere was an angle]);[148]
VIII 3: *Megas eniautos ē Astronomiē* (Great Year, or Astronomy);
XII 2: *Peri diaitēs ē Diaitētikon* (On diet [life-style], or Dietetics).[149]

Works by many other Greek authors, poets and prose writers, are also listed in ancient bibliographies and learned treatises with two titles linked by *ē* (or), some even with three or more.[150] What this means is in most cases not in doubt. The older works of Greek literature had no individual titles at all.[151] They were distinguished by their opening words, and one said "a work whose opening (*archē*) was so-and-so". For example, Diogenes Laertios cites the work by Pherekydes of Syros (6th century B.C.) on the origin of the gods in this manner.[152] Wise authors therefore used to give not only their own names but also the subject of their work in the first sentence; Thukydides still did that.[153] Only in the fifth century B.C., that is, at the time of Demokritos, Greek authors began to give individual titles to their works. The Attic playwrights did that no later than ca. 475 B.C. (Aischylos's *Persai* were performed in 472 B.C.) and probably even earlier, in order to distinguish the plays submitted to the archons from those of their competitors, and also in order to arouse the curiosity of the public to whom the performances were announced.[154] The sophists of the enlightenment in the fifth century who wrote for a broader public also published their works under distinctive titles, e.g. Protagoras in his *Alētheia* (Truth), the work that begins with the famous sentence "Man is the measure of all things".[155] Other authors soon followed the example of the playwrights and sophists, except authors of certain lyric works and those on oratory, for which individual titles could be found only with difficulty; such works were for a long time still cited by their opening words. The introduction of individual titles by the Greeks is rightly considered to be a significant innovation in the history of the book. But it had not only technical but also literary importance, because it forced authors to concentrate on the subject expressed by the title.

As can still be seen in some papyrus scrolls, the bibliographic entry (author and title) of a work was written after the text, on the inner end of a scroll where these data were best protected; sometimes they were also written in abbreviated form before the text.[156] These were known as *epigramma* or more often *epigraphē* (literally: inscription), but the author or title entry alone was also known by these terms. The verb *epigraphein* (entitle) was used accordingly. Works existing under a false name, those falsely ascribed to an author, were (and still are) called *pseudepigrapha*. The new custom was probably so widespread already in the fourth century B.C. that scholars and booksellers assigned titles on their own initiative to works which they encountered without any name.

This happened not only to older works whose authors had not given them a title because that was not yet customary at the time, but also to newer works who had already had a title but had lost it for some reason.[157] Of course, those who assigned a title to a work which lacked one based on its subject matter did not always arrive at the same results. This is true even for those scholars who had not only read the opening words of such a work, but even for those who had read it through.[158] It was therefore a common occurrence that copies of one and the same work circulated under different titles. Thus, for example, three titles are known for the work by Pherekydes on the origin of the gods, cited by Diogenes Laertios only by the opening words, and for the gastronomic epic of Archestratos (ca. 300 B.C.) no less than five titles are known.[159] If now a conscientious bibliographer found out that a certain text had different titles in the extant copies or was differently cited in the literature (provided always that the author was the same) he had to ascertain the correct title, that is, the one assigned by the author himself, if he had indeed given a title to his work. If he was unsuccessful, he had no choice but to list all titles one after the other, linked by the word *e*.[160]

Thus, the author of the list of Plutarch's works, the so-called Lamprias catalog, indicates four times, "but the title in another scroll is so-and-so".[161] A similar note is found in the list of Demokritos's works. At the end of the fourth tetralogy we read after the works *Peri nu* (On the mind) and *Peri aisthēsiōn* (On perception) that "some write these works as one and give it the title *Peri psychēs* (On the soul)".[162]

One of the different titles listed by a bibliographer for the same work may be the author's own, but not necessarily so; they may have been assigned by later scholars. Only in exceptional cases one may assume that all titles (generally no more than two) had been given by the author himself, namely when he had revised his work and had published it under a new title.[163]

At times it also happened that scholars, mostly pupils of the author, explained the short title given by the master by a second title, linked to the first one by *e*. This is the reason for the alternative title of Plato's dialogues, e.g. *Phaidon ē Peri psychēs* (Phaedon or On the soul).[164] Plato had named the dialogs only after Socrates's principal interlocutor, but the Academicians added the main subject of the dialog. Beginning at a time which has not yet been fixed, Greek authors themselves began to assign such alternative titles (as they are called by librarians) and many authors of other nations imitated them. Alternative titles are very popular to this very day.

But the two titles under which some works are listed in the Demokritos bibliography by Thrasyllos/Diogenes are evidently different titles of those works which the bibliographer had found in the extant copies and had entered in his list because he did not think that one deserved to be preferred over the other. In none of these cases should it be assumed that either Demokritos himself had given two titles to a work or that he had published it first under one, then under another title, or that his pupils had added the second title to the first one.[165] It is also very likely that the disputed titles of those works were not listed first by Thrasyllos but that they had already been known to Kallimachos who certainly encountered many works of the philosopher in at least two copies.[166]

Only regarding one of the works listed in the Demokritos bibliography there is a hint at disputed authorship. In the third tetralogy are listed: 1. *Megas diakosmos* (The great world system). 2. *Mikros diakosmos* (The small world system). For the first title it is noted that the followers of Theophrastos claim it as a work by Leukippos.[167] The bibliographer had evidently found that in all copies seen by him Demokritos was named as the author of *Megas diakosmos*. Therefore, he listed the work among those by the Abderite. He knew, however, from the literature that Theophrastos (the term "the followers of Theophrastos" meant the master himself, that was a customary paraphrase) had ascribed the *Megas diakosmos* as well as the *Peri nu* which was also known as one of Demokritos's works to Leukippos, the teacher of Demokritos.[168] It is almost certain that Theophrastos had cited both works in his *Physikōn doxai*. The Demokritos bibliographer therefore thought it necessary to mention the opinion of the famous scholar which was the opposite of his own. He probably also pointed out that the *Peri nu* ascribed to Demokritos had been written by Leukippos, according to Theophrastos, but this note is lost. Since Kallimachos in his general *Pinakes* also stated his and other people's opinion on the authenticity of certain works (as we know from information by later scholars), we need not hesitate to trace the note on the author of the *Megas diakosmos* to Kallimachos himself.

It seems to me, however, that Thrasyllos contributed the notes explaining the titles *Tritogeneia* and *Kratyntēria* which are difficult to understand,[169] because his purpose was not to compile a bibliography but to write an introduction. There is also a note on the second tetralogy, the one that deals with ethical works. The following titles are listed there in the third and fourth place: *Peri euthymiēs* (On cheerfulness) and *Hypomnēmaton ēthikōn* (Notes on ethics), followed by the remark that (the book) *Euesto* (Well-being) could not be found.[170] It seems that the bibliographer wanted to say that he would have listed the *Euesto* in the fourth place instead of Demokritos's unpublished notes on ethics, if he had been able to find it. This is reminiscent of the loss of some plays mentioned in Kallimachos's *Pinax* of Attic playwrights. Did Kallimachos also record in his Demokritos bibliography works that had been lost, that is, those not available in the Alexandrian library? Or did he still have a copy of *Euesto* whereas Thrasyllos did not have it any more? It is, however, doubtful whether a work by Demokritos with the title *Euesto* existed in addition to the one mentioned by Thrasyllos in the third place, the *Peri euthymiēs*. Several ancient scholars mention on the strength of the same information that Demokritos called the *euthymiē*, which was one of the principal concepts of his moral teachings, also by the name of *euesto*.[171] Diels assumed therefore that the philosopher had not written two works on the same subject, but that his work *Peri euthymiēs* had also been known under the title *Euesto*. This is indeed likely. But if the copies of that work which were available in the Alexandrian library had sometimes one, sometimes another title, Kallimachos probably wrote in his Demokritos *pinax: Peri euthymiēs ē Euesto* (On cheerfulness, or, Well-being). If now Thrasyllos overlooked the conjunction *ē* of if it was missing from his copy of Kallimachos's *pinax*,[172] he must have thought that there were two different works.

Thus, we can deduce several things from the Demokritos bibliography of Thrasyllos/Diogenes regarding the bibliographic methods of Kallimachos. He probably found all available copies of works ascribed to Demokritos in one single place in the library, provided there were none in the collective scrolls. His task was to distinguish between the authentic and the spurious works of the philosopher, and to ascertain their titles. In at least one case he noted that another scholar considered a work spurious which he thought to be authentic. It is quite possible that he ascribed works to Demokritos which had not been written by him. He also listed traditional titles that were different from those which he thought to be the authentic ones. He had also to check whether texts which filled an entire scroll and had their own titles were individual works or constituted parts of larger works.

There were still other problems, but it is already clear from those just mentioned that the list of Demokritos's works compiled by Kallimachos was the result of a manifold process of identification. However, it was not a monograph about Demokritos's literary remains, as Schmidt had thought, based on a false assumption.[173] There is no reason to compare it with, say, Andronikos's work on the writings of Aristotle.

But if Kallimachos compiled his Demokritos *pinax* before his general *Pinakes*, then this list of works which originated in connection with his Demokritos glossary constitutes the first bibliography based on autopsy, and generally the first bibliography of an author compiled from actual copies of his works. Based on Kallimachos's general *Pinakes* we may assume that he also collected information on the life and work of the Abderite for this purpose. This is corroborated by his note on Theophrastos's opinion on the *Megas diakosmos*.

4.4 His Lists of Greek Authors and Their Works

There can be no doubt that "the" *Pinakes* of Kallimachos, his lists of Greek authors and their works, surpass by far his other learned works, not only regarding their extent (120 books) but also in their importance. (The plural *pinakes* was used because each class of authors was listed in a *pinax* or in several *pinakes*.) The scholars of the first centuries A.D. still had copies of the *Pinakes*, but when the older literature, inasmuch as it was still of interest for contemporaries, was transcribed in the third and fourth century A.D. from scrolls to bound books (*codices*), the voluminous work was apparently disregarded, and the copies whose number was probably never very large, were ultimately destroyed.[174] This cannot simply be explained by the general decline of culture in the waning days of Antiquity. A lexicon of Greek authors was still desirable for scholars; this is shown by the *Onomatologos* (Nomenclator) compiled by Hesychios of Miletos in the 6th century. Rather, we must consider that the *Pinakes* of Kallimachos contained many authors whose works had been lost a long time ago, while those who had come on the scene since the middle of the third century B.C. were missing. Regarding the classical authors, the data in the *Pinakes* were certainly superseded in many respects by the works of the great Alexandrian philologers. Aristophanes of Byzantium had already criticized the *Pinakes* in a special work comprising several books (ca. 200 B.C.?), that is, he corrected and completed them.[175] Newer works were therefore preferred in later periods, even if they were not as voluminous as the *Pinakes* and were mere compilations. We may not reproach the people of the third and fourth century A.D. because they did not properly evaluate the documentary importance of the *Pinakes*; that would be a modern point of view.

The work is the scholarly opus of Kallimachos which is most frequently mentioned by ancient authors.[176] It is mentioned four times briefly as *Pinakes* and cited twice with an unmistakable paraphrase of this concept, each time with indication of authorship. Twenty-one other citations, in which only the author but not the work is mentioned, also relate to the *Pinakes* because of the analogous content. Finally, in one passage the authors of *rhētorikoi pinakes* (Lists of orators) are listed; this can only refer to Kallimachos and the scholars who had cataloged the library of Pergamon, the second largest Hellenistic book collection.[177]

No less than nine citations, among these the only two literal ones,[178] come from Athenaios, the polyhistor who flourished ca. A.D. 200, and who apparently still had a copy of the *Pinakes* at his disposal. Three of his citations relate to curious little books that were listed in the *Pinakes*, this is due to the general character of his multivolume work *Deipnosophistai* (The Banquet of the learned). Dionysius of Halikarnassos, an orator and historian in the second half of the first century A.D. who cites Kallimachos in his works on eminent orators of the fourth century B.C. five times, once with sharp criticism, had no doubt also seen a copy of the *Pinakes*. It is questionable whether this is also true of Diogenes Laertios, a contemporary of Athenaios, who mentions Kallimachos twice in his work on the lives and opinions of famous philosophers. The same can be said of the authors (some of which are anonymous) who cited Kallimachos sometimes in later centuries, basing themselves on older scholarly traditions.

Nowhere is the work of Kallimachos listed under the detailed title given in the *Suda* according to Hesychios: *Pinakes tōn en pasē paideia dialampsantōn kai hōn synegrapsan* (List of those who distinguished themselves in all branches of learning, and their writings). Earlier researchers, the last one being Gardthausen, thought therefore, that the words following *Pinakes* were a later addition. Today, since Schmidt, it is, however, generally assumed that Hesychios and the editor of the *Suda* preserved the original complete title of the work.[179] The explanation given for this assumption is that the noun *pinakes* needs a complement, similar to two titles from the early centuries of the Christian era which were formulated in connection with the *Pinakes* of Kallimachos.

Hermippos of Berytos, the son of a slave (first half of the 2nd century A.D.) had indeed compiled a work *Peri tōn en paideia lampsantōn dulōn* (On the slaves who distinguished themselves in branches of learning) or with a similar title, and the *Onomatologos* of Hesychios (6th century) had had the subtitle *Pinax tōn en paideia onomastōn* (List of persons renowned in branches of learning).[180] I cannot agree with this conception. The noun *paideia* (education) that appears in the three titles means there the same as scholarly learning or culture.[181] *Paideia* in this sense comprises all arts and sciences, not only those that appear in literary form.[182] As persons who distinguished themselves *en (pasē) paideia* we must therefore consider those who excelled in the arts and sciences or, in brief, in a branch of learning,[183] including those who were not active in literature, such as Socrates, Karneades (the founder of the New Academy) and other philosophers who did not write books but exercised their influence only through the spoken word, also all composers, painters, etc. who created artistic works.[184] Hesychios, for example, to name only this one witness, included in his *Pinax tōn en paideia onomastōn* not only Socrates and Karneades, but also Apelles, the most famous Greek painter. But nothing indicates that Kallimachos included in his *Pinakes* also persons who were not men of letters. One may even quite safely exclude such an assumption, because his *Pinakes* grew out of the catalogs of the Alexandrian library. On the other hand, he listed not only authors of important works in the arts and sciences (poetry, oratory, etc.) but also all persons who had written a work held by the library, even if these dealt with the baking of cakes or the relations with courtesans. The detailed title of Kallimachos's *Pinakes* is therefore not appropriate, compared with the title of Hesychios's *pinax*; it was formulated by a scholar who considered only writers as those who had distinguished themselves in the arts and sciences.[185] Such a limitation was also made by some later authors: thus, the *viri illustres* listed by Suetonius were all

151

writers; the same is probably true for the *endoxoi andres* (famous men) dealt with by some of his Hellenistic predecessors.[186] Jerome even limited his *viri illustres* to ecclesiastical writers only. But in Kallimachos's time nobody thought that lists of persons expressly containing the names of those who had distinguished themselves *en pase paideia* would name only those who had been active as writers. The detailed title of the work should therefore not be ascribed to Kallimachos himself.

But could Kallimachos publish his work under the title *Pinakes* without any addition? This is questionable, because the scholar could not permit himself what the poet had dared to do who entitled his elegies on the origins of strange customs quite simply *Aitia* (Causes). It is, however, not at all certain that he published the *Pinakes* himself. It is more likely that he worked on them until his death. Some sections were apparently not yet fully edited when he died,[187] quite apart from the fact that one could not think about a formal completion of the lists as long as the library still grew—and it grew indeed as long as he was alive and even long after his death. The huge work that became known as "the" *Pinakes* of Kallimachos was probably edited for final copying, even though not completed, only by his pupils. Even later it got the detailed title recorded by Hesychios, perhaps only at the time when Hermippos of Berytos compiled his *pinax* of slaves who had distinguished themselves *en paideia* (2nd century A.D.) The cumbersome and also somewhat pretentious formulation is similar to other titles recorded by Hesychios which were not assigned by Kallimachos either.

Several researchers, especially Schmidt, Gardthausen, Herter, Wendel, Regenbogen and Pfeiffer, demonstrated already how we should imagine the arrangement of the *Pinakes*.[188] They relied not only on the citations of those lists but partly also on comparable works of later centuries, especially that of Diogenes Laertios and the one by Hesychios of Miletos of which we have an excerpt in the *Suda*. The authors had probably not seen the *Pinakes* of Kallimachos any more, but they used the works of compilers, and those of compilers of compilers who had obtained their knowledge from the *Pinakes*. Considering the position Kallimachos had held and the task he had performed, it stands to reason that the younger Hellenistic bibliographers imitated his methods and utilized his results. It is therefore possible to draw conclusions from the later works regarding the lists compiled by Kallimachos. But first of all I would like to show what can be gleaned from the quotations of the *Pinakes* regarding the work as a whole. I am therefore presenting translations of the eight passages in which the work is quoted either expressly or in an unmistakable paraphrase.[189]

1) Fragment 429: "Eudoxos, son of Aischines, of Knidos, astronomer, geometer, physician, legislator. He studied geometry under Archytas, and medicine under the Sicilian Philistion, as Kallimachos says in the *Pinakes*. But Sotion says in his *Successors* [of the philosophers] that he had [also] heard Plato."

2) Fragment 430: "In order that I may also mention the verses of the poet and orator Dionysios Chalkus; he was called 'Bronze' because he advised the Athenians to employ bronze currency, and this statement is recorded by Kallimachos in his *List of Orators*."

3) Fragment 431: "Kallimachos incorrectly lists Prodikos among the orators; because he [appears] in those [verses] evidently as a philosopher."

4) Fragment 432: "According to Kallistratos, Diotimos claims that he [Demosthenes] delivered his first public oration before an audience of Athenians; and those who compiled the *pinakes* of orators entitled it *On the Symmories*."[190]

5) Fragment 443: "[the Athenian courtesan] Gnathaina . . . also compiled a *Rule for dining in company* (which lovers who came to her and her daughter had to follow) in imitation of the philosophers who have compiled similar rules.[191] Kallimachos recorded it in the third *pinax* of the Laws, citing the beginning of it as follows: 'The rule here inscribed is equal and fair for all'—323 lines."

6) Fragment 434: "There is also a work by Chairephon, recorded by Kallimachos in the *pinax* of Miscellaneous works; he writes as follows: 'Writers on banquets: Chairephon to Kyrebion.' Then he adds the opening words of it: 'Since you have often bidden me'—375 lines."

7) Fragment 435: "But I know also that Kallimachos in his *pinax* of Miscellaneous literature recorded books on the making of cakes by Aigimios, Hegesippos, Metrobios, and even by Phaistos."

8) Oxyrhynchus Papyri XXIII 2368, 16:[192] "[Aristarchos says . . . that] Kallimachos lists it erroneously among the paeans." (The reference is to *Kassandra* by Bakchylides which, according to Aristarchos of Samothrake, should have been listed under the dithyrambs of that poet.)

From these passages it has been deduced that Kallimachos

1. divided the authors into classes and within these classes if necessary into subdivisions,

2. arranged the authors in the classes or subdivisions alphabetically;

3. added to the name of each author (if possible) biographical data;

4. listed under an author's name the titles of his works, combining works of the same kind to groups (no more than that can be deduced from the eight citations), and

5. cited the opening words of each work as well as

6. its extent, i.e., the number of lines.

Although such generalizations are somewhat questionable, it is nevertheless possible to deduce from the cited passages some of the general principles which guided Kallimachos in his work. Some questions remain, however, still unanswered.

Regarding 1: Classification of authors. There is a class *Rhētores*, and as its equivalent we may assume a class *Philosophoi* (fr. 431). The former is also called *Rhētorika syngrammata* (Rhetoric works, i.e. speeches and writings on oratory) (fr. 430). There is also a class *Nomoi* (Laws) in at least three books, and a class *Pantodapa syngrammata* (Miscellaneous works, fr. 434 and 435).[193]

Later literary historians and critics divided the authors into poets and prose writers, and distinguished further, in accordance with the traditional literary forms and scholarly disciplines, between epic writers (often simply indicated as *poietai*, poets), elegiac, iambic, melic (song writers), tragic and comic writers, as well as historians (often simply called *syngrapheis*, that is, writers), philosophers, orators, physicians and grammarians.[194] Geographers and novelists were counted as historians, while mathematicians and natural scientists were listed as philosophers. Kallimachos probably classified authors similarly, but he probably distinguished a few more classes. The sequence of classes is not indicated by any of the citations. But since the *poietai* in the ancient and modern sense occupied undoubtedly the first rank, he probably listed the epic poets and their works in the first class. The citations let us further presume that there were *Pinakes* of melic, tragic, and comic poets, historians, philosophers, and orators, as well as legislators.[195] Presumably, astronomers, surveyors, and physicians also formed their own classes.[196] (Grammarians were not yet listed by him.) The *Pinax* of Miscellaneous works was apparently the last one. Kallimachos included in it the authors who did not fit into any of the other classes, and combined them to subdivisions within the class according to the subjects they had dealt with, by keywords as it were. One contained the authors of *deipna* (banquets), that is, the authors of cookbooks, in another there were special works on the making of cakes, *plakuntopoiika syngrammata* (fragments 434 and 435). The sequence of subdivisions is not known.

It is not clear from the citations whether there were headings that indicated the class of authors and works (e.g. *Rhētores* or *Rhētorika syngrammata*). According to the detailed title (which was not assigned by Kallimachos) the *Pinakes*, like all analogous works, were lists of persons and their works, not lists of works arranged by authors. (The end result is, of course, the same.) If Kallimachos was consistent, he must have named in the headings of each *Pinax* the class of authors, not that of subjects. If this was the case, then the citations would be inexact, which cannot be ruled out; that is, instead of *Rhētorika syngrammata* the heading would have been *Rhētores*, and instead of *Nomoi* it would have been *Nomothētai* (lawgivers). Even the last class, cited as *Pinax* of Miscellaneous works, could have had a corresponding heading. But was Kallimachos that consistent? This is rather doubtful, if indeed a subdivision of the last class was headed "Writers on banquets" and another one "Works on the making of cakes".

The headings themselves are actually unimportant, but they help us to answer another question. There were poets who had written works of different genres and in addition also works in prose — Kallimachos himself was one of them[197] — and on the other hand there were, for example, orators such as Theodektes of Phaselis, and philosophers, such as Timon of Phleius, who had written tragedies, as well as scholars who, like Eudoxos of Knidos, had published works on several different subjects. Did Kallimachos record the works of such authors in the classes to which they belonged, e.g. the works on oratory by Theodektes in the class *Rhētores*, the dramatic works in the class *Tragikoi*, etc., or did he (as Schmidt and Wendel assumed)[198] list all works by an author in one place, namely in that class in which most of his creations or the most important ones had found their place?

According to Wendel, Kallimachos preferred the latter method, so as not to have to repeat the biographical data in other classes, and referred there only to the main entry. That Kallimachos had been reproached for listing Prodikos not among the philosophers but among the orators (Fragment 431) is considered to be proof that he recorded all works of the sophist in one class. Although this is correct, it does not prove what it sets out to prove. As an orator who had also dealt with philosophical themes Prodikos was a borderline case. Where to classify him was and still is open to debate. Pfeiffer thinks that Kallimachos was right to list him among the orators;[199] I am of a different opinion. But in any case it does not follow from the classification of Prodikos that Kallimachos consolidated in one place the works of an author which belonged to different genres. Let us take Theodektos, the orator and tragedian! It is very unlikely that his tragedies were recorded together with his works on oratory in the class *Rhētores*, because otherwise it would not have been possible to call these also *Rhētorika syngrammata*, which brings us back to square one. Was it then necessary to scan all classes in order to find out whether Theodektes had written other works besides those on oratory? Not at all. The biographical data listed in each case before the bibliography contained, as we shall see, classifications of authors or relevant references to their activities. Thus, the entry Theodektes said probably *rhētor kai tragikos* (orator and tragedian); in the *Suda* he is mentioned, according to Hesychios, as *rhētor, trapeis de epi tragōdias* (an orator who changed to the writing of tragedies). From the classification it was evident that Theodektes had also written dramas which were recorded in the class of tragedians under his name. (Even in those days one had to know in which order a bibliography was arranged to find in it what one was looking for.) In the class of tragedians the biographic data pertaining to Theodektes were repeated to the extent that one could distinguish him from his namesakes, and one could see that he was also listed among the orators, where his main entry could be found. But that could already be read in the unchanged sequence of the classes to which he belonged: *rhētor kai tragikos*.

On 2: Arrangement of authors within the classes and subdivisions. The authors on the making of cakes which form a subdivision within the last class appear in alphabetical sequence: Aigimios, Hegesippos, Metrobios, Phaistos (Fragment 435). This could also be pure chance, but on the basis of other lists of authors from Hellenistic times, it may be assumed that Kallimachos arranged authors not only in the subdivision but also in the main classes alphabetically, of course only by their first letter; a more detailed alphabetization was practiced only later.

On 3: Addition of biographical data, or more precisely, data on the person of the author. From a remark by Dionysios of Halikarnassos we learn that Kallimachos generally recorded biographical data on the authors listed by him, and the authors of later comparable works, such as Hesychios of Miletos, did likewise. Remnants of such data can still be found in the quotations from the *Pinakes*. Thus, Diogenes Laertios reports in the first lines of his chapter on Eudoxos among other biographical details, that Kallimachos had stated in his *Pinakes* that the famous astronomer and mathematician, who was also a physician, had studied medicine under the Sicilian Philistion (Fragment 429). Schmidt emphasized that only such information for which Kallimachos is expressly named as an authority may be attributed to him, and Pfeiffer assumed therefore that Eudoxos had been mentioned in the class of physicians of the *Pinakes* under Philistion, as his pupil.[200] In my opinion, this stretches an intrinsically valid premise too far. Since Kallimachos knew that Eudoxos as a physician was a pupil of Philistion, he would certainly have noted that also in the entry for Eudoxos. In an analogous case, he named Lysimachos, the teacher of the future king Attalos I of Pergamon and author of a flattering report on the education of the king, as a Theodorean, that is, as a pupil of the philosopher Theodoros of Kyrene with the surname Atheos.[201] But if he mentioned the teacher of Eudoxos in medicine, he probably also indicated under whom he had studied his main subject. He probably did not neglect either to list the scholar under his full name, so as to distinguish him from namesakes,[202] i.e. besides his personal name, also that of his father (in the genitive case) and that of his birthplace (in adjectival form). The brief biographical information with which Diogenes Laertios opens his chapter on Eudoxos (personal name, father's name, name of birthplace, class of authors, teachers) could also have been given in the *Pinakes*.

If an author had a nickname, as for example, the poet and orator Dionysios of Athens who was called "Bronze", Kallimachos indicated that. For bearers of a common name such as Dionysios an additional distinguishing element was welcome. Since he also, according to Athenaios, recorded the speech in which Dionysios had counseled the Athenians to introduce bronze currency (Fragment 430), he mentioned probably also that Dionysios had therefore acquired his nickname. Hesychios did the same in analogous cases.[203]

On 4: Listing of titles. Kallimachos generally found the works which he had to record already equipped with an individual title. This provided him with a characteristic by which the works of an author could easily be distinguished. But not infrequently he may have encountered copies of one and the same work with different titles. Some works of lyric poetry and oratory were, however, still without a regular title, and certainly also some other works. Whether the banquet rules of Gnathaina (Fragment 433) were entitled *Nomos syssitikos* or whether this term, used by Athenaios, constituted the name of a certain type of works is debatable. But the collection of recipes which Chairephon had compiled at the request of Kyrebion had only a heading like a letter: "Chairephon to Kyrebion" (Fragment 434), and Kallimachos left it at that. But perhaps he constructed a title for some speeches which had been transmitted without a title. If Dionysios of Halikarnassos says in one passage that the authors of *Pinakes* on orators (by which Kallimachos and the librarians of Pergamon were meant) had named (*epigraphusi*) the first public speech of Demosthenes *Peri tōn symmoriōn* (Fragment 432), this means only that they recorded it in this form.[204] But in another passage he remarks that Kallimachos had given the title *Peri Hallonēsu* (On Hallonesos) to a speech by Demosthenes against a letter and ambassadors of king Philip of Macedonia which began with such and such words (Fragment 443). Apparently, this seemed strange to him. The title of this speech could therefore indeed have been assigned by Kallimachos.

On the arrangement of titles only very little can be gleaned from the citations. Here we must mainly rely on conclusions drawn from later lists, with one exception concerning melic poets (song writers). The remark of Aristarchos proves that Kallimachos arranged the songs of these poets by paeans, dithyrambs, etc., that is, according to types (*eidē*).[205] It is noteworthy that he listed longer poems (Pindar's odes, the dithyrambs of Bakchylides) separately. Presumably, he made analytical entries for the contents of scrolls in which such poems were written together with other poems by the same author, because he was particulary interested in them.

On 5: Indication of the opening words of a text. Kallimachos recorded, as shown by the verbatim quotations by Athenaios (Fragments 433 and 434), the opening words of the writings of Gnathaina and Chairephon. Whether the former had a title proper is questionable, as already mentioned; the latter certainly did not have one.

The other four passages in which the opening words of a work recorded by Kallimachos are quoted deal with writings whose authors or titles were disputed.[206] For this reason Wendel assumed, contrary to the current opinion, that Kallimachos had not indicated the beginnings of texts (*archē*) in all cases, but only in such disputed ones. He admits, however, that Kallimachos lists in the class *Rhētores* not only the titles of speeches but also their beginnings; otherwise Dionysios of Halikarnassos could not have identified a speech by Deinarchos which, in his opinion, had been incorrectly ascribed to Demosthenes by Kallimachos.[207] This argument is valid, but not only for speeches. Athenaios reports that Kallimachos recorded the comedy *Hairesiteichēs* (The rampart-taker) by Diphilos under the title *Eunuchos* (The eunuch), and the gastronomical didactic poem by Archestratos variously entitled by others as *Gastronomia, Deipnologia* or *Opsopoiia* under the title *Hedypatheia*; furthermore, he had listed the part on Asia in the *Perihēgēsis* (Description of the world) by Hekataios of Miletos under the name of a certain Nesiotes.[208] Athenaios would hardly have been able to identify the three works listed by Kallimachos if their beginnings had not been recorded in the *Pinakes*. It is therefore still likely that Kallimachos regularly listed the opening words of texts.

On 6: Indication of the number of lines. As can be seen from the same quotations by Athenaios (Fragments 433 and 434), Kallimachos also recorded the exact number of lines in the writings of Gnathaina and Chairephon. From the sum total of lines at the end of the bibliographies of Aristotle and Theophrastos which can be traced to the work of Hermippos, the pupil of Kallimachos, it is clear that it was common in Alexandria to indicate the extent of listed works in this manner.[209] This had already been customary in Athens in the fourth century B.C. Not only in later bibliographies, but also in many ancient papyri and in medieval manuscripts the number of lines is indicated at the end of the text.[210] Many researchers have therefore dealt with these data. Today it is certain that not the actual number of lines in a particular copy but the extent of the copied work were indicated by means of a standard measure. This standard measure had the length of a hexameter of 15-17 syllables or 34-38 letters. The lines recorded by Kallimachos—the Alexandrians called them *epē* in poetic works, and *stichoi* in prose writings—were therefore ideal or standard lines. It would indeed not have made sense to list the number of actual lines which varied from copy to copy. Rather, when the work was published the number of actual lines in the original, the exemplar for all subsequent copies, was converted to standard lines, the result was noted down at the end of the text, and was then copied together with it. The number of *epē* or *stichoi* gave the interested reader an idea of the extent of a work. Above all, the copying fee and the price of the book could be computed according to the standard lines. With the aid of these figures one could also check whether a copy was quantitatively equivalent to the original. We should, however, not entertain some exaggerated notions in this respect. The standard line was not an exact measurement, and the conversion of actual lines into epē or *stichoi*, stichometry for short, was largely based on estimates. If somebody converted the actual lines of a copy into *stichoi* and compared their sum at the end of a text with the number of *stichoi* in the original, he probably found a difference, even though not a single line had been omitted or added in the copy.[211] Only if the differences reached a certain size it could be assumed that there had been omissions or additions. (If the former balanced the latter, no difference was discernible at all.) If the indication of the number of standard lines had the purpose to safeguard the texts against insertions or deletions, as Wendel thought,[212] they served this purpose rather poorly. Their bibliographic function was more modest.

The writings of Gnathaina and Chairephon were very brief: each of these filled barely a third of a standard scroll. For works consisting of two or more books which needed two or more scrolls, Kallimachos no doubt also indicated their number. This is proven by the bibliographies of Aristotle and Theophrastos. They indicate, strictly speaking, the number of books, that is, the number of parts of which the listed works consisted, but generally a book was the equivalent of a scroll;[213] the Greek word *biblion* meant both book in the sense of part of a work and also book scroll. Since the middle of the fourth century B.C. Greek authors arranged their larger works in such a manner that each individual book filled one scroll. Later on, scholars divided also the works of the older literature in the same way and saw to it that in the production of new copies one scroll was prepared for each book. The Alexandrian grammarians certainly had a decisive influence on this process. But the copies of works of the older literature collected by the Ptolemies and cataloged by Kallimachos were probably still made during a period prior to the beginning of this process.

Starting from the quotations in which the *Pinakes* are expressly named I have tried to demonstrate the bibliographic principles of Kallimachos. In doing so, I already drew on other Kallimachos quotations which also relate to the *Pinakes*. The picture that thus emerged will only be complemented by the following three quotations:[214]

1) Fragment 442: "He [Parmenides] philosophizes in verse, just as Hesiod, Xenophanes and Empedokles . . . and it seems that he was the first to discover that the Evening star and the Morning star are the same; but others say it was Pythagoras. Kallimachos, however, says that the work was not by him [i.e. not by Pythagoras]."[215]

2) Fragment 449: Harpokration s.v. Ion: "[Ion] wrote many lyric poems and tragedies and a philosophical prose work entitled *Triagmos* (The triad) which, as Kallimachos says, has been disputed as a work of Epigenes."[216]

3) Fragment 451: Scholium to Euripides's *Andromachē*, verse 445: "The time of the creation of this drama cannot be given exactly, because it was not performed at Athens. But Kallimachos says that Demokrates was listed as the author of the tragedy."[217]

As in his Demokritos bibliography so also apparently in his *Pinakes* Kallimachos cited the opinions of other scholars who disputed the attribution of some works to certain authors whom he had listed. He also noted an indication of authorship which ran counter to the commonly accepted one, relating to the drama *Andromachē* which had not been performed in Athens, and had therefore not been mentioned in the *Didaskaliai*; yet he himself did not doubt that the tragedy had indeed been written by Euripides. (This indication of an author was probably also based on the opinion of a scholar.) If he found the same work in the several copies but with different titles, he probably also listed them, linked by the word *e*, as in his Demokritos bibliography.

No doubt the authorship and original titles of many works listed by Kallimachos were questionable or in dispute. They appeared in the copies available to Kallimachos either without indication of author and title, or under different names of authors and different titles. This began already with the "Homeric" epics. As already mentioned, one of his epigrams shows that he ascribed the "Homeric" epic on the conquest of Oichalia to Kreophylos of Samos, as other scholars had done. Like Aristotle and Zenodotos, he probably considered only the *Iliad*, the *Odyssey* and the *Margitēs* as authentic.[218] This conception must have been expressed in the *Pinakes*, though the relevant passages were not quoted.

Among the prose writings whose authorship was disputed were among others several orations by Demosthenes and by Deinarchos, who was twenty-five years younger. Since the latter had imitated the style of Demosthenes several times, some of his orations were known under the name of Demosthenes and vice versa. If all library copies of an oration by Demosthenes or Deinarchos were listed under their names and if their authenticity had not been doubted by any scholar, Kallimachos listed them in all probability under the respective name. But if the same oration existed both under the name of Demosthenes and under that of Deinarchos, of if its authenticity was in doubt, he had somehow to find out who was the real author.[219] Later scholars, especially Dionysios of Halikarnassos (second half of the first century B.C.) who specialized in this area, cited real or purported misjudgments of Kallimachos with indignation.[220] Thus, bibliographers began quite early to quarrel with their predecessors. But the Alexandrian grammarian who prepared the Demosthenes edition on which our manuscript tradition is based sided with Kallimachos regarding questions of ascription and the title of at least one oration.[221] The critical evaluation of authenticity of orations by Demosthenes was, however, at that time not yet far advanced in Alexandria.

Certainly there were also difficulties in recording the writings by scholars (philosophers, mathematician, physicians), especially of those who had been heads of schools, and particularly when all of their writings, including the unpublished ones, had been acquired by the library of the Museion. The works of Demokritos, Aristotle and Theophrastos are not the only examples. It happened not infrequently that works of pupils had found their way into those of the teachers (and vice versa), there were different versions of a treatise on the same subject, and writings which were later consolidated to larger units appeared as individual works with separate titles. The recording of such collections was beyond the capabilities of Kallimachos and his pupils.

Modern researchers are divided on the character of the *Pinakes*: some call it a catalog (with biographical data), others call it a bibliography (with biographical data).[222] According to the terminology of librarianship a catalog is a list of works and their copies, held by a particular library, whereas a bibliography is a list of works of a particular category (e.g. all works of Greek literature), no matter where they are held.[223] Now, it is quite unlikely that Kallimachos recorded in his *Pinakes* all copies of every work of Greek literature held by the Alexandrian library, and there are no hints to that effect. Rather, we must assume that he listed there only the works of Greek literature as such which were available in the library. Oddly enough, so far as I can see, there is no specific term for such a bibliographic listing; I will therefore call it a catalog of works, to distinguish it from a catalog of copies or printings. The catalog of works in the Alexandrian library was based on a catalog of copies which had also been compiled by Kallimachos, as I shall show below. But did his *Pinakes* only list the works available in the library, with biographical data on their authors, or did they also record works which were not available there, was it a bibliography of Greek literature as such? This question can only be answered if we know how the *Pinakes* came into existence. But before dealing more specifically with this issue, I am now turning to the later lists of Greek writers and their works, especially those from which we may draw conclusions regarding the work of Kallimachos. I can here refrain from a discussion of all later lists, because thanks to Regenbogen we have an excellent survey of the achievements of the Greek pinakographers.[224]

Notes to Chapter 4

1) On Hesychios and his *Onomatologos* see section 5.7 below.

2) Suidas (1928), v. 3, p. 19 f., Kappa 227:

Καλλίμαχος, υἱὸς Βάττου καὶ Μεσάτμας, Κυρηναῖος, γραμματικός, μαθητὴς Ἑρμοκράτους τοῦ Ἰασέως, γραμματικοῦ· γαμετὴν ἐσχηκὼς τὴν Εὐφράτου τοῦ Συρακουσίου θυγατέρα. ἀδελφῆς δὲ αὐτοῦ παῖς ἦν ὁ νέος Καλλίμαχος, ὁ γράψας περὶ νήσων δι' ἐπῶν. οὗτω δὲ γέγονεν ἐπιμελέστατος, ὡς γράψαι μὲν ποιήματα εἰς πᾶν μέτρον, συντάξαι δὲ καὶ καταλογάδην πλεῖστα. καί ἐστιν αὐτῷ τὰ γεγραμμένα βιβλία ὑπὲρ τὰ ὀκτακόσια· ἐπὶ δὲ τῶν χρόνων ἦν Πτολεμαίου τοῦ Φιλαδέλφου. πρὶν δὲ συσταθῇ τῷ βασιλεῖ, γράμματα ἐδίδασκεν ἐν Ἐλευσῖνι, κωμυδρίῳ τῆς Ἀλεξανδρείας. καὶ παρέτεινε μέχρι τοῦ Εὐεργέτου κληθέντος Πτολεμαίου, ὀλυμπιάδος δὲ ρκζ', ἧς κατὰ τὸ δεύτερον ἔτος ὁ Εὐεργέτης Πτολεμαῖος ἤρξατο τῆς βασιλείας. τῶν δὲ αὐτοῦ βιβλίων ἐστὶ καὶ ταῦτα· Ἰοῦς ἄφιξις, Σεμέλη, Ἄργους οἰκισμός, Ἀρκαδία, Γλαῦκος, Ἐλπίδες, σατυρικὰ δράματα, τραγῳδίαι, κωμῳδίαι, μέλη, Ἶβος (ἔστι δὲ ποίημα ἐπιτετηδευμένον εἰς ἀσάφειαν καὶ λοιδορίαν, εἴς τινα Ἶβον, γενόμενον ἐχθρὸν τοῦ Καλλιμάχου· ἦν δὲ οὗτος Ἀπολλώνιος, ὁ γράψας τὰ Ἀργοναυτικά)· Μουσεῖον, Πίνακες τῶν ἐν πάσῃ παιδείᾳ διαλαμψάντων, καὶ ὧν συνέγραψαν, ἐν βιβλίοις κ' καὶ ρ', Πίναξ καὶ ἀναγραφὴ τῶν κατὰ χρόνους καὶ ἀπ' ἀρχῆς γενομένων διδασκάλων, Πίναξ τῶν Δημοκράτους γλωσσῶν καὶ συνταγμάτων, Μηνῶν προσηγορίαι κατὰ ἔθνος καὶ πόλεις, Κτίσεις νήσων καὶ πόλεων καὶ μετονομασίαι, Περὶ τῶν ἐν Εὐρώπῃ ποταμῶν, Περὶ τῶν ἐν Πελοποννήσῳ καὶ Ἰταλίᾳ θαυμασίων καὶ παραδόξων, Περὶ μετονομασίας ἰχθύων, Περὶ ἀνέμων, Περὶ ὀρνέων, Περὶ τῶν ἐν τῇ οἰκουμένῃ ποταμῶν, Θαυμάτων τῶν εἰς ἅπασαν τὴν γῆν κατὰ τόπους ὄντων συναγωγή.

3) The date of Ptolemaios III's accession to the throne was added to the biographical data later, as Sitzler (1917) column 1091 recognized, but we do not know at which stage of the transmission.

4) On the arrangement and content of this bibliography see Daub (1880) pp. 460-466, and Callimachus (1953) Testim. 1 with Pfeiffer's note.

5) The list mentions before the *Pinakes* a work entitled *Museion* of which nothing more is known. Since there was a *Museion* by the orator Alkidamas (4th century) on extempore speeches with examples, it is assumed that the *Museion* by Kallimachos was also written in prose. I doubt this; the titles of all of his learned works were concrete, i.e. they indicated exactly the subject of the respective works.

6) All that has been preserved by or about Kallimachos was compiled by Pfeiffer in his exemplary edition (Oxford, vol. 1 1949, vol. 2 1953), in which he also gave explanations. This work is cited as Callimachus (1949) and (1953). In addition, Pfeiffer's *History of classical scholarship*, especially the chapter on Kallimachos, served as a foundation for my investigation. Very useful was also Herter's prudent article on Kallimachos in Pauly-Wissowa's *Realencyclopädie* (1931, addendum 1973) and his literature surveys in Bursian's *Jahresberichte* (1937; 1956). Among the works on literary history I mention here only the influential book by Howald (1943) who also, together with Staiger, translated the poems of Kallimachos (1955), and the work by Körte-Händel which presents Kallimachos in the framework of Hellenistic literature (1960). [English readers will find an extensive discussion of Kallimachos as a poet and literary critic in the chapter "The horizon of Callimachus" in Fraser (1972) pp. 717-793. H.H.W.] For specialized investigations on the lists of Kallimachos see below. The work by Capovilla which was sharply criticized by experts upon its publication (1967) was also consulted but my attempts to discuss it with him critically had soon to be abandoned. For a specimen of this author's method to solve problems concerning Kallimachos, see note 73.

7) Testimonia in: Callimachus (1953) pp. xviii-cvi.

8) Cicero, *De oratore* III 132. He deals there with the deplorable specialization of the disciplines. Cicero says that the scholars named by him had still mastered their discipline—*medicina, geometria, musica*, and *litterae*—in their entirety.

9) Gellius XVII 21, 41.

10) Callimachus (1949), fragment 110. The poem was translated into Latin by Catullus.

11) Callimachus (1949), Epigram 21.

12) Strabo XVII 837.

13) Callimachus (1949), Epigram 35.

14) Battiads was the name of members of a royal dynasty that ruled Kyrene for two hundred years. Bethe thought that the name of Kallimachos's father Battos, not named in his epigram 21, had been construed by later scholars from the epithet Battiad which he uses for himself in epigram 35. Herter (1931) column 386 rejected this assumption. If it were correct, then Kallimachos would indeed have considered himself to be a descendant of the first king of Kyrene. But perhaps only Strabo or the authority on whom he relied interpreted the name *Battiades* in this sense. If Kallimachos was the son of a man whose name was Battos like that of the founder of the city, he could call himself in jest a Battiad. This interpretation was already presented by Wilamowitz (1928) p. 22.

15) Thus he states in epigram 7 in order to console his friend, the poet Theaitetos who had not been successful with the general public, that Hellas would always proclaim his art.

16) Funaioli (1912).

17) Callimachus (1949), fragment 460; Herter (1931), column 388; (1973) column 185 f. (there also the older literature); also Pfeiffer (1968) p. 95, note 4.

18) Callimachus (1949), fragment 178, 30.

19) On the cultural life in Kyrene during the fourth century B.C. see Wilamowitz (1928) pp. 19-21.

20) Callimachus (1949), Epigram 32.

21) Those were the following scholars: Apollonios Rhodios, Aristophanes of Byzantium, Eratosthenes, Hermippos of Smyrna, Istros, Leon, Philostephanos. For references see Callimachus (1953) pp. xcvi-xcviii.

22) Athenaios III 72 = Callimachus (1949), fragment 465. See also Pfeiffer (1970) p. 171, who, while applying the sentence to works in general, reminds the reader that the *mega biblion* — in poetry! — constitutes the special theme of the prologue to *Aitia* in which Kallimachos proudly declares himself to be an *oligostichos*, a poet of few verses; see Callimachus (1949), fragment 1, 10. — Birt (1882) pp. 482-484 connected Kallimachos's expression with the large scrolls that were in use in pre-Alexandrian times. Wilamowitz (1924) vol. 1, p. 215 thought he heard the heartfelt sigh of a man who had read too many books.

23) Callimachus (1949), fragment 112, 8 f. with Pfeiffer's note. In English translation: "Hail, greatly hail to thee also, O Zeus: do thou save all the houses of our kings: and I will visit the haunt of the Muses on foot." According to Wilamowitz (1924) vol. 1, p. 210 Kallimachos is alluding in the last verse to the production of his great work in prose, the *Pinakes*, but according to Pfeiffer he is thinking about the writing of his poems called *Iamboi* after the meter.

24) Callimachus (1949), fragment 1, 30-36.

25) Herter (1931) column 389.

26) Callimachus (1949), fragment 392 and 228.

27) Strabo XVII, 838.

28) Herter (1931) column 391; (1942); (1956) pp. 221-230; (1973) column 198. Of the voluminous literature I mention here only the following: Hunt, in *The Oxyrhynchus papyri* vol. X (1914) no. 1241; Rostagni (1914); Wilamowitz (1914) pp. 245-247; Schmidt (1922) pp. 33-35; Wilamowitz (1924) vol. 1, pp. 160 and 206-208; Beloch (1925) vol. 4, 2, p. 595 f.; Perrotta (1925) and (1928); Wendel-Göber (1955) pp. 73-75; Eichgrün (1961) pp. 15-35 and 173-179; Pfeiffer (1968) p. 128.

29) This has been emphasized already by Beloch (1925) vol. 4, 2, p. 595 f., who arrived, however, at wrong datings, because he thought (p. 592) that Zenodotos was the teacher of the children of Ptolemaios II, contrary to the data in the *Suda*.

30) Nickau (1972) column 45.

31) Callimachus (1949), fragments 381 and 382. The poem was partially imitated by Ovid. See Eichgrün (1961) pp. 141-157.

32) Pfeiffer (1968) p. 97, who cites a satirical poem by Timon of Phleius on the scribblers of books who quarrel endlessly in the cage of the Muses.

33) Schmidt (1922) p. 34 f.

34) The so-called *Scholium Plautinum* in which Kallimachos is mentioned as an *aulicus regius bibliothecarius* may not be used as an argument.

35) The directorship of the library held by Aristarchos of Samothrake is not mentioned in the *Suda* either.

36) The text of the two brief *bioi* was published by Westermann (1845) p. 50 f. and Wendel (1958) p. 1 f. On the biography of Apollonios Rhodios see Herter (1942) and Händel (1962).

37) There were fifteen Ptolemies, who ruled during a period of some 250 years. Such a dating would not have been made by Hesychios. Wendel assumed therefore correctly that the wording should rather be "under the third Ptolemaios" as written in a younger manuscript; similarly the article on Apollonios in the *Suda*.

38) Literally: he had been together with his teacher. The verb *syneinai* (being together) was used for younger scholars who remained after the completion of their studies with their teachers as their assistants. Thus, we read about Aristotle in the *Vita Marciana* that he stayed with Plato until his teacher's death. See Aristotle, *Fragmenta* (1886) p. 427, 17; Gigon (1962) p. 2, 38. Even though Apollonios as a poet owed much to the poetry of Kallimachos, the ancient biographers considered the author of the *Argonautika* not, as was often claimed (e.g. by Händel (1962) p. 436), as a pupil of the poet but as one of the scholar Kallimachos. The *bioi* are in this respect quite unambiguous.

39) Pfeiffer (1968) pp. 146-148.

40) I see no reason to assume that there is a gap before this passage, as Wendel and Pfeiffer do. See Callimachus (1953) p. xcvi.

41) Pfeiffer (1968) p. 142, and his "Excursus to p. 142", pp. 284-285.

42) Herter (1942) p. 314 f.

43) Suidas (1928) v. 1, p. 307, Alpha 3419.

44) According to the *Suda*, Eratosthenes was born in Kyrene in the 126th Olympiad (276/272 B.C.); he lived until the era of Ptolemaios V Epiphanes (205/204-181/180 B.C.) under whom he died at the age of eighty. Against these dates the objection has been raised that a young man born ca. 275 B.C. could not have been a pupil of Kallimachos in Kyrene, because the latter had then already been in Alexandria for some time; thus, e.g. Pfeiffer (1968) p. 153. But the *Suda* says only that he was a pupil of Kallimachos, not that he was his pupil in Kyrene. According to Strabo, Erathosthenes was considered a pupil of Zeno of Kition, the founder of the Stoa, who died in 262/261 B.C.; on the date of Zeno's death see Fritz (1972) column 83; on the age of pupils of philosophers see section 3.3, note 71. If Erathosthenes had really been a pupil of Zeno, he must have been born somewhat earlier, in the 125th Olympiad, that is ca. 280 B.C. That would mean a minor copying error, similar to the one by which in Pfeiffer's Kallimachos edition, vol. 2, p. xcvii, T. 15, the 126th Olympiad appears as the 127th. It seems more likely to me that he was named as a pupil of Zeno because his teacher Ariston of Chios, who is mentioned in the *Suda*, was a pupil of Zeno. Thus Aristotle also appears in the *Vita Marciana* as a pupil of Socrates (who died long before Aristotle was born) because Socrates was the teacher of Plato, his teacher. See Aristotle, *Fragmenta* (1886) p. 427, 15 f.; Gigon (1962) p. 2, 36.

45) This can hardly mean Timachides, as suggested by Rostagni and others; see Herter (1942) p. 319.

46) This too was already emphasized by Beloch (1925) vol. 4, 2, p. 594 f., but his view was not accepted because he also assumed a return of Apollonios to Alexandria.

47) *The Oxyrhynchus papyri*, vol. X (1914) no. 1241, and the literature cited above in note 28.

48) It is generally assumed that only Zenodotos was mentioned in the last lines of the first column; see Eichgrün (1961) p. 16. This unfounded assumption is based on a reconstruction of column 1, line 16 f., suggested by Rostagni (1914) p. 248, which rests on the erroneous idea that lines 16 f. had been the last ones in the first column (which contained 36 lines); besides, it is much too long for the narrow column.

49) The Greek text follows:

ν[ι]ος Σιλλεως Αλεξανδρευς
ο [κ]αλουμενος Ροδιος Καλ
λ[ι]μαχου γνωριμος· ουτος
εγενετο και διδασκαλος του
5 πρωτου βασιλεως· τουτον

δ[ι]εδεξατο Ερατοσθενης
μεθ ον Αριστοφανης Απελ
λου Βυζαντιος και Αρισταρ
χος· ειτ Απολλωνιος Αλεξαν
10 δρευς ο ιδογραφος καλουμε

νος· μεθ ον Αρισταρχος Αρι   μεθ ον Κυδας εκ των λογχο
σταρχου Αλεξανδρευς ανω   φ[ο]ρων· επι δε τωι ενατω
θεν δε Σαμοθραξ· ουτος και   [βα]σιλει ηκμασαν Αμμω
διδ[α]σκαλος [ε]γεγε[το] των   [νι]ος και Ζηνο[δοτος] και Διο
15 του Φιλοπατορος τεκνων·   20 [κλ]ης και Απολλο[δ]ωρος γραμ
                [μα]τικοι[·]

50) On the list as a "List of diadochi" see Regenbogen (1950) column 1449-51.

51) Pfeiffer (1968) p. 212.

52) Pfeiffer (1968) p. 253.

53) Aristarchos also taught the children of Ptolemaios V.

54) The rare term *eidographos* is used for a man who wrote poems (*eide*) or who described types (*eidē*) of literary works. According to the *Etymologicum magnum* Apollonios classified the older lyric poems by musical criteria; see Pfeiffer (1968) pp. 184 and 172, note 5.

55) The second part of the article "Aristophanes Byzantios" in the *Suda* was appended by mistake to the article "Aristonymos komikos". On the dating of Aristophanes of Byzantium see Eichgrün (1961) p. 234, note 37.

56) This was clarified by Eichgrün, following combinations made by earlier researchers, especially Rostagni; see Eichgrün (1961) pp. 16-18 and 24-31, not considered by Pfeiffer (1968); see also Herter (1942) pp. 314-317.

57) Daub (1882), Index s.v. Suidas, Zusammenziehung von zwei Artikeln in einen, Zerschneidung eines Artikels in zwei. Among the persons affected by the confounding of their articles with that of a namesake was a certain Asklepiades, a pupil of Apollonios; see Daub (1882) p. 84 f.; Eichgrün (1961) p. 239, note 79. See also the fate of the *Suda* article "Aristophanes Byzantios" mentioned in note 55 above.

58) E.g. the articles "Aratos", "Aristoxenos", and "Damastes".

59) Wendel suggested to put the *akmē* data in the Apollonios article of the *Suda* before the note on the *synchronismos*; he assumed apparently that the sequence of these data as transmitted was based on a mistake. This is also possible. If we follow Wendel, only the last sentence of the article (the data on *diadochē*) may be derived from the article on "Apollonios II", and we must assume that the *akme* data given there were the same as in the article on "Apollonios I". Incidentally, also in the *Violarium* of the so-called Eudokia, which is largely consistent with the *Suda* but has sometimes a somewhat better and more detailed text, the data on the *akmē* precede the remark on the *synchronismos*. Is this perhaps an old tradition, or is it just a philological correction?

60) The contradiction cannot be resolved by the explanation that the teacher of the future Ptolemaios III had lived under him; that was just not true: he lived, i.e. he reached the zenith of his life, under Ptolemaios II.

61) E.g. Herter (1942) p. 316.

62) The *Suda* says s.v. Aristarchos "he educated the son of the sixth Ptolemaios", and s.v. Zenodotos "he educated the children of the first Ptolemaios". But s.v. Philitas: "He was the teacher of the second Ptolemaios".

63) That Aristophanes of Byzantium was the teacher or one of the teachers of Ptolemaios V, as Eichgrün (1961) p. 23 claims, is not documented.

64) Ptolemaios IV was old enough to be taught only in or close to 230 B.C.

65) Herter (1931) column 391; Pfeiffer (1968) p. 210. The differences in the enumeration are said to be due to the uncertainty about the two men called Apollonios. Incidentally, Hunt already relied on the purported statement by Tzetzes in *The Oxyrhynchus Papyri* vol. X (1914) p. 101.

66) On Rhianos see Pfeiffer (1968) pp. 122 and 148-149.

67) Wendel-Göber (1955) p. 74 stress correctly, but without giving their reasons, that the Oxyrhynchos papyrus cannot be considered a reliable testimony for the fact that Kallimachos was not the librarian of the Museion.

68) This was observed by Perrotta (1925) p. 126 f. against Rostagni (1914) p. 246. But his remark was disregarded because it was made in relation to an untenable argumentation which sought to prove that Kallimachos had been the successor of his pupil Apollonios.

69) It is not known whose pupil the eidographer Apollonios had been.

70) The linking of the two offices was particularly emphasized by Eichgrün (1961) pp. 21, 23, 26, 32, and 181-193; see also Pfeiffer (1968) p. 154. Only Jacoby (1957) T. II D, p. 705 rejected the linking of the two offices, but without giving his reasons.

71) Pfeiffer (1968) p. 154 thinks differently. This conjecture was first made very tentatively by Wilamowitz (1894) p. 30. He relied on the last lines of an epigram by Eratosthenes, dedicated to Ptolemaios III Euergetes: "Blessed Ptolemaios, when standing beside the son in youthful power, thou who bestowed upon him everything that is agreeable to the Muses and to kings. May he in future, great Zeus, also receive the sceptre from thy hand. May it be so! But whoever sees this votive offering, let him say that it had been offered by Eratosthenes of Kyrene!" Pfeiffer reprinted the Greek text. I am unable to elicit from these lines that Eratosthenes was the teacher of the crown prince.

72) Eichgrün (1961) pp. 18-21.

73) Capovilla (1967) vol. 1, pp. 368 and 371 assumes that Apollonios and Kallimachos had held their offices simultaneously: Apollonios had been the director of the library in the Serapeion, while Kallimachos had been the director of the library of the Museion and director general of both Alexandrian libraries. See above, note 8.

74) Callimachus (1949), fragment 403-464 (Fragmenta grammatica); see also Herter (1931) column 402-404; (1973) column 188; Pfeiffer (1968) pp. 134-136. My count disregards the collective titles of larger works, and includes only the separate titles and their parts. If the count is made the other way round, there are ten works.

75) Callimachus (1949), fragment 75, 53-77, with Pfeiffer's note to verse 54. Dionysios of Halikarnassos names Xenomedes among the predecessors of Thukydides in *Peri Thukydidu* 5.

76) Callimachus (1949), fragment 612.

77) Callimachus (1949), fragment 407; see also Ziegler (1949), especially column 1140 f.; Giannini (1964) pp. 105-109; Pfeiffer (1970) p. 170. Whether Antigonos is identical with the author of biographies of philosophers whose work was used by Diogenes Laertios, remains to be seen. Some researchers, lately Giannini (1963) p. 106 f. concluded from the title *Eklogē tōn paradoxōn* which is mentioned by Antigonos, that he had seen only an excerpt from Kallimachos's work. But Antigonos wants to say that Kallimachos had made a collection of selected curiosities.

78) The attempt by Giannini (1964) p. 105 f. to reconstruct from this a collective title seems to me to be futile. Kallimachos would, of course, not have written *eis hapasan tēn gēn*, but *en hapase tē gē*, probably also *thaumasiōn* instead of *thaumatōn*.

79) Whether there was a more detailed subdivision under countries is impossible to say because Antigonos arranged the curiosities by subject.

80) Callimachus (1949), fragment 407, IV and XVII.

81) Howald (1943) p. 13 f.; Kallimachos (Howald-Staiger, 1955) pp. 19 and 21; Lesky (1963) p. 754; Eppelsheimer (1970) p. 85. Howald (1943) p. 14 thinks the *Thaumasia* differed from curiosity collections of modern princes merely in that the objects existed only on paper instead of in actual showcases.

82) Körte-Händel (1960) p. 17 f.

83) Callimachus (1949), fragment 457-459. A third part probably dealt with the rivers of Libya, i.e. Africa.

84) Callimachus (1949), fragment 414-428. In the citations we read sometimes *en tō* (sc. *bibliō*), sometimes *en tois* (sc. *bibliois*) *peri orneōn* (in the book, or in the books on the birds).

85) Callimachus (1949) fragment 403; 405, 413 with Pfeiffer's notes. Another work by Kallimachos, *Peri logadōn* is also cited, but it is not clear what the title means.

86) Callimachus (1949) p. 339.

87) Christ-Schmid (1920) T. 2, 1, p. 127, note 9.

88) Jacoby (1957) no. 4, fragment 66-70.

89) Callimachus (1949), fragment 406. The wording of the two separate titles is probably distorted: transmitted is *metonomasias* (renaming) instead of *onomasias* (some researchers think, following Daub, that it should be *katonomasias*, but *onomasias* is the common expression) and *ethnos* (people) instead of *ethnē*. Similar to the parts of the *Thaumasia*, those of the *Ethnikai onomasiai* and also those on the rivers may originally have been individual works.

90) Callimachus (1949), fragment 404.

91) Wendel (1939) column 508.

92) Perhaps he had already seen works on natural science with lists of dialectal terms for the plants, etc. See Latte (1925) p. 161 f.

93) Callimachus (1949), fragment 461-464, and also Herter (1931) column 402 and (1973) column 488. On the so-called *Historika hypomnēmata* by Kallimachos, see Callimachus (1949) fragment 200a with Pfeiffer's note; Nickau (1972, Zenodotos of Alexandria) column 22.

94) Some researchers interpret the *hypomnēmata* of Kallimachos as "memorabilia" in the later sense. But for a scholar of the 3rd century B.C. the term did not have this meaning.

95) Callimachus (1949), fragment 463. The reference is to the biblical Akko (English Acre) in Israel.

96) Although this is documented only for his collection of curiosities, it is likely to have been the case also for his other collections with the exception of his collection of dialectal terms. If we did not have the 44 excerpts of Antigonos but only the few citations by other authors we would not know either that Kallimachos indicated in each case his authority.

97) Susemihl (1891) vol. 1, p. 623 and 476 f.; Kentenich (1896) pp. 25-27. The *hypomnēmata* by Istros are also called *atakta* (unordered) and *symmikta* (mixed).

98) At the time when Kallimachos devoted himself to his learned works he could hardly have played the role of the *arbiter elegantiae* at the court, which was ascribed to him by Pohlenz (1911) p. 82 without any justification. It is questionable whether he ever played that role.

99)   Plinius, *Naturalis historia*, Praefatio 17. Book 1 contains the contents of the following 36 books and the lists of authors.

100)   Callimachus (1949), fragment 421-427; missing data in fragments 424 and 426.

101)   *Pinax* (literally: tablet) was used for *anagraphē* already in the 4th century B.C. in the sense of list, register, e.g. by the Delphic Amphiktyons in relation to the list of Pythionikai by Aristotle and Kallisthenes; see Schmidt (1922) p. 47, note 4. Schmidt says that Wilamowitz wanted to omit *kai anagraphē*, but there is no need to do that. Neither is it justified to put *kata chronus* before *tōn*, as Wilamowitz (according to Schmidt) and Regenbogen (1950) column 1423 suggest. This would even give a false emphasis to the title by stressing that the poets were listed chronologically; that was self-evident because an alphabetical arrangement was at that time still not common. On *kata chronus* see Thukydides I 117, and also Porphyrios, *Bios Plotinu* 138, and the *Suda* s.v. Hesychios Milesios.

102)   Choiroboskos writes, strictly speaking, not about one *pinax* but about *pinakes* or *anagraphai (dramatōn* or *poiētōn archaiōn)*. But the plural form has no particular meaning in this case, since these were lists of poets.

103)   *Inscriptiones Graecae* XIV (1890) no. 1097 (14 lines); 1098 (18 lines); 1098 a (11 lines). In each case, only between 3 and 17 of about 72 letters in each line are extant, namely those in the middle. The most authoritative reconstruction of the text is the one by Dittmer (1923), reprinted in abridged form in Pickard-Cambridge (1968). See Körte (1905); Wilhelm (1906) pp. 195-205; 208, 255; Capps (1906); Körte (1911) pp. 227-229; Oellacher (1916) pp. 132-134; Schmidt (1922) pp. 51; 59-61; Dittmer (1923); Geissler (1925) pp. 23-26; Körte (1925); Herter (1931) column 401; Regenbogen (1950) column 1423 f.; Mensching (1964) pp. 16; 30-34; Pickard-Cambridge (1968), pp. 73; 120-122; Pfeiffer (1968) pp. 132-133.

104)   Cicero, *De oratore* III 132.

105)   Moretti (1960).

106)   Snell (1966) p. 14; Snell tried to complete the fragments of San Paolo, after Kaibel and others.

107)   Not after their first victory, as Geissler (1925) p. 13 assumed.; Capps (1906) already ruled this out because many poets had never won a victory. See also Mensching (1964) p. 30, note 87.

108)   As an example for an original entry, the beginning of the "article" Lysippos, no. 1097, lines 7-11 reads as follows:

       . . . Lysippos won in the City under . . .
       . . . under Glaukippos with the Katachenai; . . .
       . . . with the Bakchai; these only are preserved . . .
       . . . under Diophantos with the Dionysos . . .
       . . . [second] in the City under Nikoteles . . .

109) See the note above, line 9.

110) Dittmer (1923) p. 37 f. Such notes appear on two out of three fragments, namely no. 1097 and 1098 a; they could therefore not have been "occasional notes" (according to which principle?) as Capps (1906) p. 203 thought. It is not possible to decide whether the notes were in the form of adjectives or verbs, or perhaps sometimes one and sometimes the other, i.e. whether in no. 1097, line 9 should read *sōi[ai]* or *sōi[zontai]*. In no. 1098 a, line 7 an adjectival form was evidently used. In the *hypothēseis* to *Mēdeia* by Euripides and to *Achamēs* by Aristophanes which are based on Aristophanes of Byzantium there are notes on the loss of plays that had been performed at the same time; these notes use the form of verbs. See *Aristoteles pseudepigraphus* (1863) p. 559, no. 6 and 10.

111) At that time the library of Aristotle-Theophrastos-Neleus had already been brought to Alexandria.

112) In the third century B.C. there existed a comedy *Asōtodidaskalos*, (The teacher of the spendthrift), ascribed to Alexis, a poet of the fourth century, which had not been recorded by Kallimachos, according to Athenaios; see Callimachus (1949) fragment 439. Kaibel (1889) p. 43, note 2 assumed on the basis of the citation that it had been a forgery.

113) I need not dwell here on the discussion about the completion of the Roman inscription.

114) Körte (1905) p. 445; Schmidt (1922) p. 60; Herter (1931) column 401; Regenbogen (1950) column 1423 f.

115) We do not know what was the last year recorded in the copy of the *Didaskaliai* used by Kallimachos.

116) For example, it was found worthwhile to know whether a particular play had been the first or second, etc. by an author, and this was noted in the *hypothēseis*.

117) See Kallimachos's epigram 7 (to his friend Theaitetos who apparently had not been successful with the public as a playwright) and 8 (on the brief speech of the successful author, consisting of just one word: *nikō* [I am the victor]). Kallimachos himself wrote also a learned work *Peri agōnōn* (On contests) in addition to tragedies and comedies. The Athenian inscriptions on *Didaskaliai* and *Nikai* were carved in stone around 278 B.C., and Aristophanes of Byzantium in his *hypothēseis* still thought that he had to report the contest at which a particular play had been performed; he therefore mentioned the competitors of an author, the titles of their plays and their successes.

118) In a scholium to verse 445 of *Andromachē* it is said that the drama cannot be dated exactly because it had not been performed in Athens; see Aristotle, *Fragmenta* (1886) p. 389. Already in the fourth century B.C. there were plays intended for reading only, e.g. by Chairemon, as documented by Aristotle, *Rhetoric* III 12; see Ziegler (1937) column 1966.

119) Callimachus (1949), fragment 454.

120) Schmidt (1922) p. 97 f.; Herter (1931) column 401 f.; Regenbogen (1950) columns 1423 and 1441 f.; Pfeiffer (1968) p. 132.

121) The antagonism between the "idealist" Plato and the "materialist" Demokritos gave rise to an anecdote of interest for literary history. According to Diogenes Laertios IX 40, Plato wanted to buy up all works by the Abderite in order to burn them, but was told by two Pythagoreans that this would be useless, because these works were already *para pollois* (with many people).

122) Diels-Kranz (1952) vol. 2, p. 153, note to line 16.

123) Diels-Kranz (1952) vol. 2, p. 90, note to line 13.

124) Oder (1890) p. 74 wanted to write, after Hecker: *Pinax tōn Dēmokritu kai glōssōn syntagma* (List of the works of Demokritos and collection of [his] glosses). Schmidt (1922) p. 97 and Regenbogen (1950) column 1423 thought that this transposition of the title might be considered.

125) Pfeiffer uses in the English original edition (1968, p. 132) the term "obsolete words", in the German translation (1970, p. 167) he writes "ausgefallene Wörter" (strange words).

126) West (1969). On the collections of maxims by Demokrates or Demokritos see Laue (1921); Philippson (1924); Diels-Kranz (1952) vol. 2, p. 153, note to line 16.

127) A collection of maxims by an author had the title *Gnōmai tu deinos* (Maxims of so-and-so), a collection of proverbs had the title *Paroimiai* or *Synagōgē paroimiōn*; see Horna (1935); Rupprecht (1949), especially column 1770.

128) See the bibliographies in Diogenes Laertios V 26 (Aristotle); V 43 (Theophrastos); V 87 f. (Herakleides Pontikos); V 59 (Straton); on these, see Oder (1890) p. 74; Moraux (1951) p. 120. It seems that Herakleides Pontikos wrote interpretations (*exēgēseis*) on Demokritos; see Wehrli (1967), Heft 7, fragment 7 with commentary. Straton's work on the void probably dealt with one of the main concepts of atomism.

129) Pfeiffer (1968) p. 79.

130) Diels-Kranz (1952) vol. 2, no. 68 B 130-142, B 29, B 120-123.

131) Diels-Kranz (1952) vol. 2, no. 68 B 5.

132) Diels-Kranz (1952) vol. 2, no. 68 B 13. This is a passage cited by Pfeiffer (1968) p. 132, note 63 — without reference to Demokritos — in the work *Peri antōnymias* (On the pronoun) by the Alexandrian grammarian Apollonios Dyskolos (2nd century A.D.), in which it is said that Demokritos had used certain forms of the pronoun *en tois Peri astronomiēs kai en tois hypoleipomenois syntagmasi* (in his books *On astronomy* and in his remaining works); see *Grammatici Graeci* vol. 2, p. 65, 16 f. On the various

meanings of *syntagma* in relation to books see Birt (1907) p. 264 f. and (1913) p. 341 f.

133) Schmidt (1922) p. 97 f.; Regenbogen (1950) column 1423.

134) Diogenes Laertios IX 46-49; on this, see Diels-Kranz (1952) vol. 2, pp. 90-92; 130-150; 207-210. On Thrasyllos see Gundel (1936).

135) Diels-Kranz (1952) vol. 2, p. 130.

136) Diogenes Laertios IX 37, 38, 41, 46. The introductory work had the title (IX 41): *Ta pro tēs anagnōseōs tōn Dēmokritu bibliōn* (That which ought to be read before reading the works of Demokritos).

137) Thrasyllos's comparison of Demokritos with a pentathlon athlete refers to these five classes; see Diogenes Laertios IX 37.

138) Diogenes Laertios IX 45 and III 56-61; on this, see Erbse (1961) p. 219 f.; Regenbogen (1950) column 1441 f. An analogous arrangement of the works of Plato and Demokritos can be discerned only in the two first tetralogies; they deal with the philosopher's conduct of live and with ethical questions. On an Alexandrian authoritative edition of Demokritos, arranged by tetralogies (Diels-Kranz (1952) vol. 2, p. 90, note to line 17) nothing is known, as Regenbogen loc. cit. emphasizes.

139) These *Aitiai* were probably similar to the *Problēmata* in the Corpus Aristotelicum and the *Aitia physika* of Plutarch which are arranged according to that pattern; these were brief explanations of natural phenomena in various fields.

140) Diogenes Laertios IX 48.

141) Diogenes Laertios IX 49.

142) This was assumed by Diels-Kranz (1952) vol. 2, p. 91, note to line 12, but was quite rightly rejected by Regenbogen (1950) column 1442. See also Diller (1953) pp. 44-46.

143) Diogenes Laertios IX 46, 47, 48.

144) Diels-Kranz (1952) vol. 2, p. 92, note to line 6, and pp. 207-218; also Schmidt (1922) p. 97; Kroll (1934); Waszink (1954); Pfeiffer (1968) p. 132.

145) Diels-Kranz (1952) vol. 2, p. 150, note to line 8 f. Wellmann (1926) who is cited by Diels-Kranz, thought that Damokritos, who had also written a work on Jews, was identical with Bolos; he relied on the *Suda* where it is erroneously said about Bolos: *Bōlos Dēmokritos philosophos* instead of *Dēmokriteios philosophos*. According to Schwartz (1901) Damokritos wrote at the earliest in the first century B.C., but before A.D. 70.

146) Astronomical works are listed both among the works on natural science (third tetralogy) and among the mathematical ones (eighth and ninth tetralogy). Since these works are lost, we cannot pass judgment on this issue.

147)　Schmidt (1922) p. 88 f.

148)　Diels-Kranz (1952) vol. 2 no. 68 B 155 a. Therefore I accept the
conjecture of Hicks *gōniēs* instead of the transmitted *gnōmēs* which is
meaningless in this context; this conjecture is reported in the edition by
Long (1964).

149)　On further double titles, see tetralogy IV 2; IV 3/4; IV 2; XI 1; XIII 1.
In VI 3 there is probably also a double title. The existing text has *Peri
loimōn kanōn*, but this should be, following Diels-Kranz (1952) vol. 2,
p. 140, 3, analogous to Diogenes Laertios X 27, *Peri logikōn ē Kanōn*.

150)　See for example the bibliography of Antisthenes, a Socratic and a
contemporary of Demokritos, Diogenes Laertios VI 15-18, which contains
numerous examples, also of the type *Phaidon ē Peri psychēs* (Phaidon, or
On the soul), mentioned below; also the bibliography of Theophrastos,
Diogenes Laertios V 50, in which is listed as no. 218 *Peri paideias ē
Peri arēton ē Peri sōphrosynēs* (On education, or On the virtues, or On
prudence).

151)　On the following, see Wendel (1949) pp. 29-32.

152)　Diogenes Laertios I 119.

153)　Wendel (1949) p. 108, note 165; see there also older examples.

154)　Exceptions confirm the rule: in the *Didaskaliai* of Aristotle two plays by
Kallias are listed only as *kōmōdia*; see Pickard-Cambridge (1968) p. 121,
no. 1097, line 2 and 3.

155)　Nachmanson (1941) p. 9 f.; Wendel (1949) p. 30; Diels-Kranz (1952) vol. 2,
no. 80 A 21 a and 24; B 1. Plato cites the work in *Theaetetus* 152 A and
166 D, and in *Cratylus* 391 C; its title *Aletheia* was apparently well
established. Sextus Empiricus, *Prōs mathēmatikus* VII 60 (2nd century A.D.)
mentions, however, the sentence "Man is the measure of all things"
as the beginning of the *Kataballontes* (sc. *logoi*, i.e. Refuting orations)
of Protagoras. Diels-Kranz, loc. cit. apparently think that the work
which began with this sentence had had a double title, given by Protagoras
himself, namely *Alētheia ē Kataballontes*; similarly von Fritz (1957) column
919 f. But I think this is highly unlikely. If the work was known under
the title *Alētheia*, then *Kataballontes* must have been the title of a collection
of at least two works, as the plural indicates; see Usener (1868) p. 161 f.
What was the second *logos* remains to be seen. The title *Alētheia* was also
used after Protagoras by the sophist Antiphon and by the Socratic
Antisthenes; see Diels-Kranz (1952) vol. 2, no. 87 B 1-44; Diogenes Laertios
VI 16. On the other hand, Hekataios—long before Protagoras—had begun
his *Genealogiai* thus: "Hekataios of Miletos speaks thus: I am writing this
as it seems to be true to me." See Jacoby (1957) no. 1, fragment 1 a with
commentary.

156) Wendel (1949) pp. 24-29; Widmann (1967) column 564-567 (with illustrations). According to Dionysios of Halikarnassos the Younger, who wrote the *Musikē historia* the author of an epic was named before the title, but the author of a drama after the title, e.g. *Homēru Ilias* not *Niobē Aischylu*, because the epic poet tells the story of certain persons, but the persons in a drama are themselves acting. This we read in the *Aischylu bios* which is taken from the *Musikē historia* and has come down to us (with an abridged ending) in some Aischylos MSS; printed in Page's Aischylos edition (Oxford, 1972).

157) Even in the time of the Emperors, scholars such as Galen (2nd century A.D.) and Plotinos (3rd century) left copies of their work with friends and pupils without *epigraphē*, i.e. without indication of authorship (Galen), or without title (Plotinus); see Galen, *Peri tōn idiōn bibliōn* (On his own works), Preface (vol. XIX, p. 10 Kühn); Porphyrios, *Bios Plōtinu* (The life of Plotinus) 26. But I doubt whether this was commonly done, as Harder states in his translation of Plotinos's works, vol. V c, p. 90 (Hamburg, 1957).

158) According to an assumption by Nachmanson (1941) pp. 50-52 some incorrect titles are due to the fact that later scholars had read only the beginnings of the works to which they assigned them.

159) For Pherekydes, whose work is cited by Diogenes Laertios I 119 with the beginning words of the text, see the *Suda* s.v. Pherekydes; for Archestratos see Athenaios I 4 e = Callimachus (1949), fragment 436; four titles are listed there; a fifth, preferred by Lykophron is mentioned by Athenaios VII 278 a. If a work had a second title, one said e.g. (Menander's *Dyskolos*) *antepigraphetai Misanthrōpos*; see the note of the Dyskolos papyrus Bodmer.

160) This fact is not clearly brought out in the professional literature.

161) Regenbogen (1950) column 1435 f.; this list transmitted under the name of Plutarch's son Lamprias is printed in Ziegler (1951) column 696-702.

162) Diogenes Laertios IX 46.

163) This happened quite often in dramatic works, especially in comedies; see Mensching (1964) p. 20.

164) Wendel (1949) p. 30.

165) The Attic genitive forms *andragathias* and *physēos* in tetralogies II 1 and IV 1 (Diogenes Laertios IX 46) betray their foreign origin. An Abderite would have used the Ionic forms *andragathies* and *physios*.

166) The above-mentioned note to the last works of the fourth tetralogy ("some write these works, etc.") is perhaps by Thrasyllos, because it is analogous to his introduction of the appendix.

167) Diogenes Laertios IX 46.

168) Diels-Kranz (1952) vol. 2, no. 67 B 1-2.

169)   Diogenes Laertios IX 46 f.; a note on *Tritogeneia* (I 4) says that this means that three things developed from it which encompass everything human; see Diels-Kranz (1952) vol. 2, p. 132 to B 2: "Tritogeneia (Athena the 'Triple-born') = Wisdom. From being wise this threefold thing springs: to think well, to speak well, and to do one's duty." On *Kratyntēria* (VI 1), this means the confirmation of what was said before. The source of Thrasyllos may have been the Demokritos glossary of Kallimachos.

170)   Diogenes Laertios IX 46.

171)   Diels-Kranz (1952) vol. 2, p. 132, 11. Diels's assumption follows from his rendering of the title.

172)   In the title *Peri logikōn kanōn* (tetralogy VI 3), recorded by Diogenes Laertios IX 47, the conjunction *ē* was probably also omitted by an oversight.

173)   Schmidt (1922) p. 97 f.; he assumed, like Oder (1890) p. 74, that Kallimachos had recognized the spuriousness of the works known under the name of Demokritos but written by Bolos (who lived later), and that he had proved this; see also Pfeiffer (1968) p. 132, note 9.

174)   The original of the *Pinakes* perished probably already in the conflagration of 47 B.C.

175)   The work had the title *Pros tus Kallimachu Pinakas* (On the Pinakes of Kallimachos). See Schmidt (1922) pp. 27 and 101 f.; Callimachus (1949) p. 349; Pfeiffer (1968) pp. 133-134. The preposition *pros* in the title does probably not mean "against", as Pfeiffer stresses in opposition to Schmidt, but it still expresses criticism. Cf. the title of a work by Zenodotos of Alexandria, cited in the *Suda*: *Pros ta hyp' Aristarchu athetumena tu poiētu* (On the Homeric verses invalidated by Aristarchos). See also Slater (1976).

176)   Callimachus (1949), fragment 429-435. In addition, there is now an Oxyrhynchus papyrus with a citation referring to the classification of a poem by Bakchylides; see Bacchylides, ed. Snell, ed. VIII (Leipzig, 1961) p. *50 and 73; on this Pfeiffer (1968) pp. 133-134. The citations are also printed in Schmidt (1922) pp. 21-25, except for the two that were not yet known to him; Witty (1958) published a not always faithful English translation of these passages. Schmidt's monograph on the *Pinakes* of Kallimachos was the basis for all later works on this subject. Among these, the following may be mentioned: Gardthausen (1922); Herter (1931) column 396-401; Wendel (1940) pp. 9-21; Regenbogen (1950) column 1420-1426; Wendel-Göber (1955) pp. 62-68; Erbse (1961) pp. 211-217; Hunger (1961) p. 63 f.; Pfeiffer (1968) pp. 126-134. Herter (1973) column 184-188; also Wilamowitz (1924) vol. 1, p. 165 f.; Löffler (1956) pp. 15-20; Schubart (1960) pp. 46-53; Widmann (1967) column 610-619.

177)   Callimachus (1949), fragment 432.

178)   Callimachus (1949), fragments 433 and 434.

179)   Gardthausen (1922) p. 76; Schmidt (1922) pp. 47-49.

180) The work by Hermippos is cited in the *Suda* s.v. Istros, and in the *Etymologicum magnum* p. 118, 4; the one by Hesychios is cited only in the *Suda* s.v. Hesychios. The title of Hermippos's work in the *Suda* is slightly different from the one cited in the *Etymologicum magnum*, but the statements agree with each other on the fact that the work dealt with slaves who had distinguished themselves in various branches of learning. See also Christ-Schmid (1924) p. 868.

181) Jaeger (1933) vol. 1, p. 384: "The concept which denoted originally only the process of education as such expanded the scope of its meaning towards the objective, content-oriented side, exactly as our word "Bildung" or the equivalent Latin "cultura", which, starting from the process of learning, becomes a denotation of being learned, and then means the content of learning, finally encompassing the entire realm of learning and culture into which an individual human being is born as a member of his nation or a particular social environment."

182) Isokrates, *Peri tēs antidoseōs* 268 calls grammar, music, and the other branches of intellectual and artistic education of youth *paideiai* in the plural.

183) This means not only the star performers. Whoever had written a work belonged among those who had "distinguished themselves". However, those who had not written anything became known only when they had been stars.

184) Diogenes Laertios I 16 names ten philosophers who had not written any works. The realm of *paideia*, as it was commonly understood, which encompassed much more than literature, is described by Athenaios in a passage cited by Pfeiffer (1968) p. 252 f (IV 184 b f.): he reports the renewal of the entire *paideia* (*ananeosis paideias hapases*) which was brought about by those scholars who had been driven out of Alexandria by Ptolemaios VIII Euergetes II, named Kakergetes in the year 145/144 B.C.; these represented the *paideia* and were forced by poverty to work as teachers of their arts in the places to which they had fled; he names among these philologists, philosophers, geometers, (i.e. mathematicians), musicians, painters, physical training coaches (*paidotribai*), physicians and many other artisans (*technitai*).

185) It is therefore difficult to translate the title of the *Pinakes*. Pfeiffer (1968) p. 128 translates "Tables of all those who were eminent in any kind of literature and of their writings in 120 books." He ascribes this title to Kallimachos, but translates it in the same sense in which it was understood by a later scholar who formulated it, as I think.

186) Leo (1901) pp. 132-135.

187) Mensching (1964) p. 21.

188) Schmidt (1922) pp. 46-98; Gardthausen (1922) pp. 76-80; Herter (1931) column 396-401; Wendel (1949) pp. 24-75; Regenbogen (1950) column 1418-23; Pfeiffer (1968) pp. 128-134.

189) Callimachus (1949), fragment 429: Diogenes Laertios VIII 86 (beginning of the chapter on Eudoxos); fragment 430: Athenaios XV 669 D/E; fragment 431: Scholium to Aristophanes's *Birds*, verse 692; fragment 432: Dionysios of Halikarnassos, *Prōs Ammaiōn* 4; fragment 433: Athenaios XII 585 B; fragment 434: Athenaios VI 244 A; fragment 435: Athenaios XIV 643 E; see also note 192 below.

190) Groups of rich citizens for the cooperative financing of the construction and equipment of naval vessels (triremes).

191) On the "Banquet rules" of Academicians and Peripatetics see Moraux (1951) p. 129; Herter (1952) pp. 9 and 29; Jaeger (1955) p. 336.

192) The papyrus fragment was published only after the publication of Pfeiffer's Kallimachos edition; see Pfeiffer (1968) p. 130, note 5.

193) I designate the authors of works of the same literary genre (*genos*) or type (*eidos*) and of the same scientific discipline as well as their works as one class, which may sometimes consist of several subclasses. The Greeks did not distinguish sharply between levels of subclasses; for example, they equated dramatic works (tragedies, comedies) with epic works, a literary genre. The parts of philosophy were designated by some Stoics as *merē* and as *topoi*, but also as *genē* and as *eidē*; see Diogenes Laertios VII 39.

194) On this, see especially Schmidt (1922) pp. 49-57. Schemes of arrangement exist in the so-called *Canones*. The elegiac, iambic and melic poets were the equivalent of our lyric poets, but only the melic poets were also called lyric poets, because their songs were sung to the accompaniment of a lyre or other instrument, whereas the elegiac and iambic poems were spoken; see Pfeiffer (1968) pp. 183-184.

195) Melic poets: fragments 441 and 450; tragic poets: fragment 451; comic poets: fragments 439 and 440; historians: fragment 437; philosophers: fragments 438 and 442; orators: fragments 430-431; legislators: fragment 433. It is here assumed that the classes were named not after the works contained in them but by the listed authors; see also the following text. Regarding the legislators, for every law that existed in a literary form — and only those are meant here — the Greeks had a historical or mythical originator.

196) Wendel (1949) pp. 71 and 73. Wendel assumes because of the sequence of author classes to which Eudoxos belonged (he is named as *astrologos, geōmetrēs, iatros, nomothetēs*) that they were alphabetically arranged. But Eudoxos was mainly famous as an astronomer and mathematician.

197) When Kallimachos was rebuked because of the manysidedness (*polyeideia*) of his production, he referred to the very versatile Ion of Chios; see Callimachus (1949) p. 205, Iambus XIII, Diegesis.

198) Schmidt (1922) p. 58; Wendel (1949) p. 73 f.

199) Pfeiffer (1968) p. 131.

200) Schmidt (1922) p. 66 f.; Callimachus (1949), fragment 429 with Pfeiffer's note.

201) Callimachus (1949), fragment 438.

202) Diogenes Laertios VIII 90 names two such scholars.

203) E.g. in the *Suda* (Hesychios) s.v. Eratosthenes.

204) The term *epigraphei* (he entitles) is used analogously in fragments 436, 440 and 448; see Schmidt (1922) p. 68.

205) Pfeiffer (1968) p. 130 thinks that Kallimachos subdivided the *epinikia* (victory ode) further by kinds of contests and festivals. He refers to fragment 441 (ode of Simonides for victors in foot races) and fragment 450 (ode of Pindar for a victor at the Nemea). But Kallimachos already had at his disposal a collection of the odes of Simonides for victors in foot races. It is, however, possible that he collected into three groups the Olympic, Pythian and Nemean odes of Pindar. The citation says, however, only that he had recorded an ode, which afterwards had been named the second Pythian one, as one on a victory at the Nemea.

206) Callimachus (1949) fragments 436, 443, 444, 449.

207) Wendel (1949) p. 32 f.

208) Callimachus (1949), fragments 440, 436, 437. Incidentally, the *Eunuchos* was a second revised edition of *Hairesiteichēs*, which apparently began with the same words as the first one. It is said that the play was also known under the title *Stratiōtēs* (The soldier); see Wilamowitz (1875) p. 140. The work purportedly written by Nesiotes was recognized only by Eratosthenes as the second part of the *Perihēgēsis* by Hekataios of Miletos; see Jacoby (1957) no. 1, T. 11 b with commentary.

209) Pliny the Elder who reports the listing of works on magic by Hermippos also mentions the sum of lines written by "Zoroaster" as counted by Hermippos.

210) On the following, see Wendel (1949) pp. 34-44; Schubart (1960) pp. 68-70.

211) The conversion was probably made as follows (the specialists do not mention particulars): assuming a text had 800 lines with an average of 10 syllables each, therefore 8,000 syllables; 8,000 divided by 16 (the average number of syllables in a hexameter) resulted in 500 standard lines (*epē* or *stichoi*). But if only 9 syllables per line or *epē* and *stichoi* of 15 syllables were counted, the same text had a different number of standard lines.

212) Wendel (1949) p. 41; similarly already Herter (1931) column 399.

213) On this and the following, see Wendel (1949) pp. 44-59, especially p. 56: "It is indisputable that generally the book as part of a work had his own scroll, as had the book as a complete work."

214) On the following, see Schmidt (1922) pp. 91-97, and Pfeiffer's notes to the citations (fragments).

215) See Pfeiffer's note who, in my opinion, interpreted the passage correctly. It is less likely that Kallimachos had stated that the poem was not by Parmenides.

216) The end of the citation is corrupt, as has been recognized long since: "A work which is disputed as [a work] of Epigenes, as Kallimachos says". According to Clemens Alexandrinus, *Stromata* I 131, Epigenes was a scholar from an unknown period who had written an essay on the poems known under the name of Orpheus (*Peri tēs eis Orphea [anapheromenēs] poiēseōs*). (The article on Orpheus by Hesychios (in the *Suda*) still reflects the learned discussion on the real authors of "Orphic" poems, without, however, naming specific scholars.) It is out of the question that Kallimachos declared Epigenes to be the author of the *Triagmos* (in Clemens and in the *Suda*: *Triagmoi*), which had been ascribed to Ion of Chios by other scholars. Bergk suggested therefore to write *hypo Epigenus* (by Epigenes) instead of *hōs Epigenus*. Diels and Jacoby preferred to read *hōs kai Epigenes* or *hōs Epigenes* (as, or also Epigenes). Bergk's suggestion is, however, preferable not only because it is the simplest one, but also and above all because it is in accord with the facts. Kallimachos reported, as was his custom, that Epigenes denied, contrary to other scholars, that Ion had been the real author of the *Triagmos* (*Triagmoi*) ascribed to Orpheus. Epigenes did not report that this had been denied, but he denied it himself. It is not known who he thought to be the author of the work. Clemens mentions only two other works by "Orpheus" which he ascribes to Kerkops and Brontinos. Cohn (1907) column 64 f. recommended Bergk's suggestion, but Schmidt (1922) p. 94 rejected it.

217) Callimachus (1949), fragment 451: Scholium to Euripides's *Andromachē*, verse 445. See also Pfeiffer's note.

218) Pfeiffer (1968) pp. 73-74; 117; 137.

219) Callimachus (1949), fragments 444-447; see also Lossau (1964) pp. 81-86. Lossau assumes, however, that Kallimachos made decisions on authenticity, whereas, in my opinion, he simply recorded the statements in the copies at hand (which was not considered by Lossau).

220) Callimachus (1949) fragment 446. Photios, *Bibliothēkē* cod. 265, p. 491 b says about an oration, perhaps following Dionysios of Halikarnassos, that all men of sound judgment thought it certainly was by Demosthenes, but that Kallimachos, who was not capable of judging orations (*ud' hikanos ōn krinein*) thought it had been by Deinarchos. Incidentally, it seems that Kallimachos denied Plato's capability to judge poetic works in almost the same words; see Callimachus (1949), fragment 589.

221) The editor of Demosthenes included two orations which were held to be authentic by Kallimachos but were doubted by others (no. VII and VIII of the present numbering, now generally not ascribed to Demosthenes, see Callimachus (1949) fragments 443 and 444), and he omitted one oration

declared to be spurious by Kallimachos, but ascribed to Demosthenes by others; see Callimachus (1949) fragment 446; it has therefore not come down to us. But our Corpus Demosthenicum also lacks an oration considered to be authentic by Kallimachos, but judged to be spurious by others; see Callimachus (1949) fragment 445. Unless this oration was lost by accident, as Drerup (1899) assumed, the editor diverged on this point from Kallimachos. He also entitled the oration against the letter and the ambassadors of king Philip (no. VIII), following Kallimachos, *Peri Hallonēsu*; see Schmidt (1922) p. 85; Lossau (1964) p. 67. Based on this evidence we may assume with a certain degree of probability that the Alexandrian edition of Demosthenes's orations followed the *Pinakes* of Kallimachos regarding their titles and the elimination of the spurious ones, perhaps with a few exceptions. The classification into political, forensic, and epideictic ("show-off") orations followed a tradition which had certainly been observed already by Kallimachos when he recorded them. Whether the edition had more to offer on textual criticism than on authenticity is impossible to say.

222) Widmann (1967) column 618, especially note 132, Pfeiffer (1968) p. 129; Herter (1973) column 187; Widmann (1975) p. 12.

223) Blum (1980) pp. 8-9.

224) Regenbogen (1950).

5. Later Lists of Greek Writers and Their Works

5.1 The Pinakes of Kallimachos as Examples and Sources of Later Lists

AS THE GREAT Alexandrian library was far superior to any earlier Greek book collections, so also its catalog, the *Pinakes* created by Kallimachos, a repertory of the works of Greek literature held by the library with data on their authors, was unique, the more so since the library had copies of almost all works that still existed at that time. It is therefore generally assumed that all Hellenistic scholars who compiled catalogs or bibliographies after Kallimachos also used his methods and his results. His *Pinakes* were "published" in the second half of the third century B.C. (perhaps not by himself but by his pupils), that is to say, they were copied for interested scholars outside of the Museion. This can be deduced from the fact that Aristophanes of Byzantium published a separate work in several books, containing corrections and supplements to the *Pinakes*. The catalog of the library of the Museion on which this work was based, was of course continued, because the collection grew steadily, new books had to be cataloged, and the cataloging of old books had to be improved. The work by Aristophanes of Byzantium bears witness to this. We may be sure that the successors of Kallimachos followed his example, i.e. they endeavored to identify the works contained in newly acquired scrolls, to distinguish between authors with identical names, to indicate also others by relevant data about their persons, to separate authentic works from spurious ones, etc. If and when they were successful, they recorded the authors and their works in the appropriate classes, just as Kallimachos had done. Thus, the Alexandrian *Pinakes* contained also biographical data on authors who lived after Kallimachos.

The *Pinakes* of the library at Pergamon were apparently arranged according to the Alexandrian pattern. At least, two remarks by Dionysios of Halikarnassos show that the authors were listed by classes, and that the lists of their works were preceded by brief biographical data.[1] Otherwise, very little is known about these *Pinakes*. They are cited only by Dionysios of Halikarnassos and by Athenaios, altogether four times, two of these citations being negative;[2] apparently they were much less frequently used than those compiled by Kallimachos.

The hope of some modern researchers to find parts of Hellenistic library catalogs on papyri has not yet been fulfilled. Up to now, only four lists of books on papyrus fragments from the third century B.C. have come to light, and even these are difficult to interpret. The first of these fragments comes apparently from the catalog of a (public) library, the second is perhaps the draft of a catalog, the third and fourth are private copies made from library catalogs.[3] For our investigation they do not yield anything except for one point that has already been mentioned.[4]

However, a fragment of a library catalog from Rhodos in the form of an inscription carved in stone towards the end of the second century B.C., deserves attention (see below, section 5.2). Of course, this catalog of a relatively small library (probably that of the gymnasium) is not fully comparable with the *Pinakes* of the great Alexandrian library.

Not only librarians but also other scholars, especially authors of author biographies,[5] made good use of the entries in the *Pinakes* of Kallimachos. Foremost among the Alexandrian scholars who continued the biographical writings of the Peripatetics was Hermippos of Smyrna. He was probably the first among the pupils of Kallimachos who enriched biographies of philosophers and orators by adding bibliographies; his works are, however, all lost (see below, section 5.3). He as well as his successors owed their knowledge to the collections and lists of the great Alexandrian library. Later scholars used, of course, also other large libraries, especially the one in Pergamon.

The Alexandrian philologists who, beginning ca. 200 B.C., used to introduce their editions of classical poets and prose writers with biographies which were substantially different from those of Hermippos, nevertheless relied on the same sources. These biographies usually contained at the end a list of works written by the author and of writings falsely ascribed to him. In a complete edition the table of contents was actually equivalent to a bibliography of the author (see below, section 5.3).

Lists of works by individual authors were only seldom published individually. The Aristotle bibliography compiled by Andronikos of Rhodos (middle of the first century B.C.) and probably written in Alexandria, is one of the few exceptions (see below, section 5.4).

An insight into the work of a Greek scholar at the end of the first century B.C. who also dealt with biographical and bibliographical problems, is provided by the incompletely transmitted treatise by Dionysios of Halikarnassos on the life and work of the orator Deinarchos (see below, section 5.5). Dionysios utilized both the Alexandrian and the Pergamenian *Pinakes* for his work.

The biographers of earlier centuries had sought data or at least hints on the lives and creations of the poets, philosophers, etc. in their works or in those of their contemporaries. Although they sometimes interpreted these sources arbitrarily, they at least did their own research. But already since the beginning of the second century B.C. some scholars only compiled excerpts from older works that contained bibliographic data to form biographic collections; finally, in the time of the Roman emperors, biobibliographic handbooks were compiled from this and other materials, in which not only a few but all known representatives of a class of authors (e.g. grammarians, those with homonymous names, those that had been slaves) were listed. These compilations and handbooks as well as the older works on which they were based are all lost, and they can only be incompletely reconstructed from the works of later scholars who utilized them.

Outstanding among these compilations from the time of the Roman emperors is the work of Diogenes Laertios (beginning of the third century A.D.) on the lives and opinions of famous philosophers which partly contains also bibliographies, and the largely biobibliographic list of persons renowned in branches of learning by Hesychios of Miletos (middle of the 6th century) of which excerpts have been preserved in the *Suda* (see below, sections 5.6 and 5.7). Both works contain a wealth of material. It is not easy and often even impossible to name the specific authorities on whom Diogenes and Hesychios relied.[6] But it is not difficult to tell generally where the information on the lives and works of the "great" authors came from: in the last analysis, they were taken from the biographies of famous poets, philosophers, orators, etc., augmented in many cases by bibliographies of their works. But these were a minority; in addition there were many other authors who had also been known by name but had never been honored by a biography, not to mention the minor poets and writers like them. Among the more than eight hundred authors recorded in the *Onomatologos* of Hesychios, at most fifteen percent (a little more than the ten percent which had been included as classics in the so-called *Canones*) had ever had a biography with a bibliography. How did the authorities of Hesychios or their own authorities know the details of the lives and publications of the other authors? There were only very few sources for biographical and bibliographical information on authors of the second and third rank. The Alexandrian and Pergamenian *Pinakes* were certainly the best ones; especially the former were probably utilized by the compilers of biobibliographical handbooks. Some modern researchers assumed this already about a hundred years ago,[7] but it was later forgotten; at any rate, it was no longer mentioned in the publications that appeared during the past fifty years.

Among the sources on which the works of Diogenes and Hesychios and those of their authorities were based are also the products of the so-called motley writers.[8] These were large collections of information on any conceivable subject; many of these, such as the *Deipnosophistai* of Athenaios were presented in the form of table talk. Their authors had scanned the collections of large libraries (Athenaios who was born in Naukratis, about 60 miles southeast of Alexandria, had probably also used the one in the Serapeion in Alexandria) and they had collected, among other things, also valuable biographical and bibliographical information. These "motley writers" could very well claim Kallimachos as their ancestor, because he had also recorded much of what he had read in his *hypomnēmata*.

Finally, it may be mentioned that the authorities on whom Diogenes and Hesychios relied had also utilized the works of the so-called chronographers, especially the *Chronika* of Apollodoros of Athens. This author had versified the fundamental work of Greek chronology, the *Chronographiai* (Time tables) by Eratosthenes, and had continued them until his own time, i.e. until the middle of the second century B.C. Eratosthenes, a pupil of Kallimachos, had also recorded many events in literary history, following the method of Demetrios of Phaleron. Apollodoros, a pupil of Aristarchos, followed his example. Eratosthenes had probably realized that a firm chronological framework was much needed for the identification of texts, when he collaborated in the compilation of the *Pinakes*. Thus, as even this brief survey shows, Kallimachos's work had a far-reaching influence. In the following sections, I shall describe each of the works mentioned above which give us a more exact idea about Greek biobibliography, and I shall give reasons for the as yet unsubstantiated statements I made about them.

5.2 The Inscription of a Library Catalog in Rhodos

The fragment of a list of books found in Rhodos was first published in 1925 by Maiuri and then, with corrections and reconstructions, in 1935 by Segre.[9] In the view of experts, the inscription was carved in stone at the end of the second or beginning of the first century B.C. What exists is a narrow column of 29 lines and to the right of it a second column with the beginnings of 13 lines. In the left-hand column are recorded: six works by Demetrios of Phaleron (the name with at least one title is broken off, but can be reconstructed with certainty on the strength of the listed works) (lines 1-7); three works by Hegesias (of Magnesia) (lines 8-10); two works by Theodektes (the Younger, of Phaselis) (lines 11-12); fourteen works by Theopompos (of Chios) (lines 13-27); and one work by "another" Theopompos, not identical with the previously listed famous historian, who was unknown until then (lines 28-29). In the right-hand column one can make out the names of the authors Dionysios (line 20), Damokleidas (line 26) and Eratosthenes (line 29). The data are quite brief: author (only personal name, in the genitive case), title, extent (number of books). The layout of the entries is well designed: the author's name is always shifted somewhat to the left, the first title follows immediately in most cases; most data on the extent are indented far to the right, as if all these data were meant to be listed one below the other. The titles of other works by the same author always begin on a new line, somewhat indented. If a title runs to two lines, the second line is again somewhat indented. If the first title does not follow immediately after the author's name but starts only on the second line, that line is also indented like other second title lines.

The following example of a few lines in English translation shows the arrangement:

Demetrios's

    ....

5   On the Athenian
    legislation.   Five [books]

    ....

10 Theopompos's Lakonikos.[10]   [One book]
     Panionikos.[10]   One [book]

    ....

28 Theopompos's, another's
    On the reign of kings.   One [book]

The purpose of providing meaningful indentions is quite evident, even though a few mistakes have been made.

The authors are no doubt arranged alphabetically, but only by the first letter.[11] On the other hand, it is not evident whether the titles were listed according to a particular principle. Since all of the listed works are lost, it is somewhat difficult to characterize them. One could, however, say that they were mostly writings on politics and rhetoric, which does not preclude that some of them may have dealt also with other subjects. The connection between politics and rhetoric formed a link between most of them. There were learned works on political themes (e.g. the work on Athenian legislation in five books by Demetrios, line 5), political memoranda in the form of orations or letters (e.g. Theopompos's letter to Antipatros, line 22), but also several epideictic orations, especially eulogies and festive orations (e.g. Theopompos's *Maussōlos* and *Panathēnaikos*, lines 15 and 25), some of which may have had political overtones, also the *Technē* by Theodektes the Younger, a textbook of rhetoric in four books (line 11, according to the *Suda* it comprised seven books) and the *Katadromē* by Theopompos, a pamphlet against Plato and the Academy by the pupil of Isokrates (line 26); the latter was only apparently out of place, because it probably dealt with the importance of rhetoric for the *paideia* which was judged differently by Plato and by Isokrates.[12]

It seems that the right-hand column also listed mostly political and rhetorical works by authors whose names began with the letters delta and epsilon.[13] Wendel thought that these were addenda to the works of authors in the left-hand column with the initial letters delta, ēta, thēta; these could not have been works of a new class, because there was no room for the authors following Theopompos in the first class and those preceding Dionysos in a second class.[14] But it is unlikely that the right-hand column was left free for later additions. I presume therefore that the stone carver made a mistake in transferring the entries from the written copy and jumped from Demetrios to Hegesias; when he realized his mistake, he added the omitted authors with the initial letters delta and epsilon in the right-hand column.

The experts are of different opinions regarding the character of the inscription. Some think that it listed a donation of books, others explain it as a library catalog.[15] The latter assumption is, in my opinion, much more reasonable; the author of the original list evidently wished to display the contents of a book collection in a clearly arranged form for those who were interested. It would hardly have been worthwhile for someone to list a donation of books in this manner. The "Piraeus stone", with which we shall deal below, shows what an inscription looked like that listed a book donation.

Relying on another inscription from the second century B.C., discovered in the Upper City of Rhodos, in which donations and the names of gymnasiarchs are listed, and "the" library is being mentioned, those researchers who think that the above-mentioned inscription is the catalog of a library, especially Wendel and Segre, assume that this had been the library of the gymnasium situated in the Upper City.[16] The listed works would, indeed, have been in the right place in an institution that served for the education of youth in politics and rhetoric, especially since at that time Rhodos was a center for the study of rhetoric.[17]

The idea to transfer a library catalog contained in one or more scrolls onto a wall, so that all could clearly see it, was in itself not a bad one; it had already been realized by the custodian of Egyptian temple libraries.[18] To be sure, it was difficult to add new acquisitions if a catalog was carved in stone. But we do not know under what circumstances this action was taken or by whom.

The catalog reproduced in the inscription was, of course, a catalog of works. It would not have made sense to list two or more copies of the same work, if the library had such multiple copies, which was probably the case. A listing of the existing works was quite sufficient.

Since the historical works by Theopompos of Chios are not listed in the fragment of the catalog, Wendel assumed that they were recorded in another class, separate from his political writings.[19] But it is not at all sure that they were held by the library. Rather, it seems to me that the library owned only a few books other than political and rhetorical ones.[20] If that was the case, it need not have been classified, nor was there a need for a classified catalog. The works held by the library (or its classes) were at any rate arranged by authors, and these were filed alphabetically by the initial letter of their names. Since the librarian wanted to make it as easy as possible to survey the holdings of the library we must assume that the principle of alphabetical arrangement was not new but had been used for a long time. From this we may also further deduce that the alphabetical listing of the authors on the baking of cakes as given by Kallimachos was not accidental, but was based on a principle followed by Kallimachos and by other librarians of the Greek cultural sphere. (The relations between Alexandria and Rhodos were particularly close.) A more exact alphabetical order was probably not followed in Alexandria either. The *Pinakes* of Kallimachos reflected largely the physical arrangement of the scrolls on the shelves of the library; but in the long run one could not keep the scrolls in a more exact alphabetical order, because they were put on the shelves in heaps and moved as soon as one was pulled out.

The compiler of the catalog of Rhodos did not complete the name of an author with that of his father and the name of his place of birth, as Kallimachos had done, not to mention further biographic details, but he did distinguish the "other" Theopompos from his namesake, the historian. More than that did not seem to be required for his purposes. He also did not deem it necessary to record the beginning words of each work and the number of its lines. It seems also that he listed the titles quite simply one after the other, as the scrolls containing the works of a certain author happened to lie on the shelf. Most authors were represented by only a few works, except for Theopompos, but even the fourteen titles of his works were easy to scan. The Rhodian cataloger was, however, eager to indicate exactly where the entry of the next author or the next work began, by using different indentions of certain lines. This evidently seemed to be more important to him than the alphabetization of the titles, and he prescribed the indentions for the stone carver who only executed what he was told to do. The structuring of larger numbers of entries by indentation of lines—a trick known today to all librarians and bibliographers—can thus be documented already for the second century B.C. at Rhodos and may even hark back to the *Pinakes* of Kallimachos. Incidentally, the first of the three papyri from the third century A.D. (library catalogs) mentioned above is also similarly structured.[21]

The arrangement of authors in the library catalog of Rhodos confirms what Schmidt (who did not yet know of this inscription) deduced from later author lists for the *Pinakes* of Kallimachos. He relies primarily on the following three lists:[22]
1. the authors of poetic and prose works on fishery (*Halieutika*) mentioned by Athenaios; the prose writers are there listed in inverted alphabetical order after the poets, and the place of birth or the country of birth of all authors is indicated.
2. the authors of "banquets" (*deipna*) in verse, also listed by Athenaios and also in inverted alphabetical order; for these, it is almost certain that Athenaios took their names from the subdivision "Authors who wrote on *deipna*" of the main class "Miscellaneous works" in the *Pinakes* of Kallimachos, from which he cites in

another passage the description of Chairephon's cookbook. The data are decidedly in the style of Kallimachos; the class of authors or its subclass "authors of *deipnōn anagraphai*" (descriptions of banquets) is listed first, then the place of birth and, if known, any other name and the teacher: Timachides of Rhodos in eleven or more books; Numenios of Herakleia, pupil of the physician Dieuches (his work may have been a diet cookbook in verse); Matreas of Pitane, the parodist; Hegemon of Thasos, called Phakē (lentil) who is counted by some among the poets of the Old Comedy (which may presumably mean that he had been classified by Kallimachos as an old (*archaios*) poet of comedies).[23] 3. the authors of works in prose and verse on agriculture in Greek, mentioned by Varro. Varro distinguishes between 24 authors whose place of birth (*patria*) had been transmitted, and 16 others whom he knew only under their personal names. Perhaps Kallimachos already separated these because their identification was not certain, there being many bearers of common names such as Dionysios, Krates and Lysimachos.[24]

5.3 Biographies of Authors with Lists of Their Works

Hermippos of Smyrna, often called the Kallimachean, but also the Peripatetic, gained recognition by cataloging the many works on magic in the library of the Museion.[25] But he became famous through his biographical works on philosophers (e.g. Aristotle and Theophrastos), orators (e.g. Isokrates and his pupils, among which was Demosthenes) and poets (e.g. Hipponax). Judging from the citations of later scholars, these writings were similar to the works of Aristoxenos, Chamaileon and other Peripatetics. They were based on the biographical hints in the works of these authors and in those of their contemporaries, which were partly taken at their face value, partly interpreted arbitrarily; they were intended for the educated public, were written according to the rules of rhetoric, and were richly adorned by anecdotes. It is assumed that Hermippos was called a Peripatetic only because of this similarity.[26]

Two probably somewhat younger Alexandrian scholars, Satyros and Sotion, also wrote biographical works but these too are lost.[27] Satyros, who came from Kallatis on the Pontos and was called a Peripatetic like Hermippos, published biographies of poets, philosophers and orators but also of rulers; his biography of Euripides had the form of a dialog, as shown by a papyrus fragment.[28] Sotion, born in Alexandria, established with his biographies of philosophers, entitled *Diadochai* (Successors), the principle of schools of philosophers which has been followed ever since in the history of philosophy.

Wehrli, who collected and explained anew the fragments of Hermippos, i.e. the citation of his works, sees in him as a biographer merely a writer of light entertainment.[29] In my view, however, the Kallimachean, like the real Peripatetics, wanted in his works not only to entertain his readers but also to educate them, that is to say, he wanted to convey information on the lives and works of the authors he dealt with. Presumably, the citations do not convey a complete picture of his biographies, because what was mainly cited were the interesting and amusing passages. But Dionysios of Halikarnassos complains in his work on the orator Isaios that Hermippos, who had been exact (*akribēs*) about other orators, had recorded about Isaios only that he had been a pupil of Isokrates and the teacher of Demosthenes.[30] As is evident from another passage, in which

Dionysios makes the same complaint against Kallimachos regarding the orator Deinarchos,[31] he meant the lack of data on his origin, descent, period of flourishing, education, activities and fate of the orator. Thus, Hermippos did generally report these data. As Wehrli stresses, he, like his teacher Kallimachos, liked to cite his authorities for special information, namely partially unknown scholars whose works he had found in the library.[32] Wehrli calls this "foppish flaunting of erudition";[33] but it also shows a desire on Hermippos's part to obtain more detailed information on the persons he wrote about.

If the church father Jerome lists Hermippos in the first place among his Greek models in the preface to his biobibliographic work *De viris illustribus*[34] (which, despite this title, dealt only with Christian authors), then Hermippos must also have made bibliographic statements in his biographies. It is known that he compiled a bibliography of Theophrastos.[35] The list of works of this philosopher by Diogenes Laertios is probably derived from that bibliography.[36] Wehrli denies that Hermippos's bibliography of Theophrastos was connected with his biography of Theophrastos.[37] But so far as I can see, bibliographies of individual authors were not published as separate works at that time,[38] and even later this happened only in special cases.

From the work by Dionysios of Halikarnassos *To Ammaios* we can further deduce that Hermippos's biography of Demosthenes also contained a bibliography. Dionysios tries to show in this work that it was not Demosthenes who learned from the *Rhetoric* of Aristotle, but that the latter had learned from the oratory of Demosthenes. He therefore records first some (not transmitted) data on the life of the orator, second a list of the orations delivered by him until 349/348 with brief chronological notes and historical explanations, partly also with opening lines of the text, third and fourth analogous information on the life and work of Aristotle, all based on the, as he says, generally accepted results of research (*koinai historiai*) of the biographers of Demosthenes.[39] But who were the biographers on whom Dionysios relied? Regarding Demosthenes, he means no doubt mainly or even exclusively Hermippos, the best-known of the Hellenistic biographers of Demosthenes, as was noted already by Diels.[40] Thus, Hermippos included a chronological list of the authentic orations of Demosthenes in his biography of the orator, which is what we would expect from him more than from any other biographer of Demosthenes.[41] His biographies were thus probably a mixture of dry information and all manner of anecdotes, similar to those later compiled by Diogenes Laertios.

Sotion, as we learn from two citations by Diogenes Laertios, appended critical bibliographies to his biographies.[42] Whether Satyros did the same is questionable because of the dialog form of (all?) his biographies. But he, like Sotion, also dealt with problems of ascription. This was already occasionally done by the real Peripatetics. But only their Alexandrian successors who had access to the *Pinakes* created by Kallimachos in the library of the Museion, could complete their biographies by lists of works culled from those catalogs. It seems that Hermippos, who collaborated in the compilation of the *Pinakes*, introduced this innovation.[43]

Other Hellenistic biographers of authors also sought to ascertain the works that had really been written by them and to distinguish them from the spurious ones, as can be seen from the few citations of their lost writings. To mention only a few who are listed by Diogenes Laertios besides Hermippos, Satyros and Sotion because of their bibliographic information: Antigonos of Karystos (second half of the 3rd century B.C.), Neanthes of Kyzikos (3rd/2nd century B.C.), Panaitios of Rhodos (2nd century B.C.), and Sosikrates of Rhodos (2nd century B.C.).

An official at the court of Ptolemaios VI by the name of Herakleides Lembos, who had literary and philosophical interests, and who was also active as a historian, made excerpts from the biographical writings of Hermippos, Satyros and Sotion in the middle of the second century B.C.[44] Later scholars made good use of these *epitomai*, though they pretended to have seen the originals themselves. This was quite common.

In the second century B.C. a new type of author biography appeared. Leo called these "grammatical" (i.e. philological), contrary to the "rhetorical" ones by the Peripatetics and their successors,[45] because the Alexandrian grammarians as a rule put brief biographies, entitled *Bios* or more modestly *Genos* (Descent), at the beginning of their editions of the poets and prose writers who were considered as classics. In the Byzantine copies of authors included in the *Canones* as classics there are biographies which are based on those compiled by the Alexandrian grammarians.[46] Their learned authors limited themselves to a report of the most important data and facts that they had found, in a simple style, without any anecdotal frills and without a rhetorical presentation, quite different from the style of the Peripatetics. They listed: name, author class, place of birth, family, teachers, period of flourishing, contemporaries, place of activity (if not identical with place of birth), unusual events, inventions (innovations), conspicuous characteristics, death, age, works. These categories are always the same, sometimes more, sometimes less; their sequence changes somewhat.[47] The characteristics of this scheme occur in part already in the biographical data of the *Pinakes*. I consider it possible that these data served as a pattern, in individual cases even as the foundation, for the "philological" biographies.

The biographies of most authors exist in several versions of different length. The original texts were mostly condensed and edited in the course of time. The shortest versions are similar to biographical sections of articles in handbooks. Probably they are indeed nothing else but that.[48] The lists of works at the end are often omitted or they are much abbreviated and are limited to a listing of the literary genres cultivated by a particular author. For complete or partial editions a detailed list of works was indeed superfluous, because a table of contents served instead. If the editor had investigated (as was his duty) which works known under the name of an author were really his own and what had been their original titles, then the table of contents of an edition assumed even the character of a critical collective or partial bibliography.

In Byzantine manuscripts of extant dramas by Aischylos and Aristophanes there are still long lists of their plays, following the biographies of the authors.[49] The *bios* of Aischylos is rather extensive; the *katalogos* of his plays contains 73 tragedies and satyr plays (of which only seven have come down to us).[50] For Aristophanes a short *genos* is followed by a *katalogos* of 42 comedies (of which 11 have come down us).[51] The plays of both poets are arranged alphabetically according to the first letter of the title. That means that the plays of Aischylos which were performed as tetralogies (three tragedies and one satyr play) are dispersed. This must certainly have displeased most people at that time, since the trilogies of Aischylos—to name only the *Oresteia*—still formed a conceptual unit; there must have been a good reason for this method.

Among the tragedies of Aischylos two are listed with the same title, *Aitnaiai* (The Sicilians), one of which is indicated as authentic, the other as spurious. For four comedies of Aristophanes it is mentioned that there were two versions (e.g. *Plutos* b). Some plays of both authors are listed with two titles. For example, there is *Lysistratē ē Diallagai*; thus, the famous comedy of Aristophanes was also known under the title *Diallagai* (Reconciliation).

It is not immediately evident whether the two lists are based on tables of contents of editions or on *Pinakes*.[52] There is, however, no doubt that the plays themselves were arranged alphabetically by title in the editions, and those editions were similarly listed in bibliographies. The oldest testimony for such an arrangement is an inscription in two columns from the first century B.C. excavated in Piraeus, the harbor of Athens.[53] It lists several authors with a larger or smaller number of their works; apparently, this was a book donation.[54] The right-hand column records among others the contents of several scrolls with a total of thirty plays by Euripides.[55] The 38 titles of plays inscribed in the second century A.D. (?) on the back of a statuette of Euripides (today in the Louvre) are also arranged according to the same principle.[56] Remnants of alphabetically arranged editions and lists of his plays are also found on papyrus fragments from the third century A.D.[57] A part of such an edition, containing nine plays,[58] has also come down to us in a Byzantine manuscript; thus, of the seventy-five plays of the poet that are known to have existed, we have altogether nineteen, including the disputed *Rhēsos*. From papyrus fragments of the third century A.D. we learn that there were alphabetically arranged editions of Menander's comedies.[59] The lists of works of many dramatic poets which the editor of the *Suda* took from the *Onomatologos* of Hesychios, e.g., those of the tragic poet Lykophron and of the comic poet Plato, are alphabetically arranged.[60] It is therefore correctly assumed that the plays written by each dramatic poet were also arranged alphabetically in the *Pinakes* of Kallimachos.[61] It is likely that Zenodotos had already arranged the scrolls containing the plays of individual authors according to the alphabet of their titles.

It is curious that the scholars of the Hellenistic age as well as those of the early Imperial period alphabetized only by the first letter, that is, they did not file by fine alphabetization, much less by full alphabetization, but only by coarse alphabetization.[62] This is understandable for library lists such as Kallimachos's *Pinakes*, whose arrangement was intended to reflect as far as possible the arrangement of the scrolls on the shelves of bookcases, where it was impossible to maintain a more exact alphabetical order in the long run. But also in other lists no further alphabetization was used, perhaps out of sheer habit. Even in the compilation of dictionaries it was thought to be adequate to arrange all words which began with the same initial letter quite at random. It seems that this was thought to be sufficient. Perhaps it was also thought that the advantage of a more exact filing was not justified by the greater expense for labor and sometimes also for papyrus (for the making of slips), as Daly presumes.[63] Be that as it may, only in the second century A.D. were Greek reference books arranged by fine and full alphabetization, namely the great dictionary of Diogenianos (which is lost) and Galen's dictionary of Hippokrates.[64] Both authors stressed the innovations

191

that they had introduced; they clearly understood that such compilations could fulfill their purpose only inadequately unless they were arranged by a method better than the one that had been in use until then. But their works were exceptions. In the fifth and sixth century respectively, one finely and one fully alphabetical reference book was published, namely the dictionary of Hesychios of Alexandria which was based on that of Diogenianos, and the geographical lexicon by Stephanos of Byzantium. But only in the ninth and tenth century, that is in the Byzantine era, did the fully alphabetical order of entries become a common practice. Compared with the effort expected to be made by users of dictionaries it was therefore unimportant that the alphabetization of works by an author of the same *genos* or *eidos* was limited to the first letter.

The alphabetical arrangement of plays and their titles was no doubt rather practical, especially for prolific authors, but it was by no means natural, which means that it had to be established at some time. Some traces seem to indicate that it was preceded by chronological order. When Novati published the alphabetically arranged list of comedies by Aristophanes (the "Novatic index") in which under each of the letters alpha, bēta, gamma, delta, epsilon, lambda, ny, omikron, pi, and tau two or more plays are listed, Wilamowitz immediately pointed out that the titles beginning with the same letter appear in chronological order (according to the year of their performance):[65] *Acharnēs* (425 B.C.), *Anagyros* (419/416), *Amphiaraos* (414), *Aiolosikōn* (I: 410/400), *Babylōnioi* (426), *Batrachoi* (405), *Nephelai* (423), *Nēsoi* (? spurious), *Holkadēs* (423), *Ornithēs* (414). The arrangement of the titles beginning with gamma, delta, and epsilon is confused, the comedy listed before *Lysistratē* (411) cannot be identified because its title is presumably corrupt, the dating of the plays listed under pi and tau is uncertain.[66] But the chronological sequence of plays mentioned above cannot have come about by chance.

There are only few parallels to this. These observations can only be made in lists of plays which can be dated at least approximately, and their number is small. We do not know the years of preformance even for some of the plays that have come down to us. In the list of plays by Aischylos almost no traces of a chronological arrangement can be discerned. Rather, the opposite is true: *Agamemnōn* which opens the series of nine plays, was certainly performed after the eight others (458 B.C.).[67] Regarding the lists and editions of plays by Euripides, the inscription on the statuette in the Louvre lists the following titles beginning with omikron: *Oineus* (before 425), *Oidipus* (after 525), *Orestēs* (408).[68] In our best manuscripts, *Alkēstis*, performed in 438 before *Andromachē* (430/424) is also listed before it, and the four plays taken from an alphabetical complete edition whose titles begin with iota, are apparently forming a chronological series: *Iōn* (?), *Hiketides* (ca. 421), *Iphigeneia hē en Taurois* (411/409), *Iphigeneia hē en Aulidi* (after 405).

The lists of plays in the *Suda* are almost useless for this investigation, because the plays cannot be dated with certainty. Still, the lexicon lists *Monotropos* by the comic poet Phrynichos (414) and *Peisandros* by his rival Plato (422) before plays which were performed at a later time, namely *Musai* by Phrynichos (405) and *Presbeis* by Plato (4th century B.C.).

Wilamowitz stated at the time only that the Novatic index combined an alphabetical with a chronological arrangement. Nobody pursued the issue further. In my view, the Novatic index resulted either from an alphabetical rearrangement of a chronological list, or it reflects the arrangement of a library in which the comedies of Aristophanes were shelved first chronologically and were later rearranged alphabetically.[69] I think the latter to be more likely. Now, the Novatic index is probably based on the *Pinakes* of Kallimachos. The library would thus have been the Alexandrian one, and Zenodotos would have arranged the plays by Aristophanes and some other playwrights chronologically to begin with, but would soon have preferred an alphabetical arrangement because that way they were easier to find. The trilogies and tetralogies which were related to each other by their content were thus dispersed, but this was apparently considered as the lesser evil compared to the advantages from a librarian's point of view.

If the *katalogos* of the comedies of Aristophanes shows stronger traces of an original chronological arrangement than the lists of plays by Euripides, this can perhaps be explained by the fact that it was based on tables of contents of editions, whereas the Novatic index reflects a *pinax*. In any case, that catalog was at one time also listed in the *Onomatologos* of Hesychios and was transferred from this work or from its source to the Aristophanes manuscript. Rearrangements were, however, made much more frequently for purely formal reasons in editions of plays than in *pinakes*, and that is also the reason that there is no fixed sequence of plays in editions.[70]

The *Suda* occasionally also lists the titles of other poetic works and prose writings in alphabetical order. This will be treated later, but here it should be stressed that in general only the titles of works of the same literary genre or belonging to the same scholarly discipline were alphabetized. Normally it was thought to be sufficient to group them by form and content of the works. Only seldom were titles of works in various forms and with different contents listed in one single alphabet. The lists of Theophrastos's writings belong to the exceptions.

The grammatical as well as the rhetorical biographies of authors, the library catalogs, the products of the "motley writers", and the works of the chronographers constituted the sources of biographical collections and handbooks compiled by the Hellenistic scholars and by those of the Imperial period. Most of the older and younger works are, however, known to us only by title. These biographies dealt most often with philosophers, and it was common to combine biography and doxography, describing the lives and teachings of the representatives of various schools. But in addition to these works on philosophers, poets, orators, and historians there were from the first century B.C. onwards also works about authors on specific subjects and about special categories of authors. Thus, for example, Asklepiades of Myrlea (ca. 100 B.C.) wrote *Peri grammatikōn* (On grammarians), and Demetrios of Magnesia (first half of the lst century B.C.) compiled information *Peri homōnymōn poiētōn te kai syngrapheōn* (On poets and writers with the same names). The *Bioi iatrōn kai haireseis kai syntagmata* (Lives of physicians, their schools and writings) by the famous gynecologist Soranos of Ephesos (first half of the 2nd century A.D.) may also be mentioned here because its title lists the bibliographical component of his work as consisting of ten books, which is not customary in other titles. Among the scholars of the Imperial period who transmitted to posterity much biographical and bibliographical material on different authors at least two should be mentioned: Philon of Byblos (second half of the 1st century A.D.) and his pupil Hermippos of Berytos (first half of the 2nd century A.D.), the latter sometimes mistaken for Hermippos the Kallimachean. Philon wrote *Peri ktēseōs kai eklogēs bibliōn* (On the acquisition and selection of books, 12 books) and *Peri poleōn kai hus hekastē autōn endoxus ēnenke* (On the cities and the famous men that each has produced, 30 books). Hermippos wrote *Peri endoxōn iatrōn* (On famous physicians) and *Peri tōn en paideia lampsantōn dulōn* (On slaves who distinguished themselves in all branches of learning); the two works were perhaps parts of a larger one, *Peri endoxōn andrōn* (On famous men); the tradition is uncertain. Teachers and pupils apparently meant by *endoxoi andres* only those who had been outstanding *en paideia*, in branches of learning and culture. Suetonius, a contemporary of Hermippos, dealt in his work *De viris illustribus* (of which only fragments have come down to us) only with poets, orators, historians and grammarians, while Jerome (who cites Suetonius as his model) included under the same title exclusively ecclesiastical authors. The successors of the Church Father followed his terminological usage. It is impossible to say whether Neanthes of Kyzikos (ca. 200 B.C.), who was the first to use the phrase *Peri endoxōn andrōn*,[71] already limited himself to writers. Among the *viri illustres* portrayed by Cornelius Nepos (1st century B.C.) were also kings and generals.

5.4 The List of Aristotle's Writings by Andronikos of Rhodos

Among the few authors whose works were listed in a separately published bibliography was Aristotle.[72] The quantity and importance as well as the specific character of his writings were the reasons for a separate listing. As mentioned earlier, the Peripatetic Andronikos of Rhodos compiled during the first half of the first century B.C., probably in Alexandria, a new bibliography of Aristotle, intended to be a substitute for the *pinax* compiled by the Kallimachean Hermippos (from which the list given by Diogenes Laertios is derived). Andronikos did this because he had consolidated the acroamatic writings of Aristotle according to their related contents and had published them as *pragmateiai* (systematic treatises). (The Corpus Aristotelicum in the form in which it has come down to us is in all probability based on this edition.) His work in five books which contained his *pinax* of Aristotle's writings was presumably a justification of his editorial activity.[73] A certain Ptolemaios who added to his biography of Aristotle a *pinax* of his works still had access to Andronikos's compilation which is lost; he referred to it for some details, e.g. number of standard lines and beginnings of certain *hypomnēmata*. In addition, the second part of his *pinax* is almost an index to our present Corpus Aristotelicum which is based on the edition by Andronikos. Most modern researchers think, therefore, that the *pinax* of Ptolemaios is an abbreviated version of the one by Andronikos. At one time, Moraux was also of this opinion, but lately he doubted that it was correct;[74] I do not, however, share his misgivings.[75] The *pinax* of Ptolemaios diverged perhaps in details from that by Andronikos; since it is preserved only in an Arabic translation of a Syriac translation, it was certainly distorted in the course of transmission, but I think that it is quite possible that its structure still reflects that of Andronikos's *pinax*.[76]

The *pinax* of Ptolemaios consists of four parts.[77] The first part (no. 1-28) records apart from a few others mainly the exoteric writings of Aristotle, almost all of which had the form of dialogs. The most famous are listed first, apparently in no particular order (no. 1-8); the others (no. 9-28) are alphabetically arranged, i.e. by the first letter of their title. The second part (no. 29-56) lists the acroamatic writings, or more exactly, the pragmatic parts of our Corpus Aristotelicum (which appear in Ptolemaios's *pinax* only to a small extent), almost entirely in the arrangement according to the subfields of philosophy (logic, ethics, politics, poetics, rhetoric, physics, metaphysics)[78] and with the titles that have become customary since then. The writings on logic lead from the simple to the more difficult, whereas those on physics go from the higher to the lower topics. (On ethics there are only two works, on the rest of the subjects there is only one work each.) The third part (no. 57-80) contains the *hypomnēmata* in alphabetical sequence, the fourth has further *hypomnēmata* but not alphabetically arranged, as well as the huge collection of *politeiai* (constitutions) and letters. The original sequence is here disturbed.

The writings of Aristotle were thus divided by the degree of their literary completion which in turn decided the size of the audience for which they were intended: *exōterika* (for the educated public), *akroamatika* (only for the members of the Peripatos), and *hypomnēmatika* (only for the author himself and for his closest collaborators). Added to these were the collections, here represented only by the *politeiai*, that is works which contained contributions from Aristotle himself as well as from his pupils, and the letters written (and received?) by him. The compiler of the list followed in this arrangement an old tradition which can still be documented several times in Diogenes Laertios.[79]

The placing of the most important publications at the beginning can also be documented in Diogenes Laertios. The less important *exōterika* and all *hypomnēmatika* were alphabetically arranged; thus, he used this principle only for secondary writings and for those of the same kind and rank. The alphabetical order followed in each case the first noun or adjective of the title; prepositions and articles were disregarded.

The naming of the *hypomnēmatika* was more in the nature of headings consisting of keywords than real titles. Such collections of notes are already listed alphabetically by the indication of their contents in the *pinax* of Aristotle's writings that are based on the work by Hermippos.[80] Individual *hypomnēmata* of Aristotle were also internally arranged by the alphabet of key words, such as the *Physikōn* (sc. *aporēmatōn*) *kata stoicheion* (sc. *biblia*) (Physical problems in alphabetical sequence) in 38 books.[81] Thus, while Aristotle, so far as we can see, did not arrange literary works by title, he filed scientific materials alphabetically by keywords. In the *pinax* by Ptolemaios there is, however, no trace of this.

Unlike the *exōterika* and the *hypomnēmatika*, the *pragmateiai* which had been formed out of the *akroamatika* were listed in systematic order. Furthermore, the sequence of the writings on logic betrays an isagogic intention.

The arrangement of the *pinax* lacks the consistency which we expect of a bibliography today. However, the combination of formal and conceptual, systematic and mechanical principles which grew out of a tradition were not at all unhelpful: rather, they made it easier to gain an overview over the entire work and the individual writings of Aristotle. It seems to me, therefore, that they may without any doubt be ascribed to Andronikos.[82]

The above-mentioned reference by Ptolemaios seems to indicate that Andronikos recorded for each work the beginning words and the number of standard lines. This assumption is confirmed, as far as the beginnings are concerned, by Porphyrios who recorded the *archē* of each work by Plotinos for easy identification, following the example of Andronikos.[83]

Andronikos probably recorded the *pseudepigrapha*, i.e. those writings known under Aristotle's name which were considered as spurious by all scholars, in a separate list.[84] He himself thought that the *Peri hermēneias* was spurious.[85] But he probably recorded it first among the logical pragmatics in order to prove its spuriousness. This would not have been unusual.[86]

5.5 The Treatise of Dionysios of Halikarnassos on the Orator Deinarchos

Considering that all Hellenistic writings on the lives and works of Greek authors are lost, it is a stroke of luck that the treatise of Dionysios of Halikarnassos on Deinarchos, the youngest of the "ten" Attic orators, has come down to us.[87] We have here a unique biographic-bibliographic study, written in the second half of the first century B.C., on a prolific author whose work was difficult to define, because orations by him were known under the names of other authors and vice versa.

In the course of this investigation we have named Dionysios several times in connection with his quotations of Kallimachos, and have also mentioned his work *To Ammaios*, for which he presumably used the biography of Demosthenes by the Kallimachean Hermippos. About his life we know only that he dwelt in Rome since 30 B.C. Among his writings are a work on the early history of Rome in 20 books (finished in 7 B.C.) and several works on the art of rhetoric and its most important literary representatives.[88] For posterity he became the *kritikos* (critic of style) par excellence. In his writings on rhetoric he sought to show to prospective orators what they should imitate in the Attic orators of the fourth century B.C., who were held to be the classics, and what they should avoid. It is noteworthy that he was always careful to put his statements of stylistic criticism on a firm bibliographic basis, that is to say, before he described and criticized the style of an orator he endeavored to ascertain his literary property, starting with his undoubtedly genuine orations, and then distinguishing between the authentic and the spurious speeches by means of chronological and stylistic criteria.[89] If I am not entirely mistaken, he considered such studies in literary history and criticism which amounted to a biobibliography of the respective orator not as a necessary evil, a means to a goal, but as an important task in its own right, because he intended to distinguish in separate works the authentic orations of Lysias and Demosthenes from those which had been falsely ascribed to them.[90]

In the introduction to his treatise on Deinarchos he also mentions as a special point, which he wished to treat besides the life and style of the orator, the distinction between speeches actually written by him and those that were falsely ascribed to him (chapter 1).[91] He says further that Kallimachos and the grammarians of Pergamon (the compilers of the *pinakes* of that library) had not only made inexact (biographical) statements on Deinarchos—what he means by this he says later himself—but that they had even reported false things about him. In addition, he says that they had ascribed orations to him which he had not written, and had denied the authenticity of others that he had actually written.[92] That means that Dionysios had counted on finding in the Alexandrian and Pergamenian *Pinakes* exact biographical and reliable bibliographical information on Deinarchos. His expectations were hardly unfounded: the *Pinakes* of Kallimachos certainly gave the information desired by Dionysios about most other authors. His complaint points therefore to the fact that the *Pinakes* were not uniformly worked out.

Dionysios was also disappointed by Demetrios of Magnesia. This compiler, as already mentioned, had published in the first half of the first century B.C. a (lost) work *Peri homōnymōn poiētōn te kai syngrapheōn* (On poets and writers with the same names) which provided later scholars with many biographical and bibliographical details.[93] As is well known, there were many Greek authors who had the same name, and their differentiation was one of the most difficult problems of ancient literary history. The main source of Demetrios for the mass of authors of second and third rank were in all probability the Alexandrian and Pergamenian *Pinakes*;[94] at least, I would not know where else he could have found his material. About an author of whom the Alexandrian and Pergamenian librarian could not say anything "exact", Demetrios could not give any detailed information either. Thus, according to Dionysios who quotes him verbatim—the only verbatim citation from his work—he noted that aside from the orator Deinarchos there had also been other authors by that name, and then tried to characterize the style of that orator. In this connection he emphasized that it was difficult to identify orations of Deminarchos and that some people falsely ascribed to him a speech against Demosthenes, but that those actually written by him, about 160 in number, were not known.

Dionysios criticized even what Demetrios had written about Deinarchos as being inexact, because he had indicated neither his origin, nor his lifetime or place of activity. (That pertained also to Kallimachos and the Pergamenian grammarians.) For this reason, he himself then sketched the story of Deinarchos's life (chapter 2-3): Deinarchos, a son of Sostratos, was born in Korinth. He came to Athens when philosophy and oratory flourished there. Theophrastos was his teacher, Demetrios of Phaleron his school mate.[95] Through his eloquence he became in the course of time a wealthy man. His period of flourishing occurred in the time after the death of Alexander the Great (323 B.C.), of Demosthenes (322 B.C.) and of the other important orators of that era. For fifteen years, the last ten under the government of Demetrios of Phaleron, Deinarchos was active as a *logographos* (speechwriter), that is to say, he wrote forensic speeches for other people who paid him. When Demetrios was overthrown (307 B.C.) he too left Athens. Only after another fifteen years, which he spent in Chalkis, his old teacher Theophrastos succeeded in getting permission for him to return to Athens (292 B.C.). There he had first to appear before the court in his own behalf in order to sue a certain Proxenos who had embezzled his fortune. At that time, according to his own testimony, he was already an old man of feeble sight.

Dionysios took his knowledge about the life of Deinarchos from this (lost) oration against Proxenos. His predecessors, beginning with Kallimachos, had all overlooked that this speech contained much autobiographical information. The general historical framework was provided by a work cited by Dionysios, the *Atthis* (History of Athens) by Philochoros, a scholar who incidentally was also interested in literary history.[96] Since a man of seventy years was called an old man,

Dionysios assumed that Deinarchos had been born ca. 361/360 B.C. and died soon after 292/291 (chapter 4). He deducted from this that the forensic speeches ascribed to him which were written before 336/335 (when he was about 25 years old) or after 292/291 (when he was over seventy), or those written between 307 and 292 (when he dwelt in Chalkis) were not his own. This method was somewhat risky: if Deinarchos was already seventy-five or only sixty-five when he sued Proxenos, his earliest or latest orations were excluded. Still, there was now at least some negative evidence for a certain part of his speeches.

But this was not enough. In order to separate spurious orations which could not be attacked on a chronological basis, stylistic criteria were needed. Dionysios tried therefore in the second part of his treatise to characterize the style of Deinarchos better than Demetrios had done, but even he found this to be a difficult task because the orator had imitated sometimes one, sometimes another of his famous older colleagues (Demosthenes, Hypereides, Lysias) (chapters 5-8).[97]

The third part contains the list of the authentic and spurious orations of Deinarchos, compiled by Dionysios on the strength of chronological and stylistic criteria. It is preceded by a list of archons after whom the years 361/360 until 292/291 had been named (chapter 9). According to the conception of the Greeks, recognized in Aristotle's *Rhetoric*, there were three kinds of orations: political speeches (i.e. speeches in the Assembly on political matters, also known as "deliberative" speeches), forensic speeches, and epideictic ("show-off") speeches (i.e. festive orations or eulogies). Among the forensic speeches distinctions were made between public and private ones, i.e. between speeches in criminal and civil cases. Since no political or epideictic orations had been ascribed to Deinarchos,[98] Dionysios needed to record only his forensic speeches. He divided them into public and private, genuine and spurious ones. If there had been political or epideictic orations by Deinarchos, he would no doubt have listed them separately. It is probable that Kallimachos already distinguished between the political, forensic and epideictic orations of Demosthenes, as well as between public and private forensic speeches. Dionysios, who liked to emphasize his originality where it was appropriate, did not claim that his arrangement of the Deinarchos bibliography was a new one.

Dionysios lists 28 genuine and 18 spurious public speeches of Deinarchos, and 32 genuine and 9 spurious private speeches (chapters 10-13).[99] Of the last section, only the beginning exists; presumably, it was very large, because most of the speeches spuriously ascribed to Deinarchos were probably private ones. Thus, Dionysios considered sixty forensic speeches as genuine; of these, only six have come down to us, significantly enough three under the name of Deinarchos, and three under the name of Demosthenes. We do not know how many spurious speeches were known to Dionysios.

For each oration, Dionysios indicates the name of the defendant and the beginning of the text, mostly also the subject of the lawsuit, often the character of the speech (e.g. notification, plea), sometimes also the person for whom Deinarchos had written the oration. These data substitute for a title. Curiously, Dionysios never mentions the number of standard lines.[100] In one case he corrects the *epigraphē* of a speech which he had found,[101] in another he notes that Kallimachos had listed an oration among those of Demosthenes.[102] For the orations which he declared to be spurious, he gave reasons for his opinion by

means of chronological or stylistic criteria.[103] In one case he also relies on
the Pergamenian *Pinakes*, in which a particular oration has been ascribed to
Kallikrates.[104] The genuine public speeches are perhaps chronologically arranged,[105]
the genuine private ones, however, are evidently arranged by subjects of litigation —
damages, theft, defection (of a freedman from his patron), inheritance, etc. — but
within these groups the order is not chronological.[106] The spurious speeches are
arranged according to the evidence for their rejection (a. time; b. style).[107]

The treatise of Dionysios shows that he had recognized the three tasks of a
bibliographer, and had tried to achieve them professionally: 1) the critical and
historical identification of the works actually written by an author among those that
were ascribed to him and to others; 2) their exact description; and 3) the meaningful
arrangement of their titles.[108] Apparently, he was most concerned to separate the
genuine speeches of Deinarchos from the mass of those that had been ascribed to
him. His biographical researches served mainly this bibliographic purpose. Only
seldom did he try to find out the real author of an oration which he had declared to
be spurious.[109] He was therefore blamed for dismissing the orations which he had
declared to be spurious as orphans, because he could not say who had been their
father.[110]

When he dealt with the works of other orators he had, of course, also
encountered speeches which seemed to him to be by Deinarchos. Whether he
ascribed the three orations that have been transmitted in the Corpus
Demosthenicum to Deinarchos only on the strength of stylistic criteria cannot be
said with certainty. Perhaps the *epigraphai* of the copies which he had at his
disposal named Deinarchos as the author. Other scholars ascribed four other
orations to him, of which at least two had also been transmitted under the name of
Aristogeiton.[111] Dionysios started his work evidently with the Alexandrian and
Pergamenian *Pinakes*, but his Deinarchos bibliography is no doubt largely based on
autopsy, because the arguments used by him for his decisions on authenticity could
only have been derived from the orations themselves. It is not clear where he saw
the documents; perhaps in the library of Pergamon which was about 150 miles north
of Halikarnassos. But the biographic-stylistical method which he used to distinguish
between the genuine and the spurious orations of Deinarchos had already been used
by the Alexandrian librarians under the direction of Kallimachos.

5.6 The Work of Diogenes Laertios on the Lives
and Opinions of Famous Philosophers

The work of Diogenes Laertios on the lives and opinions of famous
philosophers is the most important of the three extant collective biographies devoted
to the authors of a single class.[112] It combines biography with doxography and
bibliography. The author, of whom nothing else is known, edited the notes he
had collected rather inadequately. But his work, written at the beginning of the
3rd century A.D., is nevertheless (or perhaps just because of this inadequacy)
one of the main sources for the history of ancient philosophy, because it
contains apart from all kinds of anecdotes invaluable information and documents.[113]
Diogenes dealt with 82 Greek thinkers, some of which had not left any writings
at all.[114] He arranged them by schools and within these chronologically, or more

precisely, by the principle of *diadochē* (succession).[115] There are long chapters, containing besides anecdotes also letters, last wills, epitaphs, panegyrics and bibliographies, but there are also brief articles, listing only the absolutely necessary biographical, doxographic and bibliographic data.[116]

Diogenes tried to flesh out the bare bones of the traditional scheme of biographical data, and to complement and enhance it by stories of varying degrees of credibility. His authorities and the authorities on which they had relied contradicted each other on many points pertaining to facts. Diogenes often mentions their divergent opinions, which are evidence for the endeavors of Hellenistic scholars to find out the living conditions of the ancient philosophers.

Part of the biographical scheme was also the enumeration of an author's works or the indication that he had not written anything. If a philosopher had not written many works, Diogenes cited them in the running text; if he found a longer bibliography in his sources he included it in his narrative.[117] For some of these lists he wrote a brief introductory note, stressing their importance, e.g. for those of Aristotle and Theophrastos. I have already dealt with these and with the one on Demokritos. For each listed work Diogenes generally gives only the title and the extent, i.e. the number of books; for works without a title, e.g. those of the earlier philosophers and for poems and letters he also cites the beginning of the text,[118] and for works in verse he records in addition the number of verses.[119] Sometimes he mentions the sum of the lines or books written by an author.[120] When the ascription or the title of a work was in dispute, which happened frequently, he made an appropriate note, sometimes referring to one or more scholars who represented different opinions.

Thus he writes in the brief chapter on the Socratic philosopher Phaidon of Elis that among the dialogs known under his name, *Zōpyros* and *Simon* were genuine, whereas there were doubts about *Nikias*, and *Mēdios*, the latter also ascribed to Aischines or to Polyainos, as well as about *Antimachos or the Old Ones*, and the dialogs with a cobbler, which were also ascribed by some to Aischines. In another passage he reports that Panaitios of Rhodos doubted the authenticity of any dialogs ascribed to Phaidon, and in a third passage he indicates the cobbler Simon of Athens as the author of the cobbler dialogs (between Socrates and that Simon).[121]

In the biography of his namesake, the Cynic of Sinope, Diogenes included even two bibliographies, namely a longer, anonymous one, and a shorter one, written by Sotion of Alexandria.[122] The first one lists 13 dialogs, 7 tragedies and some letters. Diogenes states that Sosikrates of Rhodos and Satyros of Kallatis declared all these works to be spurious. Sotion's list comprises 12 dialogs, of which only three appear also in the first list, as well as maxims and letters, but no tragedies. The Alexandrian thus took a position in the middle between the anonymous bibliographer who recognized as genuine everything known under the name of Diogenes, and Sosikrates who considered everything as spurious.

In the chapter on the Socratic philosopher Aristippos of Kyrene Diogenes also reproduces two bibliographies.[123] The first one is anonymous and lists a history of Libya in three books, as well as a book of 25 dialogs, partly in the Attic and partly in the Doric dialect. (The following 23 writings are, however, not dialogs.)

200

Diogenes adds that some people ascribed to Aristippos also six diatribes (treatises), but that others said he had not written anything at all; one of these had been Sosikrates. The other bibliography, also written by Sotion but approved by Panaitios, lists ten authentic dialogs, five of which appear also in the first list, as well as the six diatribes and three collections of maxims. Here too the Alexandrian Sotion is in the middle between the conservative anonymous bibliographer and the radical Sosikrates.[124]

Now, did Sotion himself compile the lists of works by Diogenes of Sinope and by Aristippos of Kyrene, relying on the holdings of the library of the Museion? It stands to reason that he copied them from the *Pinakes* that had been compiled by Kallimachos and his successors. It is, however, unlikely that the two anonymous bibliographies which deviate considerably from those of the Alexandrian scholar had their roots in the Alexandrian *Pinakes*.[125] Perhaps they were based on the Pergamenian *Pinakes* and were transmitted to Diogenes Laertios through Demetrios of Magnesia who probably used the library at Pergamon. Be that as it may, there were considerable differences of opinion among the Hellenistic scholars regarding the works purportedly written by the pupils of Socrates and their own pupils. Nobody would claim that Kallimachos and his successors had always made the right choice. But if Panaitios approved Sotion's bibliography of Aristippos (assuming that it was indeed based on the *Pinakes*) this was an important endorsement, because Panaitios, himself the author of a work on the Socratic philosophers, was a competent critic.

Regarding the arrangement of the bibliographies recorded by Diogenes Laertios, the titles are sometimes loosely grouped by the parts of philosophy according to the contents of the works, i.e. for the Peripatetics by logic (including rhetoric and poetics), ethics (including politics), physics and metaphysics in various sequences;[126] sometimes the titles seem to be listed haphazardly. Some of the lists are tables of contents of the authoritative editions of a philosopher.[127] The internal arrangement of the works is only seldom indicated.[128] The subject arrangement is sometimes subordinated to a formal arrangement, i.e. the titles are collocated according to the degree of their literary execution: thus, the dialogs written for a larger audience precede those intended only for specialists, particularly the members of the philosopher's own school; then follow lecture manuscripts, collections of materials, and finally letters and other personal pieces.[129] For some philosophers, their most important or most voluminous work is listed first, irrespective of the subject.[130] Traces of chronological or alphabetical order can be discerned only in very few lists.[131] For authors who wrote also works other than philosophical ones, these are of course listed separately.[132]

It seems that Diogenes Laertios did not change the arrangement of bibliographies which he had collected from various sources. Thus, they reflect the practices of Hellenistic scholars and their successors. Inasmuch as his authorities had utilized the catalogs of great libraries, especially those of Alexandria and Pergamon, one may say that a part of his lists was ultimately based on the Alexandrian and Pergamenian *Pinakes*. There is thus no reason to assume that the titles in all the lists recorded in his work are arranged according to a well thought-out plan. Of course, one cannot refute those researchers who think that there had once been a rational order in all these lists, but that it had been destroyed in the course of transmission; some also say that the present order may indeed be a rational one but that we cannot understand it because all the listed works are now lost. Perhaps the day may come when the arrangement of these lists which seem to lack any rational order will be cleared up. We should, however, take into consideration that the titles in these lists are recorded in the sequence in which they were listed in library catalogs. The arrangement which is still discernible in the better edited lists seems to indicate that their editors tended to group the titles according to the subject content of the writings, sometimes also by form, as for example in the Aristotle bibliography by Andronikos of Rhodos or in the Deinarchos bibliography by Dionysios of Halikarnassos.

The only exception is the alphabetical lists of works by Theophrastos with which I will deal below.[133]

At the end of many chapters Diogenes Laertios lists other bearers of the same name who had distinguished themselves in the arts and sciences, or en paideia, with a few biographical and occasionally also bibliographical data. For this he relied apparently on one or more dictionaries of namesakes; the oldest work of this kind, frequently cited by him, had been compiled already in the first century B.C. by Demetrios of Magnesia. Generally he uses the phrase "There were also other men by this name, first . . ." and so on. Thus he lists, to cite only those names that appear at least five times, five namesakes of Thales, four of Socrates, six of Xenophon, seven of Aischines, nineteen of Theodoros Atheos, nine of Krates of Athens, nine of Bion, seven of Aristotle, seven of Straton, nineteen of Demetrios of Phaleron, thirteen of Herakleides Pontikos, four of Diogenes of Sinope, five of Menippos, seven of Zenon of Kition, five of Ariston of Chios, four of Chrysippos, and five of Demokritos. Many of these were not philosophers but poets, historians, orators, grammarians, physicians or engineers; some were also sculptors, painters, composers and athletic coaches. These curious lists of namesakes remind us that the differentiation of authors with the same names was one of the biggest problems of Greek literary historians. The listing of persons who had distinguished themselves in a particular field but had not written any works was certainly intended to avoid confusions which could easily occur if someone was looking for information on a particular author.

5.7 The List of Those Renowned in Branches of Learning by Hesychios of Miletos

The Suda contains many excerpts from a reference book written by Hesychios Illustrios of Miletos, a high official of the Byzantine Empire, who had also been a historian; the work was compiled in the sixth century A.D., either under Emperor Justinian or soon thereafter. Its title was Onomatologos ē Pinax tōn en paideia onomastōn (Nomenclator, or, List of those renowned in branches of learning).[134] The noun onomatologos = onomatoklētōr was the equivalent of the Latin nomenclator; that was the appellation of a slave who knew "all" Rome (or Alexandria, or Constantinople), and whose task it was to whisper into his high lord's ear the names of important persons whom he might meet, with the necessary details.[135] The Onomatologos of Hesychios listed not exclusively but predominantly Greek authors of all genres and disciplines with brief biographical and bibliographical data. Such a comprehensive lexicon of authors had not been compiled since the days of the Pinakes of Kallimachos. Hesychios probably did not have access to those any more. His *Onomatologos* was based mainly on later compilations whose material was indeed partially derived from the *Pinakes* of Kallimachos. But Hesychios conducted also his own research on the works of individual authors in libraries.[136]

At an unknown time, an anonymous writer produced an epitome (extract, short version) of the *Onomatologos*, in which most of the articles were more or less abbreviated, and some were probably omitted altogether; this epitome apparently proved to be sufficient, because the original was no longer used and was ultimately lost. Yet even the epitome of the *Onomatologos* is no longer extant, but only the work in which it was incorporated, probably in an even more abbreviated form. Around A.D. 1000 a Byzantine scholar combined about 30,000 lexical, grammatical, historical, theological, and other articles culled from various reference works with those in the epitome of the *Onomatologos* to a fully alphabetical encyclopedia. The entries are, however, not filed according to the well-known sequence of the Classical Greek alphabet, but by the somewhat different Byzantine one.[137] Due to a misinterpretation, his work was formerly and sometimes even today known as the "Lexicon of Suidas"; actually, the work had the title *Suda* (collection? bulwark?).[138]

But not all biobibliographic articles in the *Suda* are based on the *Onomatologos*, because in the course of several centuries that work was not only abbreviated but was also enlarged by additions to existing articles and by the insertion of entirely new articles. Thus we find in the *Suda* also articles on Hesychios himself and on several authors who lived after him. Now, the article on Hesychios could perhaps be his own work (Jerome had no qualms listing himself among the famous ecclesiastical authors) but he would certainly not have written a note on the title of his *Onomatologos* which is listed first among his works, namely that the present work was a short version of it. This is an addition received by the editor from the epitomator of the *Onomatologos*. The same is true for the sentence added at the end of the article which says that Hesychios did not list any Church Fathers which raises a suspicion that he had not been a Christian but had been an adherent of the Greek (i.e. pagan) folly. Yet Hesychios was most certainly a Christian and did indeed list Christian authors, but was apparently descended from a family which remained pagan for a long time.[139] But we may conclude from this remark that the 35 articles in the *Suda* on those Christian authors who were held to be fathers of the church,[140] were not based on the *Onomatologos*. According to Wentzel, they were inserted into the epitome in the ninth century, namely by the epitomator himself.[141] Although all experts agree with this assumption, and the dating of the respective articles cannot be refuted, I see no reason to ascribe to the scholar who compiled the epitome of the *Onomatologos* also its most important additions. In my opinion, it can no longer be ascertained when the epitomator was active and whether he himself added any articles to those that he had found in the original work.[142]

More than 800 articles in the *Suda* can be traced with certainty to the *Onomatologos*; they are generally easy to spot.[143] Even though they are taken out of their original context and are often garbled, not to speak of other distortions, they still constitute a not inconsiderable excerpt from the original work. They confirm what the title of the work as cited in the *Suda* article "Hesychios" indicates: the author recorded men and women who had made a name for themselves in the arts and sciences, primarily in poetry and oratory, less often in music and in the fine arts. He dealt mainly with persons who had distinguished themselves as authors, but included also celebrities who had not been writers, such as Socrates, Karneades, the founder of the New Academy, Ammonios Sakkas, the teacher of Plotinos, and Apelles, the great Greek painter.[144] Besides Greeks and Hellenized members of other nations he included also a few Romans (altogether eleven, or 1.5%), almost exclusively those who had written in Greek, had been translated into Greek, or had themselves translated Greek words into Latin.[145] The non-authors and non-Hellenes occupy, however, such a minor space in the biobibliographic work that it can be designated unhesitatingly as a national lexicon of authors. Due to its lexical character the *Onomatologos* was thus quite different from the mere collection of biographies augmented by lists of works, compiled by Diogenes Laertios, that is, on the formal level alone, not to mention its contents. Its articles had a uniform structure; generally, some biographical data on a person were followed by a bibliography of his works; [146] in this respect, the work was similar to the *Pinakes* of Kallimachos. The original structure of the articles is still distinctly discernible in the *Suda*, despite their abridgment. This can be shown by two articles from the *Suda* which are based on the *Onomatologos*, a shorter and a medium-long one:[147] "Archigenes, son of Philippos, of Apameia in Syria, physician, pupil of Agathinos, practiced under Trajan in Rome, lived for sixty-three years, and wrote many medical and scientific books."

"Xenophon, son of Grylos, of Athens, Socratic philosopher, who was the first to write biographies and memorabilia of philosophers. He had sons by Philesia, Grylos and Diodoros, who were also called 'Dioskuroi'; he himself was called 'The Attic bee'. He was a schoolmate of Plato and flourished during the 95th Olympiad. He wrote more than 40 books, among which were the following: The education of Kyros, 8 books; The Anabasis of Kyros, 7 books; Hellenika, 7 books; Symposium, and many others."

An example of a longer biobibliography is the article on Kallimachos, quoted above on pp. 124 and 161.

In a few manuscripts of Aristophanes and Aristotle the same biographic texts as those in the *Suda* have been found, but whereas the latter lists only the eleven comedies of Aristophanes which were still studied in Byzantine times (with an appropriate note to that effect), the manuscripts record all 44 plays written by Aristophanes, except one that was inadvertently omitted, and the second version of another play with the same title as the first one. The article on Aristotle in the *Suda* concludes with the indication of his age, without mentioning the writings of the philosopher. In the manuscripts, the article on Aristotle contains different biographical information, and is followed by a note on the total number of his writings, a list of his successors, and a list of 196 works whose main part, nos. 1-139, is largely identical with the 146 numbers recorded by Diogenes Laertios, but contains in addition 27 other authentic works, 20 works which were apparently in doubt, and 10 spurious ones. These two biographies which agree with articles in the *Suda*, except for the bibliographies, are known in the professional literature by the names of their first editors as the Novatic Index (Aristophanes) and the Vita Menagiana (Aristoteles): this is not quite correct, because the index of Aristophanes is preceded by a *vita*, and the *vita* of Aristotle is followed by an index.[148] Today it is generally assumed that these two biobibliographies preserved articles from the unabridged *Onomatologos*, and that the epitomator substituted an enumeration of the eleven plays which were still studied in his own time for the original complete list of comedies by Aristophanes, while omitting the long list of Aristotle's writings entirely. This is indeed the most likely explanation of the facts.

Some researchers thought that the Vita Menagiana of Aristotle was a concoction by a Byzantine scholar who combined the Aristotle article in the *Suda* (which does not contain the data following the biographical part of the Vita Menagiana) with the bibliography inserted by Diogenes Laertios into his chapter on Aristotle (which is shorter by about 50 numbers).[149] But, quite apart from the difficulties indicated here in parentheses, it is not clear why Hesychios, contrary to his normal practice, should have given only biographical but no bibliographical data just for Aristotle. This is even less credible because the *Suda* article on Theophrastos clearly shows that Hesychios did not hesitate to include even quite long lists of works in his *Onomatologos*. In that article, the usual biographical data are followed by a list of works, beginning with five whose titles begin the letter alpha, then four main works which are not arranged alphabetically, and ends with the terse note *kai alla* (and others). The beginning of the list is entirely identical with that of the alphabetically arranged list of works reported by Diogenes Laertios in his chapter on Theophrastos, discussed on p. 59 because of its peculiar arrangement. Hesychios evidently received this list from the same source as Diogenes Laertios, but the epitomator copied only the first five titles, selected four others, and ended the enumeration in the usual manner.[150]

Researchers of Aristophanes and Aristotle assume therefore correctly that the Novatic Index and the Vita Menagiana are both based on the work of Hesychios. But curiously enough this has had no effect at all on the general ideas about the *Onomatologos*; nowhere has this work been evaluated by its real importance.[151] Although it is known that the articles in the *Suda* that are based on the epitome contain a wealth of invaluable biographic and bibliographic information on Greek authors, it has apparently not been recognized that the *Onomatologos* contained detailed bibliographies, if not for all authors, certainly for most of those whose works are not mentioned in the *Suda* at all, or not in detail or only in excerpts. Judging from the articles on Aristophanes and Aristotle, the *Onomatologos* must have been an excellent reference work, especially in the field of bibliography.

If he had the necessary information, Hesychios used to give the following details:

(1) The full name of an author, consisting of the personal name,
the name of his father (generally in the genitive case),
the name of his birthplace or country (usually in adjectival form);

(2) his class or classes (epic, lyric, tragic, comic poet,
philosopher, historian, orator, sophist, grammarian
or physician; other classifications are very rare);[152]

(3) his teacher(s) and pupils;

(4) the place of his activity, if it was not the same as his place of birth;

(5) the period of his flourishing, related to an Olympiad, a great war, the reign of a ruler, or the life of a famous contemporary "colleague"; in a pinch, the naming of a well-known teacher or pupil had to make do for an approximate chronological indication.

These were the main data on the person of an author; they identified him unambiguously, and distinguished him especially from other bearers of the same name.

The difficulties experienced by ancient biographers by the numerous namesakes have already been mentioned several times; here I wish to recall only the lists of namesakes by Diogenes Laertios. Hesychios's work highlights the dimensions of the problem. In the *Suda* 148 articles are listed under the letter alpha (including alpha iota); most of these are probably from the epitome of the *Onomatologos*. The names of 75 authors appear only once, those of 73 others (49.3%) twice or more often, most frequently Alexandros (nine times) and Apollonios (six times);[153] thus, almost every second author had a namesake who had also been a writer. Let us compare how often names which appear at least five times in Diogenes Laertios are also listed by Hesychios:

	Diogenes	Hesychios
Demetrios	20	2
Theodoros	20	4
Herakleides	14	3
Bion	10	0
Krates	10	4
Aischines	8	3
Aristotle	8	1
Straton	8	2
Zenon	8	5
Xenophon	7	4
Ariston	6	0
Demokritos	6	1
Menippos	6	1
Thales	6	1
Chrysippos	5	1
Diogenes	5	3
Sokrates	5	1
	152	36

This shows that once there were many more persons by the same name who had distinguished themselves in branches of learning than had been listed in the *Onomatologos*.

Here and there, Hesychios completed the data mentioned above by additional ones, especially for more important persons. Thus he mentioned the epithet or nickname of an author, if possible with an explanation, especially when the real name had been superseded by the epithet;[154] often he gave the mother's name which was also important for the distinction of namesakes because many sons were named after their fathers, occasionally also by the names of their grandfathers, their siblings, children or other relatives, especially if they had been "colleagues" of the author; but sometimes the reasons are not obvious.[155] He recorded also the occupation or profession of the father, if he was a nobleman or a slave, had possessed great riches or had plied a lowly trade,[156] but especially if he had distinguished himself as a scholar or poet in the same field as his son or in any other field. If the author was born in a little-known place, Hesychios briefly explained its location.[157]

Hesychios gave only seldom details about the life of an author, except for his education by a teacher, his sojourn in his primary place of activity, and his successors. His interest was primarily focused on the literary work of a scholar or poet.[158] But if an author had had an entirely different, lowly or modest occupation before devoting himself to the arts and sciences, Hesychios mentioned this.[159] Generally, he also reported special pleasant or unpleasant occurrences in the life of an author, such as holding an office (librarian, consul, teacher of a prince, being the confidant of a prince), quarrels with another author, exile, imprisonment and the like, also conversion to Christianity. Occasionally he mentioned the age of an author and the cause of his death.[160] This almost bordered on the anecdotal, to which as a rule he devoted only very little space, contrary to Diogenes Laertios. Only in exceptional cases did he say a word about an author's outer appearance or character.

The most important personalities were indicated by an appropriate attribute. Those who had distinguished themselves through an "invention" (*heurēma*), i.e. through a scientific or artistic innovation (to these belonged also the founding of a philosophical or other school) were indicated by a reference to it; for an "inventor" this took usually the form "he was the first who, etc." (*prōtos*). Furthermore, he never omitted the information that an author had been counted as one of the Seven Sages, the Ten Attic Orators, or one of the Pleiades, the seven Hellenistic tragic poets.

When Hesychios encountered in his sources conflicting data on the life of an author, which happened frequently, he listed them one after the other, connected by the word *ē* (or), or he stated that some said one thing, while others claimed otherwise. Sometimes he mentioned an authority on whom he relied, as Diogenes Laertios had done, but only rarely did he give his own opinion.[161]

The bibliographies which followed Hesychios's biographical data generally listed only the titles of works and their extent, i.e. the number of books, for epics sometimes also the number of verses.[162] For some works he also listed the dialect in which they were written.[163] If the title of a work was not indicative of its content he explained it.[164] In the *Suda* articles that are based on the *Onomatologos* it is only rarely indicated that the authenticity of a work had been in dispute, and no further data were provided.[165] This may, however, be a consequence of the abridgment of the *Onomatologos* whose bibliographies were heavily curtailed.

The epitomator abridged the biographical data (which were already quite terse) only insignificantly or not at all. This is evident from the articles on Aristophanes and Aristotle in the *Suda* which show only minor losses when compared with the *Onomatologos* as represented in the Novatic Index and the Vita

Menagiana (for Aristotle), as also from the biographic explanation (scholia) to Plato's *Republic* book X, which contain here and there somewhat but not much more than the respective article in the *Suda*.[166] On the other hand, he abridged most bibliographies. Thus we read often in the *Suda* that an author had written many other books besides those listed. Often if is only stated that he had written many works. For some persons who had evidently written works, not a word about them is said.[167] How arbitrarily the epitomator proceeded can clearly be seen in the articles on two of the most important grammarians of the Imperial period, Apollonios Dyskolos and his son Herodianos; the list of the former's writings, consisting of 25 titles, is apparently not abridged, whereas for the latter not a single work is listed, with only a note *egrapse polla* (he wrote much). The bibliography of Kallimachos, though one of the longest in the *Suda*, also suffered from deletions and transpositions.

Regarding the arrangement of the individual bibliographies, Hesychios probably followed his sources as Diogenes had done. In those, the titles were generally arranged by form and content of the works, with no further subdivision, following a tradition represented by the bibliographies of Aristotle and Aristophanes. Only the titles of works of certain kinds were alphabetically arranged, often those of dramatic works, occasionally also those of other poetic works. The titles of prose writings were only rarely alphabetically arranged.[168] Hardly any list was similar in principle to the bibliography of the works of Theophrastos.[169] Many bibliographies in the *Suda* that are based on those in the *Onomatologos* are not arranged in any discernible order, like some of those recorded by Diogenes; perhaps they are really unordered and had always been. This is impossible to decide.

Unlike the arrangement of the individual bibliographies, that of the entire list as such is Hesychios's own work. Today it is generally assumed that he arranged the authors by the customary classes and listed them in each class chronologically, whereas the epitomator combined the classes and arranged the authors alphabetically.[170] This assumption goes back to two researchers of the 19th century, Wachsmuth and his pupil Daub.[171] It was then thought that Kallimachos had listed the authors of various classes in chronological sequence; it seemed therefore that Hesychios had arranged his work like the one by the Alexandrian. Today it is, however, almost certain that Kallimachos arranged the authors within the classes in alphabetical order. The conjectural chronological arrangement of the *Onomatologos* may therefore not be deduced from the pattern of Kallimachos's work.

The arrangement of the *Onomatologos* by classes was deduced by Daub from the fact that the authors with identical names are generally listed in the *Suda* by classes, following the epitome of the *Onomatologos*: first come the poets, then the philosophers, the historians, etc. He deduced the chronological order of authors within classes from a feature of certain articles in which the expression *kai autos* (he too) refers to an author who preceded the listed one in the original chronological sequence, but who was now listed in another place because of the alphabetical order. His main example which had already been used by Wachsmuth, was the article on Hypereides in the *Suda* in which it is said that the great Athenian orator, a staunch opponent of the Macedonians, had "also" lost his life through Antipatros, i.e. like his partisan Demosthenes (who precedes him in the Greek alphabet by many letters).[172]

Wentzel proved that the namesakes in the *Suda* are arranged by classes, except in a few cases which had already been recognized by Daub, and he reinforced the conclusion at which Daub arrived.[173] But he did not mention even with a single word the chronological arrangement of authors within each class, as assumed by Daub. Did he think it was implausible? Had he noticed that Daub had in the meantime abandoned his main example (Hypereides)?[174] In any case, one may no longer rely on Daub, let alone on Wentzel, in order to claim that Hesychios arranged the authors within each class in chronological order.[175]

Thus, it would appear that only the arrangement of the *Onomatologos* by classes has been established. However, it seems to me that even this is questionable. The arrangement of namesakes in the *Suda* by classes is by no means to be taken as proof. Assuming that Hesychios listed the authors of all classes in one single alphabet, the bearers of the same name would always have come together. If he now wanted to arrange these collections of homonymous names it was easiest to list the bearers of the same name always according to a fixed scheme by classes of authors, i.e. in each instance first the poets, then the philosophers, the historians, etc. The title of Hesychios's lexicon indicated indeed that the names of authors were there united in one single alphabet: *Pinax* of those renowned in branches of learning. Thus, no *Pinakes* (lists, in the plural) are mentioned as in the classified work of Kallimachos, but only one *pinax* (list, in the singular). It could best fulfill its task, indirectly indicated in the title, when it was alphabetically arranged, as had been the individual *pinakes* of Kallimachos: because only thus could it serve its owner like a *nomenclator* without further ado, telling him who were the authors which he might have encountered in the study of literature. An *Onomatologos* arranged by classes and then in chronological order could not have done this, because the classification of many writers was problematic, and their lifetime was unknown.[176]

These general considerations are reinforced by some details, mainly by two double entries. The Alexandrian philologist Eirenaios, a not unimportant scholar of the second century A.D., whose Latin name was Minucius Pacatus, is listed in the *Suda* both as "Eirenaios, in Latin called Pakatos" and as "Pakatos, also known as Minukios and Eirenaios".[177] In the first entry there is also a biographical detail that is missing in the other one.[178] Both articles are based on the *Onomatologos*: Hesychios probably took them from two different sources.[179] That both deal with the same person could hardly have escaped Hesychios or his epitomator if the philologists had formed their own class in the *Onomatologos*, because the articles "Eirenaios" and "Pakatos" would have been separated from each other in an alphabetical arrangement by only 27 mostly brief articles,[180] and in a chronological arrangement they would even have come together. But if Hesychios listed all authors in one single alphabetical sequence, so that Eirenaios preceded Pakatos by a wide range, the double entry is conceivable, and even excusable.

The same is true for the second double entry: the philologist Sellios, also called Homeros, is identical with the philologist Homeros who called himself also Sellios. He is listed both as "Sellios" and as "Homeros", in the first entry with several works, in the second entry only with his main work.[181] The explanation is the same as for Eirenaios/Pakatos.[182]

209

It is therefore likely that Hesychios did not arrange authors by classes, as Kallimachos had done, but that he listed them from the beginning in alphabetical sequence.[183] The word "alphabetical" needs, however, further explication, if it is used in relation to ancient lists, otherwise it means too little. One must add, whether the arrangement was by coarse, fine, or full alphabetization. In the alphabetization of authors' names, keywords, etc. it was for a long time thought to be sufficient to file only by the first letter, that is, by coarse alphabetization. Only in the second century A.D. appeared a finely alphabetical and a fully alphabetical reference work, in the fifth century yet another finely alphabetical one, and in the sixth century a fully alphabetical reference work, the geographical dictionary by Stephanos of Byzantium (*Ethnika*). The literary dictionary of his contemporary Hesychios of Miletos is probably in the same category. It is unlikely that our Hesychios did not recognize the utility of the finer alphabetical order, emphasized by his namesake Hesychios of Alexandria in the fifth century; only such an order made it possible for the unclassified *Onomatologos* to answer the questions of literary scholars straightaway. Whether he arranged entries by fine alphabetization like the Alexandrian scholar (which I think is more likely) or by full alphabetization like his contemporary Stephanos of Byzantium is unimportant. In either case, his arrangement of the *Onomatologos*, the listing of all authors in a single alphabet, constituted a considerable innovation.[184] Although there was now no longer a survey of the authors of a single class (which could also be provided by tables such as the so-called *Canones*) the work enabled one to find a sought author quickly and with certainty. Evidently, this was considered more important by Hesychios. Thus he created the form of a general biobibliographic reference book which has been the usual one ever since. His *Onomatologos* belongs, together with the dictionary of his namesake from Alexandria and other works, to the great compilations of late Antiquity, which once more summarized the knowledge accumulated by earlier generations of scholars, and transmitted it to posterity. A dictionary of the (largely pagan) Greeks who had distinguished themselves *en paideia*, mostly as writers, was a remarkable undertaking in an almost completely Christianized environment, in which theology already had become dominant. Those who doubted that Hesychios was a Christian probably viewed the *Onomatologos* as a document of pagan opposition. But those who sought to combine classical traditions of learning with Christian education in the spirit of Basileios of Caesarea (who had expressly recommended to young people the study of ancient poets inasmuch as they taught and described virtue)[185] certainly considered Hesychios's work as a valuable aid for the study of the history of literature.

Notes to Chapter 5

1) Callimachus (1949) fragments 432 and 447.

2) Schmidt (1922) p. 28.

3) Wendel (1949) pp. 33 and 71 f. with references to relevant literature. No. 1: Papyrus Florence no. 371; 2. Papyrus Warsaw no. 5; 3. Papyrus Leningrad No. 13; 4. Papyrus Florence without number (*Elenco di opere letterarie*).

4) In the papyrus Warsaw no. 5 many scrolls are listed which are inscribed on both sides.

5) It seems to me that the usual expression "biographies of literati" is too narrow. For example, Aristotle and Demosthenes were not "literati" according to our conception.

6) Schwartz (1905) column 741 f.; Howald (1917) p. 119 f.

7) Daub (1880) pp. 411-413.

8) *Lexikon der Alten Welt* (1965) s.v. Buntschriftstellerei.

9) Maiuri (1925) no. 11; De Sanctis (1926); Wendel (1929); Segre (1935) and (1936); Wendel (1937) p. 585; Wendel (1949) p. 71.

10) The word *logos* must be added in each case; Lakonic oration, Panionic oration.

11) The Greek alphabet has the letter sequence delta, epsilon, zēta (these two letters are not represented in the left-hand column), ēta (a possible /h/ sound, e.g. in Hēgēsias, is disregarded), thēta.

12) On the antagonism between Plato and Isokrates see Jaeger (1933) vol. 3, pp. 105-130. De Sanctis (1926) p. 71 thought that this column listed political writings (except for two) and most researchers accepted this view, but Jacoby (1957) no. 115, T. 48 criticized it, referring to the epideictic orations. Segre (1935) p. 221, who shares De Sanctis's opinion, assumes that the *Katadromē* of Theopompos had been listed in this column only because it had been inscribed on the same papyrus scroll as the two preceding political works (orations) of the same author. But this epigraphic evidence is too weak for such a conclusion. The title of one of the two orations was evidently shifted too far to the left by an error (line 23). The *Technē* of Theodektes (four books) was certainly not combined with the essay or oration (one book) that follows it (line 11/12).

13) The author Damokleidas is perhaps identical with the Athenian orator Demokleides, who was a pupil of Theophrastos. He is represented by two works: the title of the first begins *Peri genes[eos]* (On the origin [of?])

(line 27). Segre (1935) p. 219 relates this to a work on natural science, which is probably correct. The second work, *Pros Alexandron* (To Alexander) (line 28) was apparently of a political character. The titles of two works of an unknown author (lines 17 and 18) begin with the preposition *hyper* (for) like the speeches of orators for their clients; in the left-hand column there are two analogous titles (line 19 and 20). Furthermore, the name of Hermodios, the murder of tyrants from Athens, appears in one title (line 25). Eratosthenes, who is listed in the last line, did not write any political or rhetorical works, so far as we know.

14) Wendel (1929) p. 4.

15) Wendel (1929) p. 1 f. and 4 f.; Segre (1935) pp. 219-221.

16) Nothing else is known about either this or any other library in Rhodos. Maiuri (1925) p. 7 and 15 states that the other inscription, then still in private hands, (no. 4) had been found in the area of the old acropolis, and the catalog inscription was probably also found there.

17) On the libraries of Hellenistic gymnasiums see Wendel-Göber (1955) p. 96 f.; on the study of rhetoric in Rhodos see Pfeiffer (1968) p. 266.

18) Wendel (1949) p. 15 f. The most important wall catalog still preserved in Egypt is the one in the book hall of the Horus temple at Edfu; it lists 37 titles and dates from the time of Ptolemaios VIII Euergetes II (170-116 B.C.) but is certainly based on older models.

19) Wendel (1929) p. 5.

20) See notes 12 and 13 above.

21) Gardthausen (1922) p. 79.

22) Schmidt (1922) pp. 62-66; Gardthausen (1922) p. 95 f.; Regenbogen (1950) column 1453. List 1: Athenaeus (1927) I 13 b-c; List 2: Athenaeus I 5 a-b; List 3: Varro, *Rerum rusticarum liber* I 1, 8 f.

23) This designation does not yet imply the later division of comedies by periods. Kallimachos also calls that early local historian of Keos from whom he took the story of Akontios and Kydippe, the "old" (*archaios*) Xenomedes. On Hegemon and his comedy *Philinē* see Körte (1912).

24) Regenbogen (1950) column 1454 ascribes the arrangement to Varro.

25) Wehrli (1974), fragments 1 and 3 with commentary.

26) Brink (1940) column 904.

27) Leo (1901) pp. 118-129.

28) The papyrus fragment was found in Oxyrhynchos, where Satyros later lived. See Leo (1912); Pfeiffer (1968) p. 151.

29)   Wehrli (1974) p. 78, commentary on fragment 54, and pp. 102-106. On Hermippos see also Leo (1901) pp. 124-128; Heibges (1913); Schmidt (1922) p. 99 f.; Von der Muehll (1942); Regenbogen (1950) column 1424 f.; Pfeiffer (1968) pp. 129 and 150.

30)   Dionysios of Halikarnassos, *Isaios* 1 = Wehrli (1974), fragment 69.

31)   Dionysios of Halikarnassos, *Peri Deinarchu* 1 = Callimachus (1949), fragment 447.

32)   Wehrli (1974), fragment 64; 73; 78; Hermippos also cites *adespota hypomnēmata* (ownerless notes, i.e. those written by an unknown person; according to a conjecture by Diels (1904) p. xl, anonymous commentaries on Demosthenes), fragment 71, and oral testimony, fragment 50.

33)   Wehrli (1974) p. 103 f. But Wehrli does not think that these were fabrications.

34)   Wehrli (1974), fragment 1.

35)   Wehrli (1974), fragments 54 and 55 with commentary.

36)   The same applies to the bibliography of Aristotle in Diogenes Laertios; Hermippos dealt with also with the biography of Aristotle.

37)   Wehrli (1974) p. 78, commentary on fragment 54.

38)   The bibliography of Demokritos by Kallimachos was an appendix to a glossary of Demokritos.

39)   Dionysos of Halikarnassos, *Pros Ammaion* 3.

40)   Diels (1904) p. xxxviii f.

41)   In his work on Isokrates he had reported that the philosopher had written *Philippos* when he was an old man, shortly before the death of the king and his own death; see Wehrli (1974), fragment 66 with commentary.

42)   Diogenes Laertios II 85 (Sotion) and VI 80 (Sotion and Satyros).

43)   Regenbogen (1950) column 1424 f.

44)   Bloch (1940) p. 34.

45)   Leo (1901) p. 134 f.

46)   Published by Westermann (1845). The article on Kallimachos in the *Suda* is also derived from a "grammatical" biography which was an introduction to an edition. The original was, however, severely mutilated.

47)   Leo (1901) pp. 17-34.

48) It seems that there was sometimes a circular process, as indicated by the Novatic index: a "grammatical" biography which formed the introduction to the edition of an author was included in much abbreviated form in a biobibliographical handbook, together with a bibliography; the article in the handbook or an extract from it was later copied, and formed in turn the introduction to the works of an author.

49) The lists are printed in the Aischylos edition of Page (Oxford 1972), and also in the article by Novati (1879). On both lists, see Regenbogen (1950) column 1426-1428; Daly (1967) p. 23 f.; Pfeiffer (1968) pp. 128-129.

50) According to Hesychios (*Suda*), Aischylos wrote altogether 90 plays.

51) The *genos* and the *Suda* say that Aristophanes wrote 44 comedies; in the *katalogos*, the second *Eirēnē* and the *Skēnas katalambanusai* were not listed, apparently by mistake; see Novati (1879) p. 462. The 44 plays include four spurious ones which were also ascribed to Archippos; see Gelzer (1970) column 1402.

52) Only the still extant plays are recorded, not those that had been listed in the *Didaskaliai* but had been lost; see Mensching (1964) p. 23.

53) See *Inscriptiones Graecae* vol. 2/3 2, 2 (1931) no. 2363 (previously ii 992); see also Wilamowitz (1875) pp. 137-143; Schmidt (1922) p. 71; Gardthausen (1922) p. 93; Wendel (1949) p. 44 f.; Hemmerdinger (1951) p. 87.

54) The ephebes of the Ptolemaion were under obligation to donate to the library of the gymnasium 100 scrolls after they had completed one year of service. It is, however, questionable whether the inscription recorded one of those donations; see Wendel (1949) p. 44 f. But we must agree with Wilamowitz (1875) p. 141 that the letter sequences ALAI and APHIDN[AI] in line 43 and 49 indicate Attic communities from which the donors came. Wendel is wrong to state that these letter sequences disrupt the series of titles. The difference between this list and the library catalog from Rhodos is quite obvious.

55) The scrolls were recorded in a random sequence. In addition, the distribution of the groups of plays formed by the same initial letter in the individual scrolls was also arbitrary, because the aim was only to produce scrolls of about equal length. Thus titles beginning with sigma, thēta, delta, pi, alpha and epsilon are listed one after the other; see Wilamowitz (1875) p. 142 f.

56) *Inscriptiones Graecae* vol. 14 (1890) no. 1152; see also Schmidt (1922) p. 71, note 7; Gardthausen (1922) p. 93 f.; Hemmerdinger (1951) p. 86. There are no lists of dramas by Sophokles.

57) Daly (1967) pp. 23-25; Pfeiffer (1968) pp. 129 and 195-196.

58) Namely eight tragedies and one satyr play, the *Kyklops*, which is incorrectly filed: *Helenē, Elektra, Hēraklēs, Hērakleidai, Kyklops, Iōn, Hikētides, Iphigeneia hē en Taurois, Iphigeneia hē en Aulidi.*

59) Daly (1967) p. 24 f.

60) Schmidt (1922) pp. 72-75. On the comedies of Plato see Regenbogen (1950) column 1428.

61) Schmidt (1922) p. 71; Regenbogen (1950) column 1421.

62) For lack of better terms, I call arrangement by the first letter only coarse alphabetization, arrangement by the first three to four letters fine alphabetization. and arrangement by all letters full alphabetization. The Greeks talked about order *kata stoicheion* (according to letter).

63) Daly (1967) p. 95.

64) Daly (1967) pp. 34 f. and 66 f.

65) Wilamowitz (1879) p. 464 f.

66) Under the letter pi, *Plutos* 2 (i.e. two plays, 408 and 388) is listed in the third place, and *Poiēsis* (spurious) in the fifth and last place.

67) *Agamemnōn* was the first tragedy of the *Oresteia,* the last tetralogy performed by Aischylos in Athens. Soon thereafter he went to Sicily where he died in 456 B.C.

68) The *Oinomaos* (411/408) is missing. My determination of dates follows that of Wilamowitz (1875) pp. 147-158. More recent research has led to somewhat different results, but the time relations that are of importance for my investigation are not affected thereby.

69) It was not difficult to compile a chronological list of a playwright's works, based on Aristotle's *Didaskalioi* or easier still, on Kallimachos's *Pinax tōn didaskalōn.* If such a list was rearranged alphabetically by titles, and two or more titles began with the same letter, the earliest play (e.g. Aristophanes's *Acharnēs*) filed first under the respective letter, and the latest one (e.g. his *Aiolosikōn*) filed last.

70) Daly (1967) p. 24, note 1. — Four plays by Attic dramatists appear in the *hypothēseis* with an ordinal number, two others in other passages; see Regenbogen (1950) column 1426; Mensching (1964) pp. 21 and 40; Gelzer (1970) column 1403. The discussion on these numberings has not yielded any results so far, because the researchers mostly tried to explain all numbers in the same way, and to trace them back to an edition of the respective author which was either chronologically or alphabetically arranged. I am limiting myself to only one point. The *hypothēsis* of *Alkēstis* by Euripides is unambiguous; it says there that the drama had been created as the 17th one. This datum is unassailable. The Alexandrian grammarians (e.g. Aristophanes of Byzantium) could easily find out from Kallimachos's *Pinax tōn didaskalōn* that the *Alkēstis* was indeed the 17th play of Euripides; they found that interesting from the point of view of literary history and made a note of it. It seems to me that this process was not considered during the discussion. The Roman grammarians (Varro) followed the example of the Alexandrians.

In the so-called *Didascaliae* of the comedies of Terence there is, for example, a note to the *Adelphoe*: *facta VI*. Some other numbers, also with other introductory words, indicated perhaps the place of the respective drama in an alphabetical list or edition. We must also consider that these numbers may have been distorted.

71) Leo (1901) p. 113.

72) On the Lamprias catalog of Plutarch's works see above, p. 148. Except for the detail mentioned there, this list is not remarkable from a bibliographic point of view.

73) Some researchers, e.g. Regenbogen (1950) column 1442, assume that the work by Andronikos contained also a biography of Aristotle. Although it is not unlikely that Andronikos preceded his bibliography of the philosopher with a biographical outline, similar to the Deinarchos bibliography by Dionysios of Halikarnassos, there is no evidence for it.

74) Moraux (1951) pp. 289-309; (1973) pp. 58-94.

75) See below, note 82.

76) Moraux (1973) p. 60 f. is perhaps also of this opinion when he writes that the foundation of Ptolemaios's *Pinax* might possibly have come from Andronikos himself.

77) Printed in Düring (1957) pp. 221-231; commentary pp. 241-246.

78) The *Poetics* was probably listed before the *Rhetoric* by mistake.

79) The later Neoplatonic arrangement of Aristotle's works was already discernible in the traditional scheme; see Moraux (1973) p. 71.

80) Diogenes Laertios V 24, no. 70-73; see on this Moraux (1951) p. 95.

81) Diogenes Laertios V 26, no. 120; see on this Moraux (1951) pp. 95 and 115 f. The laws collected by Theophrastos on Aristotle's suggestion, *Nomoi kata stoicheion*, were also arranged in the same way; see on this Nissen (1892) p. 185. The *Politeiai* (state constitutions) collected by Aristotle and his pupils were apparently arranged alphabetically by the names of the inhabitants of the respective cities; see Moraux (1951) p. 116. But there the situation was different: some *politeiai*, such as the *Athēnaiōn politeia* by Aristotle himself, were works in their own right which filled one or more scrolls.

82) Moraux (1973) p. 94 (Summary) states as the reason for his doubts that the arrangement by Ptolemaios is not exactly the same as the later, Neoplatonic, one; but there is no evidence that Andronikos anticipated the Neoplatonic arrangement in all respects. He also thinks that even the enumeration of the pragmatic works by Ptolemaios could hardly be based on Andronikos, but he does not explain that in detail. Furthermore, two details seem to militate against Ptolemaios's dependency on Andronikos: a) Ptolemaios lists the *Topics* (no. 31) before the two *Analytics*, whereas in our Corpus

Aristotelicum (created by Andronikos) they appear after the *Analytics*.
It may be that Ptolemaios deviated on this point from Andronikos,
following other scholars. But it is not impossible that the *Topics* were listed
before the *Analytics* by mistake, just as the *Poetics* (no. 38) were listed
before the *Rhetoric*. b) The *Peri hermēneias* which Andronikos declared to
be spurious, appear in the *Pinax* of Ptolemaios.

83) Porphyrios, *Bios Plōtinu* 26.

84) A list of *pseudepigrapha* which was perhaps compiled by Andronikos
appears at the end of the so-called Appendix Hesychiana, an appendix to
the bibliography of Aristotle as transmitted by Hesychios; see Düring (1957)
p. 91.

85) Moraux (1973) pp. 65 and 74 f.

86) The grammarians of Homer, beginning with Zenodotos, included also the
verses whose authenticity they doubted, but marked them with an *obelos*.

87) The treatise *Peri Deinarchu* has been published in *Dionysii Halicarnasei
quae extant*, ed. H. Usener et L. Radermacher. vol. V: *Opuscula*. 1.
Leipzig 1899 (Reprint: Stuttgart 1965). The conclusion of the treatise is
missing. The introduction shows harsh passages and flaws which cannot be
explained away by mere conjectures. Perhaps Dionysios left the treatise
unfinished. See also below, note 91. On the treatise see Blass (1865) pp.
207-219; Blass (1898) pp. 292-309; Radermacher (1899); Leo (1901) pp. 32 f.
and 43 f.; Thalheim (1901); Radermacher (1903); Schmidt (1922) p. 82-86;
Lossau (1964) pp. 68-75.

88) The orators were essentially writers, i.e. they wrote speeches for other
people. Only a few of them delivered (political) speeches themselves.

89) The use of stylistic criteria as a test of authenticity implied, however,
the risk of *petitio principii*; see Speyer (1971) p. 124.

90) Dionysios, vol. 5, 1, p. 284, 1-7, and p. 291, 13 f.

91) On the Greek text: I think that after *logus* p. 297, 13 there is a gap,
because *dielthein* and *diorisai* refer to the author, the following words,
however, refer to those interested in rhetoric. The participle *ama de orōn*
which opens the next sentence (in which Kallimachos is mentioned), p. 297,
14 to p. 298, 2 is not followed by a principal clause, which is peculiar
in a master of style.

92) Dionysios, *Peri Deinarchu* p. 297, 14-298, 2 = Callimachus (1949),
fragment 447.

93) On Demetrios see Schwartz (1901). His dictionary of homonymous authors
is frequently cited by Diogenes Laertios.

94) If Demetrios was born in Magnesia on the Maeander or in Magnesia on the Hermos he may have used the library of Pergamon (about 90 and 60 miles north respectively).

95) The Greek text, p. 299, 18 f. means in English "he was together with Theophrastos and Demetrios of Phaleron". The verb *syngignesthai* is also used for the relationship between teacher and pupil. But since Demetrios was ten years younger than Deinarchos, he could not have been his teacher. On the other hand, it is not impossible that Deinarchos studied dialectics and rhetoric with Theophrastos, even though he came to Athens only in 335 B.C. with Aristotle, while Deinarchos purportedly began to write speeches already in 336 B.C. The relationship of Deinarchos to Theophrastos and Demetrios was already interpreted in this manner by Photios, *Bibliothēkē* cod. 267, p. 496 b.

96) The works of Philochoros which are listed in the *Suda* show that studies in literary history were conducted in Athens ca. 300 B.C. also outside of the Peripatos.

97) For this reason, so many orations were falsely ascribed to him. That such writings were distributed and transmitted at all can only be explained by the special interest of the ancients in works of rhetoric.

98) In the article on Deinarchos in the *Suda* this is specifically noted. See also Blass (1895) p. 297.

99) Dionysios, *Peri Deinarchu* pp. 311-321.

100) In the Codex Parisinus 2934 (S) of Demosthenes the number of *stichoi* is indicated after each oration.

101) *Peri Deinarchu* p. 318, 9.

102) *Peri Deinarchu* p. 311, 21 f. = Callimachus (1949), fragment 444.

103) *Peri Deinarchu* p. 309, 18.

104) *Peri Deinarchu* p. 317, 3 f.

105) The last five public speeches, among which are the three extant ones, were made in connection with the so-called Harpalos affair. (Harpalos, Alexander's treasurer, absconded with a part of the money entrusted to him to Athens, and had purportedly bribed some politicians there.) The collection of the five speeches was therefore necessary for reasons of content as well as of time. If Dionysios arranged the public speeches of Deinarchos chronologically, then these five were the last ones which he wrote for public trials. Blass (1898) did not give any opinion on this question.

106) The first of the five speeches on damages is his own against Proxenos, which was his last or at least one of his last speeches.

107) On a speech against a certain Timokrates (indictment for overthrow of the democracy) Dionysios remarks on p. 314, 19, that the *epigraphē* alone showed that the speech was spurious, because such an indictment could only be made after Demetrios of Phaleron had been exiled. But Deinarchos had also left the city together with him.

108) According to Malclès (1950) vol. 1, p. 3, it is the task of the bibliographer to identify the documents collected by him, to describe them and to arrange them (and its descriptions) in a definite order.

109) *Peri Deinarchu* pp. 315, 17; 316, 4; 319, 21.

110) Photios, *Bibliothēkē* cod. 265, p. 491 a; see also Speyer (1971) p. 16.

111) Radermacher (1899) pp. 167-169.

112) The original title of this work is in dispute. The title was probably *Philosophōn bioi kai dogmata* (Lives and opinions of philosophers) or *Philosophōn biōn kai dogmatōn synagōgē* (Collection of lives and opinions of philosophers); see Schwartz (1905) column 738 f. The English edition, Diogenes Laertius (1925), has the title *Lives of eminent philosophers*. Long, who produced the first critical edition (1964), writes briefly *Vitae philosophorum*. The two other collections are *Bioi tōn deka rhetorōn* (Lives of the ten orators), falsely ascribed to Plutarch, and *Bioi sophistōn* (Lives of the Sophists, [i.e. the orators in Imperial times]) by Philostratos.

113) Leo (1901) pp. 35-84; Schwartz (1905); Delatte (1922); Praechter (1953) p. 19-23. A Latin translation of the work was made in the 1570s and was often reprinted; it probably had a not insignificant influence on studies in the history of literature in modern time.

114) Diogenes Laertios I 16.

115) Diogenes Laertios I 13-16.

116) Diogenes Laertios II 121-125 (pupils of Sokrates) and VIII 78-89 (pupils of Protagoras).

117) On the bibliographies see Delatte (1922) p. 59 f. and Regenbogen (1950) columns 1430-34, 1438-44.

118) Diogenes Laertios I 119 (work of Pherekydes); V 27 (poems by Aristotle); V 60 (letters by Straton).

119) Diogenes Laertios I 79 (elegies of Pittakos).

120) Diogenes Laertios V 28 (Aristotle, sum total of standard lines; VII 198 (Chrysippos, number of books on logic).

121) Diogenes Laertios II, 105; II 64; II, 122; see also Fritz (1938) column 1539.

122) Diogenes Laertios VI 80, also Natorp (1903) column 768 f.

123) Diogenes Laertios II 83-85, also Natorp (1896) column 904 f.

124) Sosikrates showed himself to be a severe critic: he ascribed to the Stoic Ariston of Chios only letters (following Panaitios), whereas he ascribed all other works known under the name of Ariston to the Peripatetic Ariston of Keos; see Diogenes Laertios II 163.

125) Thus Regenbogen (1950) column 1434 regarding the works of Diogenes of Sinope.

126) The title of works written by stoics are similarly grouped; see Dyroff (1896).

127) E.g. Diogenes Laertios VI 15-18 (List of works by Antisthenes according to an unidentified edition); III 49-51; 56-62 (List of Plato's dialogs according to the edition by Thrasyllos and a report on the various arrangements of the dialogs).

128) E.g. Diogenes Laertios V 86-88 (Herakleides Pontikos); VII 189-206 (Chrysippos). It is possible, though not certain, that these bibliographies also reproduce the tables of contents of editions.

129) E.g. Diogenes Laertios IV 11-14 (Xenokrates); V 22-27 (Aristotle).

130) E.g. Diogenes Laertios IV 4 (Speusippos); VII 4 (Zeno of Kition).

131) E.g. Diogenes Laertios II 61 (dialogs of Aischines, chronologically); IX 46 (writings of Demokritos on ethics and physics, alphabetically?).

132) E.g. Diogenes Laertios VI 80 (the tragedies purportedly written by Diogenes of Sinope).

133) Diogenes Laertios V 42-50.

134) Schultz (1913). In later Imperial times, the highest officials had the title *illustris* (Greek: *illustrios*).

135) The *Onomatologos* of the grammarian Palamedes of Elea (1st century A.D.) was probably of a different kind (dictionary of synonyms?); see Wendel (1942). The term *nomenclator* was often used during the 16th and 17th centuries as a title for biographical dictionaries; see Blum (1980) pp. 17 and 38.

136) The *Suda* article on Damophilos which is based on the *Onomatologos* says that the author, a philosopher and sophist who lived in the second half of the second century A.D., had written many works "of which I have found the following in libraries".

137) Since the pronunciation had changed, vowels and diphthongs having the same sound were combined, which resulted in the following sequence of letters:

α β γ δ αι ε ζ ει η ι θ κ λ μ ν ξ ο ω π ρ σ τ οι υ φ χ ψ

Also, double consonants were filed as single letters. This kind of alphabetization was known as *kat antistoichian* (according to the value of the letters). See also Daly (1967) p. 68.

138) Krumbacher (1897) pp. 562-570; Adler (1931), especially column 678 on the naming of the *Suda* and column 707 on the omission of articles from the *Onomatologos*: *Der Kleine Pauly* (1964) vol. 5, s.v. *Suda*. Adler also prepared the authoritative edition of the *Suda* (Leipzig 1928; Reprint: Stuttgart 1967). The humanists became acquainted with the work at the end of the 15th century through the editio princeps, edited by Demetrios Chalkondylas and printed by Joannes Bissolius and Benedictus Mangius in Milan in 1499. During the last decades of the 19th century a large number of studies on the *Suda* and the *Onomatologos* appeared, but so far as I can see, no more has been written on these works since then.

139) Presumably, his grandfather was the physician Iakobos of Constantinople, famous both for his skill and for his being a pagan, the son and father of a Hesychios. Our Hesychios reported in his *Onomatologos* s.v. Iakobos details on this man and his mother which he could have known only through family tradition. See Flach (1880) p. 213 f.; against him, but without good reasons, Daub (1882) p. 153.

140) E.g. the three great Cappadocians, Basileios of Caesarea, Gregorios of Nyssa and Gregorios Nazianzen.

141) These articles are mostly from a Greek translation of Jerome's *De viris illustribus*, supposedly translated by Sophronios; see Wentzel (1895), especially pp. 3-14.

142) Flach assumed that the epitomator lived in the 7th century; see Hesychius Milesius (1882) pp. xii-xiv.

143) In Adler's edition they are indicated. The separation of additions by later hands to the articles of Hesychios is in some cases in dispute. Also, in my opinion, one cannot always be certain whether this or that addition to the *Onomatologos* should be ascribed to the epitomator, to the editor of the *Suda* or to other scholars. Flach reproduced the *Suda* articles which are based on the *Onomatologos* in an alphabetical sequence according to the ancient alphabet. Some figures may indicate the extent of the collection. Flach lists altogether 884 articles; among those are 24 about which he has doubts, 2 doubles and 2 references; 146 are under alpha (two are missing), 9 under bēta, 12 under gamma, 68 under delta, 63 under epsilon, 14 under zēta, 17 under ēta, 44 under thēta, 45 under iōta, 51 under kappa, 24 under lambda, 50 under mu, 23 under nu, 8 under xi, 22 under omikron, 94 under pi, 4 under rhō, 78 under sigma, 38 under tau, 3 under upsilon, 47 under phi, 15 under chi, 0 under psi, 5 under ōmega. Of these, 69 are epic poets, 44 lyric poets, 45 tragic poets, 106 comic poets, 91 historians, 106 grammarians, 181 orators, 208 philosophers, 30 physicians, 7 musicians, 3 painters.

144) All famous composers named by Hesychios had also written textual works.

145) Flach (1881). Only in one or two cases it is not clear why a Roman author was included. The naming of Caesar and Brutus who had translated the *Phainomina* by Aratos and the *Historiai* of Polybios respectively, may be seen as the beginning of a bibliographic listing of translations of the national literature.

146) These articles are sometimes indicated in the professional literature as *Vitae*. Some researchers also consider the biographical data in an article as a *bios* of the respective author. This must, of course, be taken *cum grano salis*.

147) Suidas (1928), v. 1, p. 376, Alpha 4107; v. 3, p. 494, Xi 47.

148) On the Novatic index see Novati and Wilamowitz (1879); on the Vita Menagiana see Moraux (1951) pp. 195-209; 249-288.

149) Flach (1879) p. 93 f.

150) The epitomator recorded, for example, only the beginning of the alphabetically arranged bibliography of the poet Parthenios; see Schmidt (1922) p. 77 and also p. 74.

151) Schultz (1913) column 1324 mentions among the bibliographies which are based on the *Onomatologos* only that of Aristotle; other researchers who dealt with Hesychios in recent reference books do not even mention that one. Regenbogen (1950) column 1458 devoted only 13 lines to the *Onomatologos* in his otherwise excellent survey of the pinakographic literature of Antiquity, and even this in the wrong context: a dictionary that listed more than 800 authors, among which are many whose works are long since lost, did not have a "selective character".

152) Hesychios often divided the philosophers by schools: Socratic philosopher, Platonic philosopher, etc. As sophists he indicated both the orators of the so-called second sophistic school (second to third century A.D.) but also the representatives of the first sophists (fifth to fourth century B.C.). Other classifications are: *geōmetrēs, musikos, nomothetēs* (legislator), *oneirokritēs* (interpreter of dreams).

153) In addition, two names appear four times, five names three times, and seventeen names twice.

154) E.g. Eratosthenes had the nickname *Bēta*, because he ranked second in all disciplines. (The text in the *Suda* is corrupt). Xenophon was known as "The Attic bee" because of his pure Attic language. The original name of Theophrastos was Tyrtamos, but Aristotle gave him the new name because of his "divine" eloquence.

155) While it is easy to understand why Kallimachos's nephew of the same name is mentioned, we ask in vain why Hesychios (as also Diogenes Laertios) mentions by name the three daughters of the astronomer Eudoxos of Knidos. Originally there may have been a good reason for this, though it was later omitted.

156) Thus he mentions, for example, that the father of Theophrastos had been a fuller, and that the father of the Alexandrian grammarian Didymos had been a fishmonger.

157) He noted, for example, that Phaleron, the birth place of Demetrios was an Attic harbor.

158) It is characteristic that he mentions Xenophon not as the leader of the ten thousand, but as the author of the *Anabasis*.

159) E.g. the sophist Protagoras was first a porter, the stoic Kleanthes was a boxer, and Kallimachos was a school teacher.

160) E.g. Aischylos was killed when a turtle, which fell from an eagle's talons, hit him on the head.

161) Thus he wrote on Gorgias: "Porphyrios puts him [i.e. his period of flourishing] in the 80th Olympiad, but we must assume that he was older." On Kadmos, "Son of Archelaos, from Miletos, a younger historian; some also list a certain Lykinos Kadmos; but perhaps this is another man." On Pindar: "A son of Skopelinos, others say a son of Daiphantos, which is more correct; others again say a son of Pagondas."

162) E.g. the articles "Eumolpos" and "Panyasis".

163) E.g. he noted that Akron had written in the Doric dialect, Anakreon in the Ionic dialect. The dialect of a work was sometimes an important argument when the ascription was in dispute.

164) On the historian Xenophon of Ephesos he stated that his *Ephesiaka* were not a history but a love story; on Philochoros of Athens he explained which period was covered by his *Atthis* (History of Athens). His annotation on the *Ibis* by Kallimachos has no parallel, so far as I can see.

165) Thus he stated, for example, in the article on Homer that only the *Iliad* and the *Odyssey* among his epic works were truly authentic, whereas such and such works were known under his name but were spurious. In the article on Deinarchos he states that he was said to have written 160 speeches, but that according to a more correct version he had written only 60. Only in exceptional cases did he indicate why certain works of an author were thought to be spurious, e.g. in the article on Zonaios (stylistic reasons).

166) Flach (1879) pp. 87-90; Delatte (1922) p. 96.

167) E.g. in the article "Aristotle".

168) Schmidt (1922) pp. 72-91. If we consider only the unquestionable cases of alphabetization, it can hardly be said that the alphabetical arrangement of titles is predominant, as Schmidt, p. 91 states.

169) It seems that the much abridged bibliography of the physician Aristogenes of Thasos or Knidos (middle of the 3rd century B.C.) listed the titles of works from various fields of medicine in one alphabet.

170) Krumbacher (1897) p. 324 f.; Leo (1901) p. 35; Schultz (1913) column 1324; Christ-Schmid (1924) p. 1039 f.; *Der Kleine Pauly* (1964) s.v. Hesychios; *Lexikon der Alten Welt* (1965) s.v. Hesychios.

171) Daub (1880) pp. 405-410. Bergk (1872) vol. 1, p. 292 and Flach (1882 in his edition of Hesychius Milesius) p. xii still assumes an alphabetical order of the *Onomatologos*.

172) Daub (1880) p. 406. When fleeing the catchers of the Macedonian regent Antipatros, Demosthenes committed suicide in a temple; Hypereides was dragged from a temple and killed.

173) Wentzel (1895) pp. 57-63.

174) Daub (1882) p. 36: "In the following passage *aneirethē de kai autos hyp Antipatru tu basileōs* (he too was killed by king Antipatros) I thought earlier, following Wachsmuth, that the words *kai autos* were derived from the chronological arrangement of the *Onomatologos* (so that the article on Demosthenes would have preceded it there). I am no longer of this opinion and do not think that the loss of a distinct relationship of *kai autos* is to blame on the epitomator (see Rhode, *Rheinisches Museum* 34, 62); rather, it seems to me that Hesychios already found in his source on the death of Hypereides a mention on the same fate that befell Demosthenes, and that he hinted at this coincidence somewhat carelessly by the note *kai autos*." Daub's other examples can be explained analogously. His conclusions were already rejected by Flach (1880) p. 832 f.

175) Regenbogen (1950) column 1458 cites therefore Wentzel only for the classified arrangement of the *Onomatologos*. He does not deal either with the arrangement of authors within each class.

176) Hesychios once admitted his embarrassment, when he remarked on Zenon Kitieus (II) that it was not clear to him whether he had been an orator or a philosopher. Such a remark could only have been made by someone who was not forced to list this author either among the orators or among the philosophers.

177) Suidas (1928) v. 2, p. 533, Epsilon iota 190, and v. 4, p. 4, Pi 29.

178) Under Eirenaios there is a note that he was a pupil of the metrician Heliodoros, while under Pakatos it says that he called himself Minukios, i.e. Minucius Pacatus; see Cohn (1905).

179) Adler also related both articles to Hesychios. Daub (1882) p. 121 f. wanted to dispute the Hesychian origin of the article "Pakatos" but could not give any sound reasons. The interpolations of the editor of the *Suda* are of a different character, e.g. the articles "Herennios (reference to Philon of Byblos) and "Soteridas Epidaurios" (constructed from the article "Pamphile"). The author of the "fraudulent" proem to the *Suda* who lists a main work of Pakatos among the sources of the lexicon (see Adler (1931) column 681) already encountered the article "Pakatos".

180) Of the 27 articles, 18 comprise one to five lines, 6 have six to ten lines, and only 3 have more than ten lines of 18-20 syllables each.

181) The article "Sellios", one of the not infrequent brief articles in the *Suda* runs as follows: "Sellios or Sillios, who also called himself Homeros, grammarian. Before Menander." It has long been recognized that the last two words which are meaningless actually hide the title of Sellios's main work which is cited s.v. Homeros as follows (in the accusative case): *periochas [tōn] Menandru [dramatōn]*, i.e. "contents of Menander's dramas". Remnants of this work which was enriched by introductions on the literary history of the plays have come to light on papyri; see Körte (1923).

182) The two cases indicate also that in the Imperial period problems of citation began to appear which were formerly unknown. For example, should Eirenaios/Pacatus be cited under the Greek or Latin form of his name, or Homeros Sellios under the first or second part of his name? It also became necessary to include cross references; thus, in the *Suda* there is a cross reference from Herennios Philon to Philon of Byblos, also called Herennios; see also note 179 above.

183) I cite another evidence, though with some reservations. The *Suda* names s.v. Nikomachos both the son and an older relative of Aristotle: a) Nikomachos, a Stagirite [citizen of Stageiros], philosopher, etc.; b) Nikomachos, physician, also a Stagirite (*kai autos Stageirites*), etc. If we could be sure that the words *kai autos* are Hesychios's own, this would be proof that he listed the philosophers and the physicians neither in different classes nor chronologically.

184) Against the assumption that the *Onomatologos* was arranged either in finely or fully alphabetical order it may not be argued that the titles in the alphabetical bibliographies are arranged only by their first letters. Hesychios took these lists from his sources and did not rearrange them, but he himself decided on the sequence of authors. Flach pointed out that the authors of dictionaries of homonymous authors had already done some preliminary work towards a new sequence of authors, because they had collected the names of authors from all classes who had the same name; see Flach in: Hesychius Milesius (1882) p. xii. It is still not known who adapted the alphabetical order of Hesychios to the Byzantine order of the alphabet. Presumably this was not the epitomator of the *Onomatologos* but the editor of the *Suda*, because he had to cut up the epitome in any case in order to combine its articles with those that had been collected from other sources.

185) Basileios *Pros tus neus* 177 B Migne says that he had heard from a knowledgeable man that for Homer all poetry was a praise of virtue (*aretēs epainos*).

6. The Development and Character of Kallimachos's Lists of Greek Authors and Their Works

THE IMAGE of the *Pinakes* by Kallimachos which we have formed in our mind on the strength of quotations has been verified and complemented by conclusions drawn from later lists. It remains now to clarify how the *Pinakes* were compiled. To be sure, that process has not been transmitted to us, but it is possible to reconstruct it in part. It need not be stressed that every reconstruction is hypothetical. The edition of the *Pinakes* was the final stage in a process of library work which could not have been entirely different in Alexandria from those performed subsequently in later libraries. It is, however, not clear how far this process had already advanced when Kallimachos began to take part in it, and what were his own contributions to it.

Four phases can be distinguished in this process.[1]

1. The scrolls acquired since ca. 295 B.C. by Demetrios of Phaleron were probably only roughly sorted in some way. Only Zenodotos, who had become the director of the book collection, began to sort them systematically and to store them accordingly. Prior to that he had, however, to find out the contents of each scroll and had to list the entry of each work, i.e. its author and title, on a *syllibos* (title tag); this has generally not been recognized. When the scrolls were placed in heaps on the shelves of book cases[2] it was easy to read the *sillyboi* and to find out what they contained. It was, however, not always easy to determine what was contained in a scroll, because in many scrolls the author and title of a work were either not listed at all or only incompletely. Some data were also unreliable. But as long as the mass of scrolls was not sorted out, Zenodotos did not have time for investigations into literary history. He and his aides probably decided in such cases on an author and title as well as this could be done without thorough research, but otherwise they simply accepted the data found in the scrolls. It was probably only seldom possible to distinguish between namesakes mentioned in the scrolls without any additions to personal names.

We may assume that Zenodotos shelved the provisionally identified copies of Greek works of literature by author classes (epic, lyric, etc. poets, philosophers, orators . . .) and within each class alphabetically by author, that is to say, the sequence of works in the *pinakes*, the lists of books, was the same as that of the scrolls in the *bibliothēkai*, the book cases. If the principles according to which the scrolls were shelved had shown themselves to be useful, there was no reason for Kallimachos to record works according to different principles; besides, one could then have found the works listed in the tables only by "call numbers" in the book cases.

It is likely that Aristotle arranged the scrolls of his library by classes of authors, but presumably he arranged the authors within the classes chronologically. It was indeed obvious to follow the course of the history of literature, and not only to list the epic poets, whose works represented the oldest literary genre, before the lyric poets, but also to arrange them by their age.

If Zenodotos tried this method at all, he must soon have understood that it was not feasible in the Alexandrian library which was much larger. The period of flourishing of many authors was not exactly known, their chronological arrangement would therefore have been difficult, and even more so their retrieval.

The alphabetical arrangement of authors within the classes, which was introduced by Zenodotos, was apparently an innovation. Earlier examples are unknown. In the Egyptian archives, which were also called *bibliothēkai,* certain documents were perhaps already at that time shelved by places and then alphabetically by persons.[3] Kallimachos arranged the dramatists in his *Pinax* of Attic playwrights chronologically according to their first appearance; this was possible, because in this case the dates were known thanks to Aristotle's *Didaskaliai.* But a *pinax* was not a library; Zenodotos was forced by the mass of authors in all classes to choose a mechanical principle of arrangement.[4] The importance of this procedure is not insignificant, even though Zenodotos arranged the authors only by the first letter of their names. He knew probably that a more precise order was not worthwhile. Since the scrolls were placed in heaps which grew, shrank or changed every time a scroll was added or removed, it was in the long run impossible to maintain a more detailed alphabetical order, especially in a library that was constantly growing.

Regarding the order of the works by an author, one may deduce from the *Pinakes* that Zenodotos shelved scrolls with works of the same form and of related contents with those of the same kind, but that he did not subarrange these groups any further, probably for the same reason that led him to forego any fine alphabetization of authors. An exception were some categories of works of the same kind, e.g. plays, dithyrambs and elegies which Zenodotos arranged alphabetically by the first letter of their title.[5] It seems that he tried initially to shelve the plays chronologically by years of performance but that he soon abandoned this method.

A special problem was the treatment of the numerous collective scrolls, especially those which contained works by different authors and of various genres. Schmidt thought that such scrolls had been split up into their parts, or that these had been copied separately. This is quite unlikely.[6] The Alexandrian librarians treated the collective scrolls probably in the same manner in which the medieval librarians treated the collective volumes that were also not infrequent: they arranged them by the author of the first work and made a note on the title tag *kai alla* (and others).

For an easier overview of the holdings of the library, tablets (*pinakes* in the original sense) were mounted on the book cases on which the contents of each case were listed.

2. Schmidt assumed that Kallimachos began to compile his *Pinakes* immediately after Zenodotos had arranged and shelved the scrolls. He denied that the holdings of the library had been inventoried before that, because he thought that this had not been necessary at all, given that the scrolls had been put in order and that the collective scrolls had been split up.[7] He also stated that Kallimachos had not intended to compile a catalog "in which all scrolls, all doubles were recorded". His intention had rather been to record what existed in Greek literature, inasmuch as it was available in the Alexandrian library, arranged by

literary genres and authors, and with biographical data on writers and occasional critical notes on doubtful works. His *Pinakes* had therefore occupied a position in the middle between a catalog and a history of literature.[8] Gardthausen was convinced, however, that there must have been inventory lists before the time of Kallimachos, because without such lists it would have been impossible to manage a library such as the Alexandrian one. But he said that these had merely been "makeshift lists of books"; only Kallimachos had created a "scholarly catalog". His published *Pinakes*, however, had been the result of an elaboration of this catalog "to an annotated classified bibliography, or more precisely a handbook of literary history"; between these two versions there had been a great difference.[9] Wendel, on the other hand, assumed that Kallimachos had already encountered a library catalog, and had used it as the foundation for his *Pinakes*, "the first outline of the entire Greek literature which remained the most authoritative one throughout all Antiquity". He thought further that Kallimachos had complemented and improved that catalog, but above all that he had enriched it with biographical data and critical notes on authenticity; on the other hand, he had omitted the entries for different copies of the same work.[10] Wendel apparently assumed that Kallimachos had recorded also works that were not extant in the Alexandrian library. Gardthausen left that question open.

Most other researchers joined either Schmidt or Wendel; e.g. Herter followed Schmidt,[11] Regenbogen sided with Wendel.[12] The character of the book lists encountered by Kallimachos is left unclear by both researchers as well as by Gardthausen. Regenbogen ascribed to the cataloging performed by Kallimachos an order-producing function; he also thought that only Kallimachos had used the alphabetical principle of arrangement. He stated that "Kallimachos may occasionally have made also critical remarks on authenticity in his *Pinakes*". Pfeiffer apparently also assumes that there had been a library catalog before Kallimachos, but its character is not made obvious by him either. According to Pfeiffer, the *Pinakes* of Kallimachos were not a catalog but a bibliography; he states: "The distinction between a mere library catalog and a critical inventory of Greek literature is sometimes obscured in modern literature on Callimachus's great work; it was certainly based on his knowledge of the books available in the library, but he also had regard to works only mentioned in earlier literature and to questions of authenticity".[13]

Pfeiffer also thinks that Kallimachos's work had served above all to create order in the library: "His task was to find a system for arranging the texts of all writers collected for the first time in the royal library (or libraries)."[14] An objection to this is that at the time when Kallimachos was called to the court (ca. 280 B.C.) about fifteen years had already passed since Ptolemaios I had begun to acquire books on a large scale in order to create a library for the members of the Museion. Zenodotos as director of this book collection was obliged to store the scrolls in an orderly arrangement after having ascertained their contents and listing it on title tags. Otherwise it would have been impossible for the members of the Museion to use the collection, and both he and his colleagues could not have found the supporting evidence necessary for their textual criticism. It is therefore out of the question that it was only Kallimachos who brought order to the multitude of books. Rather, we must assume that he already found the scrolls arranged according to the principles indicated above and equipped with title tags. The arrangement of the library was not his work.

228

Zenodotos had probably also inventoried the shelved scrolls, as also the custodians of medieval libraries inventoried them after they had ascertained what was contained in the individual volumes and had shelved them accordingly, roughly arranged by disciplines. The so-called medieval library catalogs are not genuine catalogs at all, but merely inventory lists; all experts agree on this. Outside the circle of professionals, however, the difference between a library shelf list and a library catalog is often not recognized. The same goes for the Alexandrian library. A shelf list records the volumes extant in a library with brief descriptions and according to their place on the shelves; it serves primarily as a holdings record, a listing of what the library owns. A catalog, on the other hand, lists all copies or reprints of literary works in a library, irrespective of whether they are in a separate volume or constitute a part of a collective volume, under the names of the (real) authors and with the (correct) titles; it serves primarily for the utilization of the collection, it is an aid to scholarly work. The difference can clearly be seen especially in the manner in which collective volumes as well as works whose authors were in dispute were treated in the inventory lists of medieval libraries. Generally, when describing a collective volume, only the first work contained in it was listed, the one that had already been the criterion for the shelving of the volume, perhaps also the second work, but all others were either not listed at all or only mentioned summarily. In a catalog, not only the second, third, and further works would have been listed, but their titles would also have been inserted as cross references in those places in which they would have been listed had they been the first or only works in a volume.

If the same work was ascribed in two or more volumes to different authors, which happened not infrequently also in the Middle Ages, the inventory simply recorded what was found in each respective volume. If a catalog had been compiled, one would have tried to identify the text, i.e. to find out who was the (real) author. Most medieval libraries certainly lacked the necessary information. But the identification of disputed works and the analysis of collective volumes were not performed, mainly because this was of no importance for an inventory. Therefore no distinction was made of homonymous authors either, if the names as given in the volumes lacked any distinctive additions. The users of these libraries, who admittedly were few in number, were therefore offered only incomplete and partially also uncertain information. Nevertheless, almost all libraries throughout the Middle Ages were satisfied with the compilation of mere inventories.[15] The librarian's memory had to serve as a substitute for a catalog, in many places well into the 19th century.

The compilation of an inventory which comprised not only the books but also all other possessions was always part and parcel of a well-ordered administration. In a country such as Egypt which since Pharaonic times had enjoyed an excellent administration, continued by all subsequent rulers, the inventory-taking of the royal possessions as well as the regular control and updating of the inventory lists was certainly prescribed. These activities pertained of course also to the books acquired by the kings. The recording of large quantities of scrolls was not unusual in Egypt; in its archives it was quite customary.

The inventory, if there was one, reflected of course the order of the scrolls in the book cases. In its compilation Zenodotos relied on the *sillyboi*, and did not investigate whether or not the data of the entry were correct, because this was of no importance for the purposes of the inventory. For the same reason he probably recorded, like the librarians of the Middle Ages, not all works contained in a collective manuscript but only the first one, but he cited the beginnings of the works listed as well as their extent (the number of books and standard lines).

3. After the Alexandrian library had been inventoried, and a record of the scrolls in the book cases had been created, it was also cataloged: a survey of all copies of works by Greek authors contained in the scrolls, including the collective ones, was being compiled, arranged by classes of authors and then by individual authors. (I presume that the library had been inventoried, but wish to emphasize that this is not essential for the reconstruction of the cataloging process; the library could also have been cataloged without any previous inventory-taking.) The cataloging of the library constituted the third phrase of the process that led to the compilation of the *Pinakes*. This process is meant by Tzetzes when he reports that Kallimachos compiled the lists of books. Kallimachos thus entered into the picture at this point. The difference between the *pinakes* mentioned by Tzetzes, the catalog of copies in the library, and the catalog of works published by him or by his pupils was not very large. The catalog of works in the library would hardly have been linked for all times with the name of Kallimachos if he had not also compiled its basis, the catalog of copies. There can thus be no doubt that Kallimachos cataloged the library which had been physically arranged and inventoried by Zenodotos. In this work, he as well as Zenodotos had the help of numerous aides, some of whom also made a name for themselves as authors and are designated as Kallimachos's pupils. The catalog was a mixture of subject and author catalog, inasmuch as it allowed to find the available works of each literary genre and scholarly discipline, and within each class those written by each author.

The enterprise of Kallimachos was presumably caused by two factors. First, the contents of the numerous collective scrolls were only incompletely known. Even if the inventory had recorded the second, third, etc. works contained in those scrolls, they would still have been separated from other works by the respective authors. Only by chance or by scanning the entire inventory could it have become obvious that a collective scroll the first work of which was, say, on rhetoric (and which was therefore shelved in the class of *Rhētores*), contained also a second work on philosophy.

Second, the data on authors and titles which had been written on the *sillyboi* at the time of the preliminary identification of the scrolls, and which had been copied in the inventory, were partially unreliable. That pertained also to the data which had been taken directly from the scrolls, not to mention those which were based on the assumptions of Zenodotos and his aides. The resident experts and the authors of works on the same subjects denied the authenticity of some works, ascribed them to other authors, and cited them with other titles.

Because of the incompleteness and the unreliability of the data on the *sillyboi* and in the inventory, many works which had been acquired by the Ptolemies for a large sum remained unused. Kallimachos and his aides checked therefore once again the entire holdings of the library, prepared a sheet for each author and listed on it each of the available copies of works ascribed to him by title, beginning, number of books, and number of standard lines. A note was perhaps sufficient for "doubles". If the data were already in the inventory, he accepted them. As to collective scrolls, he had to open them if only the first work was listed in the inventory, and had to identify the second, third, or further works and then to enter them on the author sheets. Since the works of the same author were partially contained in scrolls which were shelved in different classes and under the names of other authors, he had to make a cross reference to the respective scroll, and had to note in which class and under which author it could be found, and what was the title of the work listed as the first one.[16]

The first stage of the cataloging may have proceeded more or less in this manner; it consisted of entering and transposing data:[17] the particulars of works contained in the scrolls were entered in the "account ledgers" of authors as it were, arranged as before by classes and then alphabetically by the first letter of the (real, purported or presumed) authors. This procedure confirmed that the author and title data of the inventory were in part questionable, because works whose authenticity had already been disputed, as well as many others, appeared now in the catalog also under other authors and with other titles. When scanning the beginnings of texts of works of the same kind, anyone with a good memory could discover that. Doubts about the reliability of other data were thereby reinforced. All experts realized also that works were often ascribed to the same person having a common name, such as Apollonios or Demetrios, whereas they had actually been written by namesakes. But when the author or title of a work was in question or in doubt for whatever reason, Kallimachos had to find out who (sometimes among several homonymous authors) was the real author and what had been the original title. Under the name of the author or under the title on which he had decided, he listed all copies of the respective work in the catalog, and shelved them also together in one book case and with partially corrected title tags (if they were not written in collective scrolls). If it was impossible to find out who had been the real author of a work, Kallimachos listed under the purported name as given in the copy, indicated it as spurious and shelved it with the authentic works.[18]

With the treatment of works whose authors or titles were questionable or in dispute, the cataloging entered its second stage. Unlike the recording of copies under the traditional names of authors, the testing of authenticity and the determination of the real author of the respective works was a scholarly task. For many authors, the cataloging thus led to an attempt to distinguish their genuine works from the spurious ones, and to ascertain, if possible, the real authors of the *pseudepigrapha*. Kallimachos and his aides tried to solve this task of literary criticism by collecting all data on the lives and works of Greek authors which could be found in the collection of the library. Thus, they collected not only what had been traditionally known and researched on the works of an author, but they recorded also his descent (i.e. the name of his father and his birth place), his period of flourishing, his activities and place of work as well as his teacher(s) and pupils, sometimes also his nickname and its explanation, and other details, recorded in the sources, e.g. his "inventions".[19] Evidently, he realized that he must combine bibliographic research with biographical investigations, as was later the case with Dionysios of Halikarnassos when he compiled his bibliography of the orator Deinarchos. If reliable authorities for the authenticity of a work were unavailable, the biography of an author sometimes supplied criteria on the grounds of which a work could either be ascribed or denied to him. To be sure, the negative criteria were more reliable than the positive ones, as in the case of

Deinarchos. If it transpired from a work that it had been written at a particular time or in a certain region, it could not be of an author who had not lived then or there. If a work was written in a dialect which had never been used by an author because it had not been spoken in his birth place or at the place of his activity, nor had it been a literary idiom, it must necessarily be considered as spurious.[20] The biographies of authors were of course quite indispensible when it was a question of distinguishing between homonymous authors and their works.[21]

It was not difficult to find data on the lives and works of authors of the first rank, because there were already some studies about them. The *Pinakes* of Kallimachos contained, however, also information on numerous authors of the second and third rank who had never been treated before. What has been transmitted to us about these (inasmuch as they lived before 250 B.C.) by later scholars is for the most part based on the huge work of the Alexandrian librarians. But how did Kallimachos get this material?

Similar to the earlier historians of literature he certainly drew on the works of the authors themselves and on those of their contemporaries and colleagues.[22] In addition, he used the works of scholars from the fifth and fourth century who had established important facts and data of Greek literary history, and had collected material on eminent authors. For the biography and bibliography of the Attic playwrights Aristotle's *Didaskaliai*, which he himself had edited, were of invaluable service. The works on literary history written by the Peripatetics on great poets and philosophers were also useful to him, but even from the summaries of Aristotle on rhetoric, and from the works of his pupils on the history of dogmas in natural philosophy, mathematics, astronomy, musical theory and medicine he could glean some biographical and bibliographical data.

Of course, Kallimachos did not look up the secondary literature for information on the life and work of an author only if and when he needed such data. Rather, we must assume that he perused the relevant works when he began the compilation of his catalog, so as to find useful data.[23] His *hypomnēmata* show that he knew how to scan large amounts of literature and to utilize the data; probably he also taught his pupils how to do this. It is remarkable that an *homme de lettres* such as Kallimachos has not left a single *hypomnēma* on literary history: but then, he incorporated all information on Greek authors and their works into his *Pinakes*.

In some cases, however, there were neither credible witnesses nor biographical indications which would have spoken for or against the authenticity of a disputed work. If so, a decision had to be made on the grounds of stylistic criteria. A literary critic and expert such as Kallimachos felt no doubt that he was capable to judge the authenticity of poetic works such as the "Homeric" *Oichalias halōsis* on stylistic grounds alone. It may even be that he put stylistic criteria above all others when dealing with poetic works. But he had also to decide on the authenticity of prose writings, e.g. works on rhetoric, on stylistic grounds. His competency in this area was, however, disputed.[24]

Kallimachos must also have taken a stand on the results arrived at by Zenodotos, Alexandros Aitolos and Lykophron when they made their investigations on textual criticism of the epic, lyric and dramatic poets. The editor of the works of an author had to distinguish between his genuine writings and spurious works, and had also to find out the original titles. Whether Kallimachos agreed in every respect with the opinion of his predecessor Zenodotos regarding the authenticity of works known under the names of Homer, Hesiod and Pindar, is indeed questionable. Tatianos mentions both Kallimachos and Zenodotos among the earlier scholars who dealt not only with Homer's origin and period of flourishing but who also tried to distinguish between his genuine and spurious works. As already mentioned, Kallimachos as well as Zenodotos joined Aristotle in considering only three Homeric works as authentic, namely the *Iliad*, the *Odyssey* and the *Margitēs*, and he ridiculed those who ascribed the *Oichalias halōsis* by Kreophylos of Samos to Homer. But his pupil Apollonios, later of Rhodos, who wrote a work against Zenodotos and defended in another one the authenticity of Hesiod's *Aspis* (against Zenodotos?) acted presumably in the spirit of Kallimachos. Quite by chance we also know that he did not share Lykophron's opinion on the original title of a gastronomic epic by Archestratos.

Thus, in the third stage it was decided whether a work whose author or title was questionable or disputed would be listed under the traditional author or under the name of another who was held to be the real author, and under which title it would be recorded. Or rather, Kallimachos decided on these issues on the grounds of the biographical data which he had collected about the (traditional and real) author, or by the stylistic criteria of the respective work. The result of this stage was a critical catalog, i.e. one that distinguished between authentic and spurious works of Greek authors as represented by the works available in the library.

This catalog of copies, the first library catalog that deserves this name, also contained biographical data on the authors as well as references to divergent opinions of other scholars on the lives and works of the authors, as can be deduced from the catalog of works which was based on it, namely the *Pinakes* of Kallimachos. Evidently, Kallimachos did not think that such data and references were out of place in a library catalog; quite to the contrary, he thought it useful to incorporate into the catalog the biographical and other notes which he had made during his work, since his biographical investigations were closely tied to his endeavors in the field of literary history, and to the compilation of the catalog as such. Thus, the biographical data are not, as was formerly thought,[25] a subsequently added enrichment of the catalog.

4. In the fourth and last stage, Kallimachos compiled from the catalog of copies in the library, the first *Pinakes*, an extract intended for publication, namely the second *Pinakes* which recorded only which works of Greek literature were available in the library, but did not enumerate the individual copies of those works. Other than that, the second *Pinakes* were like the first ones; this is true in particular for the biographical data and the references to divergent opinions of other scholars, which Kallimachos transferred from the first to the second *Pinakes*. The catalog of works in the Alexandrian library must have been preceded by a catalog of copies, otherwise it would not have been possible for Kallimachos to describe the works the way he did.

The arrangement of the second *Pinakes* has already been described above, and it remains only to make some additional observations or to stress the salient points once again. The authors in each class were alphabetically arranged by the first letter of their name only as had been the case in the first *Pinakes* and in the inventory list of the library. Considering the way in which the scrolls were shelved, Kallimachos thus refrained from a more detailed author arrangement. Perhaps he wrote the name of each author set off to the left, and also each title, but by a smaller space, like the later librarian of the gymnasium in Rhodos, in order to indicate the beginning of a new article and to make it easier to find specific works by the respective author.

The biographical data which preceded the bibliographies probably contained (like those transmitted by Hesychios in his *Onomatologos*) references to divergent opinions of other named or unnamed scholars. For example, Kallimachos could not indicate Homer's place of birth without noting that other scholars mentioned other cities.

The bibliographies represented the sum of decisions on literary criticism by Kallimachos. Whether he listed the works of an author which he had declared to be spurious among the others but with an appropriate note, or perhaps at the end in a separate list of *pseudepigrapha*, cannot be decided. On the other hand, we may assume that he mentioned the opinions of other scholars on disputed works, as he had already done in his bibliography of Demokritos. The passages from which this can be deduced have been listed above. Kallimachos liked to reproduce what he had found in the literature. But the quotation of opinions of earlier scholars had by then become a scholarly practice which had received its formal expression in the doxographies of the Peripatetics.

If several titles had been transmitted for the same work, he probably listed them after the one he deemed to be the original title. In the Demokritos bibliography he had recorded the various titles of the philosopher's writings, apparently connected with *ē* (or). Titles which were not expressive of the genre or subject of a work were presumably explained, as was also later done by Hesychios; in certain cases, Kallimachos probably also indicated the dialect in which a work had been written.[26]

The citation of the beginning of a work in order to ascertain its identification was problematic if it was different in various copies. This happened occasionally; the introduction to a work was especially prone to interference by different hands. Thus, there were several proems to Homer's *Iliad*,[27] and to cite its first verse was therefore not ridiculous; the Peripatetic Praxiphanes had declared the proem to Hesiod's *Erga kai hēmerai* (Works and days) to be spurious. Thus, what was the *archē* of these works?[28] Perhaps Kallimachos sided with the opinion of Zenodotos, the editor of Homer and Hesiod, regarding the *Iliad* and the *Erga*.

A similar case was the indication of the extent of a work, i.e. the number of books and standard lines; the indication of standard lines was particularly precarious if their number had not been transmitted. Some works had been abridged or enlarged in the course of time, or lines had been omitted inadvertently. The copies were therefore of different lengths. Of course, Kallimachos could take the advice of Zenodotos, Alexandros Aitolos and Lykophron for the beginnings as well as for the original extent of the epic, lyric and dramatic works that had been "corrected" by them. But in all other cases he had to make his own decision. The editor of the *Pinakes* did not just wish to describe the available copies of a work, but he intended to reconstruct their original in an outline, as it were (beginning and extent). This amounted, strictly speaking, to the philological reconstruction of the original text. One could in fact say that Kallimachos as editor of the *Pinakes* sought, like a textual critic, to recognize and capture the archetype of a literary work, hidden behind its various images—certainly a typically Greek phenomenon.

Regarding the sequence of an author's works, Kallimachos retained the traditional arrangement made by Zenodotos, mainly for practical reasons (easy identification of the scrolls). The titles of works that were related to each other formally or by content were listed in groups,[29] but within these groups only works belonging to certain categories, such as plays, dithyrambs and elegies were alphabetically arranged by their first letter. Hesychios transmitted also a few alphabetically arranged bibliographies of prose writers. These might be traceable to the *Pinakes* of Kallimachos; it is even possible that Zenodotos already shelved the scrolls of the respective works by the alphabet of their titles, that is, he sometimes extended the range of this mechanical principle of arrangement.

In this context, I would like to revert once again to the bibliography of Theophrastos, transmitted to us by Diogenes Laertios, and probably based on a bibliography of the philosopher compiled by the Kallimachean Hermippos. It consists of four lists, all of which except one are arranged alphabetically, namely the titles of works in various forms (exoteric, acroamatic and hypomnematic) and on different subjects (logic, ethics, etc.), each in alphabetical sequence, which is unusual. Alphabetization is by first letter only, but only seldom by that of the first word. This can be explained by the formulation of the titles. Whereas titles of plays either consist of a single work or at least begin with a noun that can be considered as the principal meaningful word, titles of scholarly works are often longer phrases, in which a preposition—mostly the word *peri* (on)—is followed by one or two articles and an adjective or adjectival noun before the principal noun itself. Since Hermippos or whoever edited the lists did not want to arrange them by prepositions or articles he had to choose a filing medium, and so he chose generally the first noun or adjective which was often, but by no means always, also the principal meaningful word.[30] In some cases, he preferred as filing medium a noun that followed another noun or adjective.[31] This indicates that he already encountered the problems of alphabetical arrangement of titles. Two titles each appeared twice; in the second instance, the sequence of their adjectives and nouns is reversed.[32] The four entries show that this was an attempt to alphabetize the titles of scholarly works.

It is evident that Hermippos wanted to rearrange a traditionally arranged list of works of different kinds, which had been taken from the *Pinakes* of Kallimachos, in alphabetical order and section by section. But he abandoned this enterprise before he had unified the titles of the two main sections in one single alphabet.[33] He had also already begun to list the titles of works with a common subject (which had been listed in the *Pinakes* as a larger entity under a collective title) under their individual titles at the relevant places in the alphabet.[34] It seems that an attempt to list the titles of works of all kinds in a single alphabetical sequence was here abandoned. The customary arrangement of titles of works by prolific authors like Theophrastos made it difficult to find them. It seemed plausible to combine them, despite their differences, into a single alphabetical sequence, and to arrange also the scrolls containing the works accordingly. But the other Alexandrian scholars probably did not agree to this, and thought that the customary arrangement of the scrolls in the book cases and that of the titles in the lists was more advantageous, and so everything remained as before. In my opinion, Kallimachos had nothing to do with this attempt to expand the alphabetical principle of arrangement still further.

I have tried to depict the development of the *Pinakes* of Kallimachos as a bibliothecal process, and attempted to distinguish between the contributions of two generations of Alexandrian librarians, represented by Zenodotos and Kallimachos, to the arrangement and recording of the books acquired by the Ptolemies for the Museion. What Zenodotos had done in this respect was not unusual. Only the shelving of scrolls by the alphabet of authors and in certain cases also by title of works contained in them was really new, and it was also important. But the actions of Kallimachos, which resulted in a critical catalog of the available works of Greek literature with biographical data on the authors, were altogether innovations, or inventions, as the Greeks called them. So far as I can see, Kallimachos did not have any models. The custodians of libraries in the ancient Near East, such as the one founded by Assurbanipal (668-626 B.C.) in Niniveh, never went beyond an inventory of their clay tablets; the Egyptians who had in their custody similar collections of papyrus scrolls (of which almost nothing is known) probably did not go beyond mere inventory-taking either.[35] The libraries of Greek princes in the pre-Hellenistic era were probably inventoried together with their other possessions, those of private citizens such as Aristotle hardly ever or only after their death; before that, there was no reason to make an inventory. The form in which the Greeks usually recorded a book in an inventory (indication of author, title, beginning and extent) was partially based on ancient Oriental models, as Wendel has shown. Already at the beginning of the second millennium B.C. such inventories, with other details made necessary by the material of the clay tablets, had been made, and they spread from that region throughout the Near East and until the west coast of Asia Minor, where the inhabitants of the Greek colonial cities such as Miletos became acquainted with them. Kallimachos also followed the customary form of book description. But the mere description of the copies of works of Greek literature which were available in the Alexandrian library was the least part of his enterprise; it would be wrong to draw false conclusions from Wendel's description. The main issue was literary criticism.

Even though only a few remarks of a critical nature by Kallimachos have come down to us, it is nevertheless clear from the character of his cataloging that he sought above all to find out who had been the real authors of many works whose attribution was disputed or questionable, and at least to distinguish the genuine works of an author from the spurious ones. For example, if the copies of the same work bore the name of three different authors, he could not list it under each name; this would have been inventorying not cataloging. It is therefore unlikely that he made notes of literary criticism only occasionally and as an afterthought after having finished his catalog, as some researchers have thought.[36] Rather, literary criticism constituted an integral part of the cataloging process that he performed.

As mentioned in the beginning, later Greek scholars saw in literary and textual criticism, the *kritikon*, the most beautiful part of philology. The Alexandrian grammarians in particular were praised by a knowledgeable Roman, the orator

Quintilianus, because they had distinguished the genuine works of Greek authors from the spurious ones thanks to their stringent literary criticism.[37] Kallimachos as a literary critic had some predecessors among the Greek scholars of the fourth and even the fifth century B.C.; nor was he the first Alexandrian who dealt with literary problems. But by recording the works of Greek literature available in the Alexandrian library by authors' names and from the point of view of literary criticism, he was not only the founder of cataloging beyond mere inventorying, but created at the same time also a broader documentary basis for literary criticism. This could only happen on the soil of Greek culture and under the conditions of the Hellenistic age. It was probably the incompleteness and unreliability of data on authors and titles as given on title tags and recorded in the inventory which moved Kallimachos to catalog the library in the manner described above, that is, to compile in addition to the inventory of scrolls a complete and reliable list of the works contained in them. When he wrote his *Pinax* of Attic playwrights, which must have been compiled before the edition of the *Pinakes* because of its antiquated, as it were unbibliothecal, arrangement, he had already employed a method similar to the one by which he later analyzed collective scrolls: he arranged the plays which Aristotle had listed according to festivals, by the names of each poet. And when he compiled a bibliography in connection with his glossary of Demokritos, he noticed that some works had been disputed by well-known scholars, while many others were known under different titles, and works that he had not written at all had been falsely ascribed to him.

This, however, was no surprise for him. Since the fifth century, not only the wording but also the ascription of many literary works had become questionable. Although several scholars had already tried to alleviate the uncertainty about the text and the author of many classical works, it was still in dispute (to use a formula) what was "the" *Iliad* and "who" was Homer, i.e. which of the innumerable versions of the epic was the original one, and whether Homer was the poet who wrote the *Iliad* and the *Kypria*, the *Odyssey* and the *Oichalias halōsis* as well as many other works known under his name. This must have troubled educated princes such as the Ptolemies, the more so since the study of literature was the foundation of that *paideia* which legitimized the rule of Macedonians and Greeks over the peoples subjugated by Alexander. They certainly wanted to put an end to this deplorable state of affairs. With the foundation of the Museion at Alexandria, the appointment of outstanding experts on literature, and the establishment of a huge library it seemed for the first time possible to reconstruct the text of the principal works of Greek literature which had become corrupted in the course of time. Ptolemaios II Philadelphos urged therefore his old teacher Zenodotos to edit, together with Alexander Aitolos and Lykophron, the classical works by applying textual criticism, or to "correct" them. It has not been transmitted that he induced Kallimachos to compile the *Pinakes*. But the endeavors of Kallimachos and his pupils in the field of literary criticism were no doubt analogous to the attempts at textual criticism by Zenodotos, his colleagues and successors, and in part they were even overlapping. Both Zenodotos and Kallimachos sought to overcome the uncertainty regarding the literary creations of their nation. One was concerned about the text, the other about the ascription of the works: Zenodotos wanted to reconstruct the original text of classical works, Kallimachos wanted to ascertain the authentic works of the authors. Both textual and literary criticism met the demands of the king and the Ptolemaic cultural policy.

To begin with, Kallimachos presumably wanted only to make the holdings of the library of the Museion accessible and usable as completely and reliably as possible. But the catalog that evolved was much more than a mere aid for the members of the Museion who wished to use the library; it was, as we have seen, a critical bibliography of almost all still extant works of Greek literature with biographical data on their authors. Until then, the Greek scholars had lacked an authoritative survey of the literary creations of their nation, a repertorium that showed them when and where this or that author had lived, what was the authenticity of the works known under his name, which works of a certain literary genre existed and what was available in the various scholarly disciplines. The *Pinakes* contained all desired information. Kallimachos therefore conceived the plan (perhaps already at an early stage) to publish the results of his cataloging, i.e. to edit them for copying, so that also scholars outside the Museion could use them. The king certainly welcomed and supported this project, because the *Pinakes* of Kallimachos documented impressively the literary and scholarly achievements of the Greeks, the new rulers over many peoples. The ascription of many works was still in question, but Zenodotos had not been quite successful either in the reconstruction of the original text of the Homeric epics, as the king had probably hoped. Still, both Zenodotos and Kallimachos laid the foundations for textual criticism and bibliographic work.

But it would not have made sense to reproduce the whole huge catalog of copies held by the library. Kallimachos therefore made an excerpt from it. He transferred, perhaps selectively, the biographical data; they identified the respective author, distinguished him in particular from other homonymous persons, but indicated also his position in the history of Greek literature, especially if they mentioned in addition to his origin, period of flourishing and place of activity also his innovations, his teachers and pupils. This placed the author in a spiritual chain of tradition; as is well known, the Greeks considered the history of arts and sciences from the point of view of "invention" and "succession".

On the other hand, Kallimachos did not list the individual copies of works by Greek authors acquired for the library of the Museion, but recorded only the available works, making annotations about their authenticity and in certain cases also about the opinions of other scholars regarding their ascription and titles. A listing of copies was of no value for scholars outside the Museion, given the conditions of book production and bookselling at that time. Even the members of the Museion were better served by a catalog of works than by a catalog of copies which was unwieldy because it listed all extant specimens. These were of interest only for the philologists who were concerned with textual criticism.[38]

But Kallimachos recorded also the beginnings of the text and the extent of the works as he had deduced them from the various copies, i.e. he reconstructed the originals in outline. These details too elevated his critical lists above the level of mere catalogs. But do the *Pinakes* really deserve the name bibliography?

Today we use to equate a catalog with a bibliography if the respective library possesses almost all works of a certain category. Now, the Alexandrian library probably possessed most of the transmitted works of Greek literature already at a time when Kallimachos was still a young man, and the kings sought to complete the collection by all available means. Since a part of the older literature, especially the dramatic works, had already been lost, this could only mean the acquisition of copies of the works that had not yet been purchased. When Kallimachos died, ca. 240 B.C., the Alexandrian library was an almost complete collection of extant works of Greek literature, or in modern terms a Greek national library.[39] Its catalog, the *Pinakes*, were consequently an almost complete list of extant works of Greek literature, a Greek national bibliography, nay, more than that, a national biobibliography, a national author lexicon. So far as I can see, the *Pinakes* of Kallimachos have until now never been characterized as a national author lexicon by any of the modern researchers. Even the librarians among the researchers of Classical Antiquity did not point out that the work of Kallimachos is the prototype of the much-used reference works which I mentioned in the introduction. For example, some entries in Kosch's *Deutsches Literatur-Lexikon* are in principle quite similar to those in the *Pinakes* of Kallimachos.

The *Pinakes* of Kallimachos may therefore justly be called a national biobibliography, whether he listed only works that were available in the Alexandrian library or also others, because the latter, apart from a few exceptions, could only have been works that had long since been lost. This brings me to a question with which I have not dealt so far. No doubt Kallimachos had information on works of Greek literature which were not available in the Alexandrian library, as well as on Greek authors who were not represented there. But in the older literature they were mentioned, and he had made notes on what he had found out about them. What did he do with these notes? He could not check either the ascription or the titles of such works, nor their beginnings or their extent (if these data had been mentioned). Without autopsy no literary criticism was possible. On the other hand, it is unlikely that he left this material unused. It is therefore in my opinion not impossible that he mentioned the authors who were not represented in the library, and the works that were not available there in his *Pinakes*, with a relevant annotation, if he had any information about them.

Diogenes Laertios introduced his bibliography of Protagoras with the note that his extant works were the following.[40] This seems to indicate that in the *Pinakes* of Kallimachos, from which that bibliography was ultimately derived, there were annotations to the effect that Protagoras had written also such and such works besides those that had been preserved, or at least that he had written also other works. But Kallimachos did probably not mention the many Attic playwrights and their works which were not available in the library, because all playwrights and plays which had been performed in Athens at the Dionysia and Lenaea had been listed in his *Pinax tōn didaskalōn* and it had been indicated there which plays had been preserved or had been lost.[41] Perhaps Kallimachos made these notes only during the editing of the *Pinakes* in order not to overload them with material.

Notes to Chapter 6

1) In this reconstruction I disregard the fact that the library was being added to from time to time.

2) The scrolls were probably kept in book cases; see Birt (1913) p. 341; Wendel (1949) pp. 24; 75.

3) This, however, is documented only for the archives of real estate deeds (*enktēsēon bibliothēkai*) in the Roman period; see Schubart (1918) pp. 299-301. There were also inventories (*diastrōmata*) of these archives.

4) Aristotle and Theophrastos had already arranged larger collections of scientific material in alphabetical order by keywords.

5) Schmidt (1922) p. 77.

6) Schmidt (1922) pp. 38-41. It is unlikely that the collective scrolls were split up, primarily because many of them were certainly inscribed on both sides. Furthermore, in some cases it would have been impossible to roll up the individual pieces of a dismantled scroll. But if parts of a collective scroll were copied individually, it could happen that textual evidence was copied which turned out to be inferior compared with other texts.

7) Schmidt (1922) p. 42, note 59, and p. 99.

8) Schmidt (1922) pp. 48 f.; 82, 99.

9) Gardthausen (1922) p. 77 f.; he also assumed that the library had had general author indexes and indexes to beginnings in addition to its catalog; this was refuted by Wendel (1949) p. 74 f. on valid grounds.

10) Wendel (1940) p. 14; Wendel-Göber (1955) p. 72.

11) Herter (1931) column 390; 397; Herter (1973) column 187.

12) Regenbogen (1950) column 1419-23; 1479.

13) Pfeiffer (1968) p. 128.

14) Pfeiffer (1968) p. 126.

15) Author indexes to the inventories of larger libraries were compiled in the late Middle Ages, seldom earlier, but they were of only limited value, because the inventories themselves were deficient.

16) If there were several scrolls with copies of this work, it was necessary to make a search. But the scrolls shelved under the name of the same author had perhaps been numbered when they were inventoried, and additional

scrolls were also numbered. These numbers were, of course, not call numbers (the newly added scrolls were shelved with the existing copies of the same work), but they made it easier to find a particular scroll named in a reference.

17) For the works contained in collective scrolls data were simply entered (the inventorying phase was skipped); for works in other scrolls the data were transferred.

18) I do not claim, of course, that the processes here described in their logical sequence were also always performed in the same chronological sequence.

19) Considering the importance that all Greek literary historians attached to "inventions", i.e. artistic or scholarly innovations, including the foundations of schools, we may assume that Kallimachos also took this into consideration. That he was keenly interested in finding out who had been the first to say or to do this or that needs no further proof.

20) Eratosthenes used the dialect as an argument for the elimination of spurious works by Pherekrates, a poet of the Old Comedy; see Strecker (1884) p. 16 f. Demetrios of Magnesia declared a letter by the Cretan Epimenides to Solon to be spurious because it was written not in Cretan but in Attic, even new Attic, dialect; see Diogenes Laertios I 112.

21) Kallimachos's efforts to identify persons influenced even his epitaphs (part of which he wrote to order). He evidently attempted to indicate the complete name of the deceased. Some of his epitaphs consist only of an artful connection and paraphrase of the three parts of a name. Theokritos did that only rarely. Kallimachos deals with biographical questions even in the beginning of his hymn on Zeus: the origin and grave of the god!

22) Of course, occasionally he disregarded an important source, e.g. the speech of Deinarchos against Proxenos.

23) Diels (1904) p. xxxvi f. already presumed this; see also Gardthausen (1922) p. 77, and Wilamowitz (1924) vol. 1, p. 213.

24) Lossau (1964) pp. 80-86.

25) Wendel-Göber (1955) p. 72.

26) Schmidt (1922) p. 68 f.

27) Pfeiffer (1968) p. 111.

28) There were also: a spurious proem to the *Phainomena* of Aratos; see Speyer (1971) p. 125; two prologues to the *Rhēsos*, purportedly by Euripides; see Wehrli (1967) Heft 1, p. 68; and several versions of the beginning of Plato's *Republic*; see Diogenes Laertios III 37.

29) Thrasyllos probably received the division of the works by Demokritos into five groups from Kallimachos.

30) Andronikos and Ptolemaios proceeded similarly when they alphabetized the titles of Aristotle's works.

31) Thus, for example, *Aretōn diaphorai* (Differences of virtues) and *Anhēgmenoi logoi* (Derived propositions) are filed under alpha, but *Peri paideias basileōs* (On the education of a king) is filed under bēta, and *Peri kriseōs syllogismōn* (On the evaluation of conclusions) under kappa; *Peri aristēs politeias* (On the best state) is under pi, but *Peri pseudus hēdonēs* (On the false pleasure) is under psi.

32) *Peri analyseōs syllogismōn* under alpha and *Peri syllogismōn analyseōs* under sigma (V 42 and 45); *Ēthikoi charaktēres* under ēta, and *Charaktēres ēthikoi* under chi (V 47 and 48).

33) Regenbogen (1940) column 1369 thinks that the two lists record two large purchases of works by Theophrastos (for the Alexandrian library), while the two others were supplements. In the light of the transfer of Theophrastos's (Neleus's) library to Alexandria and the organization of that library (arrangement and recording of the scrolls) I think that this is unlikely.

34) The situation is somewhat complex, and the text of the lists is partially corrupt; I shall therefore deal only with a few relatively straightforward cases. Under nos. 41-47 (V 43-44) seven different titles of individual writings on animals are listed; in five of these, the noun *(Peri)* . . . *zōōn* is missing; thereafter under no. 48 the collective title of a work *Peri zōōn* (On animals), seven books. Under no. 168 (V 48) the collective title of a work *Peri technōn rhētorikōn* (On the oratorical arts), 17 kinds, is listed, while throughout the entire alphabet 14 titles (probably to be corrected to 17) on rhetorical arts are dispersed; see Usener (1858) p. 21. Under no. 103 (V 46) we find the collective title of the work *Physika*, 8 books; under no. 58 (V 44) the title of the two first books of the *Physics*, *Peri kinēseōs* (On movement), 3 (otherwise 2) books. Titles of other books of the *Physics* do not appear. Regenbogen (1940) column 1367 f. thought that the two principles were at cross-purposes here, namely a) the recording of works under individual titles, and b) that under a collective title; he saw in the second principle the influence of the Theophrastos bibliography which Andronikos compiled about 150 years after that of Hermippos. According to this view, the collective titles would have been interpolated afterwards into the bibliography by Hermippos. In my view, they were already listed in the model copied by Hermippos. An influence of Andronikos's bibliography of Theophrastos is difficult to imagine and quite unlikely.

35) Wendel (1949), especially pp. 1-23 and 65-80; see also Milkau-Schawe (1955). The remark by Milkau-Schawe (1955) p. 40 is misleading: "after all, there was no lack of catalogs arranged by authors [in the Hethitic 'national library' of Hattusha, 14th century B.C.]". Those were not library catalogs. According to Forrer (1921) p. 36, cited by Milkau-Schawe, the library contained among other things land registers, laws, dictionaries, collections of oracles and catalogs of authors. On these catalogs, of which Forrer does not give any details, see Riemschneider (1963) p. 111 f., who does not say anything about authors. On the inventories of the library of Hattusha see

Wendel (1949) p. 8. Against the dependency of the Alexandrian library on Oriental examples, as claimed by de Vleeschauwer, see van Rooy (1958).

36) Following Schmidt (1922) p. 96, only Herter (1931) column 400 emphasized that Kallimachos was also active as a literary critic. Later researchers did not pay sufficient attention to his remark. However, in my opinion, Herter underestimated the extent of Kallimachos's literary criticism, and overestimated the preliminary work of the textual critics Zenodotos, Alexandros Aitolos and Lykophron.

37) Quintilian I 43.

38) The philologists distinguished, of course, between copies of different quality, but presumably they did not find even in the catalog of copies any data on age or quality of the copies. In the admittedly scarce remains of ancient library catalogs nothing of the kind is recorded, and such data are only rarely found in medieval library inventories.

39) Since the Ptolemies had spent large sums in order to purchase all Greek works of literature that were still extant, they certainly did not lack many older works around 240 B.C. I presume that their hunt for books was primarily aimed at obtaining good copies of those works.

40) Diogenes Laertios IX 55.

41) The data of Aristophanes of Byzantium regarding some lost dramatical works are not based on the *Pinakes* of Kallimachos but on his *Pinax tōn didaskalōn*; see Pfeiffer (1968) p. 115 (different on p. 129). It is, however, possible that Aristophanes himself declared all dramatical works not listed in the *Pinakes* to be lost.

7. The Achievements of Kallimachos in the Field of Bibliography

KALLIMACHOS "invented" the library catalog and the biobibliography, and therefore bibliography as such. These are, briefly stated, his achievements in the field of bibliography—major achievements, in my opinion, no matter whether his library catalog and the biobibliography of Greek authors which was based on it were good or bad. He created the first real library catalog, a catalog which, unlike a mere inventory, recorded not the scrolls available in the library, but all copies of works of Greek literature that were contained in them, with biographical data on their actual authors, or, in case it was not possible to ascertain those, as spurious works under their purported authors. Kallimachos did not arrange the Alexandrian library; this had already been done by Zenodotos, who was the first to arrange authors and partially also works in alphabetical order. Rather, Kallimachos tried to provide complete and reliable access to the holdings of the library. This was a large undertaking, consisting essentially of literary criticism, because of the many works whose ascription was questionable for several reasons, such as the large number of authors who had the same name. In addition to the catalog of copies Kallimachos compiled yet a second catalog, the catalog of works which, compared to the former, had the advantage of greater clarity, and still satisfied the needs of most library users.

When Kallimachos began to catalog the Alexandrian library, there were already works on the most famous Greek poets, philosophers, orators and historians. But for authors of the second and third rank no preliminary studies existed as yet. The details on their lives and works which later librarians could simply look up in the handbooks which were partially based on the *Pinakes*, had first to be discovered by Kallimachos himself. Of course, he sometimes arrived at the wrong conclusions. We cannot prove that he was a great literary historian and critic, but neither can the opposite be proven. It seems that his *Pinakes* were unevenly edited, and perhaps they were never finished. Understandably, he dealt more thoroughly with the lyric poets than, say, with the orators. There remained enough to do for his successors.[1]

The custodians of the important library of Pergamon (second century B.C.) imitated the Alexandrian *Pinakes* in every respect; for example, they also made biographical notes on authors. Other librarians, such as the one of the gymnasium of Rhodos (late second or early first century A.D.) could dispense with such notes because these data were already available in the Alexandrian and Pergamenian *Pinakes* and handbooks. The catalogs which they offered to the public were probably also catalogs of works; the catalogs of copies (the shelflists) were kept by them as working tools. This is true also for the great public libraries established in Rome under the first Emperors, which consisted of a Greek and a Latin department; their catalogs probably also contained biographical data according to the Alexandrian example. During the era of the mass migrations the cataloging of libraries in the Western world ceased, and most of its ancient libraries perished. The medieval librarians were content to inventory the volumes in their custody, and thus the art of cataloging had to be reinvented in the Renaissance.

But the *Pinakes* of Kallimachos were more than a tool for library users: they were also a biobibliography of Greek authors, classified by literary genres, not only because Kallimachos had included biographical data on the authors represented in the library, and had also tried to reconstruct the original form of the copies available in the library (beginnings and extent), but also and above all because he had recorded almost all transmitted works of Greek literature. There were probably very few older works which, though still extant, had not yet been acquired for the library. Kallimachos mentioned perhaps also lost works which had been cited by authors of earlier centuries. At any rate, even if his *Pinakes* were not chronologically arranged, they contained, as it were, a potential framework for the history of Greek literature and therefore also of the history of Greek scholarship. No doubt they had their shortcomings, but these were the reason for further biographical and bibliographical investigations by Greek scholars, especially those of Alexandria in the third and second century B.C.

In the following period, the example of the *Pinakes* of Kallimachos was emulated first for bibliographies of individual Greek authors and then for biobibliographies of Greek authors of certain classes or categories in reference books. The Romans took these works as examples for similar works on the authors of their nation. Since the end of the fourth century A.D. international biobibliographies of Christian authors began to be compiled; Jerome was the first in the long chain of their authors; he took his material largely from the ecclesiastical history of Eusebius.[2] In the sixth century it was again a Greek, Hesychios of Miletos, who compiled a *Pinax*, which recorded mainly Greek authors of all classes with biographical data and lists of their works in one alphabet. An excerpt of his work was incorporated in the *Suda*, and was transmitted through this Byzantine lexicon of the 10th or 11th century to the scholars of the Renaissance.

What Hesychios and other Greek scholars transmitted on the lives and works of the older authors of their nation is for the most part based on the *Pinakes* of Kallimachos. Kallimachos thus deserves much praise as a discoverer and transmitter of data and facts relating to Greek literary history. But now that we have come to the end of this investigation, he must also be duly honored as the founder of biobibliography and bibliography in general, because he is indeed the true "Father" of bibliography,[3] that important tool of intellectual work.

It is my hope to have shown by this investigation that Howald did not do justice to Kallimachos when he characterized him as a mere collector. But even Regenbogen and Pfeiffer who praised him as the man who brought order to large masses of books did not describe him adequately. Wilamowitz called the cataloging of the Alexandrian library "a quite colossal work", the *Pinakes* an "at least partially critical catalog", and Kallimachos an "organizer of scholarly work".[4] Following Diels, he thus pointed to a fact that had been neglected by many researchers. Howald's "hunter of curiosities" had no doubt many learned aides, and knew how to guide their work towards the goal he had set forth. The cataloging of the Alexandrian library could perhaps not be compared with the famous research into and description of 158 constitutions organized by Aristotle,[5] but it was also a great collective enterprise and was successfully led by Kallimachos. But before the execution of such a project could be organized, it had to be conceived. There can be no doubt that it was Kallimachos himself who hit upon the idea to catalog the library, and to use the information which had been collected for this purpose as well as the insights gained in order to create a biobibliography of Greek authors. If we compare his other scholarly works with his *Pinakes* we perceive a common trait: Kallimachos was always eager to convey information which he had gleaned from the holdings of the Alexandrian library to the entire world of scholarship. In the compilation of the *Pinakes* he conveyed information on the authors that were represented in the library and on their works, which were the source of his knowledge on things. The library catalog with biographical data compiled by Kallimachos and his biobibliography of Greek authors which was based on it were the new means of conveying information. Thus, his work as a scholar consisted of the transmission and dissemination of information from the literature and about the literature. But he was not merely an uncritical mediator. His collection of data culled from the writings of various scholars on marvelous and curious natural phenomena (*Thaumasia*) and related works on which Howald based his judgment are leading to false conclusions. When it was a question of literary matters on which experts had different opinions, Kallimachos reported these too, but he also expressed his own views. In the case of literary works whose ascription or title, beginning or extent were in doubt, he, as the editor of the *Pinakes* could indeed not avoid making a decision about an author or a title, the opening words of a certain text or its extent.

Scholarship rests on the work of researchers, but these need the support of other scholars who are able and willing to create the tools for scholarly work. Among these are the compilers of catalogs, bibliographies, dictionaries, and the like. Kallimachos was a scholar of this kind, one of the earliest known to us, and certainly among the most important ones, because he was not only the compiler of such tools but was also their inventor.

Notes to Chapter 7

1) Thus, Erastosthenes tried to ascertain which of the comedies said to have been written by Pherekrates were genuine.

2) Dobschütz (1912) p. 333.

3) Parsons (1952) p. 208 calls Kallimachos quite correctly the "father of bibliography", but on p. 217 he calls him incorrectly "the father of literary history". Some of the researchers who consider only printed bibliographies bestow the title "father" of bibliography on Johannes Trithemius, others honor Conrad Gessner with this epithet; see Besterman (1940) pp. 6-7.

4) Wilamowitz (1924) vol. 1, p. 212 f.

5) Jaeger (1955) p. 349 f.

Bibliography

RE = *Paulys Realencyclopädie der classischen Altertumswissenschaft.*
Neue Bearbeitung, begonnen von Georg Wissowa.

1827

EUSTATHIUS. *Commentarii ad Homeri Iliadem.* Edited by Georg Stallbaum. Leipzig, 1827.

1843

GRÄFENHAN, August. *Geschichte der klassischen Philologie im Altertum.* Bonn, 1843-50.

1845

WESTERMANN, Anton, ed. *Biographoi. Vitarum scriptores graeci minores.* Braunschweig, 1845.

1857

DIOMEDES. *Ars grammatica.* (In: *Grammatici Latini.* Ex recensione Henrici Keilii. Leipzig, 1857, pp. 297-509.)

1858

USENER, Hermann. *Analecta Theophrastea.* Leipzig, 1858.

1863

Aristoteles pseudepigraphus Valentini Rose. Leipzig, 1863.

1865

BLASS, Friedrich. *Die griechische Beredsamkeit in dem Zeitraum von Alexander bis Augustus.* Berlin, 1865.

1868

USENER, Hermann. "Lectiones Graecae." *Rheinisches Museum für Philologie* 23 (1868): 147-169.

1872

BERGK, Theodor. *Griechische Literaturgeschichte.* Berlin, 1872.

1875

WILAMOWITZ-MOELLENDORFF, Ulrich von. *Analecta Euripidea.* Berlin, 1875.

1877

DÜBNER, Friedrich, ed. *Scholia graeca in Aristophanem.* Paris, 1877.

1879

DIELS, Hermann. *Doxographi graeci.* Berlin, 1879.
FLACH, Hans. *Untersuchungen zu Eudokia und Suidas.* Leipzig, 1879.
NOVATI, Francesco. "Index fabularum Aristophanis." *Hermes* 14 (1879): 461-464.
WILAMOWITZ-MOELLENDORFF, Ulrich von. "Index fabularum Aristophanis." *Hermes* 14 (1879): 464 f.

1880

DAUB, Adam. "De Suidae biographicorum origine et fide." *Jahrbücher für classische Philologie.* Suppl. XI. Leipzig, 1880, pp. 401-490.

FLACH, Hans. "Über den
gegenwärtigen Stand der
Quellenkritik des Hesychius von
Milet." *Jahrbücher für classische
Philologie* 26 (1880): 821-833.
KOCK, Theodor, ed. *Comicorum
Atticorum fragmenta.* Leipzig, 1880.

1881

FLACH, Hans. "Die Vitae römischer
Schriftsteller im Suidas." *Rheinisches
Museum für Philologie* 36 (1881): 316-
321.
WILAMOWITZ-MOELLENDORFF,
Ulrich von. *Antigonos von Karystos.*
Berlin, 1881. (Philologische
Untersuchungen, 4.)

1882

BIRT, Theodor. *Das antike Buchwesen
in seinem Verhältnis zur Litteratur.*
Berlin, 1882.
DAUB, Adam. *Studien zu den
Biographika des Suidas.* Freiburg
i.Br., 1882.
HESYCHIUS MILESIUS. *Onomatologi
quae supersunt. Cum prolegomenis
ed. Johannes Flach. Accedunt
Appendix Pseudohesychiana, Indices.*
Leipzig, 1882.

1883

DIONYSIUS THRAX. *Ars grammatica.*
Ed. Gustavus Uhlig. Leipzig, 1883.
(Grammatici Graeci. 1, 1.)

1884

LUDWICH, Arthur. *Aristarchs
homerische Textkritik.* Leipzig, 1884.
STRECKER, Carl. *De Lycophrone,
Euphronio, Eratosthene comicorum
interpretibus.* Greifswald, 1884.
(Ph.D. thesis)

1886

ARISTOTLE. *Aristotelis qui ferebantur
librorum fragmenta.* Collegit
Valentinus Rose. Leipzig, 1886.
HILLER, Eduard. "Die Fragmente des
Glaukos von Rhegion." *Rheinisches
Museum für Philologie* 41 (1886): 398-
436.

1887

DIELS, Hermann. "Leukippos und
Diogenes von Apollonia."
Rheinisches Museum für Philologie 42
(1887): 1-14

1889

HAEBERLIN, Carl.
"Voralexandrinische
Homerausgaben." *Centralblatt für
Bibliothekswesen* 6 (1889): 481-503.
KAIBEL, Georg. "Zur attischen
Komödie." *Hermes* 24 (1889): 35-66.

1890

DESSAU, Hermann. "Zu Athenaeus."
Hermes 25 (1890): 156-158.
HAEBERLIN, Carl. "Einfache und
Mischrollen in den antiken
Bibliotheken." *Centralblatt für
Bibliothekswesen* 7 (1890): 1-18.
*Inscriptiones Graecae. XIV: Inscriptiones
Italiae et Siciliae.* Ed. Georgius
Kaibel. Berlin, 1890.
ODER, Eugen. "Beiträge zur
Geschichte der Landwirtschaft bei
den Griechen." *Rheinisches Museum
für Philologie* 45 (1890): 58-99.
ZACHER, Konrad. "Dia Kallistratu."
Philologus 49 (1890): 313-337.

1891

DZIATZKO, Karl. "Johannes Tzetzes
und das Plautusscholion."
Rheinisches Museum für Philologie 46
(1891): 349-362.

SUSEMIHL, Franz. *Geschichte der griechischen Literatur in der Alexandrinerzeit.* Leipzig, 1891-92.

1892

NISSEN, Heinrich. "Die Staatsschriften des Aristoteles." *Rheinisches Museum für Philologie* 47 (1892): 161-206.
USENER, Hermann. "Ein altes Lehrgebäude der Philologie." *Königliche Bayerische Akademie der Wissenschaften. Philosophisch-Philologische und Historische Klasse. Sitzungsberichte.* (1892): 582-648.

1893

DIELS, Hermann. "Über die Exzerpte von Menons Iatrika in dem Londoner Papyrus 137." *Hermes* 28 (1893): 407-434.
IHM, Max. "Die Bibliotheken im alten Rom." *Centralblatt für Bibliothekswesen* 10 (1893): 513-532.

1894

WILAMOWITZ-MOELLENDORFF, Ulrich von. "Ein Weihgeschenk des Eratosthenes." *Nachrichten von der Königlichen Gesellschaft der Wissenschaften zu Göttingen, Philosophisch-Historische Klasse* (1894): 15-35.

1895

WENTZEL, Georg. *Die griechische Übersetzung der Viri illustres des Hieronymus.* Leipzig, 1895. (Texte und Untersuchungen zur Geschichte der altchristlichen Literatur. 13, 3)
WILAMOWITZ-MOELLENDORFF, Ulrich von. *Euripides' Herakles. 1. Einleitung in die griechische Tragödie.* 2. Aufl. Berlin, 1895.

1896

DYROFF, Adolf. *Über die Anlage der stoischen Bücherkataloge.* Würzburg, 1896.
KAIBEL, Georg. "Aristophanes." *RE* 2 (1896): 971-994.
KENTENICH, Gottfried. *Analecta Alexandrina.* Bonn, 1896. (Ph.D. thesis)
NATORP, Paul. "Aristippos von Kyrene." *RE* 2 (1896): 902-906.

1897

KÖRTE, Alfred. "Zu attischen Dionysos-Festen." *Rheinisches Museum für Philologie* 52 (1897): 168-176.
KRUMBACHER, Karl. *Geschichte der byzantinischen Literatur.* 2. Aufl. München, 1897.

1898

BLASS, Friedrich. *Die attische Beredsamkeit.* Leipzig, 1898.
WENTZEL, Georg. "Hesychiana." *Hermes* 33 (1898): 275-312.

1899

DIONYSIUS HALICARNASEUS. *Dionysii Halicarnasei quae extant.* Ed. Hermanus Usener et Ludovicus Radermacher. Leipzig, 1899.
DRERUP, Engelbert. "Antike Demosthenesausgaben." *Philologus.* Suppl. VII (1899): 531-588.
KAIBEL, Georg, ed. *Comicorum Graecorum fragmenta.* Berlin, 1899.
RADERMACHER, Ludwig. "Dinarchus." *Philologus* 58 (1899): 161-169.

1900

ARISTEAS. *Aristeas ad Philocratem epistula.* Ed. Paulus Wendland. Leipzig, 1900.
——. *Der Brief des Aristeas.* Uebersetzt von Paul Wendland. (In: *Die Apokryphen und Pseudepigraphen des Alten Testaments.* Tübingen, 1900. 2. Bd., pp. 1-31.)
BAUMSTARK, Anton. *Aristoteles bei den Syrern vom fünften bis achten Jahrhundert.* Leipzig, 1900.
ROBERT, Carl. "Die Ordnung der Olympischen Spiele und die Sieger der 75.-83. Olympiade." *Hermes* 35 (1900): 141-195.

1901

HILGARD, Alfred, ed. *Scholia in Dionysii Thracis Artem grammaticam.* Leipzig, 1901. (Grammatici Graeci. 1, 3.)
LEO, Friedrich. *Die griechisch-römische Biographie nach ihrer literarischen Form.* Leipzig, 1901.
SCHWARTZ, Eduard. "Damokritos." *RE* 4 (1901): 2070.
——. "Demetrios von Magnesia." *RE* 4 (1901): 2814-2817.
THALHEIM, Theodor. "Deinarchos." *RE* 4 (1901): 2386-2388.

1903

NATORP, Paul. "Diogenes von Sinope." *RE* 5 (1903): 765-773.
RADERMACHER, Ludwig. "Dionysius von Halikarnassos." *RE* 5 (1903): 961-971.
REISCH, Emil. "Didaskaliai; Didaskalos." *RE* 5 (1903): 394-401; 401-406.

1904

CAPPS, Edward. "The 'Nemesis' of the younger Cratinus." *Harvard Studies on Classical Philology* 15 (1904): 61-75.

DIELS, Hermann; SCHUBART, Wilhelm, eds. *Didymos: Kommentar zu Demosthenes.* (Pap. 9780.) Berlin, 1904. (Berliner Klassikertexte. 1.)

1905

COHN, Leopold. "Eirenaios." *RE* 5 (1905): 2120-2124.
CRUSIUS, Otto. "Dithyrambos." *RE* 5 (1905): 1203-1230.
KÖRTE, Alfred. "Inschriftliches zur Geschichte der attischen Komödie." *Rheinisches Museum für Philologie* 60 (1905): 424-447.
SCHWARTZ, Eduard. "Diogenes Laertios." *RE* 5 (1905): 738-763.

1906

CAPPS, Edward. "The Roman fragments of Athenian comic didascaliae." *Classical Philology* 1 (1906): 201-220.
KÖRTE, Alfred. "Aristoteles' Nikai Dionysiakai." *Classical Philology* 1 (1906): 391-398.
WILAMOWITZ-MOELLENDORFF, Ulrich von. *Urkunden dramatischer Aufführungen in Athen.* Hrsg. von Adolf Wilhelm. Wien, 1906.
WILHELM, Adolf. *Urkunden dramatischer Aufführungen in Athen.* Wien, 1906.

1907

BIRT, Theodor. *Die Buchrolle in der Kunst.* Leipzig, 1907.
CAPPS, Edward. "Epigraphical problems in the history of Attic comedy." *American Journal of Philology* 28 (1907): 179-199.
COHN, Leopold. "Epigenes." *RE* Halbbd. 11 (1907): 64-65.
REISCH, Emil. "Urkunden dramatischer Aufführungen in Athen." *Zeitschrift für die österreichischen Gymnasien* (1907): 289-315.

WILHELM, Adolf. "Inschrift aus Athen." *Jahreshefte des Österreichischen Archäologischen Instituts in Wien* 10 (1907): 35-40.

1909

GUDEMAN, Alfred. *Grundriss der Geschichte der klassischen Philologie.* 2. Aufl. Leipzig, 1909.
JACHMANN, Günther. *De Aristotelis didascaliis.* Göttingen, 1909. (Ph.D. thesis)
KROLL, Wilhelm. *Geschichte der klassischen Philologie.* Leipzig, 1909.

1910

BETHE, Erich. "Die griechische Poesie." (In: *Einleitung in die Altertumswissenschaft.* Leipzig, 1910, pp. 275-328.)
LIPSIUS, Justus Hermann. "Didaskalika." *Rheinisches Museum für Philologie* 65 (1910): 161-168.

1911

KÖRTE, Alfred. "Bericht über die Literatur zur griechischen Komödie aus den Jahren 1902-1909." *Jahresbericht über die Fortschritte der klassischen Altertumswissenschaft* 152 (1911): 218-312.
POHLENZ, Max. "Die hellenistische Poesie und die Philosophie." (In: *Charites. Friedrich Leo zum 60. Geburtstag.* Göttingen, 1911, pp. 76-112.)

1912

DOBSCHÜTZ, Ernst von. *Das Decretum Gelasianum de libris recipiendis et non recipiendis.* Leipzig, 1912. (Texte und Untersuchungen zur Geschichte der altchristlichen Literatur. Reihe 3, Bd. 8, 4.)
FUNAIOLI, Gino. "Hermokrates von Iasos." *RE* Halbbd. 15 (1912): 887-888.

HOMERUS. *Opera.* Ed. Thomas W. Allen. Oxford, 1912.
JACOBY, Felix. "Glaukos von Rhegion." *RE* Halbbd. 13 (1912): 1417-1420.
—————. "Hellikanos von Lesbos." *RE* Halbbd. 15 (1912): 104-155.
KÖRTE, Alfred. "Hegemon von Thasos." *RE* Halbbd. 14 (1912): 2595-2596.
LEO, Friedrich. "Satyros' bios Euripidu." *Nachrichten von der Königl. Gesellschaft der Wissenschaften zu Göttingen, Philosophisch-Historische Klasse* (1912): 273-290.
REISCH, Emil. "Zu den Listen der Tragödiensieger." *Wiener Studien* 34 (1912): 332-341.

1913

ACHELIS, Th. O. H. "De Aristophanis Byzantii argumentis fabularum." *Philologus* 72 (1913): 414-441, 518-545; 73 (1914-16): 122-155.
ARISTEAS. *The Letter of Aristeas.* Tr. by H. T. Andrews. (In: *The Apocrypha and Pseudepigrapha of the Old Testament in English . . .* Oxford, 1913, vol. 2, pp. 83-122.)
BIRT, Theodor. *Kritik und Hermeneutik. Nebst Abriss des antiken Buchwesens.* München, 1913. (Handbuch der klassischen Altertumswissenschaft. 1.)
HEIBGES, Stephan. "Hermippos der Kallimacheer." *RE* Halbbd. 15 (1913): 845-852.
PASQUALI, Giorgio. "Die schriftstellerische Form des Pausanias." *Hermes* 48 (1913): 161-223.
PFISTER, Friedrich. "Die Lokalhistorie von Sikyon bei Menaichmos, Pausanias und den Chronographen." *Rheinisches Museum für Philologie* 68 (1913): 529-537.
RZACH, Alois. "Homeridai." *RE* Halbbd. 16 (1913): 2145-2182.
SCHULTZ, H. "Hesychios Illustrios." *RE* Halbbd. 16 (1913): 1322-1327.

1914

The Oxyrhynchus Papyri. Ed. by
Bernard P. Grenfell, Arthur S. Hunt.
London, 1914.
ROSTAGNI, Augusto. "I bibliotecari
alessandrini nella cronologia della
letteratura ellenistica." *Atti della R.
Accademia delle Scienze di Torino.* 50
(1914/15): 241-265.
WILAMOWITZ-MOELLENDORFF,
Ulrich von. "Neue lesbische Lyrik.
(Oxyrhynchus-Papyri 10.) [Anhang:
Die Liste der alexandrinischen
Bibliothekare, Pap. 1241.]" *Neue
Jahrbücher für das klassische Altertum*
33 (1914): 245-247.

1915

BRINKMANN, August. "Die
Olympische Chronik." *Rheinisches
Museum für Philologie* 70 (1915): 624-
637.
DITTENBERGER, Wilhelm, ed.
Sylloge inscriptionum Graecarum.
Leipzig, 1915-24.

1916

OELLACHER, Hans. "Zur
Chronologie der altattischen
Komödie." *Wiener Studien* 38 (1916):
81-157.

1917

HOWALD, Ernst. "Handbücher als
Quellen des Diogenes Laertius."
Philologus 74 (1917): 119-130.
SITZLER, J. "Die alexandrinischen
Bibliothekare." *Wochenschrift für
klassische Philologie* (1917): 1087-
1096.

1918

SCHUBART, Wilhelm. *Einführung in
die Papyruskunde.* Berlin, 1918.

1919

JACOBY, Felix. "Kallisthenes."
RE Halbbd. 20 (1919): 1674-1707.
————. "Kallixeinos."
RE Halbbd. 20 (1919): 1751-1754.

1920

CHRIST, Wilhelm von. *Geschichte der
griechischen Literatur.* 6. Aufl.
München, 1920. (Handbuch der
klassischen Altertumswissenschaft. 7,
2, 1.)

1921

CALLIMACHUS. *Hymns and epigrams.*
Tr. A. W. Mair. Cambridge, MA,
1921. (Loeb Classical Library)
   The numbering of epigrams in this
edition differs slightly from that in
Pfeiffer's edition (Callimachus
[1949]).
FORRER, Emil. "Ausbeute aus den
Boghazköi-Inschriften." *Mitteilungen
der Deutschen Orient-Gesellschaft* 61
(1921): 20-39.
GUDEMAN, Alfred. "Satyros." *RE*
Reihe 2, Halbbd. 3 (1921): 228-235.
KÖRTE, Alfred. "Komödie
(griechische)." *RE* Halbbd. 21
(1921): 1267-1275.
LAUE, Heinrich. *De Democriti
fragmentis ethicis.* Göttingen, 1921.
(Ph.D. thesis)

1922

DELATTE, Armand. *La Vie de
Pythagore dans Diogène Laërce.*
Bruxelles, 1922. (Académie Royale
de Belgique. Classe des lettres.
Mémoires. Série 2, T. 17, 2.)
GARDTHAUSEN, Viktor. "Die
alexandrinische Bibliothek, ihr
Vorbild, Katalog und Betrieb."
*Zeitschrift des Deutschen Vereins für
Buchwesen und Schrifttum* 5 (1922):
73-104.

SCHMIDT, Friedrich. *Die Pinakes des Kallimachos.* Berlin, 1922. (Klassisch-Philologische Studien. 1.)

1923

DITTMER, William A. *The fragments of Athenian comic didascaliae found in Rome.* Leiden, 1923. (Ph.D. thesis)
KÖRTE, Alfred. "Sellios." *RE* Reihe 2, Halbbd. 4 (1923): 123-124.

1924

ARISTOPHANES. *The Acharnians. The Knights. The Clouds. The Wasps.* Tr. Benjamin B. Rogers. Cambridge, MA, 1924. (Loeb Classical Library)
CHRIST, Wilhelm von. *Geschichte der griechischen Literatur.* 6. Aufl., bearbeitet von Wilhelm Schmid. München, 1924. (Handbuch der klassischen Altertumswissenschaft. 7, 2, 2.)
COLSON, Francis H. *M. Fabius Quintilianus: Institutionis oratoriae. 1.1.* Ed. with introduction and commentary. Cambridge (England), 1924.
PHILIPPSON, Robert. "Demokrits Sinnsprüche." *Hermes* 59 (1924): 369-419.
PREUNER, Erich. "Aus alten Papieren." *Mitteilungen des Deutschen Archäologischen Instituts. Athenische Abteilung* 49 (1924): 102-152.
WILAMOWITZ-MOELLENDORFF, Ulrich von. *Hellenistische Dichtung in der Zeit des Kallimachos.* Berlin, 1924.

1925

BELOCH, Karl Julius. *Griechische Geschichte.* Berlin, 1925-27.

DIOGENES LAERTIUS. *The lives of eminent philosophers.* Tr. R. D. Hicks. Cambridge, MA, 1925. (Loeb Classical Library)
GEISSLER, Paul. *Chronologie der alten attischen Komödie.* Berlin, 1925. (Philologische Untersuchungen. 30.)
KÖRTE, Alfred. "William Anthony Dittmer. The fragments of Athenian comic didascaliae found in Rome . . ." *Philologische Wochenschrift* 45 (1925): 1-6.
LATTE, Kurt. "Glossographika." *Philologus* 80 (1925): 136-175.
MAIURI, Amedeo. *Nuova silloge epigrafica di Rodi e Cos.* Firenze, 1925.
OTTO, Walter. *Kulturgeschichte des Altertums. Ein Überblick über neue Erscheinungen.* München, 1925.
PERROTTA, Gennaro. "Studi di poesia ellenistica. V. Callimaco, Teocrito e Apollonio. 3. Apollonio." *Studi italiani di filologia classica.* Nuova serie 4 (1925): 118-129.

1926

DE SANCTIS, Gaetano. "La biblioteca di Rodi." *Rivista de filologia e d'istruzione classica.* Nuova serie 4 (1926): 63-73.
ROSTAGNI, Augusto. "Il dialogo aristotelico perduto Peri poiētōn." *Rivista di filologia e d'istruzione classica.* Nuova serie 4 (1926): 433-470; 5 (1927): 143-173.
WELLMANN, Max. "Zu Demokrit." *Hermes* 61 (1926): 474-475.

1927

ATHENAEUS. *The Deipnosophists.* Tr. Charles B. Gulick. Cambridge, MA, 1927. (Loeb Classical Library)
BÜRCHNER. "Skapsis." *RE* Reihe 2, Halbbd. 5 (1927): 445-446.
SCHUBART, Wilhelm. *Die Griechen in Ägypten.* Leipzig, 1927. (Beihefte zum Alten Orient. 10.)

1928

PERROTTA, Gennaro. "Il papiro d'Ossirinco 1241 e la cronologia dei bibliotecari d'Alessandria." *Athenaeum.* Nuova serie 6 (1928): 125-156.

SUIDAS. *Lexicon.* Ed. Ada Adler. Leipzig, 1928-38.

WILAMOWITZ-MOELLENDORFF, Ulrich von. *Kyrene.* Berlin, 1928.

1929

SCHMID, Wilhelm; STÄHLIN, Otto. *Geschichte der griechischen Literatur.* München, 1929. (Handbuch der Altertumswissenschaft. 7, 1, 1.)

STRABO. *The geography of Strabo.* Tr. Horace L. Jones. Cambridge, MA, 1929. (Loeb Classical Library)

WENDEL, Carl. "Spuren einer alten Bibliothek auf Rhodos." *Zentralblatt für Bibliothekswesen* 46 (1929): 2-6.

1931

ADLER, Ada. "Suidas." *RE* Reihe 2, Halbbd. 7 (1931): 675-717.

HERTER, Hans. "Kallimachos." *RE* Suppl. V (1931): 386-451.

Inscriptiones Graecae. II/III 2,2. Inscriptiones Atticae Euclidis anno posteriores. Ed. Johannes Kirchner. Editio minor. Berlin, 1931.

LAQUEUR, Richard. "Menaichmos." *RE* Halbbd. 29 (1931): 698-699.

1932

ARISTOTLE. *The Poetics.* Tr. W. Hamilton Fyfe. Cambridge, MA, 1932. (Loeb Classical Library)

SOLMSEN, Friedrich. "Drei Rekonstruktionen zur antiken Rhetorik und Poetik. II: Theodektes." *Hermes* 67 (1932): 144-151.

1933

JAEGER, Werner. *Paideia: die Formung des griechischen Menschen.* Berlin, 1933-47.

MANTEUFFEL, Georg. "De novo quodam librorum inventario." (Pap. Varsov. 5.) *Aegyptus* 13 (1933): 367-373.

MÜLLER-GRAUPA, Edwin. "Museion." *RE* Halbbd. 31 (1933): 797-821.

1934

DILLER, Hans. *Wanderarzt und Aitiologe. Studien zur hippokratischen Schrift Peri aerön hydatön topön.* Leipzig, 1934. (*Philologus* Suppl. xxvi, 3.)

KROLL, Wilhelm. "Bolos und Demokritos." *Hermes* 69 (1934): 228-232.

SCHMID, Wilhelm; STÄHLIN, Otto. *Geschichte der griechischen Literatur.* München, 1934. (Handbuch der Altertumswissenschaft. 7, 1, 2.)

SOLMSEN, Friedrich. "Theodektes als Rhetor." *RE* Reihe 2, Halbbd. 10 (1934): 1729-1734.

1935

EDELSTEIN, Ludwig. "Hippokrates." *RE* Suppl. VI (1935): 1290-1345.

FRITZ, Kurt von. "Neleus." *RE* Halbbd. 32 (1935): 2280-2281.

HORNA, Konstantin. "Gnome." *RE* Suppl. VI (1935): 74-90.

SEGRE, Mario. "Epigraphica. I. Catalogo di libri da Rodi." *Rivista di filologia e d'istruzione classica.* Nuova serie 13 (1935): 214-222.

1936

GUNDEL, Wilhelm. "Thrasyllos." *RE* Reihe 2, Halbbd. 11 (1936): 581-584.

SEGRE, Mario. "Ancora sulla
biblioteca del ginnasio di Rodi."
*Rivista di filologia e d'istruzione
classica.* Nuova serie 14 (1936): 40.

1937

HERTER, Hans. "Bericht über die
Literatur zur hellenistischen
Dichtung aus den Jahren 1921-1935.
I. 1. Allgemeines. 2. Kallimachos."
*Jahresbericht über die Fortschritte der
klassischen Altertumswissenschaft* 255
(1937): 65-217.
WENDEL, Carl. "Neues aus alten
Bibliotheken." *Zentralblatt für
Bibliothekswesen* 54 (1937): 585-589.
ZIEGLER, Konrat. "Tragoedia."
RE Reihe 2, Halbbd. 12 (1937):
1899-2075.

1938

FRITZ, Kurt von. "Phaidon von Elis."
RE Reihe 2, Halbbd. 38 (1938):
1538-1542.

1939

WENDEL, Carl. "Onomastikon."
RE Halbbd. 35 (1939): 507-516.

1940

BESTERMAN, Thedore.
*The beginnings of systematic
bibliography.* 2d ed. rev. London,
1940. (Reprinted: New York, 1968.)
BLOCH, Herbert. "Herakleides Lembos
and his Epitome of Aristotle's
Politeiai." *Transactions of the
American Philological Association* 71
(1940): 27-39.
BRINK, Karl Oskar. "Peripatos."
RE Suppl. VII (1940): 899-949.
REGENBOGEN, Otto. "Theophrastos."
RE Suppl. VII (1940): 1354-1562.

WENDEL, Carl. "Das griechisch-
römische Altertum." (In: *Handbuch der
Bibliothekswissenschaft.* 3. Bd. *Geschichte
der Bibliotheken.* Leipzig, 1940, pp. 1-63.)

1941

HESTER, Franz. "Aristoteles und die
Siegerlisten von Olympia."
Gymnasium 52 (1941): 29-38.
KÖRTE, Alfred. "Phrynichos, Dichter
der alten attischen Komödie."
RE Halbbd. 39 (1941): 918-920.
NACHMANSON, Ernst. *Der
griechische Buchtitel.* Göteborg,
1941. (Göteborgs Högskolas
Årsskrift. 47, 19.)
ROSTOVTZEFF, Michail. *The social
and economic history of the Hellenistic
world.* Oxford, 1941.

1942

BAYER, Erich. *Demetrios Phalereus der
Athener.* Stuttgart, 1942. (Tübinger
Beiträge zur Altertumswissenschaft 36.)
HERTER, Hans. "Zur Lebensgeschichte
des Apollonios von Rhodos." *Rheinisches
Museum für Philologie* 91 (1942):
310-326.
VON DER MÜHLL, Peter. "Antiker
Historismus in Plutarchs Biographie
des Solon." *Klio* 35 (1942): 89-102.
WENDEL, Carl. "Palamedes. (3)."
RE Halbbd. 36 (1942): 2512-2513.

1943

HOWALD, Ernst. *Der Dichter
Kallimachos von Kyrene.* Zürich, 1943.

1944

SNELL, Bruno. "Die Nachrichten über
die Lehren des Thales und die
Anfänge der griechischen
Philosophie- und Literatur-geschichte."
Philologus 96 (1944): 170-182.

1946

SCHMID, Wilhelm; STÄHLIN, Otto. *Geschichte der griechischen Literatur.* München, 1946. (Handbuch der Altertumswissenschaft. 7, 1, 4.)

1948

GERSTINGER, Hans. *Bestand und Überlieferung der Literaturwerke des griechisch-römischen Altertums.* Graz, 1948.

WENDEL, Carl. "Tyrannion." *RE* Reihe 2, Halbbd. 14 (1948): 1811-1819.

—————. "Tzetzes, Johannes." *RE* Reihe 2, Halbbd. 14 (1948): 1959-2010.

1949

CALLIMACHUS. Ed. Rudolfus Pfeiffer. Oxford, 1949-53.

JACHMANN, Günther. "Vom frühalexandrinischen Homertext." *Nachrichten der Akademie der Wissenschaften zu Göttingen, Philosophisch-Historische Klasse* (1949) Nr. 7: 167-223.

JACOBY, Felix. *Atthis. The local chronicles of ancient Athens.* Oxford, 1949.

RUPPRECHT, Karl. "Paroimiographoi." *RE* Halbbd. 36 (1949): 1735-1778.

WENDEL, Carl. *Die griechisch-römische Buchbeschreibung, verglichen mit der des Vorderen Orients.* Halle, 1949. (Hallische Monographien. 3.)

ZIEGLER, Konrat. "Paradoxographoi." *RE* Halbbd. 36 (1949): 1137-1166.

1950

KÖRTE, Alfred. "Platon, Dichter der alten Komödie." *RE* Halbbd. 40 (1950): 2537-2541.

MALCLÈS, Louise-Noëlle. *Les sources du travail bibliographique.* Genève, 1950.

REGENBOGEN, Otto. "Pinax." *RE* Halbbd. 40 (1950): 1409-1482.

ZIEGLER, Konrat. "Plagiat." *RE* Halbbd. 40 (1950): 1956-1997.

ZUCKER, Friedrich. "Athen und Ägypten bis auf den Beginn der hellenistischen Zeit." (In: *Aus Antike und Orient. Festschrift Wilhelm Schubart zum 75. Geburtstag.* Leipzig, 1950, pp. 146-165.)

1951

ARISTEAS. *Aristeas to Philocrates (Letter of Aristeas.)* Ed. and tr. by M. Hadas. New York, 1951.

HEMMERDINGER, B. "Origines de la tradition manuscrite de quelques auteurs grecs." *Studi italiani di filologia classica* 25 (1951): 83-88.

MORAUX, Paul. *Les listes anciennes des ouvrages d'Aristote.* Louvain, 1951.

RADERMACHER, Ludwig, ed. *Artium scriptores. (Reste der voraristotelischen Rhetorik.)* Wien, 1951. (Oesterreichische Akademie der Wissenschaften, Philosophisch-Historische Klasse. *Sitzungsberichte.* 227, 3.)

ROHDE, Georg. "Über das Lesen im Altertum." (In: *Ansprachen und Reden zur Feier der Uebergabe der Spende der Ford Foundation.* Berlin, 1951, pp. 16-28.) Also in his *Studien und Interpretationen zur antiken Literatur, Religion und Geschichte.*

ZIEGLER, Konrat. "Plutarchos." *RE* Halbbd. 41 (1951): 636-962.

1952

DIELS, Hermann, ed. *Die Fragmente der Vorsokratiker. Griechisch und deutsch.* 6. verb. Aufl. hrsg. von Walter Kranz. Berlin, 1952.

HERTER, Hans. *Platons Akademie.* 2. Aufl. Bonn, 1952.

PARSONS, Edward A. *The Alexandrian library, glory of the Hellenic world.* London, 1952.

PASQUALI, Giorgio. *Storia della tradizione e critica del testo.* 2. ed. Firenze, 1952.

1953

ARISTOPHANES. *Aristofane. Le commedie.* Edizione critica e traduzione a cura di R. Cantarella. 1. Prolegomini. Milano, 1953. (Classici greci e latini. 9.)
MENANDER. *Menandri quae supersunt.* Ed. Alfred Körte. Leipzig, 1953.
PRAECHTER, Karl. *Die Philosophie des Altertums.* 13. Aufl. Basel, 1953.
ZUCKER, Friedrich. "Selbstbehauptung und Versagen der Griechen in Ägypten bis zum Ende der Ptolemäerzeit." *Gymnasium* 60 (1953): 7-19.

1954

BUCHNER, Edmund. "Zwei Gutachten zur Behandlung der Barbaren." *Hermes* 82 (1954): 378-384.
SEXTUS EMPIRICUS. Rec. Hermannus Mutschmann. 3. *Adversus mathematicos.* Ed. Jürgen Mau. Leipzig, 1954.
WASZINK, Jan Hendrik. "Bolos." (In: *Reallexikon für Antike und Christentum,* 2. Bd., 1954, pp. 502-508.)

1955

CHRIST, Carl. "Das Mittelalter." Ergänzt von Anton Kern. (In: *Handbuch der Bibliothekswissenschaft.* 2. Aufl. 3. Bd. *Geschichte der Bibliotheken.* Wiesbaden, 1955, pp. 243-498.)
JAEGER, Werner. *Aristoteles. Grundlegung einer Geschichte seiner Entwicklung.* 2. Aufl. Berlin, 1955.

KALLIMACHOS. *Die Dichtungen. Griechisch und deutsch.* Übertragen, eingeleitet und erklärt von Ernst Howald und Emil Staiger. Zürich, 1955.
MARROU, Henri-Irénée. *Histoire de l'éducation dans l'antiquité.* 3e éd. Paris, 1955.
MILKAU, Fritz. "Der alte Vorderorient." Neu bearb. von Josef Schawe. (In: *Handbuch der Bibliothekswissenschaft.* 2. Aufl. 3. Bd. *Geschichte der Bibliotheken.* Wiesbaden, 1955, pp. 1-50.)
NILSSON, Martin P. *Die hellenistische Schule.* München, 1955.
ROSTOVZEFF, Michail. *Die hellenistische Welt. Gesellschaft und Wirtschaft.* Stuttgart, 1955. [English ed. 1941.]
VLEESCHAUWER, Herman Jean de. "Les bibliothèques ptoleméennes d'Alexandrie." *Mousaion* 1 (1955): 1-40.
WENDEL, Carl. "Das griechisch-römische Altertum." Ergänzt von Willi Göber. (In: *Handbuch der Bibliothekswissenschaft.* 2. Aufl. 3. Bd. *Geschichte der Bibliotheken.* Wiesbaden, 1955, pp. 51-145.)

1956

DÜRING, Ingemar. "Ariston or Hermipos." *Classica et Mediaevalia* 17 (1956): 11-21.
FRITZ, Kurt von. "Die Bedeutung des Aristoteles für die Geschichts-schreibung." *Fondation Hardt. Entretiens sur l'antiquité classique* 4 (1956): 85-128.
HERTER, Hans. "Bericht über die Literatur zur hellenistischen Dichtung seit dem Jahre 1921. II. Apollonios von Rhodos." *Jahresberichte über die Fortschritte der klassischen Altertumswissenschaft* 285 (1956): 213-410.
LÖFFLER, Karl. *Einführung in die Katalogkunde.* 2. Aufl. Stuttgart, 1956.

1957

DIHLE, Albrecht. "Der Platoniker Ptolemaios." *Hermes* 85 (1957): 314-325.

DÜRING, Ingemar. *Aristotle in the ancient biographical tradition.* Göteborg, 1957. (Göteborgs Universitets Årsskrift. 63, 2.)

FRITZ, Kurt von. "Protagoras." *RE* Halbbd. 45 (1957): 908-921.

JACOBY, Felix, ed. *Die Fragmente der griechischen Historiker.* Leiden, 1957-64.

MARROU, Henri-Irénée. *Geschichte der Erziehung im klassischen Altertum.* Freiburg i.Br., 1957. [French ed. 1955.]

MICHAELIS, Wilhelm. "Aristeasbrief." (In: *Die Religion in Geschichte und Gegenwart.* 3. Aufl. Tübingen, 1957. vol. 1, col. 596.)

1958

DI BENEDETTO, Vincenzo. "Dionisio Trace e la Techne a lui attributa." *Annali della Scuola Normale Superiore di Pisa. Lettere, storia e filosofia.* Serie 2, 27 (1958): 167-210; 28 (1959): 87-118.

HABICHT, Christian. "Die herrschende Gesellschaft in den hellenistischen Monarchien." *Vierteljahresschrift für Sozial- und Wirtschaftsgeschichte* 45 (1958): 1-16.

ROOY, C. A. van. "Die probleem van die oorsprong van die groot alexandrynse biblioteek." *Acta classica* (Capetown) 1 (1958): 147-161.

WENDEL, Carl, ed. *Scholia in Apollonium Rhodium vetera.* Berlin, 1958.

WITTY, Francis J. "The Pinakes of Callimachus." *Library Quarterly* 28 (1958): 132-136.

1959

BLUM, Rudolf. "Vor- und Frühgeschichte der nationalen Allgemeinbibliographie." *Archiv für Geschichte des Buchwesens* 2 (1959): 233-303.

ERBSE, Hartmut. "Über Aristarchs Iliasausgaben." *Hermes* 87 (1959): 275-303.

QUINTILIANUS, M. Fabius. *Institutio oratoria.* Ed. Ludwig Radermacher. Leipzig, 1959.

TARN, William. *Hellenistic civilization.* 3d ed. London, 1959.

1960

KÖRTE, Alfred. *Die hellenistische Dichtung.* 2. Aufl., bearbeitet von Paul Händel. Stuttgart, 1960.

MORETTI, Luigi. "Sulle didascalie del teatro antico rinvenute a Roma." *Athenaeum.* Nuova serie 38 (1960): 263-282.

SCHUBART, Wilhelm. *Das Buch bei den Griechen und Römern.* 3. Aufl. Leipzig, 1960.

1961

EICHGRÜN, Egon. *Kallimachos und Apollonios Rhodios.* Berlin, 1961. (Ph.D. thesis)

ERBSE, Hartmut. "Überlieferungsgeschichte der griechischen klassischen und hellenistischen Literatur." (In: *Geschichte der Textüberlieferung der antiken und mittelalterlichen Literatur.* Zürich, 1961, pp. 209-283.)

HINTENLANG, Hubert. *Untersuchungen zu den Homer-Aporien des Aristoteles.* Heidelberg, 1961. (Ph.D. thesis)

HUNGER, Herbert. "Antikes und mittelalterliches Buch- und Schriftwesen." (In: *Geschichte der Textüberlieferung der antiken und mittelalterlichen Literatur.* Zürich, 1961, pp. 27-147.)

1962

GIGON, Olof, ed. *Vita Aristotelis Marciana*. Berlin, 1962.
HÄNDEL, Paul. "Die zwei Versionen der Viten des Apollonios Rhodios." *Hermes* 90 (1962): 492-443.
RUSSO, Carlo Ferdinando. *Aristofane, autore di teatro*. Firenze, 1962.

1963

JAEGER, Werner. *Diokles von Karystos*. 2. Aufl. Berlin, 1963.
LESKY, Albin. *Geschichte der griechischen Literatur*. 2. Aufl. Bern, 1963.
MENSCHING, Eckart. *Favorin von Arelate. Der erste Teil der Fragmente*. Berlin, 1963.
RIEMSCHNEIDER, Margarete. *Die Welt der Hethiter*. 6. Aufl. Stuttgart, 1963.
VLEESCHAUWER, Herman Jean de. "The library in the Hellenic world." *Mousaion* 71 (1963): 33-99.
VORLÄNDER, Karl. *Geschichte der Philosophie. 1. Philosophie des Altertums*. Hamburg, 1963.

1964

DIOGENES LAERTIUS. *Vitae philosophorum*. Ed. H. S. Long. Oxford, 1964.
EISSFELDT, Otto. *Einleitung in das Alte Testament*. 3. Aufl. Tübingen, 1964. [English ed. 1965.]
GIANNINI, Alessandro. "Studi sulla paradossografia greca. II." *Acme* 17 (1964): 99-139.
Der Kleine Pauly. Lexikon der Antike. Stuttgart, 1964-75.
LOSSAU, Manfred Joachim. *Untersuchungen zur antiken Demosthenesexegese*. Bad Homburg, 1964. (Palingenesia. 2.)
MENSCHING, Eckart. "Zur Produktivität der alten Komödie." *Museum Helveticum* 21 (1964): 15-49.

RITCHIE, William. *The authenticity of the Rhesus of Euripides*. Cambridge (England), 1964.
STEINMETZ, Peter. "Gattungen und Epochen der griechischen Literatur in der Sicht Quintilians." *Hermes* 92 (1964): 454-466.

1965

EISSFELDT, Otto. *The Old Testament: an introduction*. New York, 1965.
Lexikon der Alten Welt. Zürich, 1965.

1966

DÜRING, Ingemar. *Aristoteles. Darstellung und Interpretation seines Denkens*. Heidelberg, 1966.
SNELL, Bruno. "Zu den Urkunden dramatischer Aufführungen." *Nachrichten der Akademie der Wissenschaften in Göttingen. Philosophisch-Historische Klasse* (1966) 2.
TARN, William. *Die Kultur der Hellenistischen Welt*. 3. Aufl. Darmstadt, 1966. [English ed. 1959.]

1967

CAPOVILLA, Giovanni. *Callimaco*. Roma, 1967. (Studia philologica. 10, 1, 2.)
DALY, Lloyd W. *Contributions to a history of alphabetization in Antiquity and the Middle Ages*. Bruxelles, 1967. (Collection Latomus. 90.)
DÖRRIE, Heinrich. "Xenokrates." *RE* Reihe 2, Halbbd. 18 (1967): 1512-1528.
SCHNEIDER, Carl. *Kulturgeschichte des Hellenismus*. München, 1967-69.
WEHRLI, Fritz, ed. *Die Schule des Aristoteles: Texte und Kommentar*. 2. Aufl. Basel, 1967-69. Suppl. 1, 1974.
WIDMANN, Hans. "Herstellung und Vertrieb des Buches in der griechisch-römischen Welt." *Archiv für Geschichte des Buchwesens* 8 (1967): 545-640.

1968

DÜRING, Ingemar. "Aristoteles."
RE Suppl. XI (1968): 159-336.
LESKY, Albin. "Homeros."
RE Suppl. XI (1968): 687-846.
PFEIFFER, Rudolf. *History of classical scholarship: from the beginning to the end of the Hellenistic age.* Oxford, 1968.
PICKARD-CAMBRIDGE, Arthur. *The dramatic festivals of Athens.* 2d ed. Oxford, 1968.
WEHRLI, Fritz. "Aristoxenos."
RE Suppl. XI (1968): 336-343.

1969

BENGTSON, Hermann. *Griechische Geschichte: von den Anfängen bis in die römische Kaiserzeit.* 4. Aufl. München, 1969. (Handbuch der Altertumswissenschaft. 3, 4.)
BLUM, Rudolf. "Bibliographia: eine wort- und begriffsgeschichtliche Untersuchung." *Archiv für Geschichte des Buchwesens* 10 (1969): 1009-1246. [English ed. 1980.]
WEST, M. L. "The sayings of Demokritus." *Classical Review.* New series 19 (1969): 142.

1970

EPPELSHEIMER, Hanns W. *Geschichte der europäischen Weltliteratur.* Frankfurt a.M., 1970.
GELZER, Thomas. "Aristophanes."
RE Suppl. XII (1970): 1392-1569.
PFEIFFER, Rudolf. *Geschichte der klassischen Philologie: von den Anfängen bis zum Ende des Hellenismus.* Hamburg, 1970. [English ed. 1968.]

1971

SPEYER, Wolfgang. *Die literarische Fälschung im heidnischen und christlichen Altertum.* München, 1971. (Handbuch der Altertumswissenschaft. 1, 2.)

1972

FRASER, P. M. *Ptolemaic Alexandria.* Oxford, 1972.
FRITZ, Kurt von. "Zenon von Kition."
RE Reihe 2, Halbbd. 19 (1972): 83-121.
GOTTSCHALK, H. B. "Notes on the wills of the Peripatetic scholars." *Hermes* 100 (1972): 314-342.
LYNCH, John P. *Aristotle's school: a study of a Greek educational institution.* Berkeley, 1972.
NICKAU, Klaus. "Zenodotos von Alexandreia." *RE* Reihe 2, Halbbd. 19 (1972): 20-23.
————. "Zenodotos von Ephesos."
RE Reihe 2, Halbbd. 19 (1972): 23-45.
STARK, Rudolf. *Aristoteles-Studien.* 2. Aufl. München, 1972.

1973

HERTER, Hans. "Kallimachos."
RE Suppl. XIII (1973): 184-266.
MORAUX, Paul. *Der Aristotelismus bei den Griechen: von Andronikos bis Alexander von Aphrodisias.* Berlin, 1973.

1974

WEHRLI, Fritz, ed. *Die Schule des Aristoteles: Texte und Kommentar. Suppl. 1. Hermippos der Kallimacheer.* Basel, 1974.

1975

KALLIMACHOS. Hrsg. von
Aristoxenos D. Skiadas. Darmstadt,
1975.

WIDMANN, Hans. *Geschichte des
Buchhandels vom Altertum bis zur
Gegenwart.* Teil 1. Wiesbaden, 1975.

1976

SLATER, W. J. "Aristophanes of
Byzantium on the Pinakes of
Callimachus." *Phoenix* 30 (1976):
234-241.

1978

MEJER, Jørgen. *Diogenes Laertius and
his Hellenistic background.*
Wiesbaden, 1978. (Hermes-
Einzelschriften 40.)

1980

BLUM, Rudolf. *Bibliographia: an
inquiry into its definition and
designations.* Tr. Mathilde V.
Rovelstad. Chicago, 1980.

1982

KRISCHER, Tilman. "Die Stellung der
Biographie in der griechischen
Literatur." *Hermes* 110 (1982): 51-64.

Name and Subject Index

Subscripts following page numbers refer to notes.

In order to aid the reader in the identification of persons, their profession, occupation or other distinction has been added to most names, even in the case of very well-known ones, because of the many homonyms (and see the author's discussion of the problem). Greek and Hellenistic authors are identified only by their profession, etc., but for authors of other nationalities or periods this is indicated, e.g. "Roman orator", "Byzantine grammarian".

Aristophanes of Byzantium (grammarian) 4, 6, $11_{20, 21}$, 26, 39, 40, 49, 65_{10}, 163_{21}; 166_{65}, 167_{63}, 182; library director 111, 122_{71}, 131, 243_{41}; *Hypothēseis* 26-29, 137, 171_{117}; *Pros tu Kallimachu Pinakes* 150, 176_{175}

Aristotle 4; bibliographies 55, 61-63, 71_{57}, 90_{242}, 91_{245}, $92_{255, 260, 261, 264}$, 183, 194-196, 202, 216_{73}, 242_{30}; biography 20; doxographies 43-46; edition of, by Andronikos 55, 63, 93_{273}, 194; his edition of *Iliad* 21, 22, 110; his interpretation of poets 22-23; library 22, 52-64, $90_{242, 243}$, 99, 102, 171_{111}; arrangement 64, 226, 240_4; cataloging 59, 64; contents 53; destiny after A.s death 53-63; inventory 90_{242}, 94_{278}; literary history 20-23, 33, 42-43, 46-47; nickname "reader" 22, 52, 70_{47}; official copies of works of three classical tragedians 42, 83_{155}; on Empedokles 44, 71_{56}; on grammar 17, 20-23; on Homer 15, 21, 22; on Onomakritos 17, 43; on Orpheus 17, 43, 44; teleological conception of literature and philosophy 42-43; textual critic 15, 22, 45-46; Vita Marciana 15, 69_{45}, 164_{38}, 165_{44}; Vita Menagiana 92_{260}, 204-205, 207, 222_{148}; will 53;

works: *Analytics* 216_{82}; *Aporēmēta Homērika* 21, 22, 69_{45}; *Constitutions* 21, 69_{42}, 216_{81}, 245; *Didaskaliai* 23, 24-43, 49, 76_{96}, 79_{125}, 159, 232; adaptation by Kallimachos 24, 41, 139-142; dating 29, 32; reconstruction 28-32; reliability 35-36, 39, 41, 42, 78_{116}; scope 29, 66_{97}; sources 29, 78_{112}; *Hypomnēmata* 53, 61, 92_{255}, 195; *Metaphysics* 44; *Nikai Dionysiakai* 23, 24, 30-32, 171_{117}; *Olympionikai* 19, 23, 71_{58}; *Peri hermēneias* 217_{82}; *Peri philosophias* 43, 44; *Peri poiētikēs* 22, 43, 70_{52}, 84_{157}; *Peri poiēton* 22, 44; *Peri tragodion* 41, 84_{157}; *Peri zōōn moriōn* 84_{158}; *Politika* 96, 114_3; *Pythikos* 71_{60}; *Pythionikai* 19, 23, 29, 33, 71_{60}, 170_{101}; *Technē rhetorikē* 46, 189, 198; *Technēs tēs Theodektu synagōgē* 85_{177}; *Technon synagōgē* 46, 85_{177}; *Topics* 216_{82}

Aristoxenos of Tarentum (philosopher) 42, 44, 47-50, $87_{189, 191, 195, 198}$; *Harmonika stoicheia* 84_{163}

Arrangement: alphabetical, *see* Alphabetization; by subject or form 202; classified 46, 153-154, 208-209, 224_{175}, 226-227; chronological 192, 193, 201, 208-209, 226-227; scrolls 187, 226; titles 187, 191-193, 195, 202, 208, 216_{82}, $223_{168, 169}$, 227, 235, $242_{30-32, 34}$

Arrianos (historian): *Anabasis Alexandru* 97

Artistic contests 18, 19, 24-26, 33-40, 49

Artists: lists 20, $68_{37, 40}$

Asklepiades of Myrlea (grammarian) 10_{12}, 11_{24}; *Peri grammatikōn* 193

Assos (city) 61

Assurbanipal 236

Astydamas (tragic poet) 75_{89}

Athenaios (grammarian) 56-58, 68_{40}, 89, 157, 187; *Deipnosophistai* 56, 151, 184

Athens: archives 29, 35; constitution 60_{42}, 216_{81}; *Didaskaliai* inscription 27-28, 171_{117}; dithyrambic contests 25, 31, 33-34; dramatic contests 24-26, 34-40, 49; *Fasti* inscription 31-33, 40, $77_{103-106}$, $79_{122, 123, 125}$; *Nikai* inscription 27, 30-31, 171_{117}, 74_{83}, 76_{98}, 171_{117}, Greek text 74_{85}; official copies of classical tragedies 42, 83_{155}; Ptolemaion 83_{155}, 214_{54}

Attalids 54, 106, 117_{28}

Attalos I, king of Pergamon 103, 119_{49}, 156

Attic playwrights, *see* Kallimachos: *Pinax tōn didaskalōn*

Authenticity 4-8, 15-17, 42, 51-52, 146, 148, 158-159, 176_{173}, 196-198, 200, 231-234, 236-238, 241_{20}; *see also* Literary criticism

Author indexes 240_{15}

Authors: biographies of 17-18, 41, 50, 188-210; classification 46, 153-154, 208-209, 224_{175}, 226-227, 233; data in catalogs and bibliographies 153, 155-156, 183, 189, 196, 207, 231-232; lexicons of 204; names, *see* Names

Autobibliographies 92_{261}

Bakchylides (lyric Poet) 19, 156, 176_{176}; *Kassandra* 153
Basileios (bishop of Caesarea) 210, 221_{140}
Beginning words of works 146, 156-157, 196, 200, 219_{118}, 230, 234
Bibliographies 2, 3, 41, 42, 51, 190; alphabetization, *see* Alphabetization;
  annotations 228, 234; author entries 155-156, 225_{182}; autobibliographies 92_{261};
  biographical data 155-156, 182-184, 188-194, 206-207, 231-235; chronological
  arrangement 192, 193, 201, 208-209, 226-227; classification of authors 46, 143-155, 208-
  209, 224_{175}, 226-227, 233; cross-references 225_{182}, 231; dialects used 200, 207, 223_{163},
  234, 241_{20}; distinguished from catalogs 160; "fathers" of 247_{33};
  of authors: Aischines 220_{131}; Aischylos 190-191; Antisthenes 220_{127}; Apollonios
  Dyskolos 208; Aristippos 200-201; Aristophanes 190-191, 204; Aristotle, *see* Aristotle:
  bibliographies; Chrysippos 220_{128}; Deinarchos 183, 196-199; Demokritos 92_{255}, 143-150,
  $172_{122-124}$, 220_{131}, 234; Demosthenes 196, 198-199; Diogenianos 191; Euripides 191;
  Herakleides Pontikos 220_{128}; Isokrates 188; Kallimachos 124-125, 108; Lykophron
  191; Lysias 196, 198; Parthenios 222_{150}; Phaidon 200; Plato (philosopher) 220_{187}; Plato
  (poet) 192; Plotinos 196; Plutarch 148, 216_{72}; Protagoras 239; Speusippos 63, 91_{225},
  93_{270}, 271; Straton 63, 92_{255}; Theophrastos, *see* Theophrastos: bibliographies;
  Xenokrates 63, $91_{254, 255}$; Xenophon 204; Zeno 220_{130}; Zoroaster 103, 179_{209};
  of famous men 1, 152, 202-210; of grammarians 193; of philosophers 199-202,
  222_{152}; of physicians 193, 194; of playwrights 137-142, $170_{103-108}$, $171_{109, 110}$
Bibliophylax 102, 105, 109, 112, 127
Biobibliographies 1, 57_{30}, 183-184, 188-210, 239, 245
Biographies of authors 47-52, 190, 193-210; data in catalogs & bibliographies 155-156,
  182-184, 188-194, 206-207, 231-235; quotation of divergent opinions 200, 207, 233, 234
Boethos of Sidon (philosopher) 55
Bolos of Mendes (philosopher) 146, 173_{145}, 176_{173}
Books, *see* Extent of works, Scrolls
Brontinos (poet) 180_{216}
Brucheion 97; *see also* Alexandrian libraries: Museion
Brutus, Marcus Junius (Roman statesman and orator) 221_{145}
Byzantine alphabet 203, 220_{137}

Caesar, Gaius Julius 99, 221_{145}
Cataloging 63, 64, 105, 106, 108, 230-239; of Aristotle's library 59, 64; of
  medieval manuscripts 3-4
Catalogs: distinguished from bibliographies 160; distinguished from inventories 229,
  236, 237; of libraries: Alexandria, *see* Kallimachos: *Pinakes*; Edfu 186, 212_{18};
  Pergamon 182, 196, 199, 201, 244; Rhodos 85_{177}, 185-188, 244; Rome 102, 244
Catullus, Gaius Valerius (Roman poet) 162_{10}
Chairemon (playwright) 171_{118}
Chairephon (writer on banquets) 153, 156, 157, 188
Chamaileon of Herakleia (philosopher) 47, 48, 49, 51, 67_{21}, $87_{189, 190, 197}$, 88_{200}, 188
Choirilos of Athens (playwright) 22
Choiroboskos, Georgios (Byzantine grammarian) 26, 33, 73_{78}, 137, 170_{102}
Choregoi (chorus leaders) 24, 26, 29
Chronographers 184
Chronological arrangement of works 192, 193, 201, 208-209, 226-227
Chrysippos (philosopher): bibliography 220_{128}
Chrysogonos (flutist) 52
Cicero, Marcus Tullius: on Aristotle 46; on Kallimachos 125, 138, 162_8, 170_{104};
  Brutus, De oratore 12_{27}
Classical tragedies: official copies in Athens 42, 83_{155}
Classification of authors 46, 153-154, 208-209, 224_{175}, 226-227, 233

267

Dramatic contests 24-26, 34-40, 49
Dramatists, *see* Playwrights

Edfu library, 186, 212$_{18}$
Editions 15, 109
Egypt: archives 227, 229, 240$_3$; temple libraries 186, 212$_{18}$; *see also* Ptolemaic empire
Eirenaios/Pacatus (grammarian) 209, 224$_{178}$
ekdoseis (editions) 15, 109
Empedokles (philosopher) 23, 45, 49, 70$_{54}$, 71$_{56}$, 158; *Peri physeōs* 22, 44
Ephoros of Kyme (grammarian) 67$_{21}$
Epicharmos (comic poet) 52
Epigenes (tragic poet) 158; *Peri tēs eis Orphea poiēsōs* 180$_{216}$
epigraphai (inscriptions) 147-148, 219$_{107}$
Epikuros (philosopher) 45
Epimenides of Crete (poet) 241$_{20}$
Epiphanios, St. 100, 106; *Peri metrōn kai stathmōn* 116$_{20}$
Erastos (philosopher) 54, 61, 90$_{241}$
Eratosthenes of Kyrene (scientist & library director) 9$_{11}$, 73$_{80}$, 78$_{116}$, 82$_{151}$, 105, 112, 113, 120$_{52}$, 123$_{74}$, 128, 129, 131, 133, 142, 163$_{21}$, 165$_{44}$, 167$_{71}$, 185, 241$_{20}$, 247$_1$; *Chronographiai* 184
Eubulos of Anaphlystos (comic poet) 79$_{121}$
Eudemos (historian) 44, 47; *Arithmetikē historia, Astrologikē historia, Geometrikē historia* 84$_{163}$
Eudoxos of Knidos (scientist) 152, 154-156, 178$_{196}$
Euphorion (poet) 121$_{65}$, 129
Eupolis (comic poet) 25, 82$_{151}$, 142; *Kolakēs* 27, *Marikas* 142
Euripides (editor of Homer) 15, 65$_6$
Euripides (tragic poet) 22, 25, 26, 28, 39, 41, 42, 49, 51, 53, 76$_{94}$, 82$_{152}$, 83$_{155}$, 104, 141; bibliographies 191; chronology of plays 192; library 52; works: *Alkēstis* 76$_{94}$; *Elektra, Helenē, Hērakleidai, Hēraklēs* 214$_{58}$, *Hikētides, Iōn, Iphigenia hē en Aulidi, Iphigenia hē en Taurois* 192, 214$_{58}$; *Kyklops* 214$_{58}$; *Mēdeia* 51, 171$_{110}$; *Oidipus, Oineus* 192; *Oinomaos* 215$_{68}$; *Orestēs* 192; *Rhēsos* 41, 42, 51-52, 82$_{152}$, 241$_{28}$
Eusebios (bishop of Caesarea, historian) 100, 245; *Historia ecclesiastica* 116$_{27}$
Eustathios (Byzantine scholar) 15, 65$_{6, 8, 10}$
Extent of works: books 146, 179$_{213}$, 200, 207, 230, 234; lines 59, 60, 91$_{253, 254}$, 92$_{255, 263, 264}$, 120$_{58}$, 146, 157-158, 179$_{209-211}$, 230

Famous men 1, 151-152, 194
Fasti inscription 31, 33, 40, 79$_{122, 123, 125}$
Filing, *see* Alphabetization, Arrangement

Galen, Claudius (physician) 46, 83$_{155}$, 92$_{261}$, 103, 117$_{28, 191}$; *Peri tōn idiōn bibliōn* 175$_{157}$
Gellius, Aulus (Roman grammarian) 88$_{210}$, 99
genos (origin) 17, 50
Georgios Synkellos (Byzantine historian): *Chronographia* 116$_{19}$
Gessner, Conrad (Swiss bibliographer) 247$_3$
Glaukos of Rhegion (historian) 20; *Peri archaiōn poiētōn* 19
Glossography 111, 143-144
Gnathaina (Athenian courtesan) 102, 153, 156, 157
Gorgias (philosopher & orator) 85$_{173}$
Grammar, *see* Philology
Grammarians 5-7, 15, 48, 109, 111, 127, 129, 190, 215$_{70}$; bibliographies 193

Hypereides (orator) 198, 208, 224_{172}
hypomnēmata (notes) 61-63, 136-137, 145, 149, 195
hypothēseis (summaries of plays) 26-29, 137, 171_{117}

Inscriptions: Athens 27-28, 30, 31-33, 40, $74_{83,\ 85}$, 76_{98}, $77_{122,\ 123,\ 125}$, 171_{117}; Edfu 186;
  Piraeus 186, 191; Rhodos 85_{177}, 138, 185-188; Rome 137-142, $170_{103\text{-}108}$, $171_{109,\ 110}$
Inventories 227-230, 236, 240_{15}; Aristotle's library 90_{242}, 94_{278}
Ion of Chios (tragic poet) 178_{197}; Triagmos 158, 180_{216}
Iophon (tragic poet) 5, 11_{20}, 80_{138}
Irenaeus (bishop of Lyons) 99, 100; Adversus haereses 116_{27}
Isaios (orator) 188
Isidorus of Seville (historian) 99
Isokrates (orator) 95-96; bibliography 188; Panegyrikos 114_2; Peri tēs antidoseōs 177_{182};
  Philippos 95, 114_2, 213_{41}
Istros (pupil of Kallimachos) 136, 163_{21}, 169_{97}

Jerome, St. 152, 189, 194, 203, 221_{141}, 245; De viris illustribus 1, 2
Josephus Flavius (historian) 100
Juba II, king of Mauretania 12, 17; Theatrikē historia 12_{25}

Kallias (comic poet) 174_{154}
Kallikrates (orator) 199
Kallimachos: adaptation of Didaskaliai 24, 41, 139-142; bibliographer 142-160, 231-246;
  bibliography of 124-125, 208; biobibliographer 155-156, 231-246; biography of 2, 124-
  126; cataloger 105-113, 119_{52}; innovator 236-237, 244; library director 112, 127, 132,
  133, 168_{73}; literary critic 232, 234-236, 243_{36}, 244-246; Mega biblion (big book) citation
  127, 163_{22}; poet 98, 114_9, 125, 127; posthumous fame 125, 138; pupils 126-127, 164_{38},
  165_{44}; scholarly works 133-137; teacher of Ptolemaios III 127, 133;
  works: Aitia 127, 134, 152, 163_{22}; The arrival of Io, Arcadia, The colony of the
  Argonauts 124; epitaphs 241_{21}; Ethnikai onomasiai 135, 169_{89}; Glaukos 124;
  hypomnēmata 136-137, $169_{93,\ 94}$, 232; Ibis 125, 128; Ktiseis ... kai metonomasiai 135;
  Museion 161_5; Nomina barbarika 135; Peri agonōn 171_{117}; Peri anemōn, Peri orneōn,
  Peri nymphōn, Peri ... potamōn 135; Pinakes of Museion library (catalog of copies)
  105, 108, 119_{52}, 126; Pinakes of Greek authors (catalog of works) 2, 64, 108, 124-160,
  176_{176}, 233-239; arrangement 153-156, 191, 233-239; as bibliography 228, 245; as
  example and source 182-184, 245; classification of 153-154, $178_{193,\ 195}$; listing of lost
  works 139; quotations from 151-158; reconstruction 226-233; title 2, 151-152; Pinax
  tōn didaskalōn 24-28, 33, 68_{39}, 137-142, 227, 239, 243_{41}; Pinax of glosses and works by
  Demokritos 143-150, 234, 237; Plokamos Berenikēs 125, 127; Semelē 124; Thaumasia
  134, 168_{81}, 169_{89}, 246
Kallimachos, the Younger (poet, nephew of K.) 124
Kallisthenes (philosopher, nephew of Aristotle) 23, $71_{59,\ 60}$, 170_{101}
Kallistratos (director of plays) 27, 28, 34, 35, 37-39, $78_{119,\ 121}$, 81_{138}, 153
Kallixeinos of Rhodos (historian) 100; Peri Alexandreias 58
Kantharos (playwright) 79_{121}
Karneades (philosopher) 151, 204
Kartinos (playwright): Pytinē 27
Keos (island) 134
Kerkops (poet) 180_{216}
Keywords 195, 240_4
Kinesias (dithyrambic poet) 33
Kleanthes (philosopher) 92_{255}
Klearchos (philosopher) 86_{182}

270

Title Index

Acharnēs (Aristophanes) 27, 34, 37, 38, 39, 78$_{119}$, 171$_{110}$
Adversus haereses (Irenaeus) 116$_{27}$
Agamemnōn (Aischylos) 192, 215$_{67}$
Agōn Homēru kai Hēsiodu 17
Aiolosikōn (Aristophanes) 35, 40, 81$_{143, 146}$, 192
Aithiopika (Philon) 135
Aitia (Kallimachos) 127, 134, 152, 163$_{22}$
Aitia physika (Plutarch) 173$_{139}$
Aitnaiai (Aischylos) 191
Alētheia (Protagoras) 147, 174$_{155}$
Alexandra (Lykrophron) 98
Alkēstis (Euripides) 76$_{94}$, 192, 215$_{70}$
Alkibiades (Plutarch) 70$_{46}$
Amphiaraos (Aristophanes) 34, 192
Anabasis Alexandru (Arrianos) 97
Anagyros (Aristophanes) 192
Analytics (Aristotle) 216$_{82}$
Andromachē (Euripides) 41, 141, 158-159, 171$_{118}$, 180$_{217}$, 192
Antigonē (Sophokles) 5, 11$_{20}$
Antilogika (Protagoras) 51
Antimachos (Aischines or Phaidon?) 200
Anyllos (Nikostratos or Philetairos?) 52
Apology of Socrates (Plato) 26
Aporēmata Homērika (Aristotle) 21, 22, 69$_{45}$
Arcadia (Kallimachos) 124
Archonton anagraphē (Demetrios of Phaleron) 52
Argonautika (Apollonios of Rhodos) 103, 118$_{39}$, 128
Arithmetikē historia (Eudemos) 84$_{163}$
Arrival of Io, The (Kallimachos) 124
Asōtodidaskalos (Alexis) 171$_{112}$
Aspis (Hesiod) 6, 128, 233
Astrologia (Kleostratos) 121$_{66}$
Astrologikē historia (Eudemos) 84$_{163}$
Astronomia (Demokritos) 147
Athenian constitution (Aristotle) 69$_{42}$, 216$_{81}$
Atthis (Philochoros) 197, 223$_{164}$

Babylōnioi (Aristophanes) 34, 37, 38, 40, 192
Bakchai (Euripides) 28
Batrachoi [Frogs] (Aristophanes) 11$_{20}$, 25, 34, 40, 80$_{138}$, 192
Bibliothēkē (Photios) 12$_{27}$, 180$_{220}$
Bioi iatrōn (Soranos) 193
Bioi sophistōn (Philostratos) 219$_{112}$
Bioi tōn deka rhētorōn (Pseudo-Plutarch) 83$_{155}$, 219$_{112}$
Bios Homēru (Herodotos) 17
Bios Homēru (Plutarch) 17
Bios Plōtinu (Porphyrios) 175$_{157}$, 257$_{83}$
Brutus (Cicero) 12$_{27}$

277

279

280

WISCONSIN STUDIES IN CLASSICS

General Editors
Barbara Hughes Fowler and Warren G. Moon

E. A. THOMPSON
Romans and Barbarians: The Decline of the Western Empire

JENNIFER TOLBERT ROBERTS
Accountability in Athenian Government

H. I. MARROU
A History of Education in Antiquity
Histoire de l'Education dans l'Antiquité, translated by George Lamb
(originally published in English by Sheed and Ward, 1956)

ERIKA SIMON
Festivals of Attica: An Archaeological Commentary

G. MICHAEL WOLOCH
Roman Cities: Les villes romaines by Pierre Grimal,
translated and edited by G. Michael Woloch,
together with A Descriptive Catalogue of Roman Cities
by G. Michael Woloch

WARREN G. MOON, *editor*
Ancient Greek Art and Iconography

KATHERINE DOHAN MORROW
Greek Footwear and the Dating of Sculpture

JOHN KEVIN NEWMAN
The Classical Epic Tradition

JEANNY VORYS CANBY, EDITH PORADA, BRUNILDE SISMONDO
RIDGWAY, and TAMARA STECH, *editors*
Ancient Anatolia: Aspects of Change and Cultural Development

ANN NORRIS MICHELINI
Euripides and the Tragic Tradition

WENDY J. RASCHKE, *editor*
The Archaeology of the Olympics: The Olympics and Other Festivals in Antiquity

PAUL PLASS
Wit and the Writing of History: The Rhetoric of Historiography in Imperial Rome

BARBARA HUGHES FOWLER
The Hellenistic Aesthetic

F. M. CLOVER and R. S. HUMPHREYS, *editors*
Tradition and Innovation in Late Antiquity

BRUNILDE SISMONDO RIDGWAY
Hellenistic Sculpture I: The Styles of ca. 331–200 B.C.

BARBARA HUGHES FOWLER, *editor and translator*
Hellenistic Poetry: An Anthology

KATHRYN J. GUTZWILLER
Theocritus' Pastoral Analogies: The Formation of a Genre

VIMALA BEGLEY and RICHARD DANIEL DE PUMA, *editors*
Rome and India: The Ancient Sea Trade

RUDOLF BLUM
Kallimachos: The Alexandrian Library and the Origins of Bibliography
Kallimachos und die Literaturverzeichnung bei den Griechen,
translated by Hans H. Wellisch